ALEXANDER THOM
Cracking the Stone Age Code

ALEXANDER THOM - CRACKING THE STONE AGE CODE

'It seldom happens that a single book, by an author who makes no claim to be an archaeologist, compels archaeologists themselves to re-examine their assumptions about a whole section of the past. This one does. If we accept the evidence here presented by Professor Thom (in such detail that the reader can check all the stages of the argument), and if we concur in even a part of his conclusions (which are drawn with the most scrupulous regards for the limits of inference), we must alter radically our current view of the intellectual calibre of man in Britain in the later third and second millenia BC'

Professor Richard Atkinson,
Review of *Megalithic Sites in Britain*, *Antiquity* (1968, vol 42, 77)

"As archaeologists we are sometimes accused, as other people are in specialised disciplines, of being a closed shop, and preventing unorthodox and new ideas. I don't think this is the case at all, we're perfectly prepared to accept new ideas, if they are examined and stated in the terms of archaeological evidence. In other words, you've got to be an archaeologist before you can start putting forward new ideas about archaeology."

Professor Stuart Piggott,
BBC *Chronicle* programme: *Cracking the Stone Age Code* (1971).

'It is hardly surprising..that many historians either ignore the implications of Thom's work, because they do not understand them, or resist them because it is more comfortable to do so. I have myself gone through the latter process; but I have come to the conclusion that to reject Thom's thesis because it does not conform to the model of prehistory on which I was brought up involves also the acceptance of probabilities of an even higher order. I am prepared, in other words, to believe that my model of European prehistory is wrong, rather than that the results presented by Thom are due to nothing but chance.'

Professor Richard Atkinson,
Megalithic Astronomy - a prehistorian's comments,
Journal of the History of Astronomy (1975, 6; 51)

ALEXANDER THOM
Cracking the Stone Age Code

Robin Heath

Author of
Sun, Moon & Stonehenge,
The Measure of Albion, (with John Michell)
Sun, Moon & Earth
Stonehenge

Bluestone Press
St Dogmaels, Pembrokeshire
Wales

Alexander Thom [signature]

ALEXANDER THOM

Cracking the Stone Age Code

First Edition 2007

ISBN No. 978 0 9526151 4 9

Robin Heath asserts his moral rights to be identified as the author of *Alexander Thom: Cracking the Stone Age Code*, in accordance with the Copyright and Data Protection Act, 1988.

All rights reserved. No part of this book may be reproduced or transmitted in any form or by any means, electronic or mechanical including photocopying, recording or by information storage and retrieval system, without permission in writing from the publisher.

Original parts of the manuscript, up to 500 words, may be quoted if due acknowledgement is made as to the source, author and publisher. Larger sections and use of the original graphical material within this book may be reproduced by arrangement with the publisher.

Every reasonable attempt has been made to contact the copyright holders of certain illustrations found within this book. If any person or organisation subsequently contacts the publisher with information concerning permissions or copyright information, we will gladly make the appropriate acknowledgements and amend future editions of this book.

To order further copies of this book or information about other Bluestone Press publications, or details of forthcoming *Sky & Landscape* events, visit our website,

www.skyandlandscape.com

Copyright © 2007 by Robin Heath

With 60 photographs, 85 illustrations and 42 survey plans.

Bluestone Press - Published in Wales
Printed by Gomer Press, Llandysul, Carmarthenshire

Acknowledgements

The author is in debt to many people for their help and kindness during the preparation and writing of this book. My gratitude is conveyed to the relatives of Alexander Thom, in particular his late son Dr Archibald Thom, who sent me and freely gave me permission to use the meticulous plans that he and his father collated over forty years. Grateful thanks to Thom's daughter Beryl Austin and his granddaughter Susan MacColl, who together with her husband James and their children, Eòghann, Duncan and Shona have assisted in supplying anecdotes, family photographs and biographic details, all with customary Scottish warmth and hospitality. My grateful appreciation is acknowledged for a contribution towards the cost of printing this book, donated by Mike Bossom of *Encaustic Arts*, Glogue. (www.encaustic.com).

For various reasons I would also like to thank Dr Aubrey Burl, Dr Euan MacKie (interviews), Graham Challifor, John Michell, Michael Postins, Lesley Ferguson and Ian Frazer (RCAHMS), John Martineau, David Handford, Professor Keith Critchlow and Professor Roger and Irene Earis (my long-suffering and much appreciated editor). My partner Tricia Osborne is last but not least in this list, for providing proof-reading at inconvenient times and helpful comments at every stage of researching and producing this book.

Photographs are credited where the source is other than the Thom family or my own collection. The cover portrait (*reproduced also on page 162*) is from a photograph taken by Hamish Gorrie at Carnac, Brittany.

Survey drawings supplied to the author by Archibald Thom. Thom's painting on page 74 from Thom family archives. The two illustrations, of Kintraw and Ballochroy, were commissioned from Janet Lloyd Davies by the author in 1997. Concentric ring illustration on page 158 courtesy of John Martineau and the late Anne Macaulay. Portraits by Rose Marshall. Stonehenge paperweight and mechanical calculating engines (*page 29 & 30*) are from author's own collection.

Copyright

Most of the photographs and plans in this book have been supplied by friends and relatives of Alexander Thom. Every effort has been made to trace and to acknowledge ownership of copyright of the other photographs, wherever possible. The publishers would be glad to make suitable arrangements with any copyright holder(s) whom it has not been possible to contact, so that any future editions may be amended, and sources acknowledged.

Cover

Cover design is based on 'Calanais' by artist Eòghann MacColl, Alexander Thom's great-grandson, with many thanks for his permission. The photograph on the cover is of Thom at Carnac in 1970, taken by Hamish Gorrie.

Alexander Thom - Cracking the Stone Age Code

Childhood in a Victorian Family. Alexander Thom, just four years old (*left*), during a family reunion in summer 1898.

Immediately above Alexander in the family photograph above, are his parents, father Archibald Thom and mother Lilias Thom (*née* Strang). In the top row, second left, is William Strang - Uncle Willie of Mugdoch Castle - who gave great encouragement to his nephew during his early years. At the extreme right of the top row is another Uncle, Sam Strang, who taught Alexander how to sail.

Alexander's mother suffered greatly from depression, which may explain the curious posture of both his parents in the photograph.

- *frontispiece* -

CONTENTS

Foreword by Beryl Austin (*née* Thom) (iii)
Introduction (vii)

Chapter One	*A Man of Nine Decades*	1
Chapter Two	*A Passion for the Past*	27
Chapter Three	*The Thomist Paradox*	75
Chapter Four	*The Quest for the Megalithic Yard*	103
Chapter Five	*Megalithic Designs*	131
Chapter Six	*Disposing of the Evidence*	163
Chapter Seven	*A Fitting Tribute*	185

APPENDICES

Appendix One 210
 - *A Brief History of British Archaeoastronomy*
Appendix Two 215
 - *Alexander Thom: Archaeoastronomical Publications*
Appendix Three 216
 - *Glossary of Astronomical Terms*
Appendic Four 217
 - *Formulae Used in Archaeoastronomical Work*
Appendix Five 220
 - *A Newly Discovered Megalithic Site on Lundy*

BIBLIOGRAPHY 221

INDEX 225

Alexander Thom - Cracking the Stone Age Code

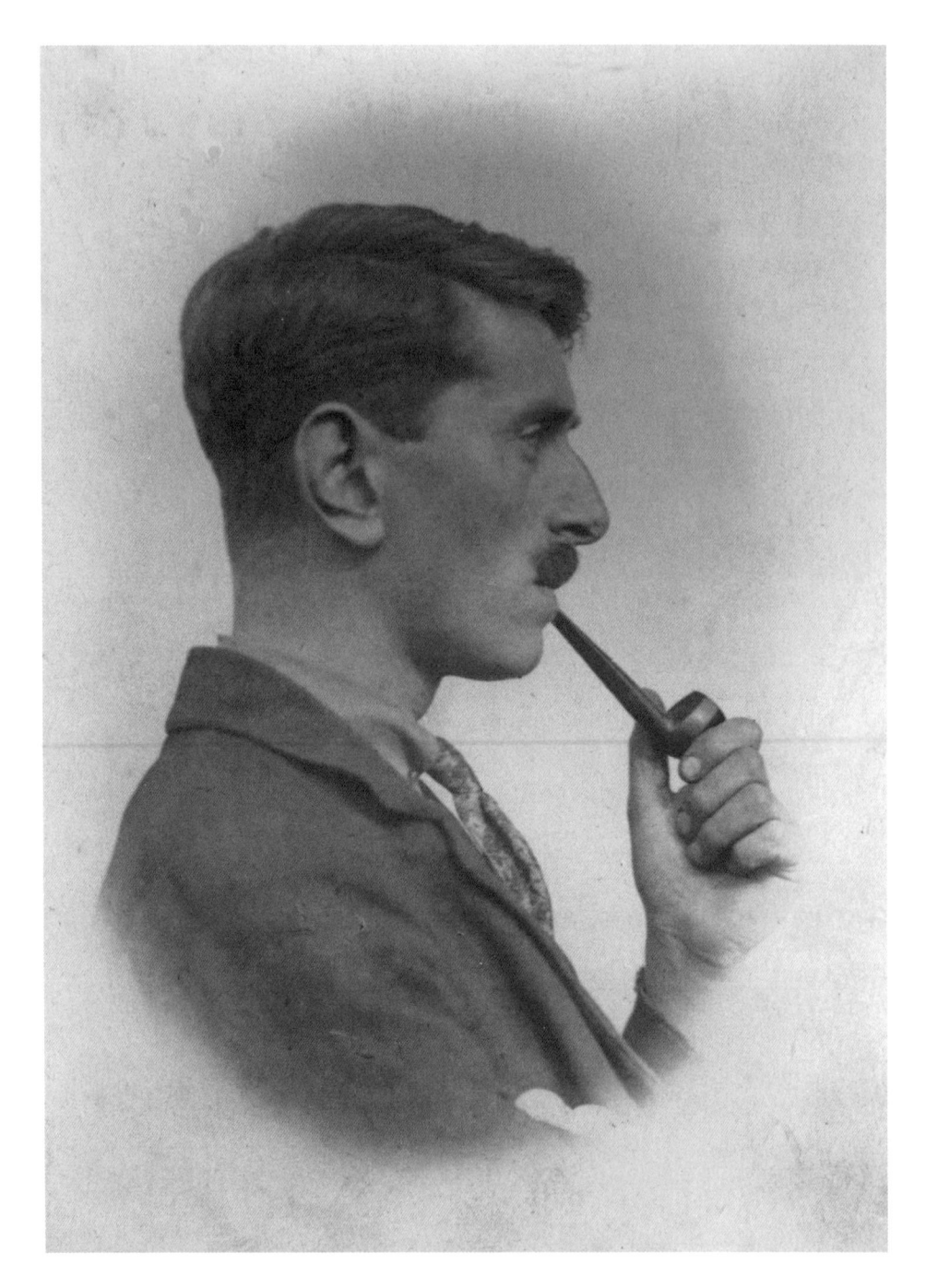

Alexander Thom
(about 1930)

Foreword

Foreword
by
Beryl Austin (*née* Thom),
[Alexander Thom's Daughter]

My father was a complex person. He had an enquiring mind and questioned *everything*. The extent of his interest was wide-ranging and he never had a lazy moment. He was always working at something. He could be very charming to people but he could also be very intolerant, which made a consistent relationship difficult. His childhood must have been strange in that his mother was a classic depressive with ups and downs having a five year cycle. She was from a large family, the daughter of a Victorian muslin manufacturer, and had seven brothers and four sisters. Their mother was Lilian Symington - a name taken from the lands of Symington in Ayrshire which were given to them by Robert the Bruce.

My father's father was a practical farmer, a clever man who should have been an engineer. He farmed as a tenant farmer the Mains farm for Carradale House, where he met Lily Stevenson Strang, (the same Stevenson as the lighthouse Stevensons and Robert Louis Stevenson) when she was staying with her family in the summer in Carradale. Grandfather trained the Church choir and my Grandmother was a pianist.

My father was born at Carradale on 26th March 1894 and spent his childhood, up to the age of seven years, at the Mains. My mother was born on the same date three years later, in 1897, in the Parish of Dunlop, Ayrshire. My father's family left the Mains to come to the 'Mainland' to be nearer Glasgow and my grandmother's family rather than living out on the Kintyre peninsula. Lily's father bought her *The Hill* farm at Dunlop. The farmhouse had been built in 1692 by one of our covenanting forebears who had returned to Ayrshire from Ireland following the 'Troubles', bringing with her the recipe for 'Sweet milk cheese', now known as Dunlop cheese.

My grandfather and a helper brought their entire stock from Carradale by ship to Largs and drove them over the Kilbirnie hills to *The Hill*. There is a 300 yard avenue up to the farmhouse and as they were coming up the the avenue in the dark the departing owner opened one of the top windows of the house and stuck a gun out, threatening to shoot them, thinking they were raiders! Grandfather later bought a cartload of Snowdrop and Daffodil bulbs, and flanked the entire avenue banks with them. It became one of the sights of Ayrshire. My Father saw all this work going on around him and hence developed a strong work ethic.

Once married, my father and mother moved immediately to Gosport. After his job designing flying boats for the Gosport Aircraft Company had finished, following the cessation of hostilities in the Great War, they returned, and in 1922 built an asbestos and wood house, *Thalassa*, adjacent to *The Hill* following their return to Scotland. My father was appointed lecturer at Glasgow University. In *Thalassa* he built a study, a room where he prepared all his lectures, wrote the Field Theory book with C J Apfeld, the thesis for his D.Sc. and designed the water turbine which was to power the farm with electricity.

At weekends we all helped with the free-range hens as the farm helper was off. Hens everywhere to be let out, fed and watered, eggs collected and then shut in at night to protect them from marauding foxes. My father was involved in all of this, as was my mother, meanwhile undertaking all the gardening, and working out the correct water flow for the turbine. In addition to this they undertook, using spades, the excavation and construction of the turbine house installation deep in the earth.

In the early Thirties my father was not well, and could get no help from the doctors. Eventually, he went to a Dr Balfour, a 'Nature curist' in Glasgow, who encouraged him to become a vegetarian, to take a cold bath each morning, swim twice a week, to exercise and to have a course of massage. My father subsequently made an outside cold plunge from a cast iron bath fed by rainwater, a device which he used until he was over 80. His health improved. Having endured the food shortages during the Great War he foresaw what would come when the 1939 war began. He said to us all - "start eating meat, eat everything you can lay your hands on!" But he himself never ate a lot of meat and was careful to eat as much fruit and green vegetables as possible. In the 30s it was not at all easy to be a vegetarian in Scotland, so we grew as much as we could, eating kale in winter and greenhouse tomatoes in summer, etc. Everyone thought we were quite mad! However, my father lived well into old age and was very active.

My father was always interested in paintings and if we were near an art gallery we would visit together. He had dabbled in painting in his younger days but did not concentrate on that. Woodwork was his hobby - very exact and precise woodwork. He once made a dodecahedron box, all mortice and tenon joints. Amazing! He was also an expert lathes-man.

Having acquired expertise in the design of aeroplanes, my Father applied himself to starting the Department of Aeronautics at Glasgow University. As a consequence of this, at the onset of World War II in August 1939, he was directed to the Royal

Foreword

Aircraft Establishment (RAE) at Farnborough. He found the first year difficult, he was not being stretched and there was a lot of internal politics. But eventually he was asked to design and build the High Speed Wind Tunnel, and that was him off.

During the war we lived in Fleet and my father cycled to Farnborough daily because he loved cycling. Before many goods became unobtainable due to the war he ordered a special bike on which he rode many thousands of miles, and on which I'm sure he did a lot of thinking. We had cold, cold winters during the war and Fleet Pond froze each winter and we skated there. Previously the family had skated on Loch Libo in Ayrshire but my Father always went over it with a rope before we were allowed onto the ice.

My father was a great yachtsman, taught the craft by his Uncle Sam, and he loved the west coast of Scotland and knew all the anchorages and islands in detail. He was a careful yachtsman, wary and respectful of our weather. The yachts and cruises were an important part of his life and I remember our first cruise when the last war was over, in 1946. We sailed out of the Crinian Canal Basin and my father stretched out his arms and shouted 'We are *FREE*!". A most touching moment for us all after the dark, dreadful days of the war. Of course his skills as a yachtsman coupled with his knowledge of the Hebrides later assisted him greatly in finding and reaching the stone circles there.

My brother Alan's death just at the end of the war had affected my father greatly. He felt that Alan had had an exceptionally good brain and his death was a great loss to him, while my mother was heartbroken and never really recovered from his death. We soon moved to Oxford, which was an enjoyable and fulfilling time for my father, having the challenge of enlarging the Department of Engineering and then planning what became the Thom Building. He found college life as a Fellow of Brasenose College interesting and he rebuilt and improved the sundial that graces the wall of the courtyard there.

On retirement, in 1961, he came back to his beloved Scotland and got down to his standing stone research, collating the information which he had been gathering and thinking about since 1930. He and my brother Archie, his devoted and supportive son, worked tirelessly. Although twenty-four years separated them, they were always great friends and together they developed the name astro-archaeology. As someone on the fringe it saddened me to witness the opposition to the subject which they constantly had to overcome. My Father once said to me, "If only the critics would learn maths instead of criticizing something which they do not understand I could get on with my work." Of course, Professor Atkinson did just that and became a faithful supporter, as did Bob Merritt. Strange that an American lawyer should become so involved with my father's work!

My father was meticulous in replying to all letters of criticism but this had the effect of holding him back considerably, and was so time consuming. This was such a shame, as he had developed quite an understanding of "the Boys" as he and Archie referred to the stone builders. In addition, having been raised in a Highland community with no lights at night he was intensely aware of the night sky - as his "Boys" would have been.

Because of the the different backgrounds of his parents my father was a curious mixture of conventionality and non-conventionality. Around the house and garden he would be very informally dressed but was always correctly dressed for professional work and formal occasions. As children he insured we learned our table manners as in his numerous uncles' and aunts' houses the meals were formal and waited upon.

My father was not interested in sport and not at all competitive. The rape of the planet worried him greatly. He said to me, "I will vote for any party which will leave the oil under the North Sea. What is under the sea and soil should stay there." At the time he said this there was no thought or word concerning global warming.

One evening in the early sixties my father and I went to a reception at the Royal Society in London. He wished to find out about the Bristlecone Pine research (calibrating radiocarbon dates). Going back to Oxford on the Train he was very quiet and I asked him why. "Their dates don't coincide with mine. There is a difference of several hundred years. But I cannot change anything because my dates are what my measurements and calculations tell me." A few months later he told me that their dates had changed and were now in line with his.

During the final years of my father's long life, he moved to live with me. He had always been a great *raconteur*, and during these final days the visiting nurse would frequently break out into gales of laughter at his stories. Our Doctor here in Fort William once described my father as a free thinker. I agree with him.

Banavie, Fort William, December 2006

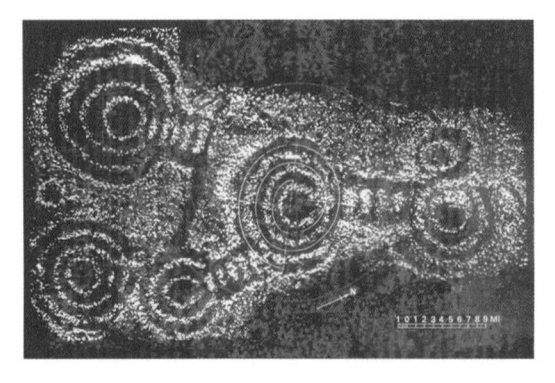

The Panorama Stone, Ilkley, Yorkshire. A rubbing taken from the stone and subsequently analysed by Thom confirmed a relationship between the units of length picked into the cup and ring-marked stones and the unit of length used to lay out the stone circles.

Introduction

This is the story of one man's quest to understand our legacy from prehistory. For nearly half a century, Alexander Thom amassed a formidable collection of accurate data on aligned sites, stone circles, rows and fans in order to assess their astronomical, geometrical and metrological properties. This package comprised the most accurate surveys ever undertaken of over 500 sites and included Britain's most important prehistoric monuments - Avebury, Callanish and Stonehenge.

Once the cause of an astonishing rumpus in archaeology, Alexander Thom's researches led him back into the minds of the megalith builders, yet this pioneering work, together with its implications, was subsequently rejected *en masse* by mainstream archaeologists and historians. The whole Thomian package has been neatly and effectively airbrushed out of the academic study of prehistory.

This books tells the story of what happened to Thom and his data both during and after his remarkable life, in order to discover why his work was very quickly and perhaps rather too conveniently forgotten and shunted off into an academic *cul de sac*.

My first aim in writing this book was to present anew the research, methodology and conclusions of Thom's prodigious output. Presently scattered widely throughout a myriad of out of print or rare books and specialist journals, the original material suffers from being largely inaccessible to a non-specialist reader, although the implications from it are clear enough. Twenty one years after his death, at age 91, it seemed timely to re-evaluate Thom's researches and repackage them into a more palatable and accessible form.

But this book is also about something else - *change*. More specifically, it deals with how the introduction of new and radical ideas, in this instance concerning the origins of civilisation, are resisted by cultural forces inherent within our society. Thom's conclusions and their implications were vigorously rejected by people determined to maintain a different model of prehistory. Thom never fully understood this resistance to the new ideas he willingly offered to the archaeologists, partly because no one was more sure of the reliability of his data, but also because within his own discipline, scientific research and engineering, change at an exponential rate had become the norm, and adapting to rapid change had been the only way to survive in that profession during the twentieth century.

Following the Second World War, Britain upheld a curiously stuffy establishment which, in a time of fading Empire, fought vigorously to resist change to its values and to its way of life. Yet curiously, during this same period, Britain also had in place a breed of scientists and engineers that were unmatched anywhere else in the world, of which Alexander Thom was a supreme example. Rising from the ashes left by the war the inventions and innovations of these people germinated within the fertile tilth of commercial expansion. This sort of change was welcomed with open arms in a Britain suffering from austerity and loss of the Empire, often at a remarkable pace. But ideas or research which threatened in some way the social paradigm were ignored or, should they persist, were ruthlessly rejected. Alexander Thom experienced both sides of this polarity with considerable frustration and bewilderment, having received high honours for his industrial and academic career and virtually complete rejection over his later work with the megaliths.

During the revolutionary times of the 1960s, the turmoil in social and cultural beliefs that characterised this astonishing decade saw a concerted attack on the conservatism of the post-war era. And in archaeology, then, as now, an extremely conservative profession, an almighty revolution was under way as the traditional dating framework, and the cultural model which resulted from it, was revealed to be grossly in error as the new radiocarbon dating techniques revealed massive cracks in that model. The leading prehistoric archaeologist of his generation, Dr Colin Renfrew, cited this issue in the very first paragraph of his seminal book, *Before Civilisation* (Cape, 1973),

> 'The study of prehistory today is in a state of crisis. Archaeologists all over the world have realized that much of prehistory, as written in the existing textbooks, is inadequate; some of it is quite simply wrong.'

Right in the middle of this turmoil in archaeology, Thom's first book, *Megalithic Sites in Britain* (Clarendon Press, Oxford, 1967), was published. It revealed an astonishing picture of ancient Britons well versed in astronomy, surveying, metrology and geometry. It too suggested that the current model of prehistory was sadly deficient and had not accounted for the abilities of Neolithic and Bronze Age Europeans in astronomy and geometry. And, unlike many of the rising numbers of New Age 'alternative archaeology' books of this period, Thom's tome was rigorous and objective, not at all an 'easy read', nor intended to be, especially for the lay person. It read like a scientific textbook, because, essentially, that is precisely what its author intended it to be.

Megalithic Sites in Britain amounted to a second front in exposing fault lines in the archaeological model of prehistory, this time not as 'quite simply wrong' - Thom was too much of a gentleman to indulge in overt criticism of archaeology and archaeologists - but as massively incomplete. Paradoxically, the timing of its publication was both perfect and perfectly awful. Why this and his subsequent books upset the archaeological establishment so much forms a further theme within the story unfolded here.

Alexander Thom, often called 'Sandy', 'A.T.' or 'The Skipper' by his family and friends was driven to find out how things worked and why things were made

Introduction

the way that they were made. This motivation lies at the very core of a scientist, inventor or engineer, and Thom was all three rolled into one very energetic and wiry Scot. During the second half of his long life, his passion became stone circles. He recognised, perhaps for the first time, that the megalithic remains that survived across northwestern Europe had been *engineering projects* and were, from an engineer's perspective, little different from being given a complex piece of equipment with no service manual. Hardly a remarkable problem within an engineer's mundane working environment, Thom, a supremely qualified engineer scientist, set himself the task of writing, perhaps more accurately one might say re-writing, the service manuals for many of the megalithic designs he investigated. The consequences of this innovative approach took him on an astonishing journey, revealing to him a wholly new perspective on the past and an unexpected take on prehistory.

Thom's 'well-constructed parcel bomb', as Richard Atkinson described Thom's first book, became one of the central pieces of evidence fuelling the rising New Age interest in 'earth mysteries.' Although 'the bomb' went off, resoundingly, within the archaeological world, and was largely contained within the profession, the explosion managed to leak out into the public domain. Unfortunately, because the book was so inpenetrable to the layperson, who often has no choice but to rely on 'experts' to assess complex technical information, many non-specialists outside of the archeological profession were later swayed away from their original interest in this material by archaeologists who declared it unworthy of study. Thereby was the explosion ultimately contained and this goes some way to explaining why today Thom's name is more widely known, though his work not better understood, outside of academia than within, as any popular bookshop with a 'New Age' or earth mysteries section will reveal. One has only to look up 'Thom' in the index of almost any title within this *genre* to confirm the truth of this statement. Within books on prehistoric archaeology he almost doesn't exist, he has become *persona non grata* and we will discover why.

Thom was no popularist. As he himself said of *Megalithic Sites in Britain*, in response to a question asked by his cousin, Jack McLay, about the accessibility of his work, "I published one book, but there were not more than five people in the world who understood it." He then added that that he had received a number of letters, following a BBC documentary about his work, which had enquired after a 'Child's Guide' to the whole subject, and that he was attempting to provide such, only this time he was, "...rather afraid that there might be no more than twenty-five people who might understand it." Unfortunately, Thom's 'Child's Guide' never saw the light of day - as often is the case with innovators and pioneers he probably wasn't the right man to present such a work. And as he was also approaching 80 years of age at the time, it was probably too late anyway.

So just who was this man who claimed to have penetrated so deeply into the mindset of our megalithic ancestors, yet who so doubted our abilities when it came to understanding his findings? And how did it come to pass that the very man who effectively fathered the subject of astroarchaeology, now generally referred to as archaeoastronomy, and presented it as a wholly respectable subject - we now have a Chair in the subject at Leicester University - has been almost forgotten within that same subject? And how did a retired engineer/scientist/academic whose conclusions briefly became a popular talking point amongst the entire nation manage to rattle more cages within the archaeological establishment than almost anyone else?

I shall attempt to answer these questions honestly and fairly as the man and his pioneering work gradually emerge and are brought into focus within these pages. Detailed accounts of Thom's methodologies and results are intermingled with the criticisms and objections to his revealed view of prehistory. I have endeavoured to interview and/or quote from those archaeologists, specialists and family members who took part in the original and often turbulent debate surrounding his work, once referred to as the *Thomist Paradox* by archaeologist Dr Euan MacKie. Their comments, even their photographs, will, I hope, inject the story with an added dimension, assisting the reader to understand better the mood of the time. This is a story well worth the telling and long overdue.

Alex Thom was primarily a scientist and engineer, a Scottish one at that, ideally qualified academically and also experienced practically to undertake and analyse the accurate astronomical observations and surveys described within his books. The environment to which Alexander Thom had contributed during his years at Glasgow University and then holding the Chair of Engineering Science at Oxford was the rigorously academic world of the world-class university. His earlier industrial career had included skilled topographical surveying, the designing of flying boats, and the successful undertaking of the design and construction of one of the most advanced wind-tunnels ever built, at the Royal Aircraft Establishment (RAE), Farnborough.

In contrast to his glittering record in both the industrial and academic world, Thom's family tree was rooted in a farming tradition, and he thus held fast to that traditional approach to the matters of mundane and family life that has now almost entirely vanished, but which may be glimpsed in many of the photographs embedded within the book. Today, such a way of life is often seen as unsophisticated, and even in Thom's heyday it contrasted vividly with the social patina of the rising post-war consumer society. The *waste not want not, make do and mend* practical approach spawned of the agricultural way of life was an essential aspect of Thom's background, a traditional philosophy which never left Thom even after he had risen through the ranks and was enjoying the relative affluence conferred on him by his senior status. As a consequence he was always improving equipment, repairing broken machinery and inventing better ways to make things, *anything*, more functionally effective.

In his own words, "the art of successful living is to perform unimportant tasks gracefully", and while Alex Thom kept his mundane life simple, one

Introduction

could never use that word to describe either his intellect or his aspirations. A true engineer and craftsman, he built his own house, then powered it from a windmill he designed himself. He was always adapting or fabricating things, including the mirrors of large astronomical telescopes.

The traditional upper and middle-classes had long eschewed practical skills and a practical or scientific education for a 'classical' education, and even today in Britain engineers are still imagined as men, almost never women, with oily overalls and dirt in their fingernails. This curiously British class prejudice can be seen operating just under the surface at key stages in the dismissal of Thom's researches - being 'academic' was seen as incompatible with being an engineer.

Another mistake was that some people mistook A.T.'s apparently quiet spoken and reserved nature as a weakness. Thom was no self-publicist. For example, he repeatedly disclaimed any competence as an archaeologist, which led Professor Richard Atkinson to write, in his obituary for Thom in the *Journal for the History of Astronomy*, 'His critics have fastened on these (occasional archaeological errors) quite disproportionately'. Some archaeologists went further, inferring that he was completely deluded over his megalithic discoveries. But Sandy Thom had a good sense of humour, even against a constant rain of such opinions. He once introduced himself to archaeologist Jack G Scott, who was, at the time, excavating the chambered cairn at Kintraw with: "Hello, I am Alexander Thom. I expect that you think I am mad!" Scott said later that he had found this 'utterly disarming'.

All Thom ever did was report what he had found. His only sin was that he dared to encroach into another profession's territory. His researches began to reveal to him huge omissions in the model of prehistoric life taught in our schools and universities. Many sites revealed the same skills and the same intent, despite often being built hundreds of miles of distance or hundreds of years in time apart. His data became a log-jam of inferences that shrieked out that archaeologists had missed an astonishing and colourful dimension related to Neolithic and Bronze Age culture. And most of them just couldn't hack it, even worse, most had not the astronomical knowledge nor the technical abilities of an engineer's brain to be qualified to judge the material that A.T. had laid so impeccably before them.

Every single one of Thom's major conclusions were refuted, despite one of the most respectable and respected archaeologists of the time, Professor Richard Atkinson, author of the then definitive and classic book, *Stonehenge* (1956), 'coming out' and admitting that his previously held views concerning prehistoric Britain were seriously in need of revision since Thom's work had become known to him. One of the great missed opportunities in the history of archaeology may one day centre on why the remainder of the profession, with very few notable exceptions, failed to pick up Thom's baton and run with it, following Atkinson's green light.

Alexander Thom - Cracking the Stone Age Code

As I have seldom met anyone, historian, archaeologist or layperson, who appears to have fully grasped the implications of either the astronomy or the accuracy and consistency of the geometry of megalithic sites, a text accessible to specialist and non-specialist alike seemed long overdue. I have lost track of the number of times I have heard people qualified enough to know better dole out the phrase, 'But of course, Thom's ideas have all been dismissed now'. Asking "By whom?", "When?", and "How has this opinion been arrived at?" usually leads to an uncomfortable silence and a change of subject. This kind of statement needs to be informed, not drawn from blind belief or professional bias.

During half a lifetime measuring and recording the megalithic remains of Britain and Brittany, Thom was more or less on his own, the only player on a decidedly non-level playing field, kicking the megalithic ball uphill and struggling against a full side of censoring academics. This was a further factor that encouraged me to write this book. Twenty years after Thom's death, it is surely time to encourage more players, perhaps even some transfers, to his team. This can only happen if his work is better explained and then understood, both in context within the period during which it appeared and by an appraisal of where it has been applied since Thom's death in 1985. Only thus can Thom's contribution to understanding prehistory become integrated within mainstream archaeology, where it belongs. It is high time that this material came out of the cold, for as we shall see it has much to offer.

Fortunately, throughout Thom's work one discovers an evidence-based world of repeatable measurements absent from many other disciplines. One may enjoy a real sense of objectivity in studying Thom's life-work, and even in checking it out oneself, as the author has been doing for over twenty years. From such work, and that undertaken by some other researchers, it has been possible to extend the boundaries of Thom's work beyond those set during his own lifetime. The subject is not sealed in a time-capsule, a curio dating from the middle of the last century, but has evolved dramatically to reveal, as I shall show in later chapters, an astonishing new picture of the intentions and capabilities of prehistoric society. This new work augments the earlier material and confirms Thom's conclusions in a manner that will surely prove quite embarrassing to some of his surviving critics.

The reader has every right to enquire of the position of the author in all of this. My own background is quite similar to that of Thom. By education I am an engineer, and have been a research scientist (in electronics), a departmental head of engineering in three colleges of further education, and lecturer in five, (one of which - Farnborough - was heavily dependent on the RAE student apprentice intake), a keen amateur sailor and much interested in astronomy. In the course of a fifteen year teaching career I have also taught surveying, mensuration, geometry and navigation. While all of these things have been undertaken at a considerably lower level than that realised by Thom, this background has placed me within the same kind of thinking environment as AT and better enabled me to understand his work and the technical content of the criticism directed at much of it. Most recently I have been awarded an honorary research fellowship within the Department of Archaeology and Anthropology at the University of Wales, Lampeter.

My personal views on the value of Thom's research matter less than a firm conviction that the whole package is worthy of a re-appraisal, and holds wide interest beyond the normal boundaries of archaeology, which still has not answered why so many circles and other Neolithic monuments were constructed, nor their function. There is no single volume tracing the history of Thom's contribution to the subject of archaeoastronomy, nor explaining how it became so marginalised so quickly during his last decade. I have attempted not to burden the reader with a succession of my own opinions, preferring instead to present the evidence almost entirely through the quotes and comments of those people who engaged in the theatre of operations during the latter half of the last century. I have attempted at all stages of the text to follow the axioms of good journalism, one of which is to recognise personal bias as inevitable while attempting to minimise its interference in presenting an accurate storyline.

Although of necessity quite heavily biographical in places, this book is not primarily a biography. That task was undertaken by Thom's son Archibald (Archie) whose *Walking in all of the Squares* was published by Argyll Publishing in 1995, in the same year as Archie's untimely death. My first published book, *A Key to Stonehenge* (Bluestone Press, 1993) had been dedicated to the memory of Alexander Thom and during its preparation Archie had supplied me with his father's large scale plans of Stonehenge. Archie was delighted with both my book and its dedication and, as a result, during one long telephone conversation, I innocently asked him if anyone had written a biography of his father. Archie paused and then laughed, as this was the work in progress at the time, and we subsequently went on to discuss together the likely costs of together publishing Archie's biography of his father. Regrettably, Archie's advancing illness at that time precluded any further involvement with this project.

It is a matter of much sadness, beyond the personal family tragedy, that Archie had become too ill to adequately coordinate the final stages of the biography of his father, although he did see the finished book before his death. One consequence of this is that the book is patchy, incomplete in places with repetition in other places. Some of it was generously completed by a long-standing professional colleague and friend, Professor Archie Roy, a formidable astronomer, based at Glasgow University.

Filled with invaluable biographic material, Archie's book, hereinafter referred to as *WIATS*, demonstrates the filial devotion Archie gave freely to his father. Without Archie's book, this one could not have been completed. Similarly, without constant assistance from Archie during hundreds of surveys and visits to the wilder places of Britain, often in terrible weather, Alexander Thom could not have achieved one half of his remarkable forty-year output. Surveying needs at least two people, and Archie is undoubtedly the unsung hero of this story.

Alexander Thom - Cracking the Stone Age Code

The surviving Thom family, in particular Archie's daughter, Susan MacColl (*nee* Thom), had the wisdom to recognise the historical value of the huge collection of survey plans amassed over forty years, which were stored at *The Hill*, the Thom's family home in Dunlop, Ayrshire. Through the assistance of Dr Euan MacKie these were donated, with other memorabilia, to the Royal Commission for Ancient and Historic Monuments, Scotland, (RCAHMS) in Edinburgh. The 'Thom Collection', as it has become known, was catalogued by Lesley Ferguson, who has kindly made the material available to me during several visits to Scotland during the preparation of the book. The Thom family, particularly the MacColls and Thom's daughter Beryl, have been wholly generous in both their time and hospitality while I have collated the biographic material within this book. They have given me an insight into the man which could have been gleaned from no other source.

There are, and will no doubt remain, objections and justifiable criticisms of Thom's methodology, data and conclusions. Peer group critiques are a necessary, normal and entirely healthy aspect of scientific debate, a process by which a subject advances. In the history of science, Newton's spat with Sir Robert Hook showed how awful can be the consequences of this becoming a personal feud. The critical process can and should be non-personal. It was in this spirit that Thom initially endorsed astrophysicist Dr Clive Ruggles' Science Research Council grant application towards a project to check his surveys. Thom welcomed this offer to revisit and recheck many of the Scottish sites, yet the consequences of this work were to launch a long decline in acceptance of his findings, and appeared to cast doubt on the conclusions and even the methodology of the original surveys. Despite operating on a narrow front - the reality and precision of prehistoric astronomical alignments, this had the unfortunate effect of consigning the whole gamut of Thom's work to near oblivion as far as the archaeological profession was concerned. This painful episode in Thom's twilight years, when his health was fast failing, will be revisited, for it sheds much light on a major theme within this book.

Finally, in writing this book I wanted to present Thom's material in a way which hasn't been attempted before - accessible to the non-specialist reader and a 'good read'. If the specialist reader feels that in so doing I have diluted the original research, I would refute that vigorously and insist that popularisation and simplification have always followed pioneering research in any innovative field. The success of the BBC programmes, *Meet the Ancestors*, *Time Watch* and *Time Team* prove this point for archaeology, and have introduced the fascination of this subject to a national audience. As the editor of the similarly popular magazine, *Current Archaeology*, wrote recently, 'the subject may now be regarded as a popular commodity.'

In addition, I felt that the *Thomist Paradox* needed a fresh influx of energy in order to stimulate a new generation into debate and discussion about the nature and implications of Thom's megalithic units of length, and the astronomy and

Introduction

geometries of stone rings, fans and alignments. New ideas, like seeds, take time to grow into their culture. Forty years ago, the science of electronics was relatively new, now it is taught in our schools. One had to be an undergraduate to study transistor circuits in 1967; today the same material is taught, albeit greatly simplified, to fourteen year olds. And forty years ago computers were the stuff of boffins and science fiction films, today that same fourteen year old owns and uses several. And forty years ago, 'Sandy' Thom wrote and subsequently published an epic book, of which he himself reckoned only five people understood. It is high time more people from many disciplines understood this work, if only to enable them to understand what it reveals about prehistoric culture in these lands, and the reasons why Thom has become so marginalised. There are repercussions in the history of science, geometry, mathematics and even art which range far beyond the boundaries of conventional archaeology.

Today, I believe anyone may understand both the research and the implications of Thom's researches. In following through this process I hope to bring Alexander Thom into the public eye as one of the outstanding scientists of the last century. If that can be achieved then I, for one, will celebrate by raising a glass to the memory of a great Scotsman - Alexander Thom, the father of modern archaeoastronomy and the first person to provide scientific evidence of the true capabilities of our far distant ancestry.

Megalithic alignment near Burrator, Dartmoor, (*photograph by David Handford*).

Alexander Thom - Cracking the Stone Age Code

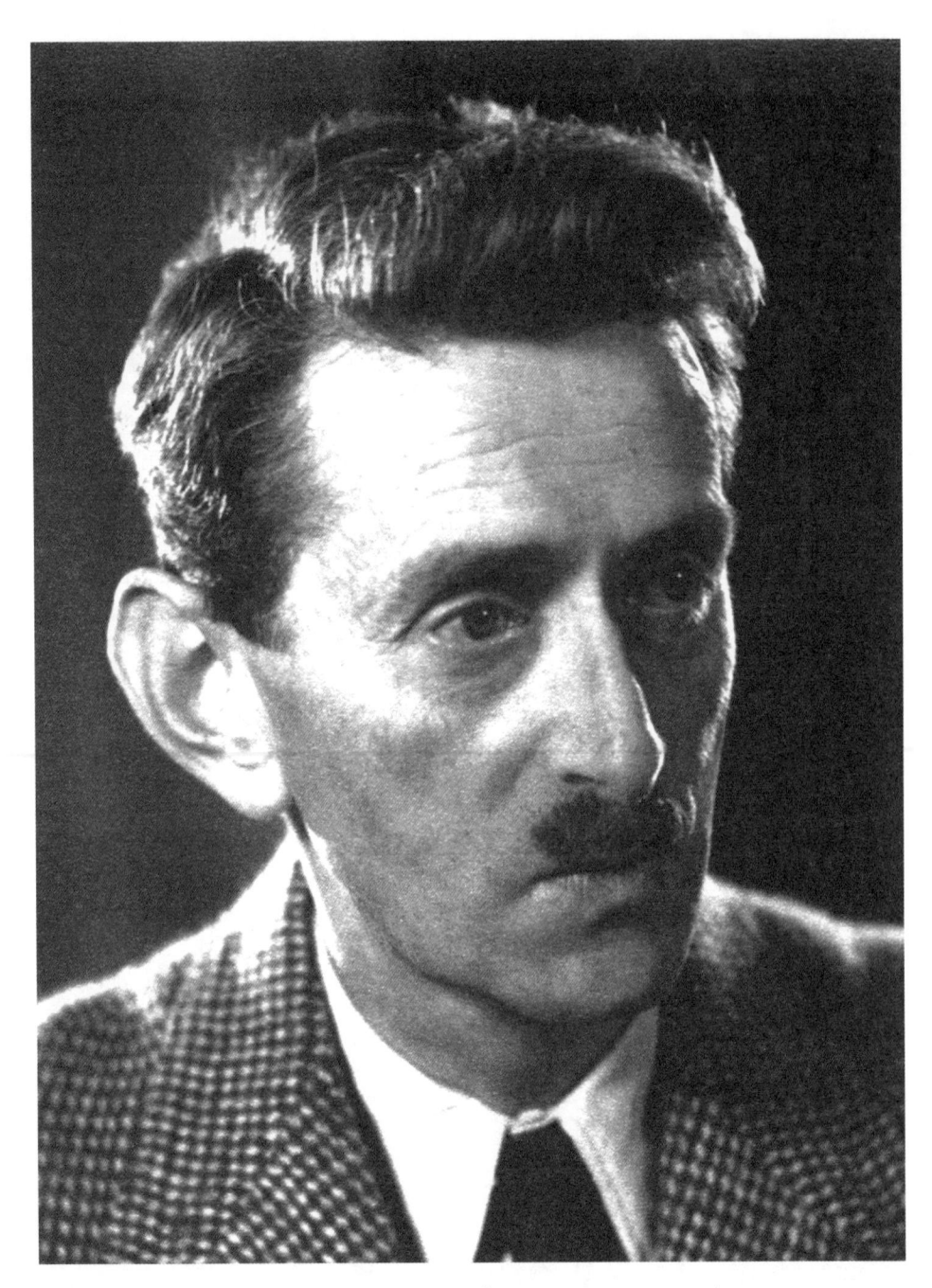

Alexander Thom, 1946

One of a sequence of portraits taken in 1946 in connection with his appointment as Chair of Engineering at Oxford, and Fellow of Brasenose College. Thom was then 52 years of age and moved to Oxford from his war-time post at the Royal Aircraft Establishment at Farnborough.

CHAPTER ONE

A Man of Nine Decades

Born on the 26th of March 1894, at Mains of Carradale, Argyllshire, into a farming family, Alexander 'Sandy' Thom became the classical self-taught industrial engineer, pulling himself up through the academic ranks by his own bootstraps. Thom was first and foremost an extremely able scientist and engineer, with a publications list and a *curriculum vitae* which would have been the envy of anyone.

Thom was born a Victorian, during that astonishing period of engineering achievement, particularly in his native Scotland. Thom was also of that almost vanished breed of men both practical and academic, artistic and scientific, who in a previous era have been called Renaissance men. 'Sandy' Thom spread his interests, applying his scientific knowledge through a wide range of hobbies. His knowledge of astronomy was renowned, and he was an expert at the unbelievably tricky task of shaping large telescope mirrors. He was a competent woodworker, and although not a religious man in a formal sense, loved nothing more than to explore the architecture of old churches and Cathedrals. AT was a considerable gardener and a good shot. He could also play a violin and be entirely at home fabricating metal parts on a lathe. He was an expert sailor and navigator of the notoriously tricky coastal waters around Scotland, completely at ease in many types of boat, powered or under sail. His nickname of 'The Skipper' was well earned and those who had sailed with Thom never felt any unease with him at the helm. Thom loved sailboats and sailing, an art he learned from his uncle, Sam Strang. One of the earliest photographs of him (*overleaf*) shows a very determined young man hauling up a gaff-rigg sail.

In 1911, Thom entered the Royal Technical College in Glasgow, where he sat alongside John Logie Baird, who is known as the inventor of television. Sandy and other classmates took notes for Baird in his frequent absence due to 'working his way through college' (financing his studies by taking a part-time job). Thom's name is mentioned twice in *The Secret Life of John Logie Baird*.

Alexander Thom - Cracking the Stone Age Code

As a young man, during the summer of 1912, he attended a summer school at Loch Eck, where no less than Professor Moncur and Dr David Clark personally taught him the surveying skills and field astronomy which were to be so important later in revealing the secrets of the megalithic culture. The fee for this course was also paid for by Thom's family mentor, his mother's brother, William Strang.

Support of this kind proved invaluable to the growing boy, and in 1917 Uncle Willy even gave Thom an *Albion* motor car. In the summer of 1913, aged 19, Thom sailed to Canada, for just £12, again paid for by his uncle, where he assisted in the surveying and siting of the Canadian Pacific Railway network. Civil engineering students were obliged to do practical work as part of their 'sandwich course' and Sandy worked as a chainman and again learned surveying. On graduating in 1914 from the Royal Technical College (RTC) in Glasgow, he finished his B.Sc. with 'Special Distinction' in Engineering at Glasgow University, where he also took a course in astronomy. He built himself his first telescope, and established an observatory at *The Hill*.

A potentially serious heart 'murmur' precluded any possibility of being called up for active service when the Great War started. Instead, in 1915, Thom joined the engineering firm of Sir William Arrol and Company, the company that undertook the building of the Forth Bridge, that supreme symbol of Victorian heavy engineering skill. Feeling the need for a career change, he suddenly took off and moved south into England and joined The Norman Thompson Flight Company and, later, the Gosport Aircraft Company, where he designed flying boats.

On one weekend in August 1917 he returned home to Scotland and married his sweetheart, Jeanie Kirkwood (*photo opposite with marriage announcement*). Jeanie was called 'Sis', having the unfortunate pleasure of being the only girl in a family of older brothers. They knew she had been out with Sandy and were savouring all the routine *double entendre* and sniggering that boys display where courtship is concerned. Nonchalantly, but with deliberate emphasis, one

Chapter One - A Man of Nine Decades

of her brothers asked his sister "And what have *you* been doing today?" Sis immediately wiped out the entire family with her equally nonchalant reply, "I got married", shortly before catching the train down south with her new husband. Jeanie was forever a "huge support' to Sandy Thom, and their long marriage was a lively and interesting one.

In 1921, A.T. returned to Scotland and was appointed as lecturer in engineering at Glasgow University, rapidly gaining Ph.D and D.Sc. degrees. An increasing interest in the new science of radio led A.T. to build increasingly complex crystal sets, each with tuning capacitors (condensers) he had learned to make himself. Long lengths of aerial wire were stretched across the garden, and efficient electrical earthing rods driven into prepared earth. He built crystal sets for his family and friends. Later, when valve sets became available he received transmissions from stations broadcasting from the USA. He constructed a two-valve TRF set, later modifying it to a super-regenerative design, and adapted reception to include the new shorter wavelengths. An Ekco superheterodyne wireless set from about 1935 may be seen in some of the old photographs. Yet he was not partial to television, '*What a misuse of a marvellous invention!*' he would exclaim, just loudly enough for viewers to have heard him!

THOM—KIRKWOOD.—At Glasgow, on the 10th of August, 1917, Alexander Thom, B.Sc., A.R.T.C., of The Hill, Dunlop, to Jeanie Boyd, eldest daughter of Mr and Mrs Allan Kirkwood, Glencairn, Dunlop.

In 1922, Thom built his own home, *Thalassa*, (*below right*) and powered it with electricity from a windmill he designed and built himself (*below left*). He became a family man, and always treated himself and his family to a few weeks hard sailing every summer off the coast of Scotland. When his father died in 1924, he actively took over and assisted in the running of the family farm at *The Hill*, Dunlop. He fathered three children, Archibald, Alan and Beryl (*see family photo*

on page 7). Alan was to perish in a civilian flying accident in 1945, Jeanie never totally recovered from this tragic event, while Sandy went in on himself and buried himself in his work. Archie died of a brain tumour in 1995.

Above: 'Commencing the motor'. Alexander Thom at the controls of a single cylinder motorcycle at the gate leading to the bungalow at *The Hill*, around 1932. Thom's love of machinery made motorcycling a joy, and both he and his wife undertook long distance runs on various solo and sidecar machines.

Below: A mighty mechanical beast! Thom's four-cylinder FN combination, with his brother-in-law, David McCardle in the saddle. Location and date remains unidentified, but according to Thom's daughter Beryl, it is clearly not at *The Hill*.

From 1921 until the outbreak of the war in 1939, Thom was employed first as a lecturer in engineering at Glasgow University, and took part in the development of the new Department of Aeronautics there. In addition he taught statistics, practical field surveying and astronomy. He also lectured in the theory and practice of theodolite design and use, and made the interesting quote to his students that, "the instrument is almost unique in that it can be made to check its own adjustment". Thom's university duties coupled with the onerous task of managing the farm following his father's death left little time for other pursuits. However, the job did provide a long summer break, ideal for an outdoor man who would, within ten years, begin surveying scores of stone circles all over Britain.

Like all mechanically minded people, Thom loved motorcycles. For a family, it was common to add a sidecar to the machine, and the Thoms owned two at

Chapter One - A Man of Nine Decades

this time. More unusual, his wife Jeanie also drove, and was adept at driving their *Precision* sidecar outfit over long distances. Her husband owned the four-cylinder FN combination displayed at the bottom of the previous page and various solo machines at various times during this period.

The 'Skipper' making good way through the waters of the Western Isles, with wife Jeanie and two young relatives of his Uncle, Sam Strang, as crew. The clinker-built tender in tow enabled the crew to beach onto tiny islets, and other places of interest where no easy harbour existed. This same mode of transport was later to prove invaluable, enabling access to megalithic sites in remote places. How Thom kept the cap on remains a mystery.

The sailing trips remain very much part of the Thom family legend. Thom was a first rate sailor and knew intimately well both the waters and the weather off the west coast of Scotland. On the BBC *Chronicle* documentary, aged 76, he was filmed again sailing into East Loch Roag, the inlet near Callanish on the Isle of Lewis. This delightful piece of filming shows the 'Skipper' in action, the sole record we have, and the voice-over has him describing this as a "filthy coast", and that "Tyree has five times the gale frequency of most of Britain." Thom had been sailing this tricky coastline 'for nearly fifty summers' when he wrote his introduction to *Megalithic Lunar Observatories*. He stresses the dangers to small boats sailing here, describing the extreme tidal rips and the 'amphidromic point' where the two high tides meet out of phase. Both represent potential fatal hazards, and Thom recognised that prehistoric people must inevitably have made connections between the tidal state and the moon. Why? Because at a

Alexander Thom - Cracking the Stone Age Code

AT enjoying a pipe while the sails idly luff in a becalmed sea, with happy wife Jeanie, elder son Archie and an unidentified woman leaning on the mainsail. The yacht is probably *Hadassah*, date about 1937, location unknown.

given location the moon's position in the sky is synchronized to the tides - the moon is always found in roughly the same area of the sky when it is high tide.

The dangers of getting the timing wrong in small boats must have provided a crucial impetus to understanding lunar motion. The lunar phases determine the heights of the tides (the tidal range) and indicate the amount of available light during the night, whilst the moon's position in the sky told those in the know when to expect high and low water. For these reasons Thom knew that prehistoric marine traders and travellers must have had the strongest of reasons to study the moon. Succinctly he writes, "The relation between the phase of the Moon and the time, direction and violence of the tide must be clearly understood'.

'The Skipper' rowing back to the yacht across a calm sea, following a shopping trip ashore.

Chapter One - A Man of Nine Decades

The Thom family in the garden of their new rented home in Fleet, Hampshire, probably in autumn 1939. A grumpy looking Alexander Thom is perhaps due in part to problems with the timed shutter on the camera. In addition he was finding the politics at the Royal Aircraft Establishment, where he had been sequestered for the War, very difficult to deal with during his initial period at the RAE. Until the High Speed Wind Tunnel (HST) project came along, he felt under-occupied.

Sandy and wife Jeanie make up the top row. The second row finds son Alan (left) and daughter Beryl, while elder son Archie and his future wife Margaret are kneeling on the grass.

1939 AND THE MOVE TO FLEET, HAMPSHIRE

Immediately following the outbreak of World War II, Thom was directed to the Royal Aircraft Establishment in Farnborough. The family moved there during the autumn of 1939, renting a house in nearby Fleet, Hampshire. During the war, in the post of Principal Scientific Officer, Alex Thom headed the Royal Aircraft Establishment (RAE) team which developed the first high speed wind tunnel, thereafter known as the HST. It was in use almost every day at RAE Farnborough during the latter part of the war. Thereafter it provided an invaluable research facility for the development of almost every post-war British military aircraft and many civilian airliners, including the first passenger jet airliner, the ill-fated Comet 1.

Thom's specialist practical knowledge of the laminar flow around surfaces brought him into contact with the work of Barnes Wallace, later Sir Barnes Wallace, the designer of the revolutionary 'geodetic' Wellington bomber and of the 'bouncing bomb' made famous by the Dambuster raids. Archie Thom relates that Thom had told him that he "knew Wallace",

Alexander Thom - Cracking the Stone Age Code

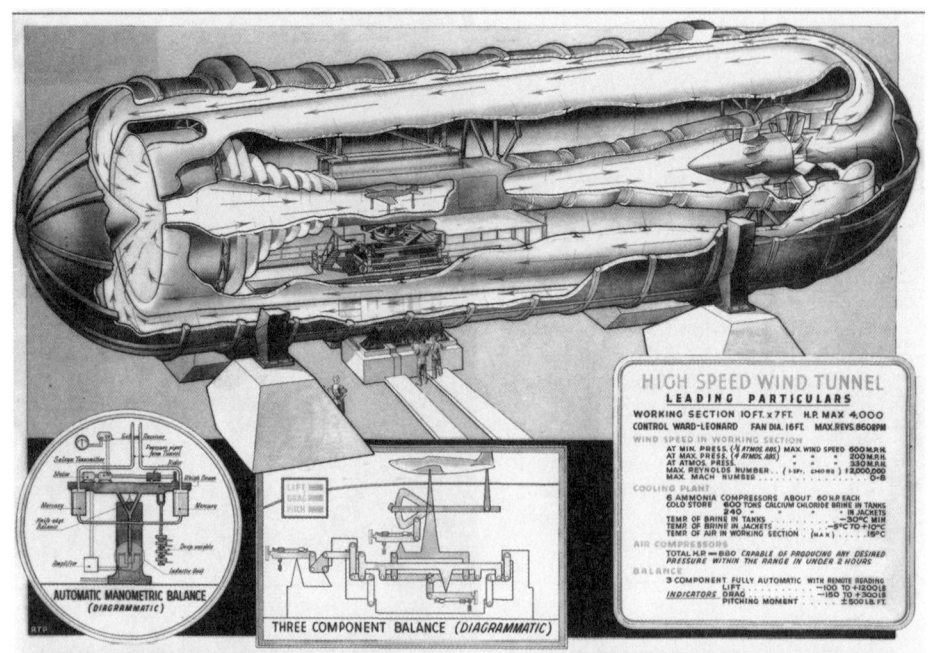

HIGH SPEED WIND TUNNEL —— DIAGRAM OF OPERATION

'Sandy had met Barnes Wallace, inventor of the 'spinning bomb'. There was no discussion at RAE about Sandy's pre-war work on spinning cylinders, but Austin Mair remembers "a day when a man from the Armaments Department of the RAE came to see AT and asked him about the work he had done at Glasgow on flow past cylinders and whether he had worked on spheres. I think he also asked about rotation but I am not sure of this. After the news came about the the raids on the dams AT realised what had been the reason for the enquiry."

The photographs opposite give some account of the magnitude of the HST project. Both resemble stills from a Fritz Lang film, although the lower picture is of the inauguration ceremony, with Thom seated at the end of the third row (*inset bottom left*) and the government top-brass on the podium. One can only wonder if Thom's decidedly *hitlerian* moustache caused a few security problems at Farnborough!

[*Acknowledgement and grateful thanks are due to DERA for the supply of both photographs of the HST. These are held under Crown Copyright, (2000 DERA), and reproduced with the permission of the Controller, HMSO.*]

THE POST WAR PERIOD - BRASENOSE COLLEGE, OXFORD

In 1944, Thom successfully applied for the Chair of Engineering Science at Brasenose College, Oxford. To be appointed to this post indicates the highest professional assessment of his skills. The family again moved house, and made arrangements to rent out *The Hill*. Thom converted two large hen houses into live-in cabins, for use by the family during holiday periods and during the long summer break. Daughter Beryl describes these cabins as being 'very comfortable'. Archie was working at Glasgow University by this time, and he and his family moved first into *Thalassa*, then into *The Bungalow*, a property at *The Hill,* upon Thom's retirement in 1961.

The engineering block at Oxford, a contemporary glass and steel building completed after he had retired, is named 'The Thom Building' in his honour. At Brasenose he used his management abilities to enlarge his initially small department to an academic staff of fifteen with 160 undergraduates. In 1961, on his retirement, he was appointed Professor Emeritus, and published a classic text, *Field Computation in Engineering and Physics*, with Dr C. J. Apeld as co-author.

But Thom also left his astronomical mark at Oxford. At Brasenose College he realigned the sundial on the wall of the main quadrangle and made an engraved *Equation of Time* on the opposite wall in the main Dining Hall entrance. It remains there to this day. This enables students and staff to correct for local meridian time, and estimate the time to within a few minutes, but only when the sun is shining.

Alexander Thom - Cracking the Stone Age Code

What was to become Thom's second career began in parallel with his academic and industrial careers. It gradually led him to discover 'Megalithic Science'. From about 1937 until 1961, much of his spare time was spent surveying megalithic remains. When he retired from academia in 1961 he devoted the rest of his active life to the surveying and analysis of those surviving megalithic sites which still litter northwestern Europe. A.T. enjoyed a real *Indian summer*, enjoying an active career at an age when many people think of donning their pipe and slippers and taking things easy. Apart from the omnipresent pipe, this was not Thom's way of approaching the world. He was an active man always working on practical outcomes to domestic and professional matters.

Thom always smoked a pipe, consuming about an ounce of *Erinmore Mixture* or *Gold Block* per week. He never smoked cigarettes. From his early thirties until his late seventies, following another health scare, Thom took his daily cold dip in an old bath installed outside *Thalassa*, fed from rainwater stored in an ancient whisky barrel. The bath remains there, although Thalassa was demolished in the 90s. His wife took up the habit as well, and neither seemed to do other than thrive on this spartan activity, even though at times they had to break the ice on the surface of the bath. If Sandy was invited to stay in the homes of friends and, later in his life, those of admirers of his work on the megaliths, he would always immediately open the window in his room, whatever the weather.

Alexander Thom could be excellent company amongst friends, some of whom were archaeologists. But he was never one for small talk, preferring to sit with a pipe and spend time contemplating his next project. He was by all accounts very well read, including many of the classics, and could recite *Tam O'Shanter* by heart. He often chose to read novels in German translations because 'they take longer that way.' In compiling this book, not a single person I spoke with appeared to have disliked the man, nor knew anyone who did. Yet, at the same time, he could be irascible, blunt, bawdy and impatient to a high degree and he suffered fools not at all, yet alone gladly - he was no saint. But he could be very witty and something of a master at *double entendre*. His son Archie related a story about a dinner party in West Kilbride. Thom and Jeanie were enjoying an aperitif, when Helen, the hostess, excused herself saying she "had a tart to cover in the kitchen". Quick as a flash, Sandy replied, "I think I'd make a better job of that than you, Helen". (*WIATS*, p 143).

At work in *The Cabin*, a converted hen house at *The Hill* in Dunlop where the Thom family spent their holiday periods. About 1948.

According to his notebooks, from about May 1938, Thom began accurate theodolite surveys of many Scottish and Lake District sites (*photo of Castle Rigg opposite*). Assisted by his family, wife Jeanie ('Sis'), son Archie, daughter Beryl

Chapter One - A Man of Nine Decades

The earliest Thom photograph of a stone circle, Castle Rigg in the English Lake District. It shows the midsummer setting alignment from a stone (named 'B' on the plan given in MSIB and on page 58 and 188 here). The alignment then passes through the top of the foreground stone, through the centre of the ring and leaves *en route* for the top of the hill in the background via stone 'A". Thom was clearly undertaking a survey here, ropes are laid from the centre where a survey stave can be seen. The man and boy cannot be identified. The photograph was developed and printed by Thom before the war, around 1938. Badly deteriorated, it has required much restoration.

and latterly, even grandchildren, Thom's regimented surveys were a mixture of work hard and play hard. Later, as the work became more demanding, a string of fascinated helpers from outside the family circle volunteered their services, seduced by the charm that Sandy exuded whenever he became head of a team of people. Yet here was a hard task-master unremitting in his requirements for diligence and accuracy over even the most trivial of details. Although normally a polite and reserved man, he could become quite grumpy and curt with chattering on-lookers when taking bookings from his theodolite - he would simply say "do you mind?" with increasing intensity until they shut up or went elsewhere.

With half a century of man-management skills under his belt, Thom knew perfectly well how to mix with people and extract the best efforts from his helpers. He radiated charisma, he took command quietly. His energy for structuring and organising surveys set an example to all who knew him. Like some latter-day Pied Piper, he enchanted people into a world not of music and dance, but instead of hour angles, azimuths, closed traverses, datum points, vernier scales and the daily pirouette of the earth, reflected in the risings and settings of sun, moon and stars.

Through his field work and diligent analyses, Thom regularly published a stream of monograms and papers revealing his findings. These were published by such august bodies as the *Institute of Navigation*, the *Royal Statistical Society*, and the *Journal for the History of Astronomy*. It is regrettable that so little of this work was known about nor ever made available to the non-specialist. Sandy didn't see the point, and was far too busy collecting an ever increasing corpus of data. Ever the head-strong pioneer, this data satisfied his increasing awareness that his 'Megalithic man' was a skilled astronomer and geometer.

Archaeologists eschewed this aspect of the past relating to stone circles and ancient astronomy, and Sandy was not much concerned that they found increasing difficulty in integrating his findings within their model of prehistory. He almost certainly saw his quest as a specialist task, largely outside of archaeology, with no requirement to inform anyone other than fellow specialists. This was a serious misjudgement on his part, for it certainly led to an inaccessibility whereby the lay public could only look to 'experts' for help in deciding whether Thom's thesis was correct. This was a serious misjudgement on their part - prior to the sixties, Thom *was* the sole expert in this field and the archaeologists were by and large fazed by the whole thing.

Another early survey around 1951. A lightweight theodolite has staves at the base of the tripod laid flat as if indicating important perimeter stones. The site appears to be either a treeless Rollright stones or Stanton Drew, both of which are built with conglomerate stones similar to those above.

THE 1960s - THE ARRIVAL OF ASTRO-ARCHAEOLOGY

Up to 1965, Thom's researches were unheard of outside of a few specialists and a small *coterie* of friends and helpers. Then, circumstances were to change the entire tack of his career. In the social ferment of the sixties, archaeology and 'earth-mysteries' began to become popular as a whole generation of young people strove to find new and 'alternative' social pathways, eschewing the industrial culture. The word 'ley-line' became infused into popular culture, as Alfred Watkins' *The Old Straight Track*, originally published in 1924, became available in a popular new edition. Although Watkins never once used the word ley-line within his book it entered popular culture and it suddenly became

Chapter One - A Man of Nine Decades

extremely 'trendy' to search out the older traditions, calendar rituals and folklore of Britain. Naturally, up surfaced the hoary question of what all those stone circles were about. Nobody seemed to know why they were built nor what they were for. The stage was set, and as often happens when the public wants answers, the key players in the drama which was about to unfold were already in place and not long in coming forward. *Come the time, come the man*. As the editor of *Archaeoastronomy* was to eloquently put it, in his obituary on Thom,

'The world was ready for Thom, and Lord knows, Thom was ready.'

In 1965, a British born American astronomer, Dr Gerald S. Hawkins, published a popular book which entirely captured public imagination. *Stonehenge Decoded* became a best selling book about the relationship between the world's most famous megalithic monument and the astronomy above Salisbury Plain, around 2000 BC. In 1963, Hawkins shared his emerging theory with Cambridge archaeologist, prehistorian and editor of *Antiquity*, Dr Glyn Daniel, who immediately wrote to the leading astrophysicist of the day, Professor Fred Hoyle, 'Either this man is mad, or it will cause a revolution in our thinking about prehistoric Britain.' Hoyle wrote back, 'I have checked the calculations. Hawkins is not mad. And you considerably underestimate the impact.' Whilst Hawkins was decreed not to have been mad, neither was he the discoverer of the key alignments at Stonehenge that had provided the basis for his book. That title goes to a retired Gas Board manager, Mr C. A. ('Peter') Newham, [*photo overleaf*] from Tadcaster in Yorkshire. We shall meet the tale of Newham's ill-fated booklet on Stonehenge later. Although Newham was acknowledged in *Stonehenge Decoded*, all the glory went to Hawkins. Hawkins never mentioned (nor has anybody else) that Newham was an active and experienced amateur astronomer, running the Leeds Astronomical Society. Happily, once published, Newham's little booklet '*The Astronomical Significance of Stonehenge*' remained the best selling publication at Stonehenge for decades.

Gerald S Hawkins, the British born astronomer who started the fuss about Stonehenge in 1965, with the publication of *Stonehenge Decoded*. He used a computer to determine alignments.

When *Stonehenge Decoded* hit the bookshops, the archaeological world was shaken, the more so because this young and dashing astronomer was taking the then revolutionary step of analysing all his alignments with an IBM computer.

Alexander Thom - Cracking the Stone Age Code

In the 1960s computers were still novel enough to be held in awe. Hawkins' timing could not have been better, and he caught the whole archaeology profession napping, arguably doing more to popularise Stonehenge than had Atkinson a decade previously with his seminal book, *Stonehenge*. The outcome of their inevitable spat is discussed in a later chapter - enough here to say that, predictably, Atkinson was decidedly miffed at this young upstart kicking up the dirt on his patch!

Much of Hawkins' book concerned itself with exactly the same kind of precision measurement that Thom had been routinely undertaking since 1933. Inevitably, in view of what had happened to Newham, Thom must have sensed the danger of his own discoveries being usurped, with the consequent risk of him becoming a secondary player in the race to reveal 'his' Megalithic Science. He must have seen plainly that he had amassed more than enough convincing material to write and then publish a full length book. In 1965 he published a well received 'trial run' of his astronomical material in *Vistas in Astronomy* (Vol 7, 1-57) then grasped the nettle, and wrote to Oxford University Press. The result was *Megalithic Sites in Britain*, published by Clarendon Press, Oxford in 1967. It was followed in 1969, by *Megalithic Lunar Observatories* and in 1978 the final large scale work to be published in his lifetime, *Megalithic Remains in Britain and Brittany*, was published.

Posh frocks at Stonehenge. Cecil August Newham, who understandably preferred to be known as 'Peter', here flanked by early 1960s fashions. A retired gas board manager and adept amateur astronomer from Yorkshire, in 1961 Newham surveyed Stonehenge looking for alignments other than the well known midsummer one, and Hawkins took it from there, (*photo from Michael Postins*).

Chapter One - A Man of Nine Decades

These books were totally unlike Hawkins' work, either in content or style. Thom's books were not for the faint-hearted, and never could have been popular texts in the same league as *Stonehenge Decoded*. They were hard, dry, academic textbooks, an extreme read, and the going was so tough that many mathematically challenged academics, and this category included most archaeologists of that era, fell at the first fence. But if these books never really entered the public arena, the lectures and talks given by the seventy-odd year old retired professor certainly began to capture public imagination. A froth of debate ran around the nation in 1968 and 1969, fuelled by lecture tours undertaken by both Sandy and Archie, usually together, and people were openly discussing the possibilities that early man was capable of a high level of astronomy, geometry and observational skill, certainly much more than the neolithic barbarian image still prevalent from Childe's and Clark's popular archaeology books. Some of these folk became dubbed 'Stone-Age Einsteins', a phrase that Magnus Magnusson was to pick up on in the later *Chronicle* documentary on Thom.

The archaeological profession as a whole treated Hawkins and Thom to the time-honoured manner of the professional snub. However, several of the weightier names in the field of megalithic archaeology became Thom's personal friends. In an obituary, perhaps the greatest old-school archaeologist of the twentieth century, Richard Atkinson, warmly described Thom as a 'most generous man' who had 'single-handedly created a new academic discipline'. His quotes at the very beginning of this book eloquently describe his conversion process. Dr Euan MacKie remains convinced that Thom's researches discovered a hidden dimension in neolithic culture and has continued to provide archaeological evidence to support that view. And the greatest living authority on stone circles, Dr Aubrey Burl, wrote in his obituary that 'Alexander Thom was a modest, unaggressive man and in many ways a great man'. In an interview I held with Dr Burl, he continually stressed that "Thom made us all think. About astronomy, about geometry..." Yet despite doing all that thinking, the archaeological profession as a whole sat on the fence, and has managed to airbrush Thom and his conclusions out of mainstream archaeology, the subject of a later chapter.

These same leading archaeologists stood in awe of Thom's technical skills, and evidently, as this quote by Atkinson indicates, his energy and commitment,

> *'I took part in his survey of Stonehenge (1973), and found it hard to keep up with him..'.*

Thom was 79 at the time. Atkinson was 26 years his junior and commanded an immense respect. The fact that 'Sandy' once asked to use Atkinson's cigarette holder to temporarily mark a datum point during the Stonehenge survey suggests that they were on pretty good terms. Atkinson agreed to the request. On occasion Thom and Burl loaned theodolites to each other, and freely swapped information, again demonstrating a *camaraderie* that existed between them, out of the increasingly unkind limelight of the archaeological press. MacKie worked on site with both Alex and Archie Thom, the only archaeologist that has ever attempted to support Thom's evidence with conventional archaeological techniques on site. MacKie also visited Sandy during his final days.

Thom's public forays were unfortunately often billed alongside the gurus of the then rising craze for the older traditions, ufology, and the hippy philosophies of that era. In 1968, this was the fate of any speaker in the then nascent subject which became known as 'earth mysteries', once referred to by Atkinson in the now notorious phrase, "The loony fringe of dotty archaeology". By no stretch of the imagination would Thom have identified himself as a New Age guru. Yet, in truth, that is precisely what was bestowed upon him by the New Agers. One could reasonably expect that there would be no link whatever between a Victorian-born cartesian scientist and the marijuana flavoured culture that so warmly embraced his radical model of prehistory. Yet even if most could not understand the detail, they saw the picture on the box. His books lay alongside the 'hugely influential' New Age classic by John Michell, *The View over Atlantis* (1969), Guy Underwood's *Pattern of the Past (1974),* the beautifully graphic work by Keith Critchlow, *Time Stands Still* (1973) and a popular 'overview' book by author, Francis Hitching, *Earth Magic* (1976).

The irony of Thom's role as ageing Oxbridge professor to these people is that he was more of a proto-hippy than many of them could have ever imagined. The alternative movement had welcomed into their midst a man who had, up to forty years previously, become a lifelong vegetarian, had powered his self-built wooden home with a self-built windmill, grew most of his own produce as a routine way of life and was "vehemently against what he saw as the rape of the planet". Sandy had been 'back to the land' before most of the hippy generation's parents had been born, indeed, he had never left it! Perhaps more importantly, unlike them, he had no problem mixing this with technological advances. In their language, his right and left brain talked freely to each other, man.

The author once heard Thom lecture at a university arts festival. He was timetabled against a gentleman who claimed to have been abducted by the occupants of a UFO, and who thereby drew a capacity audience. However, as his anti-gravity demonstration was somewhat less than successful, perhaps as many as 100 disillusioned festival goers rapidly became unimpressed and attempted to gate-crash Thom's lecture midway through. It was remarkable to witness this seasoned lecturer taking all this additional influx and shuffling of feet in his stride as he continued to deliver his painstaking accounts of neolithic geometry as if nothing was happening.

Slow, measured and spoken with his quiet yet melodic Scottish accent, Thom expected his audience to be already familiar with the main themes of his work. So, compared to our abductee, this lecture was hard work, even for those who had been in from the start. Thom came across, with cardigan and pipe, as the classic 1950s professor, an archetype later to be perfectly portrayed by Anthony Hopkins in *Shadowlands*, the film about another Oxford academic, C.S.Lewis.

Chapter One - A Man of Nine Decades

Predictably, after a further twenty minutes or so, an increasing number of those same feet which had shuffled in at half-time, shuffled out to the exits, presumably thoroughly disillusioned with both UFO abductees and the geometry of stone rings. But no-one in from the start left and questions were going strong for a good three-quarters of an hour after the lecture. The Student Union was buzzing with discussions about Thom's theories for weeks afterwards.

The one problem that Thom never overcame was that despite intense public interest in his ideas on prehistory - his work, or rather the proof of his researches, was never really presented so as to be understood by the general public or non-specialist. Thom belonged to that generation of academics who didn't think that popularisation was really necessary nor even advisable if it compromised the scientific approach to research. Old school - new ideas, always a difficult combination, and for a man approaching seventy-five years of age, probably doubly so.

THE BBC *CHRONICLE* DOCUMENTARY

Help was at hand, however, and two years later the BBC *Chronicle* series produced a documentary about Thom's work, entitled 'Cracking the Stone Age Code'. *Chronicle* was one of those rare TV documentary series that attempted, without compromising depth, to bring complex subjects to a wider cross section of the population. Produced by the master of the *genre*, Paul Johnson, the presenter was the amiable Magnus Magnusson, who wove his informality and magic into the programme. Thom and Magnusson clearly got on well together, both pipe smoking their way through the difficult terrain of Thom's findings and theories. The result was probably the best treatment of Thom's researches and conclusions ever carried out in his lifetime.

Serendipity played its part in this popularisation of Thom's work, and from an unlikely source. The open-mindedness of Cambridge archaeologist Dr Glyn Daniel catalysed the original meeting between Thom and the BBC team, and the result was that the documentary now represents a superb time-capsule of the attitudes of archaeologists of that period. The viewer was treated to a forest of well known names in the archaeological profession, Dr Glyn Daniel, Professor Richard Atkinson, Dr A H A Hogg, Professor Stuart Piggott, Dr Jacquetta Hawkes, Dr Humphrey Case, and Dr Euan MacKie all discussing, from various vantage points, the paradox between archaeology as was (in 1970), and the radical ideas of Professor Thom.

Some of these eminent archaeologists later came over to acknowledge and validate Thom's findings, Atkinson doing this publicly on more than one occasion. MacKie picked up on many of Thom's researches and developed them. Some jumped ship, as in the case of Daniel, who had been kindly disposed to Thom at the time of the programme, yet later turned strongly away from Thom's model of prehistoric Britain. The *Chronicle* programme was remarkably fair, both to archaeology, as we might have expected, but also to our retired professor, which for once made for a level playing field. There were some surprising 'voice-overs', beginning with Professor Glyn Daniel,

"Firstly, all professional archaeologists are beset by the lunatic fringe. Secondly, Professor Thom is not part of this."

Duly exorcised and somewhat patronisingly having had his sanity vouched for, Thom then pronounced on megalithic astronomers,

"I think they were, as far as brain power is concerned, my superiors."

No respected scientist or engineer had previously ever uttered words like these on a mainstream television programme! As a counter statement to the popular 'woad-covered savages' belief concerning ancient Britons, this was heady stuff and it must have shocked many viewers, for Thom was clearly, as far as brain power was concerned, vastly superior to the average modern human.

Dr Glyn E Daniel (Cambridge)

Earlier on in the programme, Atkinson made this revealing statement,

"No-one I am sure is going to question the accuracy or the comprehensiveness of the evidence which Professor Thom has put before us. Where people are going to have difficulty is with the implications. If we accept the implications we are going to have to accept something which to us archaeologists sounds pretty improbable but I still think we have got to take it seriously simply because if we reject it we are in fact flying in the face of a great deal of evidence which cannot be explained away simply as the result of chance or accident."

Professor R J Atkinson (Cardiff)

Chapter One - A Man of Nine Decades

Quite. Then Dr Euan Mackie entered the debate. Asked by Magnusson what the chances were that Thom's 'observation platform' at Kintraw had been man-made, he gave this *libranesque* reply, "I'd say about 50:50", to which Magnusson demanded that the scales tip by asking, "What would have proved it one way or the other?", MacKie replying, "Well, some concrete sign of human activity like potsherds or a post hole or a stone socket. Perhaps a piece of charred timber: something like that. We haven't had any of those."

With Thom's reputation still left swinging in the balance, viewers were then treated to a delightfully non-committal epithet,

Dr Euan W MacKie (Glasgow)

> "I think the evidence that Professor Thom has given us makes it overwhelmingly probable that astronomy could have been practised."

This underwhelming endorsement was perhaps about as much grace as orthodox archaeologists could grant Thom in 1970 and MacKie was apparently unable to offer an unqualified green light. Yet despite this non-committal start, MacKie becomes one of the heroes of our story, and went on to promote Thom's ideas more than any other single person in the profession, probably to the detriment of his career opportunities. He remains the only archaeologist to have used conventional archaeological techniques in order to support and confirm Thom's astronomical theories.

The *Chronicle* documentary mixes graphics and prehistoric sites in a remarkably lucid account of other aspects of the professor's researches. The major alignments are there, solar and lunar, and the producer wisely involved Thom in the then rising controversy within archaeology. The alignments, geometries, metrology and the controversy form the subject of later chapters of this book. However, well worth a mention is the lesson Thom gave Magnusson on laying out megalithic designs. Using a sandy beach, some pegs and a marked rope, he drew a 'Type I egg' from two 3:4:5 Pythagorean triangles. Graphics then showed the viewer how this and the other shapes could have been laid out prior to importing the large stones that then defined the geometry. At one point

Alexander Thom - Cracking the Stone Age Code

the cameraman is evidently getting wet feet as waves lap up the beach in the foreground of the shot!

Magnusson offered Thom the challenge of proving his theories by undertaking a survey to Carnac, in Brittany, perhaps the most important megalithic site of them all and where megalithic remains abound. This was a wonderful opportunity for Sandy, for it gave him the chance to see whether or not the Brittany 'Boys' were using the same units of length and pursuing the same kinds of astronomy as the 'Boys' over here. It appears on the film as if the entire Thom clan went to Brittany. Initially totally apprehensive at the possibilities of conducting such a huge survey on such a difficult site, Thom rose to the challenge, and this must have been his finest hour. Sitting at the head of a long camping table, the obvious patriarch, Thom looked triumphant, allowing himself a glass of the local *vin ordinaire* and sporting a suntan rarely to be found so readily in his native Scotland.

In a curious montage of short takes, the film shows a flurry of theodolites, tape measures, and note-taking undertaken by the younger members of the family. Clad variously in hot pants, flared jeans and wellies, accompanied by both ethnic music and early *electronica*, all this endeavour was to be later rigorously checked over by the eagle eyes of Sandy and Archie, whilst Glyn Daniel and Bob Merritt*, who respectively had initially set up and partly funded the whole venture, watch on in some amusement. And despite at times resembling Glastonbury festival with added megaliths and theodolites, thus did Thom finally get to deliver his message to the public directly, on mainstream television.

Historically, the *Chronicle* programmes represented a high pinnacle of television documentary making in the 1970s. Shot entirely onto film, many of the team responsible were later to become implemental in launching the super-successful *Horizon* flag ship, and the theme music for the Thom programme was partly composed by the then unrecognised *doyenne* of electronic music, Delia Derbyshire, who had previously composed a major component of the now world famous *Doctor Who* theme under the *cache* of Ron Grainger and the BBC Radiophonic Workshop. This was curiously appropriate, since Thom came across as very much something of a *Doctor Who* figure, someone wise and from a distant vanished time - Victorian Britain - like the original *Doctor*.

The Thom programme resolved itself entirely happily back in Uncle Thom's Cabin at *The Hill*, where a relaxed Sandy and the jovial Magnusson are filmed doing some male bonding with pipes over survey plans of *les alignements* at Carnac. The survey had indeed found the same units of length, the same kinds of alignments for lunar astronomy, and the same geometries, based on the same Pythagorean triangles in the stone rings, vindicating entirely Thom's theories. Eventually, amidst swirls of tobacco smoke, Magnusson asked Thom the obvious final question,

*Robert L Merritt's crucial role in this story is amplified on pages 119 -121, with an ensemble photograph taken during the 1973 Stonehenge survey, which he helped to fund.

Chapter One - A Man of Nine Decades

Happy pipe smokers. Magnus Magnusson and Alexander Thom clearly enjoyed each other's company during the filming of the BBC *Chronicle* documentary. Here they are in *The Cabin* at Dunlop discussing the results from the Carnac trip. Whatever happened to documentaries like *Chronicle*?

> *"Your theories about Stone Age Einsteins have got up the backs of some archaeologists. The idea that the cup and ring marks were used as writing has got up the backs of a lot more. Does it worry you?"*

Thom replies, and breaks out into spontaneous and very engaging laughter,

> *"Not in the slightest. I just go right on.. measuring and recording what I find."*

And at seventy-five years of age, one probably would have expected that kind of response from a man who had spent his entire working life recording what he had found. However, it was not really a true answer. By 1971 Thom was already becoming deluged with criticism from archaeologists and historians, and it was clear to friends and family that it upset him greatly. In his entire professional career he had never been attacked so vehemently nor so personally. Euan MacKie recently shed light on Thom's independent pioneering character, which must have sustained him through all the criticism,

> *'I never really knew him (Thom) well, and we both being rather reserved personalities I didn't find it easy to do so. In any case I suspect that he thought archaeological support was rather irrelevant; he had collected and analysed the data to his own satisfaction and if someone like me came along and did a dig to investigate, that was fine but it was only peripheral. He knew he was right!'*[*]

[*] Personal communication to the author.

Sandy undertook his final surveying trip with his daughter Beryl in 1977, to Balinaby, after which his eyesight gradually deteriorated to the point where he could no longer perform such tasks. His daughter Beryl related to the author that, "My father was thrilled. He came around the corner and saw the enormous stone.. I suppose you would call it a monolith... and a grin slowly spread right across his face". Jeanie, who for forty years had supported and endured his constant returnings from cold, wet and windy moors with the comment that he was 'old enough to know better", had latterly changed her tack and begun to joke that Sandy had become "too old to know any better" and frequently likened her husband to the 'molecatcher', a profession notorious for always leaving a pair of moles to breed so there would have to be a revisit to the site the following year. Although Jeanie was a good match for Thom, born on the same date and three years his junior, she eventually became tired of her husband's passion for stone circles. Even so, she provided massive support for each survey trip AT and Archie undertook. Jeanie was an independent woman. A story related to the author by her grand-daughter Susan's husband, James relates how she was once observed shooting pigeons attacking the family cabbages clad only in her underwear! Sandy and Sis spent 58 years together before she passed away in August 1975, and living alone began to prove more and more arduous for Thom.

Now confined pretty much to barracks, Thom then jointly wrote *Megalithic Remains in Britain and Brittany* (Oxford, 1978) with his son, Archie. The tenor of this book is different, urgent. Jointly penned, with Archie as co-author, it is pure essence of Thom, the style terse with not a single unnecessary word, once again an *extreme read*. But who was it written for? By 1978, the archaeological world had all but slammed the door firmly shut on Thomian ideas, and the book was impenetrable to all but a very few hardy academics and specialists in other fields. Containing many gems of understanding, this *Cinderella* of a book fared very badly, despite being well loved by Thom devotees. The book contains all the findings from the latter surveys on the major sites: Stonehenge, Avebury and Carnac.

A hopeful sign of an independent test of his alignments raised its head in 1977. Dr Clive Ruggles, who had graduated as a mathematician from Cambridge and obtained a D.Phil in Astrophysics from Oxford applied to the Science Research Council for a £14,000 grant to 'measure up the circles in all the important districts in Britain'. Thom supported Dr Ruggles in his application. In a letter to his friend Bob Merritt, in February 1978, Thom wrote,

> 'His idea is quite sound. Our work must be independently checked but I do not see the SRC giving him £14,000 for the two years' work and I do not know of anywhere else he can apply. It is a pity because I believe he is a very good man with a theodolite and I think he read astronomy at Cambridge. It will be very difficult to find a more suitable man to make an independent check on our work, and it is obviously going to be expensive. I have written a very strong recommendation to the SRC.'

Chapter One - A Man of Nine Decades

This letter contrasts sharply with a letter dictated six years later by Thom just a year before his death, in November 1985. Previously quietly pleased that Ruggles' resurveying of many sites had revealed no serious errors or mistakes, on reading Ruggles and Whittle's paper, *A Critical Examination of the Megalithic Lunar Observatories*, he then wrote to Merritt,

> 'Clive Ruggles has shown that he has surveyed a large number of sites on the west coast of Scotland. In the book he carries out a careful analysis of these surveys. He finds that these indicate certain declinations and avoid other declinations. This does not make sense and we must look further.
>
> But he pays no attention to the unequivocal metrological conclusions arrived at by myself, namely that these people were capable of working to a precision of an arc minute.
>
> If they used the same precision in their astronomical work then Ruggles' conclusions must be wide of the mark.
>
> It is to be noted that Ruggles work is to $\pm 1°$. It seems to me that he has introduced a new set of problems for statisticians to solve when they try to explain his peculiar results.'

Ruggles' original work is discussed later on in this book, but as a direct consequence of his conclusions, it appeared to many archaeologists, and suited their cause well, that Thom had been over enthusiastic in his claims for megalithic astronomy. An astrophysicist surveyor was just the ticket - what archaeology had been waiting for - to get permission to drop the whole astronomical alignments issue. Ruggles was apparently just the man to take Thom on at his own game and suggest that he had been over-enthusiastic in his findings.

By winter 1981 it was necessary for Sandy to undergo an eye operation, which was successful but left him weak. His convalescence was marred by having unsuitable spectacles to wear, through which he could not see at all well. In January 1982, he took a bad fall on ice and broke a femur, after which, despite still enjoying the benefits of an active mind, it was becoming clear that Sandy was finding it increasingly difficult to manage on his own. Notwithstanding this, he continued to submit papers, and undertook correspondence and interviews, using a tape dictaphone and employing an audio typist, Hilda Gustin, who died in November 2006, in Stroud.

By the end of 1983, Alex could cope no longer. His son Archie took him to live with his daughter, Beryl, at Banavie, some 120 miles away (*photo of Beryl Austin on page (iii)*). Leaving his beloved *Thalassa*, the home he and his wife had built themselves at *The Hill*, could not have been easy. After a day's quiet reflection on what he would need, Archie's Range Rover was laden to the gunwales with his books, calculators, essential possessions and even a favourite armchair. He knew he was leaving *The Hill* for the final time, for as he was being driven down the long driveway he remembered "coming up the first time in 1901", and added, "I'll not be back".

At Banavie, and registered as blind, he concluded the draft of his 557 page book, *Stone Rows and Standing Stones*, published posthumously as two volumes in 1990, assisted by Aubrey Burl. His daughter Beryl's home backs directly onto 'Neptune's Gates', that remarkable canal lock system which connects the North Sea to the Irish Sea through the Caledonian Canal. All manner of interesting sailing vessels pass through these locks. It was perhaps the ideal setting for a lifelong sailor to spend his last days and Alexander Thom passed away peacefully on November 7th 1985 at Fort William Hospital, aged 91. His funeral took place shortly afterwards, near Ayr.

Alexander Thom, aged 91, in the summer of 1985

Alexander Thom had lived an astonishingly full and active life, right into his tenth decade. A true pioneer, he has rightly become known as the founding father of modern archaeoastronomy, even if at the time of his passing this discipline had been firmly criticised, placed on ice and had effectively disappeared from academic view. But like the Devil when ignored, it did not go away.

In *The Theory of Culture Change*, (University of Illinois Press, 1944), the anthropologist Julian Steward wrote,

> *'Fact-collecting of itself is insufficient scientific procedure; facts exist only as they are related to theories, and theories are not destroyed by facts, they are replaced by new theories which better explain the facts. Therefore criticisms...which concern facts alone and which fail to offer better formulations are of no interest.'*

Thom well understood this statement. It was the nub of the whole matter. As a scientist, his whole professional life had been about acquiring objective data around which theories could be grown or diminished. Renfrew's book, *Beyond Civilisation* had proclaimed the unwelcome message that the current archaeological model of prehistory was 'in crisis' and 'simply wrong'. Thom's research, like radiocarbon dating, had provided prehistorians with new techniques and data with which to enhance what little was known about prehistoric culture in Britain. Unlike the developers of radiocarbon dating techniques, he was made unwelcome for his trouble. Yet despite being heavily criticised, often at a personal level, he also understood the futility in himself criticising the archaeologists' facts and theories concerning the prehistoric model. He therefore never indulged his frustration by criticising the archaeological profession, indeed he made friends

Chapter One - A Man of Nine Decades

from within the profession and freely shared his facts and theories wherever possible. As Thom himself said, in the *Chronicle* programme, "I just keep on reporting what I find".

Thom spent over forty years acquiring his data. His note-books remain, over 250 of them, filled with objective data that responds particularly well to scientific analysis and from which a radically different model of European prehistory emerges. That model is Thom's legacy - the subject of the following chapters.

'The Skipper', around 1936

Alexander Thom - Cracking the Stone Age Code

From around 1933 onwards, Alexander Thom began compiling survey plans of many of the surviving megalithic monuments in Britain. Many were in ruinous condition, with fallen or removed stones, but in all regions he was able to discover the size, orientation and geometries of well-preserved examples of stone circles, stone rows, fans and long distance alignments to key solar, lunar and stellar rise and set positions on the horizon. His previous professional expertise in engineering, astronomy and surveying uniquely placed Thom into the position of being able to amass the complex data, analyse it, and draw sensible theories concerning what the sites were for and why they had been constructed. His is undoubtedly the finest collection of survey plans ever amassed on the subject, and most of it now resides in Edinburgh, at the Royal Commission on Ancient and Historic Monuments (RCAHMS) of Scotland), donated by the Thom family and the assistance of Dr Euan MacKie.

CHAPTER TWO

A Passion for the Past

In 1933 Alexander Thom first became aware of the complex legacy left by the megalithic builders. Fate played her trump card and thereafter, Sandy Thom was a man on a mission. His propulsion into the world of stone circles started from an astronomical realisation that people were familiar with and were closely observing the sky in prehistory, building astronomical alignments into their monuments. We are blessed to have Thom's own account of his initiation into matters megalithic, written as a foreword to Dr Neil Thomas' interesting book, *British Neolithic Calendar Buildings*. Dated 1985, and with Thom aged 91, these were his last published words, typed up by Hilda Gustin from a dictation into his tape recorder. They may also be found word for word in Margaret Ponting's later essay in *Records in Stone*, published after Thom's death. The story takes us right back to the beginning of the whole adventure,

> 'Each summer for over sixty years, I have cruised in the waters of the Hebrides, exploring out-of-the way places, many of them normally inaccessible by public transport. In the year 1933, I cruised in the sailing yacht Hadassah with my son and four friends; we left the sound of Harris and after a long day's sail in the North Atlantic we arrived in the twilight at East Loch Roag, that beautiful secluded inlet to the north-west of the Isle of Lewis. I was seeking a quiet anchorage for the night and navigating with care between rocky islets and promontories. I finally made up my mind where to anchor, as far up East Loch Roag as my chart allowed me to go with safety. We stowed sail after dropping anchor, and as we looked up, silhouetted between the stones of Callanish, was the rising moon. I had been concentrating on the navigation as darkness was approaching, and I did not know how near we were to the main site of the Callanish megalithic monument.
>
> After dinner, we went ashore to explore. I saw by looking at the Pole Star that a north-south line existed in the complex. That fascinated me, as I knew that when the site was built no star of any magnitude had been at, or near the celestial pole. Precession had not yet brought Polaris as near to the celestial pole as it is now. I wondered whether the alignment was a chance occurrence or whether it had been deliberately built that way. If it were deliberate it would probably be found at other megalithic sites. I had

> *of course known about the complex of stones and menhirs at Callanish since 1912 when Somerville's paper had greatly intrigued me.*
>
> *'The Outer Hebrides have a charm all of their own, not the least being their remoteness. To realise that megalithic man had lived and worked there as well as on the mainland of Britain aroused my interest in the working of his mind and so, my interest having been stirred, I began to make detailed surveys of all the sites I could find.'*

As for everything else Thom attempted in his life, he now threw himself into his new calling with passion. A.T. didn't dabble, ever, and the 'interest' cited twice above in the final paragraph is surely a euphemism for this passion. His interest lay in 'the working of his (megalithic man's) mind', his primary goal being to get inside the heads of prehistoric Britons.

Thom's evaluation of the Megalithic unit of length formed the spine of his research throughout the period from 1938 to 1967, and also drove much of the work at his last surveys at Stonehenge and Carnac in the early seventies. It also forms the backbone of this book. But this was merely one aspect of his researches, and there were other projects, such as the dating techniques derived from assumed astronomical alignments, which demanded the same scrupulous data gathering and frequent visits to difficult sites armed with his specially lightened 'off road' theodolite.

This chapter identifies the various projects by which Thom came to understand these 'workings'. Each major area of work is categorised here in brief, an overview approximately in the chronological order in which it appeared in his notebooks and publications. For each, I have attempted a brief explanation as to the nature and importance of the work undertaken, to be further elaborated on in later chapters.

THE MEGALITHIC YARD

> *"Undoubtedly it was universally used, perhaps universally sacred."*
>
> Alexander Thom, *The Glasgow Herald*,
> 12th December 1967,
> (Article by Samuel Hunter)

The prodigious collection of notebooks and diagrams that preceded the discovery of the Megalithic yard now resides in the *Royal Commission for Ancient and Historic Monuments of Scotland* (RCAHMS) in Edinburgh. At weekends and every holiday period from about 1933 until 1977, A.T. was lugging his surveying and ranging kit up and down the mountains and moors of western Britain, often assisted by Archie and/or other members of his family.

It is impossible to work with a theodolite without at least one other person in attendance. The duties of this active and often accursed soul are to hold ranging

Chapter Two - A Passion for the Past
The Megalithic Yard

poles, make runs with tapes or chains, take bookings, and walk mile upon mile in the course of a survey which may only be of a few tens of square yards in area, whilst being shouted at continuously by the theodolitist. Provided that the bookings are made in the standard way, then a typical stone circle measured radially will take three to four hours to survey to an accuracy of one part in 1000. (99.9% accuracy). If a closed traverse or other complex survey is undertaken, the operation will normally take in excess of a day, even under ideal conditions. To take a 360 degree horizon profile needs several hours to perform adequately, and this depends on good visibility. Thom's survey of Stonehenge, the most accurate ever undertaken, took weeks to complete; Avebury, a seven-station closed traverse, took two months.

Once these bookings were taken, the rest, in Thom's words, was 'office work'. Almost all his research was analysed and written up in a converted chicken house in his garden near *Thalassa*, the house he built in 1922 at *The Hill*. The younger reader needs to be aware of another important historical detail. In Thom's time, at least prior to the later surveys at Stonehenge, Avebury and Carnac, the calculations involved slow, huge and heavy 'Brunsvega' mechanical calculating machines in *lieu* of modern electronic calculators. 'Guestimates' (to perhaps 0.5% accuracy) were taken with a slide rule, essentially a simple analogue logarithmic calculator and the stock-in-trade issue to any engineer until about 1972. Before this date, 'office work' was slow and tedious. A.T. also owned a Curta calculator, an ingenious mechanical device manufactured in Liechtenstein and based on Charles Babbage's original computing engine. This beautifully constructed small machine was used to obtain final results to an accuracy of a modern electronic calculator or a computer. The author's Type 1 Curta is illustrated below.

After the first affordable electronic calculators arrived, around 1972, the 'Brunsvega', slide rule and Curta were practically made obsolete overnight and destined for the history books. Thom bought a Hewlett Packard '25' programmable calculator in 1975, and it opened up a new world of faster calculating possibilities. At 81 years of age, he still managed to write all his own

The Curta calculating engine, a "cross between a coffee grinder and a Tibetan prayer wheel".

- 29 -

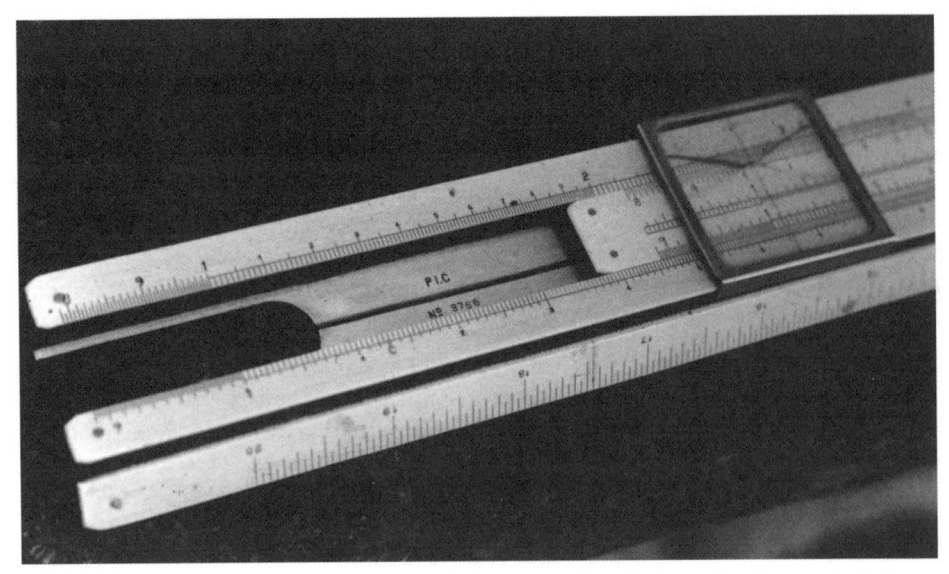

Batteries not included. A 24 inch (60 cm) engineer's slide rule, the basis for all fast calculations before the advent of the electronic calculator around 1972. Capable of accuracies of better than half of one percent, every scientist and engineer routinely employed the 'slip-stick' to perform almost all the functions of a modern scientific calculator. It became totally obsolete in less than a year (author's collection).

programs, but the machine arrived too late to facilitate the arduous calculations of a working lifetime. Unless the reader understands the vast amount of calculation work involved in undertaking over 500 surveys in about 40 years, then the dedication, tenacity and stoicism required of an archaeoastronomer from the pre-electronic era will never be properly appreciated.

The outcome of these surveys revealed much that had remained hidden for four millennia. Thom discovered that the stone circles formed groups which displayed the same geometric shapes over and over again, using the same unit of length, and that integer values of this same unit had been used in defining both the radii and perimeters of the circles. Pythagorean triangles (right-angled triangles whose sides are in whole number ratios to each other) appeared to have been employed to mark out and thereby define the resulting geometry.

Thom's identified unit of length he called the *Megalithic fathom*, which he defined as having been used to mark out the diameters of stone circles. The radii then became half that unit, a length which Thom called the *Megalithic yard*, 2.72 feet (0.829 metres). This length is approximately the length of a human step, and two such lengths, the 'fathom', measure approximately, the outstretched span of the arms, or a human pace, a half-pace being metrologically a step, two and a half times the length of its defining or 'root' foot. In the final chapter, on page 199, the metrology of the Megalithic yard will be discussed in more detail, to let the reader see how it is placed within the canon of ancient measure.

Chapter Two - A Passion for the Past
The Megalithic Yard

Twelve years before Thom published *Megalithic Sites in Britain* he had asked two of the most respected statisticians in Britain to assist in the statistical treatment of his data. The outcome of this correspondence is covered in full in chapter four (*page 103*). This correspondence led, during the mid 50s, to a succession of papers published in the *Journal of the Royal Society of Statistics* and *Biometrika*, each based on Thom's existing data set derived from surveys of over 100 stone rings.

The perimeters of most stone rings was found to be an integer multiple of 2.5 MY, a dimension which Thom named the *Megalithic rod*. Thom's data and methodology, again discussed in detail in a later chapter, showed that there was nothing approximate about the rulers or tagged ropes used throughout Europe to mark out circles. He claimed that the builders were all using the same length, to an astonishing tolerance. This result Thom placed within his 'parcel bomb', *Megalithic Sites in Britain* (1967), where he told his readers,

> *'..there is a presumption amounting to a certainty that a definite unit of length was used in setting out these rings. It is proposed to call this the Megalithic yard (MY). It will appear that the Megalithic yard is 2.72 feet (0.829 m), and gives a tolerance spread of plus or minus 0.003 feet (0.9 mm).'*

'Office work'. Before the electronic era calculations were a long hard slog, Alexander Thom is seen here twiddling away on his *Curta* calculator while son Archie, hand on head, reads out the numbers and writes in the results. (*photograph taken at the Hotel Celtique, Carnac, in 1970*).

THE ALIGNMENTS

"They were able to split a minute of arc, and that's better than a modern surveying theodolite."

Alexander Thom, *Cracking the Stone Age Code*,
Chronicle, BBC

When Thom began work on the megaliths he had already seen Somerville's accurate plan of Callanish and read the associated paper where a lunar alignment had been proposed. One may assume that he had been aware of Sir Norman Lockyer's 1904 theodolite measurements of the 'midsummer alignment' at Stonehenge, where the Heel Stone (originally one of a pair of stones) marked the solstitial sunrise. The press had latched onto Lockyer's work at Stonehenge and it became somewhat sensationalised, immediately firing public desire to know more about Stonehenge.

Archie Thom informs us (*WIATS*, page 292) of his father's interest in Egyptology, from which we might assume that Petrie's theodolite survey of the Great Pyramid would have stimulated Thom's interest in ancient metrology. One of Petrie's surveys had revealed the high accuracy of the alignment of the pyramids to the four points of the compass, as Thom was later to observe having been incorporated into the design of Callanish. Later, on the same page, we learn that A.T. was 'extremely interested' in Greek Mathematics, from which we must assume an interest in the work of the Pythagoreans, Archimedes, Plato, Aristotle, Eudoxus and Eratosthenes. He also owned a set of 'Smoley's Tables', which amongst many other things included the side lengths for all the lower integer Pythagorean triangles, laid out in feet, inches and 1/32nds of an inch. As a trained scientist, Thom would certainly have studied the known history of his chosen career.

"Shooting the Sun". Thom taking a theodolite reading from the sun. This technique is essential to any serious archaeoastronomical work and the most accurate way to determine true north at the site under investigation. The horizontal angle of the sun is recorded along with the time. Reference to *Nautical Almanac* tables then gives the true angle for this time to be found (*photograph by Robert Merritt*).

Chapter Two - A Passion for the Past
The Solar Alignments

It was therefore inevitable that when Thom began to let loose on the megalithic sites of his native Scotland, he would attempt to relate these ancient monuments, of uncertain origin, with the sole information in existence about the ancient sciences of southern Europe and the Middle East. Furthermore, despite the fact that Archie had told me that his father 'began with a clean sheet of paper', Sandy's mind was already well primed with many aspects of both ancient scientific thought and recent scientific measurements on the astronomy of ancient sites. Regrettably, we shall never know how much any earlier 'homework' had influenced him during his formative research on alignments and stone rings. We can however be assured that when he began this work he hit the ground running, this being Thom's way.

The aligned monuments we are about to discuss here were built by engineers with a knowledge of astronomy, they were not built by archaeologists. Thom clearly recognised this advantage conferred on him by his professional background. Only an astronomer-mathematician-engineer possessed the skills to both understand and then crack any megalithic code - 'it takes one to know one'. Thom was extremely well if not uniquely placed to undertake this work.

The Solar Alignments

Sunrises and sunsets swing annually back and forth along an arc of the horizon whose angular range is wholly determined by the latitude of the observations. Because this angle changes with latitude, long distance horizon alignments at megalithic sites tend to confirm the astronomic intention of their builders because of their unique angular relationship to the local extreme solar angles of midwinter and midsummer (called *solstitial angles*).

In southern Britain, this range of angles between midsummer and midwinter is about eighty degrees, whilst in Scotland it enlarges to ninety degrees, a right angle.

Many examples of neolithic sites which are aligned to solstice and equinox positions of solar rise or set may be found within the works of Lockyer, Somerville, Lewis and others. Thom catalogued scores of additional such sites and then, after about 1964, concentrated on finding alignments which marked the extreme lunar positions.

A persistent complication in all such work is that the change of the earth's angle of obliquity - the earth's tilt angle - has reduced by about half a degree since Neolithic times, requiring some quite advanced trigonometrical calculations to ascertain where the sun, moon and stars rose and set along the horizon at a given locality during the era when the monuments were thought to have been erected. This is why Thom needed a theodolite while the megalithic astronomers did not - the rising and setting points of sun, moon and stars have moved since neolithic times.

Cerrig Gorwel

Azimuth of 'last flash', 223°37'
Elevation 2°48'
21st December 2002, 15:25 hrs,
Mold, North Wales

This photograph of the midwinter setting sun in the mountains of North Wales demonstrates that the naked eye can easily discriminate between the two human figures, spaced just five minutes of a degree apart and half a mile distant from the camera. The sun's disc occupies an angle of just over half a degree. A theodolite is not required to accurately record the 'last flash' position.

Five important requirements are needed to discover these original bearings:

1. A site where an alignment appears to have been set up to a distant foresight during the megalithic period.

2. A theodolite of accuracy at least to one minute of a degree.

3. An observer who can set up and use this theodolite.

4. The mathematical ability to calculate where along the horizon the various rises and sets occurred at the date when the site was erected.

5. A sunny day in order to 'shoot the Sun' whereby, with reference to the *Nautical Almanac*, one may use the theodolite to establish the azimuth angle of the alignment to high accuracy, within one minute of a degree.

The megalithic 'theodolite' was, of course, the local horizon at the site itself, where no correction or calculation was needed, just the ability to build or mark the backsight at the correct position to observe the alignment.

"I can't go back and look at it in 1800 BC. They could but I can't, that's why I need a theodolite."

Alexander Thom, BBC *Chronicle*.

A theodolite is essential in this work. Using a theodolite to 'shoot the sun' (*see photo on previous page*), enables the *azimuth*, the angle from true north, of the proposed alignment and all other relevant angles of the site, to be very accurately determined. Because the axial tilt of the earth has significantly changed since the Neolithic, the risings and settings of celestial bodies are no longer aligned to the sites. *The sites no longer work!* The measured angles of a proposed alignment must therefore now be related to where on the horizon the relevant rise or set occurred *at the estimated date of erection of the site* under investigation.

The theodolite, having enabled an accurate determination of the alignment angle(s) at the site, is also used to obtain a profile of the local horizon - both horizontal and vertical angles are measured.

Chapter Two - A Passion for the Past
The Solar Alignments

St David's Alignment : Feb 18th 2006
QuickAz HOZA -0.4394, ECOR 0.1234
Refraction 0.6, Parx 0.002 (sun)

First touch 252.3339 degrees
Half-set 252.6679 degrees
Last flash 253.3332 degrees

Solar Fire gives 252°08' -0°46' (centre disc or half-set)
for 17:38:20 hrs

Any suitable natural feature some miles from an observer reveals the year length as 365 days, In time, the ¼ day annual 'slip' will be noticed, making the year length 365 ¼ days. The 'egg-cup' shown here delivers the year length to 11 minutes just with naked eye and by counting days. Range 17 miles.

These angles may then be converted to astronomical *declinations* in order to effectively remove the latitude variation from site to site. Declination is the angle measured from the equator. Thom built up a catalogue of declinations for aligned sites, first throughout his native Scotland, then in England, Wales and finally in Brittany. Many of these sites consisted of an *indicated foresight* - a notch in a distant hill or mountain, indicated by an oriented slab-sided stone pointing towards the foresight. Often a standing stone, cairn or platform formed the *backsight*, the place where the observer had to stand in order to make the crucial observation.

As the distance between foresight and backsight increases, the potential angular resolution increases. For example, two stakes having a 10cm (four inch) separation and at a distance of just 300 metres (1000 feet) offer a resolution of about an arc minute (one sixtieth of one degree), while a foresight 16 Km (10 miles) away theoretically offers resolution down to a couple of

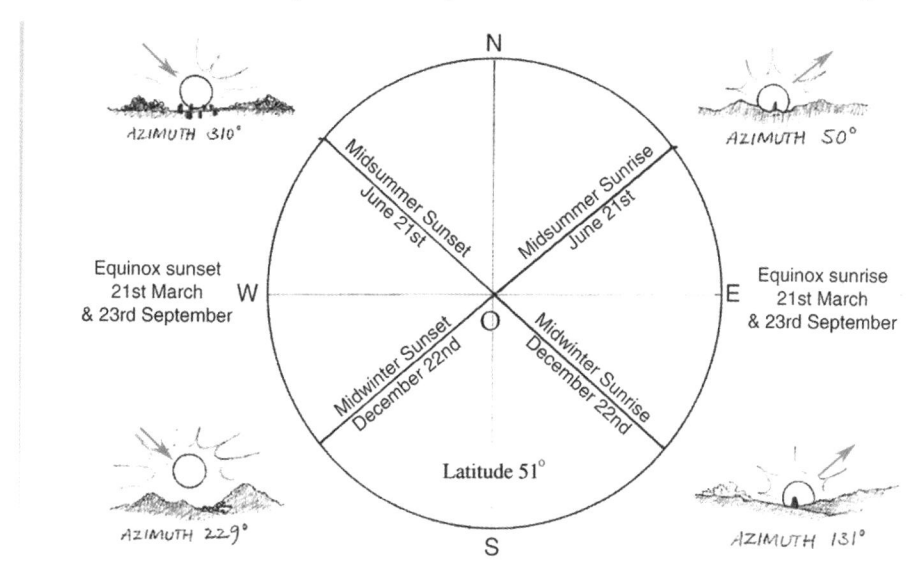

AZIMUTH 310°
AZIMUTH 50°
Midsummer Sunset June 21st
Midsummer Sunrise June 21st
Equinox sunset 21st March & 23rd September
Equinox sunrise 21st March & 23rd September
Midwinter Sunset December 22nd
Midwinter Sunrise December 22nd
Latitude 51°
AZIMUTH 229°
AZIMUTH 131°

An observer standing at a location (O) in southern Britain offering a panoramic view of a level horizon observes the solstitial sun rises and sets at the angles (azimuths) shown above. The range of sunsets and sunrises is about ±40 degrees either side of east and west. However, if similar observations are made in Scotland, at 57 degrees latitude, this angle increases to 90 degrees. Each latitude thus has four unique angles for the extreme sunrises and sunsets - an *astronomical signature* for the latitude. The sun never rises or sets north or south of these angles. (*sketches by Janet Lloyd Davies*)

Alexander Thom - Cracking the Stone Age Code

One of Thom's most publicised solar alignments, at Kintraw, Argyllshire. As the winter solstice approaches, each consecutive sunset moves to the left until, on the day of the solstice, it slips down the right hand slope of Ben Shiantaidh (*shown above*), and an observer standing at the backsight - a level platform of stones above a ravine bordered with two large boulders laid down end to end - sees the sun make a final appearance, for a few seconds, further down the slope. The ravine is not shown. It lies directly beneath the observer here. The alignment is indicated by the cairn and standing stone shown directly in front of the observer, but is not visible from either. (*artwork by Janet Lloyd Davies*).

seconds of a degree of azimuth. In practice, as Thom points out, in *Megalithic Lunar Observatories*, atmospheric refraction causes much larger fluctuations in measurements of altitude. Indeed, he devotes an entire chapter in *MLO (Chapter 3)* to a discussion of refraction effects, based on two papers submitted to *The Institute of Navigation* (1954 and 1958). Thom took over 500 measurements of near-horizon refraction sequences over a period of several years and under a wide range of weather conditions and during the night-time as well as during the day. Details on refraction can be found in appendix three and four.

The separation needed to observe and differentiate between consecutive sunsets (or rises) on the days either side of the solstice is half a minute of arc, and this is just realisable under favourable conditions at Thom's identified observatories. However, at the equinoxes, when the rate of change of daylight is greatest, this daily separation rises to 0.8 degree in southern Britain, more than the angle occupied by the sun's disc itself. Differentiation between the equinox sunset position and the sunsets either side of it requires only a clear sky, a good eye and suitable horizon marks. A day count - notches or tags spaced evenly on a rope - between a repeat event at the same time of year around the equinox will, in a few years, reveal a count of 365 days for the length of the year (*see diagram above*). The extra quarter day will naturally emerge from the observations. The prehistoric astronomers needed only a keen eye and a tally counter - either notches on wood or stone, a collection of stones or a tagged rope.

Chapter Two - A Passion for the Past
The Solar Alignments

Thom produced compelling evidence that the circle builders were accurately observing both the equinox and solstitial rising and setting points of the sun, together with the extreme lunar rise and set points against the local horizon. At site after site, he discovered that a distant mountain slope, a notch in a range of mountains or a man-made feature such as a large standing stone or row of stones provided rifle-barrel accuracy to the precise azimuth of the solstice or extreme lunstice points during the dating range given to him by archaeologists for the site in question. Often the slope angle of a mountain side was chosen to provide an 'amplifier' of the declination at the azimuth angle of rise and set. Because these extreme angles of the sun (and moon - see later) vary with the latitude of the site, they provide considerable proof of deliberate intent when, at site after site from Brittany to the Orkneys, Thom accurately measured their azimuths and compared the obtained figure with the calculated azimuths for the archaeological dating of the site, duly corrected for the change in the angle of the earth's tilt, lunar parallax and atmospheric refraction effects.

Good examples of solar sites set up in this way include Ballochroy (summer solstice) and Kintraw (winter solstice), both in Argyllshire, Scotland. This latter site was investigated further by Dr Euan MacKie, who for the first time in Thom's lifetime, took Thom's astronomical and surveying work and satisfactorily mixed it with conventional archaeological techniques, excavating a level stone platform at the backsight Thom had identified as having been the location for observing the alignment. The platform was exactly the correct size and location for the

At Ballochroy, three stones mark the backsight of a summer solstice alignment. The middle stone is slab-sided, and angled such that it is aligned to the foresight position (*shown above*). On the days prior to the solstice, each consecutive sunset moves to the right until, on the solstice, as the disc of the sun rolls down the right-hand slope of Corra Beinn, the intended foresight, a final 'flash' is observed. Archaeologists remain sceptical that this kind of arrangement does not provide proof of intent by Neolithic astronomers, and have accused Thom of 'selection bias'. Due to changes in the earth's tilt angle, an observer today would need to stand ¼ mile to the right (*artwork by Janet Lloyd Davies*).

purposes of observing an approaching winter solstice sunset in a V-shaped coll in the Paps of Jura in 1800 BC. It was assessed by another specialist, Aberdeen soil scientist S J Bibby, who carried out a petrofabric analysis on it, and deemed it likely to have been man-made.

With a 27.2 mile distant foresight, the width of the platform to detect the angular shift of successive sunsets at the solstice needed to be 21 feet (7 m) to the left, and this is what MacKie found under the peaty topsoil. The platform was bounded in front of a precipitous gorge by two large boulders placed end to end and forming a notch at the crucial solstice viewing position. MacKie, recognising the importance of this complementation of techniques, found another, in his words, "astronomically meaningless boulder" further along the ridge and excavated there to establish that any 'platform' was confined to the identified site and not a random ice age scree deposition. No deposition and hence 'platform' was found at this second off-axis boulder, the probe sinking a full metre into the topsoil. MacKie's rigorous scientific methodology on site may be fully appreciated in a Glasgow University film, *Astronomy in Prehistoric Britain*. As a result of MacKie's work, Kintraw remains the most thoroughly investigated example of a long distance solar alignment made by early man. A further stone placed on the alignment but above the platform has been investigated more recently by MacKie. A nearby equinoctial alignment, at Brainport Bay, investigated by MacKie, Fay and Gladwin offers further confirming evidence concerning the astronomical precision of megalithic solar observatories.

These sites all utilised features on a distant horizon to accurately identify a rare cyclic event which manifested as an extreme and therefore highly significant rising or setting angle for either the sun or moon. The sun observations translate into knowledge of the calendar and seasons, those of the moon to an understanding of the 18.6 year 'draconic' cycle of the moon, knowledge of which is essential in predicting eclipses. Because the foresights are often many miles from the intended observing site, they offer a potential accuracy to within a minute of arc, a sixtieth of a single degree, and Thom confirmed that many sites were set up exactly to the correctly predicted azimuth, calculated after surveying the site. Because of the inexorable and known reduction in the earth's angle of tilt, this then offered him the added opportunity to date the original erection of the site. Aware that he was working with two dependent variables - azimuth and date of site - he continuously sought advice from archaeologists concerning dating, and this information was often wrong. During the middle of the last century, there could hardly have been a worse time to seek such advice. The dating of the European Neolithic and Bronze Age period was in no little chaos.

Those critics who, in the words of Atkinson had, 'fastened on these occasional archaeological errors' need to recognise that Thom's datings came from within their own camp. Once Thom had become aware of the earlier dating for many Neolithic and Bronze Age sites, he reviewed and in some cases rejected his earlier work, particularly that on stellar alignments. However, his data consistently informed him that the solar and lunar sites had been actively used during the period 2000 - 1600 BC.

The Lunar Alignments

There are essentially four major observable events of the moon which become apparent if her motion is observed over time. The reader needs to be familiar with these, and commence a regime of observing the moon over some time in order to understand the following discussion of Thom's work on lunar alignments. Our present educational system fails to provide much relevant material on the motion of the moon or the cycle of its risings and setting positions, nor its link with the state of the tides.

1. The most obvious observable event is that the moon completes a rotation of the earth -passes by the same star - every 27.32 days - the *sidereal* or *tropical month*. It appears to travel at thirteen times the rate of the sun against the backdrop of the stars. Because of this, during the sidereal month the moon completes a sequence of rising and setting positions against the horizon which more or less emulate those of the sun during the whole of its annual cycle.

2. Secondly, *the phases* of the moon complete a cycle in just a few minutes over 29.5 days in length. Because the earth moves around the sun, one sidereal month after a full moon finds the moon 2.2 days short of again becoming full - the sun, earth and moon in an alignment - which then completes a *lunation cycle* or a *synodic cycle* (one *lunar month*) of average duration 29.53 days.

3. The full moon each month is always opposite the sun. One effect of this is that in winter the full moon reaches its highest position in the sky, when the sun is at its lowest, whilst in summer, the full moon is at its lowest, when the sun is at its highest. The full moon thus 'mirrors' the position of the sun at the opposite time in the calendrical cycle of the year.

4. The fourth effect is an 18.6 year cycle of position of monthly extreme risings and settings caused by the offset angle (i) of the moon's orbital plane (5.145°) in comparison to the Earth's axial tilt angle of 23.47° (ε) . This cycle is observed as a slow change in the two extreme positions of both the rising and setting of the moon every sidereal month. Every 18.6 years these reach an ultimate extreme position rather like the midsummer and midwinter solstice extremes, where the moon rises and sets many degrees outboard of the solar extremes. 9.3 years later it rises and sets many degrees inboard. Thom called these two sets of extreme angles the major and minor *standstill,* avoiding the confusing and wholly oxymoronic term *lunar solstices,* which may still be found in some textbooks. The extreme northerly monthly rise and set always occurs when the moon is transiting the stars near Orion; the southerly rise and set in Capricorn.

Alexander Thom - Cracking the Stone Age Code

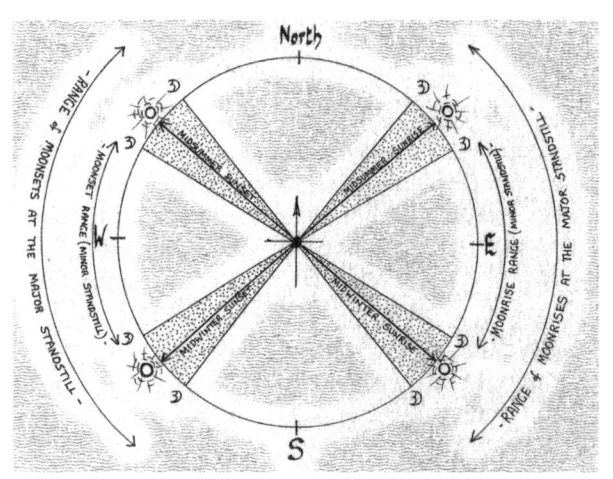

The 18.6 year cycle of the moon's orbital behaviour with respect to that of the earth around the sun causes its monthly extreme rise and set positions to change position against the horizon. In effect, they 'breathe' in and out either side of the extreme solar solstice positions taking 18.6 years to complete a 'breath'. This cycle also governs at what dates during the year eclipses might be expected to occur. Major stand-stills occurred in 1951, 1969, 1988, and 2006, when the moon rose and set at its extreme northerly and southerly positions. (*author's diagram from Sun, Moon & Earth, courtesy of Wooden Books*).

The following diagrams explain *what is observed on the landscape* due to the 18.61 year cycle of the moon. The sidereal month is split into two distinct halves, one period when the moon has positive declination and is above the ecliptic (earth's orbital plane with the sun) and a second period when it travels below the ecliptic. The former period can be compared to the moon's 'summer half' of the month, because it is seen to be higher in the sky; whilst when below the ecliptic (the 'winter half') it is observed lower in the sky. However, twice every sidereal month the moon cuts the ecliptic when the two orbital planes, that of the earth-sun and that of the earth-moon intersect. These two diametrically opposite points where the moon crosses the ecliptic are termed by astronomers the *lunar nodes*. The *north node* is the point where the moon crosses from beneath the ecliptic to above it, the *south node* is where the moon crosses from above to beneath the ecliptic. At both points the moon has *zero declination* - it is located

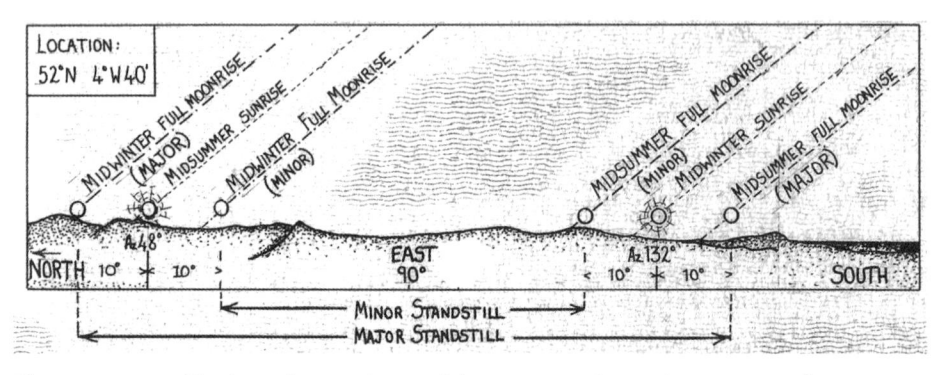

The extreme monthly rise and set positions of the moon are observed occurring within a narrow band either side of the extreme solar positions. In Britain this band is about 8 - 10 degrees, and is easily calculated - it is 5.145 degrees, the lunar orbital obliquity, (termed (i)) divided by the cosine of the latitude of the site. Thus, prehistoric lunar observatories, like the solar observatories, are uniquely defined in terms of the latitude of the site, (*from Sun, Moon & Earth, courtesy of Wooden Books*).

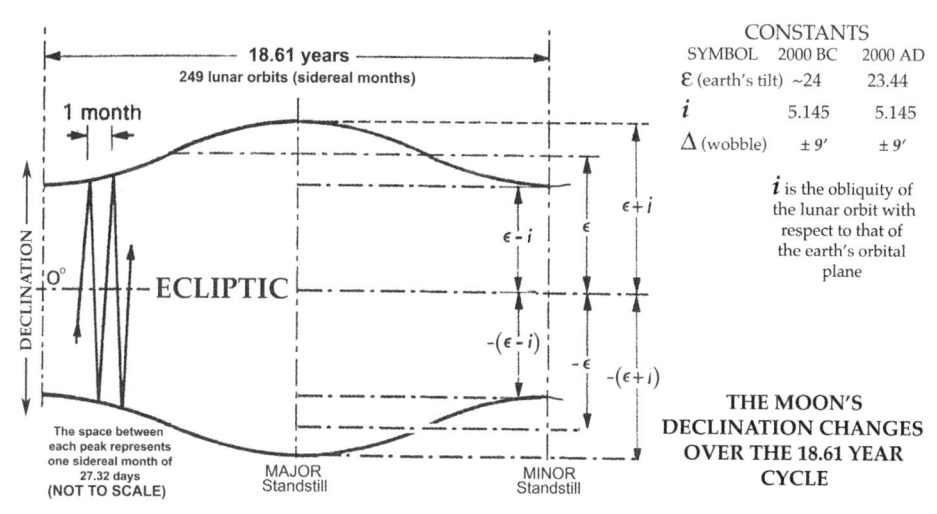

Chapter Two - A Passion for the Past
The Lunar Alignments

CONSTANTS

SYMBOL	2000 BC	2000 AD
ε (earth's tilt)	~24	23.44
i	5.145	5.145
Δ (wobble)	± 9'	± 9'

i is the obliquity of the lunar orbit with respect to that of the earth's orbital plane

THE MOON'S DECLINATION CHANGES OVER THE 18.61 YEAR CYCLE

on the plane of the ecliptic. The astronomy of this is shown on the diagram above. This diagram in turn may be linked to the extreme lunar rising and setting positions *(see below)*, connecting declination with azimuth so that the astrophysics comes down to earth and relates to what is actually observed on the landscape.

At this point it is necessary to point out that there is no signpost in the sky saying 'Node here'! The exact nodal positions have to be calculated using hard won formulae perfected over many years by astronomers. Ancient astronomers knew where they were, and called them the dragon's head and dragon's tail, those places in the zodiac where the sun or moon were swallowed by a giant cosmic dragon during an eclipse. We do not know how far back such knowledge began, but we can assert that prehistoric astronomers could readily have noted what an observer on the landscape can readily accumulate today from regular observance of the moon.

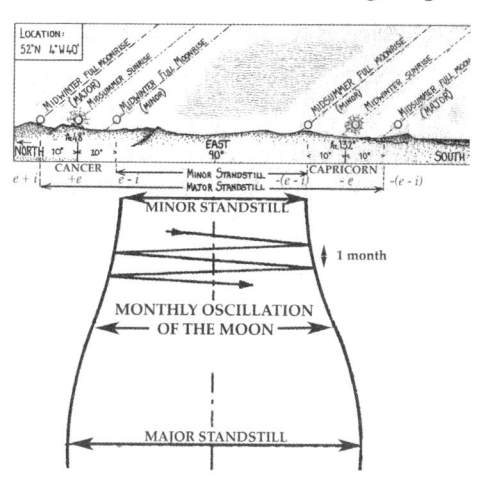

For example, an experienced observer can usually tell when the moon is *near* to the nodes by noting its position relative to the stars and noting how closely the moon rises and sets to exact east and west. And there is sometimes a spectacular event that indicates that the moon is near to one of the nodes: *eclipses can only occur when the moon is near the nodal positions*. It is also obvious

THE CONNECTION BETWEEN THE MOON'S DECLINATION & EXTREME RISE AND SET POSITIONS

Alexander Thom - Cracking the Stone Age Code

when the moon is *furthest away* from the nodes - at its maximum or minimum declination during the month - because its rising and setting positions take up their extreme values for that month (*see diagrams on previous page*).

Thom felt sure that Neolithic astronomers could have made the connections between the extreme monthly rising and setting positions of the moon and the occurrence of eclipses. His work at sites (*see opposite*) confirmed that they had done these things, and more.

5. The fifth factor in observing the moon is that an eclipse is not seen each and every full and new moon. Because the moon is typically well above or below the plane of the earth's orbit (the ecliptic) no alignment of sun-moon-earth (solar eclipse) or sun-earth-moon (lunar eclipse) can occur at full or new moon, the prerequisite conditions for an eclipse. But a further effect of lunar motion must now be taken into account. *The two lunar nodes, the points around where eclipses do occur if the moon comes to full or new while passing through them, rotate backwards around the calendar* also taking 18 years and about 7 months to complete one circuit.

There are thereby created two 'eclipse seasons' a year, one for each node (the north node and the south node), each lasting 34 days and spaced about 173.3 days apart. These 'eclipse seasons' rotate backwards around the calendar, by just under 20 days a year. Eclipse tables show this regular change in the two periods during the year when eclipses can take place. Two 'eclipse seasons' make up an 'Eclipse year' of 346.62 days. This is the period between the sun transiting over one of the nodes.

6. The sixth factor (Δ) in lunar motion is a tiny oscillation of the moon's path by about ± 9 minutes of a degree, synchronized to the eclipse season cycle. *Only when the moon is at a standstill position can this small oscillation be observed, and only when it is very near its maximum positive value can eclipses occur.* Thom found many sites ideally set up to observe this 'wobble'.

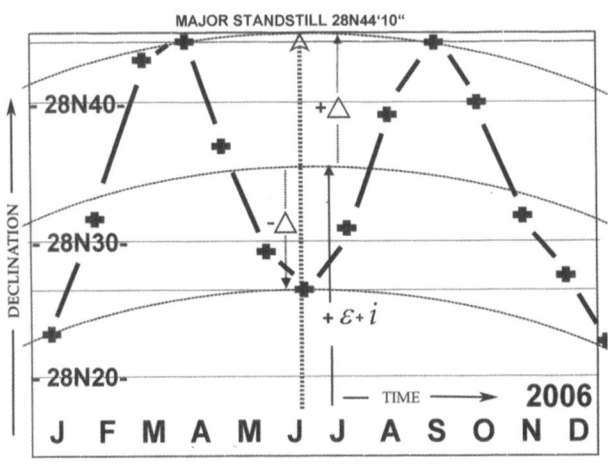

Only during the year of a major or minor standstill period is it possible to observe the small 'wobble' (Δ) of the moon. Eclipses can occur only when the wobble reaches its maximum value, here seen occurring in March/April and September, 2006. This diagram is a tiny section of the diagram at the top of the previous page. The wobble has a period of 173.3 days, half the 'eclipse year' of 346.62 days.

Many sites (*some opposite*) suggested to Thom that the wobble was being observed by Neolithic astronomers.

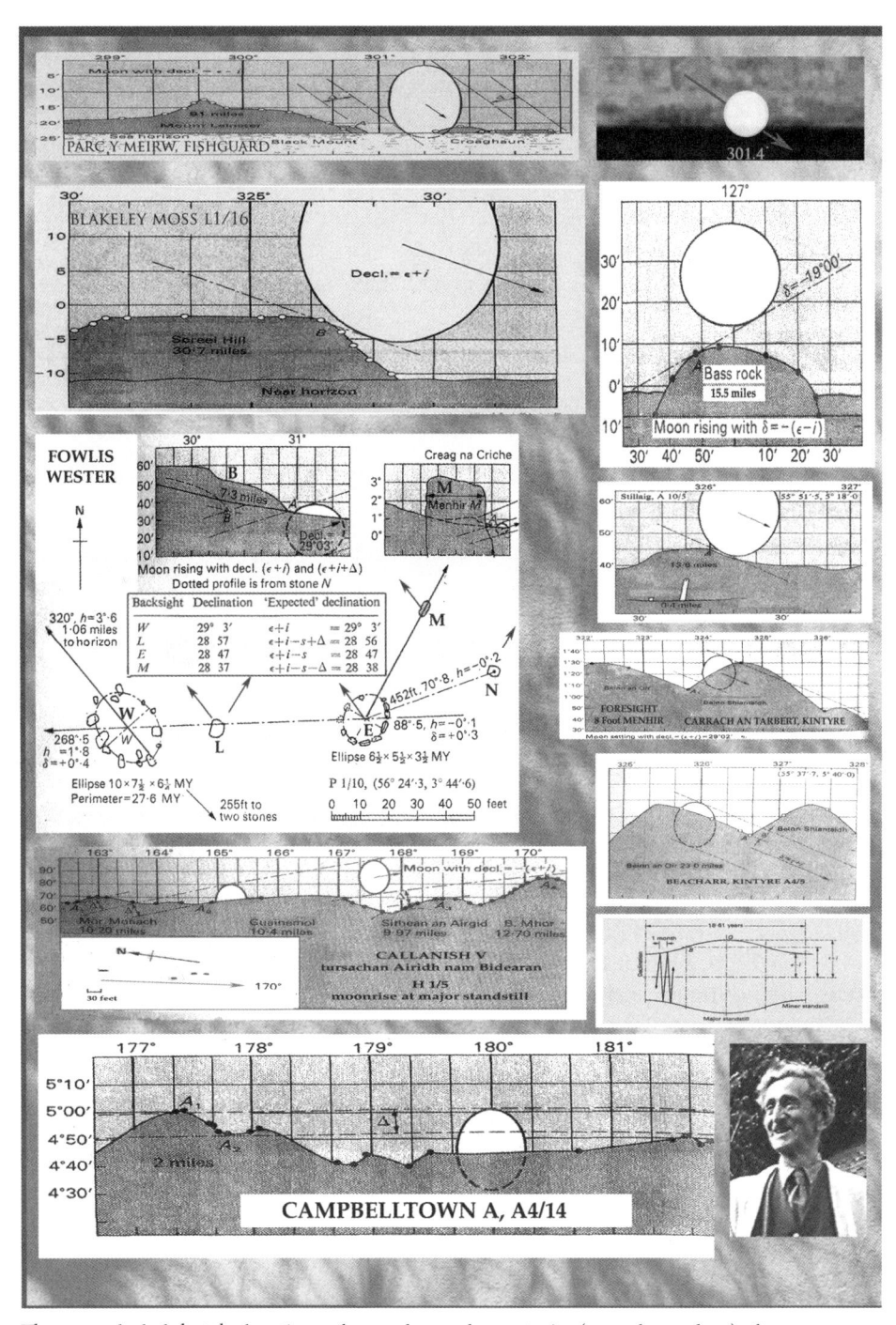

Chapter Two - A Passion for the Past
The Lunar Alignments

Thom concluded that the locations of many lunar observatories (*some shown above*) often gave near-perfect topology to enable the lunar wobble to be observed, and hence eclipses predicted.

- 43 -

Alexander Thom - Cracking the Stone Age Code

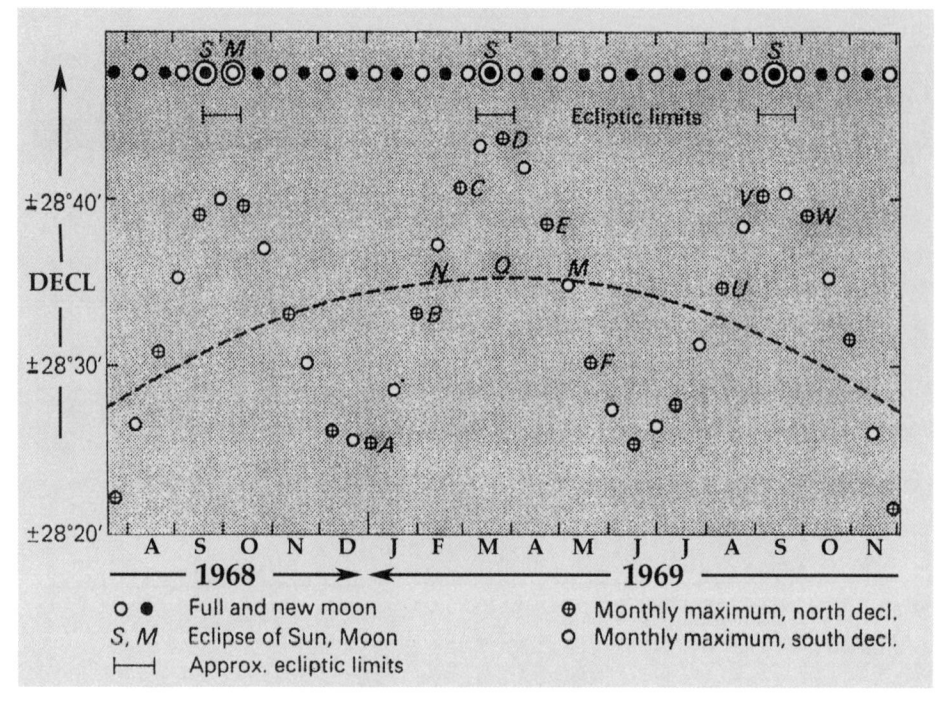

Only when the moon's 'wobble' (Δ) is at its maximum value are the conditions right for an eclipse to occur. The connection is illustrated above, where the full and new moons (top) during the 1968/1969 major standstill period are seen aligned to the wobble. Only when the wobble reaches its maximum, every 173 days, can the conditions for eclipses occur.

Written descriptions of the motion of the moon are much better understood through regular observation and by experiencing what is *actually seen from the surface of the earth*. The nodes are invisible, and the ecliptic a non-visible circle, a cosmic motorway along which the sun and most of the planets trundle at their respective rates. But in a few months of observing the moon, it is possible to observe both when it crosses the ecliptic (i.e. it is positioned on one of the nodes), by noting its position relative to the fixed stars, and also to assess when it is in quadrature (90 degrees) to the nodes, because the extreme monthly risings and settings occur.

The wobble may only be observed at a standstill, and from scratch would require observation at the kind of sites identified by Thom and others (and shown on the previous page) over two or three standstill periods to enable the link to be made between its maximum and the occurrence of eclipses. As Thom reminded his viewers to the *Chronicle* documentary, "Well, if you missed it, well, you'd just have to wait." However, by the time this programme was made, Thom already knew that there was another major observational hurdle to be overcome, the fact that the times of the extreme maximum and minimum declinations of the moon each month are not synchronised to the time of moonrise or moonset. This difficulty, and it represents a major obstacle in observing the wobble and hence

Chapter Two - A Passion for the Past
The Lunar Alignments

linking it with eclipses, is covered in a later chapter, where artefact evidence at lunar sites suggest that the astronomers had addressed and solved this problem. Exactly as for the solar alignment sites, the lunar sites comprise a backsight and a distant foresight. Thom noted that larger stones were normally employed in the architecture of a lunar backsight than for solar sites. He also recognised that the occurrence of stone fans and rows at identified lunar sites was significant, and this led him to a solution to finding where the moon would rise or set at the moment of the monthly maximum declination.

Understandably, this difficulty has been fastened onto by several of Thom's critics and together with the complex explanations and diagrams for lunar motion found within Thom's *Megalithic Lunar Observatories*, the lunar 'package' has been easily misinterpreted as being beyond the capacity of neolithic astronomers to solve. The reader is forced to relate to very complicated diagrams that intimidate and overshadow the importance of the research being described. In addition, most astronomy books show the moon's motion as seen from space, using the celestial sphere as the teaching aid. This is a terrible way to connect to neolithic skywatchers. To rectify this issue was one of my primary intentions in writing and illustrating the book *Sun, Moon and Earth* (*Wooden Books* and *Walker & Co, New York*, 1999). Joachim Schultz's book *Rhythm of the Stars* (Floris Press, Edinburgh) is also recommended.

Thom's initiation into matters lunar is an essential part of the history of archaeoastronomy. His grand-daughter Susan MacColl (*née* Thom) tells of a single memorable night when she was quite young and A.T. ran excitedly from *Thalassa* into the back door of *The Bungalow* asking after Archie's whereabouts and shouting "It's lunar, It's lunar!". He had realised for the first time, based on exhaustive calculations, that many sites were indeed aligned to lunar standstill rises and sets - A.T. enjoyed a 'Eureka moment'. Susan is only able to date this historic event approximately, to around 1962 or 1963. In Chapter 14 (Conclusions) of *MSIB*, we learn from Thom,

> *'through a fear of building evidence subjectively, I resisted accepting lunar lines until the final evidence came objectively. When the first histogram of the possible lunar lines was plotted it showed a double peak corresponding to the two limbs of the moon.' (histogram, MSIB, page 120, shown overleaf).*

More importantly within the context of this book, he continued,

> *'This result was unexpected and it was so unlikely to have happened by accident that it seemed desirable to look more closely into a number of sites where the indication of the necessary azimuth at the site itself was weak. This study showed up that Megalithic man was well acquainted with the small amplitude ripple on the moon's declination and has left such definite indicators that we can, with their help alone, determine its magnitude. We do not know of any technique which could have been used*

to examine this oscillation with the moon at the nodes, but they could have made a measurement of its period and may have connected it with the eclipse year. (the eclipse year is 346.63 days in length, the time between successive passages of the apparent path of the Sun past the north node of the moon).'

Thom's original 'curvigram' from *Megalithic Sites in Britain*, page 120, showing the difference between the observed declination (δ) and expected declination (δ e) of the moon, taken from a variety of sites he had identified as being megalithic lunar observatories. The result was wholly unexpected, which suggested to Thom the crucially important fact that no selection bias had been applied to the alignments. In addition the two peaks occupied the angular diameter of the moon, a further confirmation that megalithic observers were using both the upper and lower limb of the moon at sites. Müller (1970), Heggie (1981) and Ruggles (1984) have challenged this data, while no one has attempted to repeat the measurements.

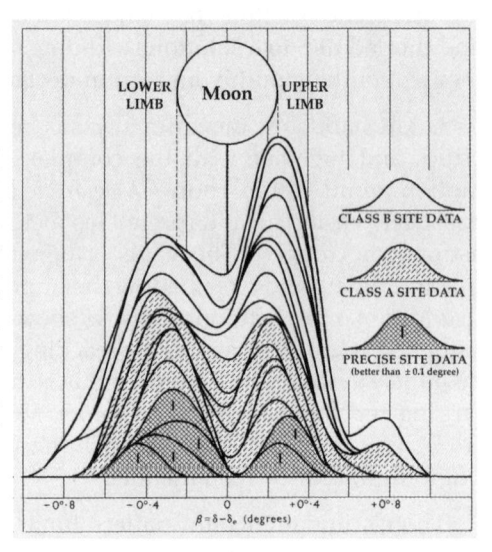

Following a letter Thom wrote to *New Scientist* in July 1964, suggesting that his data might give 'independent confirmation' of Dr Gerald Hawkins' work, there commenced a correspondence between these two pioneers of archaeoastronomy. Dr Gerald Hawkins later claimed that correspondence between himself and Thom had led to the discovery of the lunar standstill sightlines and the nine minute 'wobble." (*Archaeoastronomy*, Vol 8, No.1-4). However, as the Thom family point out, the revelation above occurred before 1964, and as C.A. ('Peter') Newham made the original lunar sight-line discovery at Stonehenge in 1962, and was in communication with Thom about matters megalithic prior to his article in the *Yorkshire Post*, in August 1963, we have some reason for supposing that Thom, and particularly Newham, were the joint discoverers of significant lunar intent at megalithic sites during this critical period in the history of archaeoastronomy.

There is a further strange story to tell concerning the publication of Newham's original discoveries about lunar and solar sightlines at Stonehenge. His original manuscript was mislaid, the photographs became damaged and then the whole self-funded business venture foundered when a fire in the print shop of the publisher destroyed the whole booklet. As one author baldly put it,

'when publication eventually came in 1964, the astro-archaeological thunder had been stolen by Hawkins and Nature.'

Riddles in the British Landscape,
Richard Muir. Thames and Hudson, 1981

Chapter Two - A Passion for the Past
The Lunar Alignments

Thom discovered many observatories whose function was wholly lunar. The most impressive of these was probably *le Grand Menhir Brisé*, a 330 ton mega-megalith erected near Carnac, also known as *Er Grah*, providing a foresight for all eight key standstill positions of the moon. It was not possible to identify all the backsights, although Thom discovered enough evidence to identify the probable positions of these backsights. At one, near St Pierre, there was a surviving stone fan, which, as we shall see later, he found to be an essential component of a lunar observatory.

The huge Ring of Brogar, in the Orkneys was another lunar observatory. In the preface to *Megalithic Remains in Britain and Brittany*, the authors write,

> *'Here, as in no other place, there are enough remains to prove conclusively that the movements of the moon were being fully observed.'*

Lest this unambiguously worded citation be thought to disprove the validity of all the other sites, the reader should take account of the word *fully*. Brogar was unique: a site whose remoteness had largely protected it against the ravages of farming techniques, land development and vandalism.

We are fortunate to have a reliable witness to testify to Thom's assertions. Oxford scientist Professor Hans Motz wrote in *Records of Stone* the following account of Thom 'on-site', at the Ring of Brogar itself,

> *'..I do want to give account of a most impressive episode. The Brogar Ring is surrounded by foresights, both in the shape of cairns and in features of the not-too-distant hills such as the Kame of Corrigal, a steep part of which has the same slope as that of the moon at maximum declination at a major standstill.*
>
> *This had been investigated by the team on previous occasions, but this time many things needed to be checked. In particular the azimuth angle under which the feature of the Kame of Corrigal appears, when viewed from the circle, had to be measured with great accuracy to identify it with the azimuth expected at the major standstill during a night observation by Neolithic man.*
>
> *The skies were too cloudy for optical observation in daytime and the following strategy was employed. The Range Rover was driven up as high as possible near the Kame. The headlights were then screwed off and carried, together with the car battery, up to a cairn which stands at the site. The Thoms had not examined the site before, but inspection revealed a platform to which large stones had been brought. If this platform could be identified as being of megalithic origin this would strongly support Thom's hypothesis, that the Brogar Ring had amongst other functions that of a lunar observatory. We were equipped with walkie-talkies and it had been agreed that a car light should be lit in the darkness of the night, when the professor had set the hair-line of the theodolite precisely at the azimuth*

setting predicted by the astronomical theory. I was with him when the signal was given and the light spot appeared, exactly on the hair-line.'

' ..Witnessing confirmation of a prediction is indeed very impressive.'

It is also good science, Herr Professor.

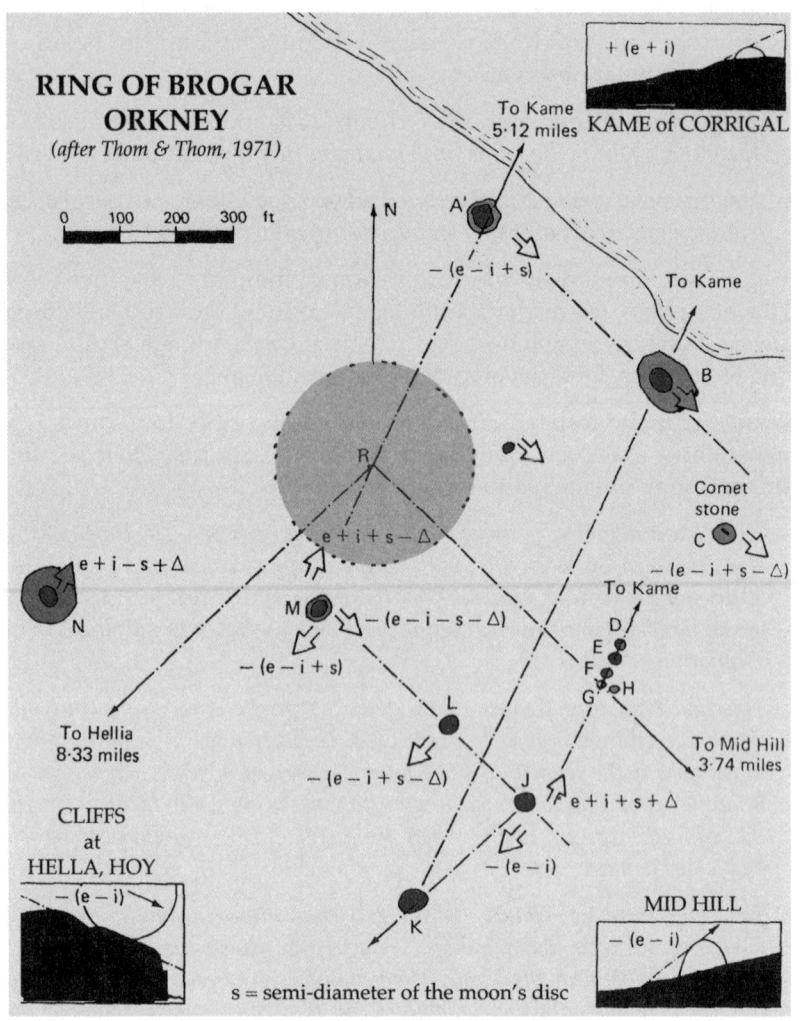

RING OF BROGAR ORKNEY
(after Thom & Thom, 1971)

The Ring of Brogar site as a lunar observatory. This giant ring (60 stones and 340 feet in diameter), plus the surrounding cairns (*shown shaded*) and horizon features (*insets*) gave Thom an unprecedented opportunity - an almost unspoiled site that offered several precise lunar alignments to standstill rises and sets.

Not all sites were as complex as Brogar. Thom identified the huge aligned stones of Parc y Meirw (field of the dead) near Fishguard in West Wales as a lunar alignment to the minor standstill moonset, proposing that the intended foresight was a mountain in Ireland, some 93 miles away. The author has observed both

Chapter Two - A Passion for the Past
The Lunar Alignments

the moonset (in January 1996, now misaligned due to changes in the tilt of the Earth's axis) and the mountain, but not simultaneously (*see photograph, top right, on page 43*).

Other lunar observatories were found in various states of ruin and surveyed. Some had other megalithic evidence adjacent to where the backsight once stood. Temple Wood, in Argyll and part of the Kintraw/Ballochroy/Brainport Bay complex, is one such, and it took A.T. many years to solve, before its intentions became crystal clear to him: "*If you put me here, in megalithic times, knowing what I know now, I could have worked this thing*". Temple Wood, also known as Half-moon Wood, lies close to the Kilmartin House Museum, Kilmartin, Argyll, Scotland.

Today, whilst most archaeologists agree that ancient sky-watchers were aware of and were observing the extreme lunar standstills and key solar risings and setting points, they suggest that these were *symbolic* alignments, and remain in doubt that *precision* observations were made in order to fuel a Neolithic 'scientific' astronomy. This point has become something of a log-jam in the whole subject. Whilst the short range alignments within many stone circles fall into the class of being symbolic, often down-graded to *orientations* as these can only yield poor angular resolution, one must raise an eyebrow when the same blanket conclusion is drawn about an alignment many miles, or tens of miles, in length. At site after site, Thom demonstrated that these long range alignments were made, and that they were pointed precisely where they should be in order to make the required observation during the late Neolithic period.

The periodic nine minute (of arc) wobble of the moon is a phenomenon of little importance to modern astronomy. Thom had discovered that 'the Boys' (his ever so slightly sexist name for the megalithic astronomers - he was, after all, born in 1894!)) had set up sites where this small amplitude wobble could be observed. It can *only* be observed as a variation in the height of the moon, at the standstills. At maximum height, it heralds an eclipse season and one can only conclude, as Thom did, that the purpose of such a precise observation was probably to perfect a knowledge of eclipse prediction. He even suggests (*MLO*, page 106), rather quaintly and as a hoary old academic himself, that,

> '*It will be assumed that the observatories were built primarily for eclipse prediction, but it is possible that the Megalithic scientist was using this as an excuse to 'obtain funds' to enable him to make a deeper study of astronomy.*'

If he is correct, these astronomer-priests represent the beginning of an unbroken line of academics and scientists systematically extracting resources from funding bodies by 'blinding 'em with science'! In Neolithic times, being able to predict eclipses would, one supposes, have provided a 'wow factor' sufficient to promote support for other types of astronomical research and observation. And accurate solar observation was essential in providing that most essential time-keeping tool for any culture, the calendar.

Stellar Alignments

The sun or moon rising and setting is something that draws the attention of even the most casual observer. It is an awesome spectacle of the natural environment that often moves people to tears. Unconcerned with refraction and parallax, the observation becomes simply a focus on the horizon where the luminary concerned passes from the above world to the underworld or vice versa. The horizon marks a boundary, a liminal space 'twixt two quite separate states - day/night or moon/no-moon. To observe this spectacle, either by accident or design, there needs to be no obscuring cloud.

For stars a rather different set of conditions apply. Stars rise and set at the same horizon angles for generations. But most stars disappear two or three degrees above the horizon when they set, and a similar angle is observed between the horizon and their emergence. This crucial angle, which depends on the brightness or *magnitude* of the star, is called by astronomers the *extinction angle*.

In the northern hemisphere, only the star Sirius can be observed setting right down to the horizon, and then only under exceptional viewing conditions. To design a suitable alignment to note star risings and settings requires that the foresight is elevated above the atmospheric haze adjacent to a level horizon. Worse, variable atmospheric conditions make even this a problem in any attempt to define an alignment to a rising or setting star.

Thom recognised this problem, writing an entire chapter in *MSIB* addressed to the subject,

> 'We can only expect to find a nice tidy line if we were in a position to assign the correct date to each site (page 160)' and 'There is not enough material for a fully fledged statistical calculation of this kind and an overall mean date is all that could be obtained (page 163)'

Despite these formidable hurdles, Thom was sure that four or five of the brightest stars had been observed in this way by prehistoric astronomers. In particular the star Deneb appeared several times in his list of possible alignments. Deneb's declination hardly changes over epochs of time and consequently Thom was more confident in determining its extinction angle.

Because of the archaeological dating available in the mid-sixties, Thom was strapped between dates 2000 BC and 1600 BC in his search for alignments. He did not consider the declinations for the major stars earlier than this period and, as a direct consequence, when the dates for some of the sites were pushed back following the publication of radiocarbon calibration dates, Thom's stellar alignments represented the weakest card in his hand, for which he was not entirely to blame. Compared to the slow inexorable reduction in the earth's tilt angle, some stars change their declinations quite quickly. If a site set up to a proposed stellar alignment is not accurately dated, one can never be certain of the alignment's validity.

Chapter Two - A Passion for the Past
Stellar Alignments

Alignments - So Many Choices?

It was the extreme stations of the sun and moon which were most often marked by the long alignments, and there are just four solar and eight lunar extreme positions, whose angles were defined uniquely *according to the latitude of each site*. Knowing the latitude and the date of the site one can calculate the precise angle to look for in an astronomical alignment, then find a site in the landscape or on a map which is aligned to one of these angles. Alternatively, one can work backwards, discover a site that appears ideal for observation and perform the necessary calculations to confirm its suitability.

Whichever approach is adopted, these directions amount to *only about two per cent of the whole compass*. To the uninformed, however, it appears that almost any bearing must encompass some star, sun or moon rise or set. It must have been irksome for Thom, on the set of the BBC *Chronicle* documentary, to have to listen to Jacquetta Hawkes (*below*), sharing her lack of knowledge of basic astronomy dressed up in the polished patina of academic superiority.

"I believe the thing is he gives himself so many choices. I feel he is a man surrounded by loopholes. That he has so many instruments on the one hand, it can be the top in a stone, the gap between stones, it can be something in the foreground, it can be what he calls a foresight, some natural thing you pick out on the horizon. And then also, so many objectives - different phases of the moon, sun rises and sets summer and winter, twelve major stars. And really there's a vast amount of choice there so that if you don't find one thing, you find another."

Dr Jacquetta Hawkes

When academics haven't done their homework we may all raise an eyebrow, and there was no excuse for this display, as Thom had already covered this matter on the very first page of the introduction to *Megalithic Sites in Britain*, the book upon which the whole documentary was based.

No challenge or debate on Hawkes' comment took place on air, and A.T. would have been too much of a gentleman to deliver the appropriate ruffling of Hawkes' feathers. But one senses that Hawkes was enjoying dismissing Thom's findings, particularly as she later disrespectfully referred to him as 'Mr Thom'. Two percent of the horizon profile, calculated beforehand and corrected for latitude of the site, horizon altitude, refraction and parallax is hardly 'so many choices', and the loopholes belonged entirely to Hawkes' failure to grasp Thom's methodology.

Thom sometimes had cause to change his mind concerning the purpose of a particular megalithic site, as its complexities and idiosyncrasies were revealed to him. This was no weakness nor vacillation, it merely confirmed the pioneering nature of the work in hand and his own flexibility to change tack when results suggested it. There was no *terra firma* and there were no textbooks, no academic references, just a landscape to be explored, original research to be undertaken. As Archie relates, Sandy was increasingly criticised by 'smaller minds' for these occasional changes of tack - apparently it was not by loopholes that he was surrounded.

THE CALENDAR

"Just as today, our astronomers like to produce a calendar which is exact, to a fraction of a second if you like, these people were working to a fraction of a day, and they wanted to be accurate, just the same as our scientists today want to be accurate. They wouldn't have been scientists if they hadn't tried to be accurate"

Alexander Thom, *Cracking the Stone Age Code*,
Chronicle BBC

Thom wrote an entire chapter in *Megalithic Sites in Britain* devoted to the calendar. He began by pointing out that the Egyptian technique of observing the heliacal rising of a bright star (Sirius) was wholly unsuitable for the long twilights of temperate latitudes. Instead he proposed that the large annual range of rising and setting azimuths of the sun on the horizon in Britain provided an easily observable phenomenon whereby an observer could fix an individual date within the year - in other words, to derive a calendar accurate to the day.

He also suggested, from the evidence he accrued, that megalithic astronomers were able to count the number of days in the year. His proof was remarkably simple and may easily be verified, drawing on two facts. Astronomically, the equinoxes are defined as the instant when the declination of the Sun is zero, i.e. the sun appears to be on the celestial equator, rising exactly in the East and setting exactly in the West, independent of the latitude of the observation. The day and the night are then of equal duration, as the word equinox tells us. But because the earth's orbit around the sun is not circular, the two halves of the year, summer and winter, are unequal in duration and the halfway points between the two solstices do not fall on the astronomical equinoxes.

The division of the year exactly into two equal halves in time either side of the solstices occurred in neolithic times when the sun's declination was about half a degree above zero, an angle which translates to nearly a whole degree in azimuth on the horizon at British sites. This angular discrepancy had been already recorded by Thom at site after site. From this he concluded that megalithic astronomers had been comfortable with the manipulation of large numbers, and were able to conceive of the concept of half or division by two.

Chapter Two - A Passion for the Past
The Calendar

To emphasise the importance of this point: such a marked and easily observed deviation from true east and west at identified equinoctial sites shows that megalithic man was counting the days from solstice to solstice and then halving the result to define a 'megalithic equinox'. There is no other way by which this 'megalithic equinox' could have been determined. It was then built into the equinoctial alignment sites as the location of the backsight.

Secondly, the alignments Thom measured in the field suggested that the astronomers had then repeatedly divided the year up into halves, ending up with a 16 month year (the year halved four times). Thom found evidence for this practice throughout Britain and beyond and his calendar emerged from the data from all the aligned sites, presented below as a 'curvigram'.

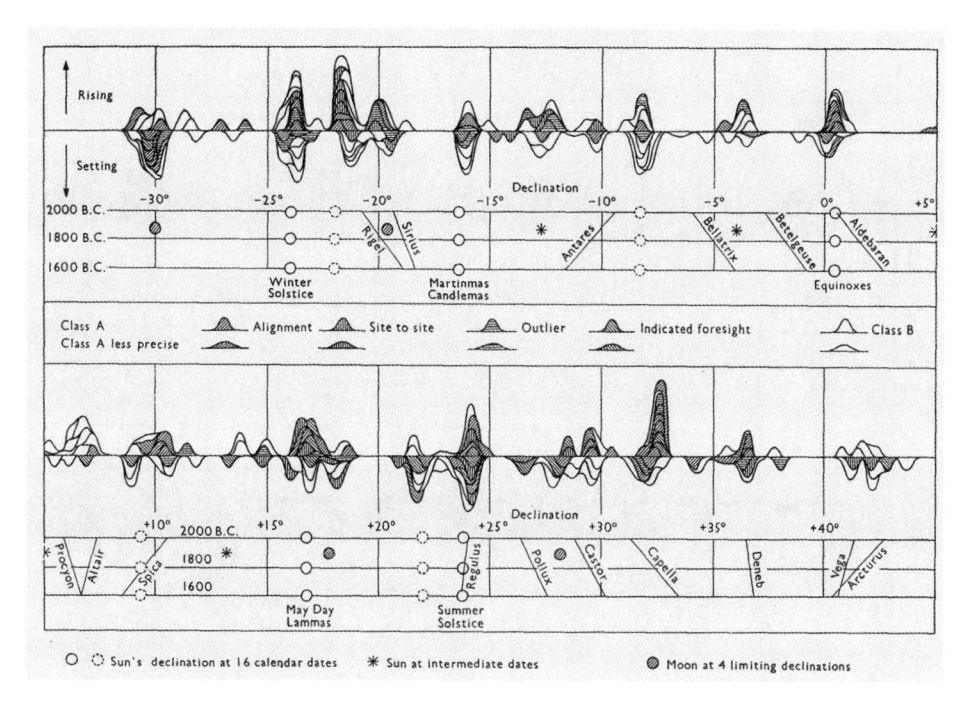

Over many years Thom's surveys at aligned sites built up into the histogram-style chart shown above. Many sites incorporated an indicated foresight, and this data built up into the distinct declination pattern shown above suggesting to Thom that megalithic astronomers had repeatedly divided the year into two, to derive a 16 'month' calendar. Some major star alignments and the minor standstill of the moon are included, unconnected to the solar calendar, which is shown overleaf.

Supposing that we ourselves are the megalithic astronomers wishing to set up the best solution to a seasonal calendar, he noted (*MSIB*, page 107) that,

> 'What we can do is to define the equinoxes as those two days which divide the year into two equal parts and on which the sun has the same declination - that is the same rising point.'

Alexander Thom - Cracking the Stone Age Code

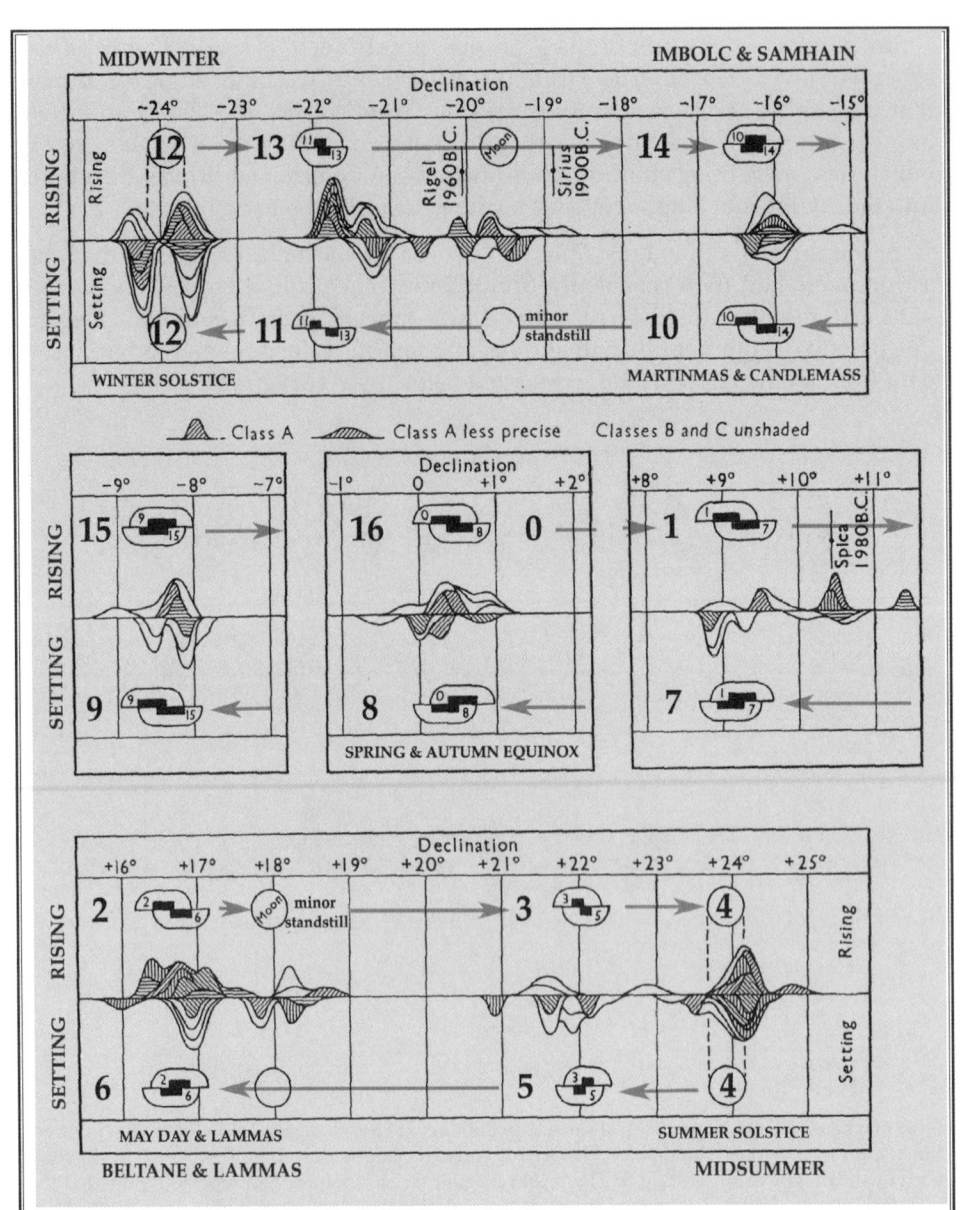

The 16 month solar calendar proposed by Thom in *Megalithic Sites in Britain*. The month numbers begin at the spring equinox (marked zero) and the count increments to the summer solstice (month 4), back to the autumn equinox (month 8), then to the winter solstice (month 12) and finally returns to the spring equinox (month 16/month 0). The quarter days, Mayday/Beltane, Lammas, Halloween/Samhain and Imbolc are respectively the beginning of months 2, 6, 10 and 14. There remains a wide traditional use of the quarter days in Church rituals and pagan festivals. Starting from Mayday the month lengths are (in days) 24, 23, 23, 23, 23, 22, 22, 22, 22, 23, 23, 23, 23, 23, 23, 23, totalling 365. This sequence is 1 of 24 days, 4 of 23 days, 4 of 22 days and 7 of 23 days. This numerical sequence is similar to the markings of the 16 fold pattern pictogram on the outer rim of the pictogram 'fan' (*shown overleaf*), at Knowth in Ireland.

- 54 -

Chapter Two - A Passion for the Past
The Calendar

Thom, ever the practical engineer, was quick to note that if this was the case, then one marker can serve for both equinoxes, spring and autumn - a single ten ton stone could serve as the backsight (or foresight) for two months instead of only one. At a site set to observe the day of any one of the 'months', a single alignment would always record the day of another month equally spaced in time either side of the solstice, i.e. symmetrically placed. The advantages of such an ingenious technique would have been obvious. He concluded (*MSIB*, p 107-8),

> *'It is true that these people, having set up the mark, might have stopped keeping a tally of days, simply leaving the marks to give the indications. But the Megalithic culture was widespread and communication essentially slow. To transfer the 'date' from one end of the system to the other meant that the messengers must have counted days as they travelled and having arrived at an isolated community the counting had to go on until a year with suitable weather allowed the marks to be set up. The alternative is to assume that each community began independently the arduous task of establishing its own calendar epochs. This is indeed possible, but when we find indications of the same declinations in Cumberland, Lewis, Wales and Caithness we must consider the possibility that the calendar dates throughout this wide area were in phase.'*

Thom presented his case, backed up by extensive work on site, to indicate that a sixteen-month calendar year was in force in megalithic times - the original division by two was continued to enable a single set of markers to indicate the 'months' for each half of the year. The moon was not involved in this 'solar' calendar, and these 'months' have nothing to do with lunar phases or the moon's position.

The move from simple visual astronomy to the counting and recording of astronomical events by Stone-Age astronomers was no small cultural step for mankind. Had it been proclaimed with far more emphasis by Thom, his evidence would surely have attracted much more interest by historians. When Thom suggested that the calendar year was divided into two, we need not assume that long division was applied, perhaps a long rope marked in days (365 marks - midsummer solstice to midsummer solstice) was simply folded in half to attain the required number of days for each half of the year. The same technique may then be applied to quarters, eighths and sixteenths.

The Celtic calendar, the Church and the modern neo-pagans still celebrate the four 'quarter' days, still referring to the same (astronomically defined) dates: Imbolc (February), Beltaine (May Day), Lugnasadh (August; Lammas) and Samhain (November; All-Saint's Day, Halloween and even Bonfire Night). These all fall closely halfway between the four salient turning points in the year, the two solstices, midsummer and midwinter and the two equinoxes, spring and autumn. Long term changes in the earth's orbit mean that any calendar will eventually require to change the date on which these quarter-days occur.

Is Thom's 'Stone-Age' calendar a mere fantasy, as some have suggested? Why, for example, has not a site been identified where *all* the dates are indicated from a single backsight? One answer may well be provided by Stonehenge, which contains all the ingredients to indicate, albeit at a low accuracy, eight of the sixteen months, as suggested by C A 'Peter' Newham's work there.

But we can go further than this in support of a Neolithic calendar. At Knowth, in the Boyne Valley, many kerbstones suggest the numerical periods of solar and lunar timekeeping, in days, along with the lunar month, the 19 year metonic cycle, and even a seven day week within a 28 day month. One inscribed kerbstone may describe the 16 month calendar. It is reproduced here, courtesy of Dr Neil Thomas. The correct number of days for each of the months suggested by Thom are to be found on the outer rim of the semi-circular 'fan' pictogram, in anticlockwise order and commencing at Mayday, at the end of the second month. As for all interpretations, it is impossible to confirm absolutely the intentions of the creators of these strange pictograms, but the design below could be used to track Thom's 16 month calendar - "*..I could have worked this thing*".

There must have come a time when the ritual of the calendar became abstracted from actual observations of the sky, when counting or geometry replaced the need to observe the sky. Many sites contain numerical and geometrical designs which suggest such a step had already taken place by the late Stone-Age. During such a change of approach, the sky would have become much less valued as a source of information, while the mental skills of mathematics and geometry would have become emphasized, not just in understanding the calendar, but also in weaving and pottery designs.

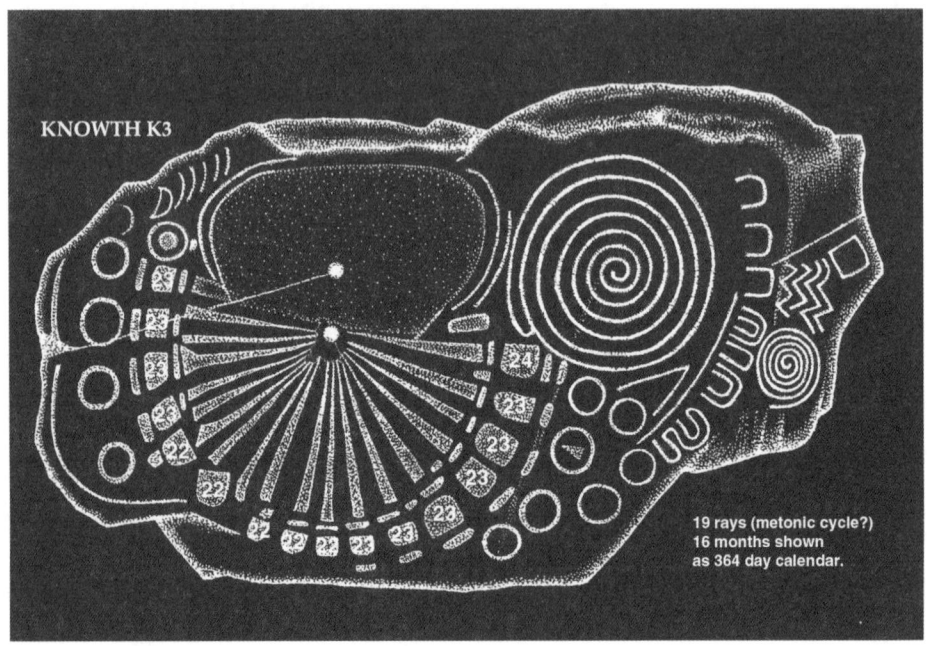

KNOWTH K3

19 rays (metonic cycle?)
16 months shown
as 364 day calendar.

Chapter Two - A Passion for the Past
The Geometries

THE GEOMETRIES

"Well, it might have been geometry for its own sake. These people were, well, they were researching into geometry. All the time they were controlled by this convention that they had to have it in whole numbers."

Alexander Thom,
Cracking the Stone Age Code, Chronicle BBC

Once the theodolite survey of a circle had been undertaken with sufficient accuracy, Sandy would spend many a evening in his cabin at *The Hill* draughting out an accurate plan of the site from the theodolite survey bookings. He insisted on working to an accuracy of one part in a thousand, reckoning that the constructors were capable of maintaining half this accuracy. To attain this level of accuracy in his plans, he had made a special pantograph, adapted to fit his large drawing board.

Although two-thirds of all stone circles were found to be true circles, the rest formed a fascinating collection of shapes based on blending arcs of different radii together. Whatever their shape, Thom discovered that the same general rules almost always applied - the diameters were in whole integers of a basic length, usually the Megalithic yard or sometimes half that measure, and the perimeters were often made to become an integer multiple of 2.5 times the same length - i.e. measured in Megalithic rods. Thom discovered that the shapes were laid out according to certain simple geometrical rules, often incorporating an internal 'Pythagorean' triangle. These are right-angled triangles having whole number side lengths. Because such triangles regularly had integer side lengths of the same or multiple units of length as the diameters of the final stone ring, Thom was assured that he had discovered both the geometrical construction method and the metrology employed by the circle builders. Quite independently of any astronomical alignments they may have possessed, the circles spoke of a knowledge of the 3:4:5, the 5:12:13, the 8:15:17, the 12:35:37 and possibly the 9:40:41 Pythagorean triangles, plus knowledge of many approximations, for example, 8:9:12 where the accuracy is to 99.967%.

With the geometries in the bag, Thom thought he possessed a three-pronged spear with which to prod the whole weary giant of archaeological indifference and wake it to a new dawn of exploration of the European megalithic culture. Yet many critics attacked his geometric constructions, most notably, Arthur Hogg, who had criticised A.T.'s geometry together with the basis for the Megalithic yard on the BBC *Chronicle* programme,

'Just because the circles could have been laid out that way does not mean that they were laid out that way'

Alexander Thom - Cracking the Stone Age Code

While true to a degree, some sites did reveal exactly how they were marked out. Stones in their perimeters are positioned on the key positions of Thom's proposed geometrical construction. In these show-piece sites, the layout had been exactly as Thom describes.

For example, at Castle Rigg (*above*), a Type A flattened circle, nine stones are found accurately placed at 30° intervals around the 240° section where the design is truly circular. This reveals two facts, firstly that the geometrical construction of dividing a circle into six and hence twelve was known to the builders and, secondly, that ropes and pegs were the method used to lay out Castle Rigg.

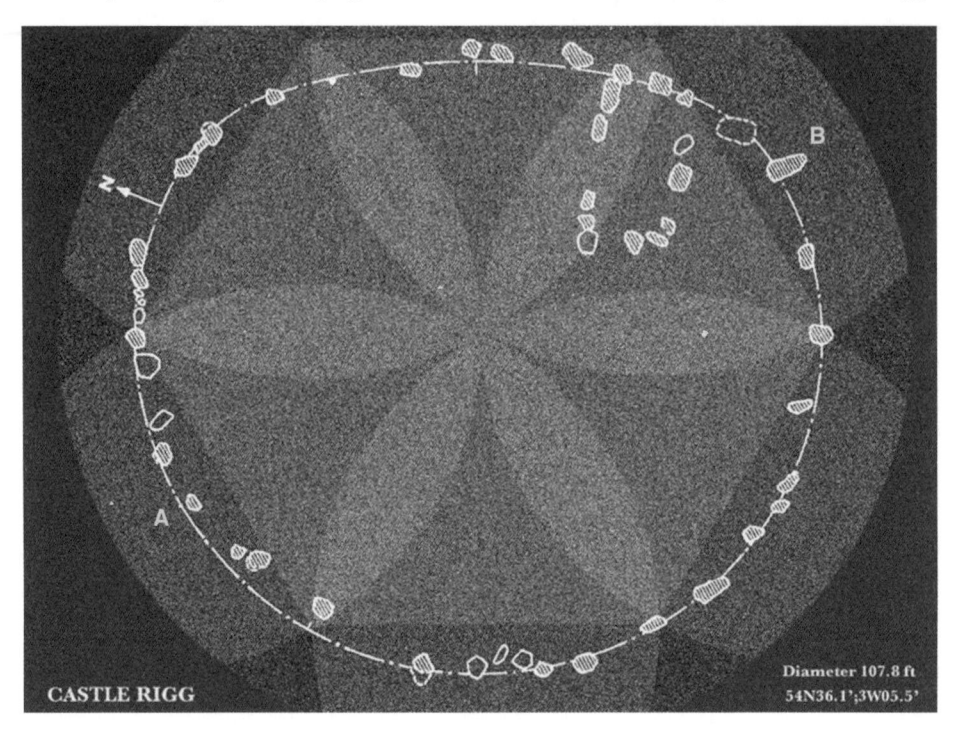

CASTLE RIGG

Diameter 107.8 ft
54N36.1';3W05.5'

Chapter Two - A Passion for the Past
The Geometries

Anybody who has even a remote interest in the history of science would, one might think, be astonished at this earliest known indicator of the division of a circle into twelve (or six) using the same geometrical construction to be found in every school text-book ever since Euclid. Such a discovery by Thom relocated a once giant cultural leap for mankind away from the Middle East, and plonked it firmly in the English Lake District (Castle Rigg also has interesting astronomical and locational properties. In chapter seven this link is explored further)

Moel ty Uchaf is another example, one of Thom's 'compound rings'. Based on two concentric circles, the inner one 4 and the outer 7 megalithic yards in radius (*below left*). These circles are then divided into ten equal divisions prior to constructing a complex pentagonal geometry (*below right and below that*).

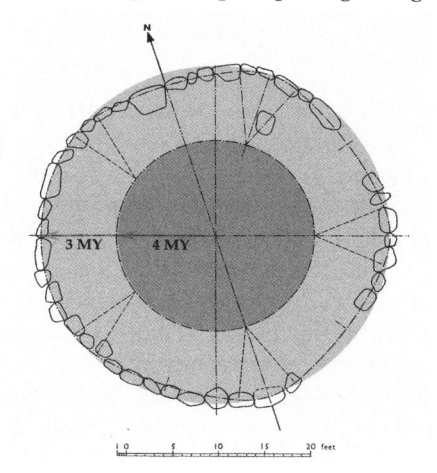

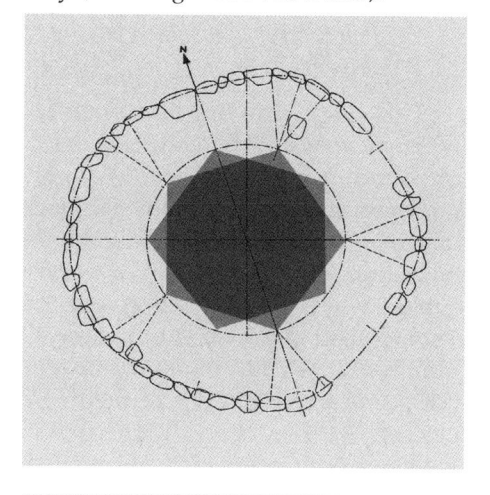

Moel ty Uchaf is described as a kerbed cairn, located high up in the Welsh hills above Llandrillo, near Bala. Its geometry is exquisite - two concentric circles of radii 4 and 7 Megalithic yards (*above left*) are divided into ten (*above right*) and a complex pentagonal perimeter form is constructed using long arcs whose axis is struck from the opposite 'corner' of the pentagons points (*right*). Smaller arcs round off the resulting corners.

The builders of Moel ty Uchaf were evidently consciously aware of the geometrical steps they placed within their design, and to perform their art, must have been using ropes and pegs marked up in units of the Megalithic yard.

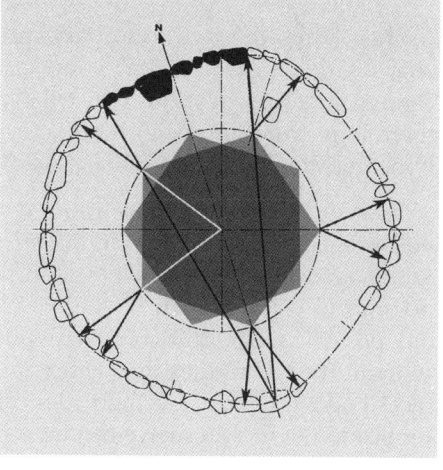

It is possible to verify the geometry today, using ropes, to discover that the perimeter remains within an inch or two of Thom's proposed constructional geometry. This proof of a ten-fold division of a circle located high up in the remote hills of Wales and constructed prior to 3000 BC should have been heralded by historians and mathematicians alike. It was not.

For some geometrical designs the required internal stone marker 'pegs' used in forming the final shape were left by the builders and have been discovered. They remain in place on Dartmoor, the Welsh hills and elsewhere and the author has found several examples. But during the 70s this was an under-reported yet remarkable confirmation for Thom's geometries, and the response from academics was predictable, unsubtly criticised in the words of one mutinous archaeologist, Dr Ian Orkney, who was working with a colleague, Jack G. Scott, at the time of one similar discovery, which converted him to Thom's ideas,

> '..the establishment's brainless inability to take in the significance of the stone marker pegs which Jack and I found at the arc centres of the Temple Wood egg.'

This single true but below the belt remark symbolises the whole problem with the subject. The cultural significance of this artefact evidence is indeed profound, while the 'establishment' (whoever they were!) probably never understood the reason why so, because Thom's ideas and findings were so far removed from the archaeological paradigm of the time. An enormous educational promotional drive was needed, including the "Child's Guide" to the subject, which the two archaeologists above, along with everyone else, including Thom, failed to provide at the time. One result of this failing is that the several hundred stone balls, ploughed up over several areas of Scotland, each of which has been carved into one of the five Platonic solids, remain classified as 'ritual objects'. Yet these are yet more proof that the contemporaneous circle builders were indeed "researching into geometry", as Thom had always claimed.

Chapter seven explores these fascinating geometries of megalithic man much further, while the two examples above provide a taster to show that Thom's surveys demonstrated that stone circles were much more than crude ovals thrown together by primitive tribespeople. They incorporated geometry and metrology from an epoch when current academic thought believes there was none in Britain, preceding the classical Greek culture by two millennia.

During my own megalithic workshops and tutorials, I have always encouraged students to undertake their own "research into geometry", usually with somewhat smaller stones than those used on megalithic rings, in order to attempt to recreate their shapes first *without* using Thom's geometries. Forget any possible megalithic context awhile and just attempt to recreate these shapes without the techniques that Thom uncovered. Be prepared to face some loss of face! Following this, by then replicating Thom's suggested geometry, perfect replication of the geometry can be achieved.

Thom eventually surveyed nearly 500 stone circles. It is quite remarkable that so little interest has been shown in the circles as storehouses of geometrical, astronomical and metrological wisdom since Thom published these surveys.

Chapter Two - A Passion for the Past
The Extrapolation Devices

THE EXTRAPOLATION DEVICES

"They knew what they were doing alright! This thing wasn't set out without endless headaches and trial and worry and calculation, if you like, only the calculation was done on the ground, geometrically. If you put me here, in megalithic times, I could have worked this thing, knowing what I do know now."

Alexander Thom,
Cracking the Stone Age Code, Chronicle BBC

In addition to the circular geometries of stone rings, Thom surveyed several sites where curious stone rows and fan shaped stone arrays were to be found adjacent to the astronomical alignment(s). Perhaps the most famous of these in Scotland is the Hill o'many Stanes, Mid-Clyth, where a 200 by 100 foot fan may be found adjacent to the alignments Thom had identified as being observatories of lunar standstills. Other good examples of lunar sites with stone fans include Dirlot, Caithness, Loch of Yarrows, Camster and St Pierre, Baie du Morbihan, in Brittany (*shown below*).

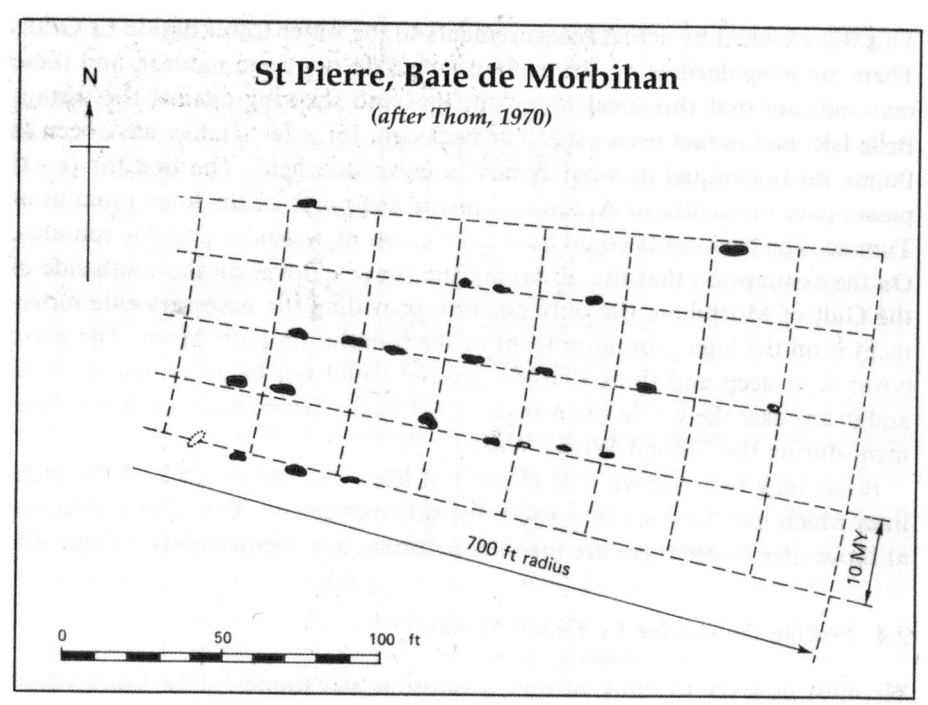

St Pierre, Baie de Morbihan
(after Thom, 1970)

700 ft radius

10 MY

0   50   100 ft

Thom made the reasonable assumption that the stone arrays were once part of whatever had been going on at the observatories, and owed their existence to them, for they are found only at lunar observatories. He pointed out (*MLO*, page 95), concerning Mid Clyth, that, *'The chance is remotely small that these stones are situated by accident at a spot which provides foresights of e + i and - (e - i) [these terms are explained later] with perturbations, and provides them accurately. As has been pointed out, such a site is useless without a means of extrapolation.'*

So, what is extrapolation? Once again, Sandy did not begin at square one for his astronomically challenged readers, making quite a complex meal out of his explanation for what is essentially a simple technique for establishing where on the horizon the extreme moonrise or set occurs each month. John Edwin Wood, in *Sun, Moon and Standing Stones*, (OUP 1980) does a whole lot better, but the subject remains in need of a simpler explanation to demonstrate the practical need for megalithic astronomers to grapple with the vagaries of lunar motion in understanding eclipses and lunar standstills.

The next few paragraphs and their associated diagrams offer an understanding of why the fans and stone rows might have been built and how they could have been used to assist accurate lunar observation. They would have been essential to any precision astronomy. However, the whole subject can be detached from any megalithic context and approached as a modern exercise in positioning and timing the maximum monthly moonset.

DRAWING DOWN THE MOON
SETTING UP A MODERN LUNAR OBSERVATORY

Observing where the moon rose and set may have begun as a mere curiosity. If the moon is observed whenever weather conditions permit, over a period of years, one cannot fail to notice that, every month, its extreme rising and setting positions on the horizon vary, and that each extreme rise and set would occur at a different phase of the moon. Such observations would surely have developed into a recognition that there were two pairs of limiting positions beyond which the moon never rose or set. These ultimate extreme positions, which Thom termed the major and minor standstills, would surely have held a significance worthy of being celebrated or marked in some way.

In our present epoch the extreme set in the northwest always occurs at the point in the sidereal month when the moon is passing the easily identifiable stars of Orion and the twin stars, Castor and Pollux - the Zodiacal constellation of Gemini and the Sign Cancer. At the approach of the major standstill, each and every month the moon's most northerly set occurs a little further to the northwest. This would continue until the major standstill is reached. Then, the moon having reached its extreme northwesterly set position, would very gradually, month on month, return back from whence it had arrived and then return once more 18.6 years, or 230 months later.

Having watched the moon reaching the period of extreme monthly setting positions, every 18.6 years, an attempt could then be made to mark its approach

Chapter Two - A Passion for the Past
Lunar Observatories

by placing a sequence of stakes or marker stones in the ground at the point at which, each set, it aligns the moonset to a prominent foresight. This sequence of stakes would slowly move to the left, the gap between them narrowing all the while until, following the monthly extreme set, the most northerly set position for that month, the stakes would turn around and increasingly move to the right, past those stakes already placed.

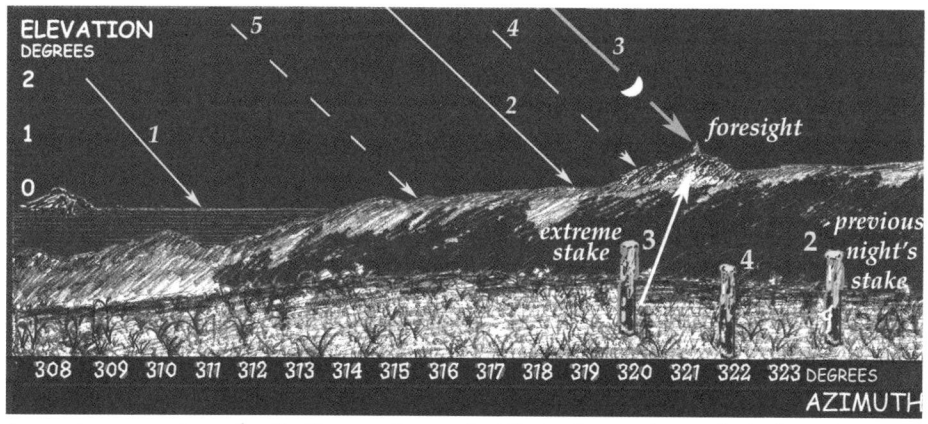

Successive moonsets reach a limiting position against the horizon each month. At the major standstill, every 18.6 years, an ultimate limiting position is observed. The moon never sets any further to the north than this. The diagram above shows the position of five successive moonsets including the extreme position for the month (3), at the standstill. The set positions prior to this are numbered 1 & 2, those after are numbered 4 & 5 and the setting track is shown as a dashed line.

If an attempt were made to align each of the above moon sets with the foresight it would be necessary to move to the right, except for the extreme set. If the locations for the other sets are staked out, a pattern of stakes is produced, as shown in the foreground of the diagram above and in more detail below. For both diagrams, the extreme stake (3) marks the best estimate for the position of the backsight in order to be aligned to the major standstill moonset.

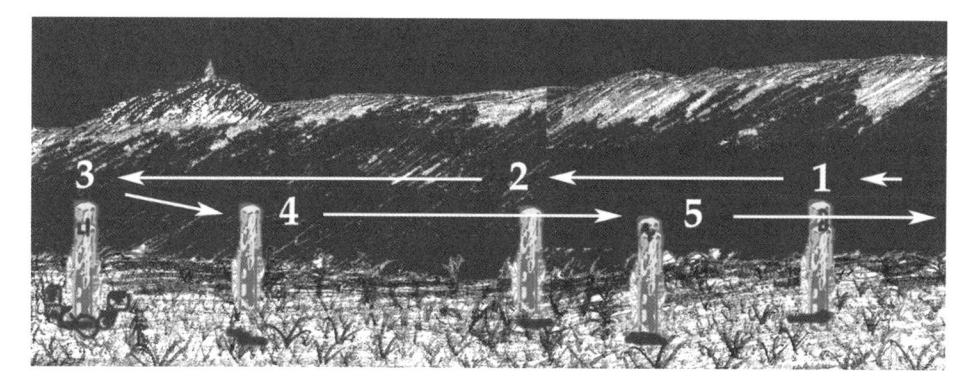

Each month, in order to guarantee that the monthly maximum had occurred, a minimum of one or two setting positions either side of the monthly maximum set position would need to be placed - there would be stake placements prior to the monthly maximum because we are still awaiting its arrival, and stakes afterwards to confirm that the maximum for that month had indeed passed.

- 63 -

Patterns would begin to emerge. These stakes would soon spell out that the distance from the furthest left stake (the monthly extreme set) to the midpoint of the nearest adjacent two stakes placed before and after the maximum *is always the same*. This distance would have been seen as special in some way, and it would always be the same length *at a given observatory*. At another observatory it would be a different length, being a function of the spacing between foresight and backsight. Thom allocated it a symbol, the letter G, signifying this distance.

Another pattern would appear. The maximum possible spacing of any two stakes in the sequence would be found to be 4G in length, a distance that Thom termed the *characteristic distance* of the site. And for an alignment at the standstill, the lunar diameter on the ground, found by staking the lower and upper limb positions as the moon set (often termed 'first touch', when the lower limb of the moon touched the horizon, and 'last flash', when the upper limb of the moon disappeared), would always be just over 2G (major standstill) or about equal to 2G (minor standstill).

At the standstill itself an absolute 'maximum ever' left position could be staked, the place where, ultimately, a permanent backsight should be erected, indicating the place where an observer should thenceforth stand to observe subsequent standstills - a highly significant place marking the spot where the moon is seen to set onto the foresight *only* at the major standstill (every 18.6 years). The moon will *never* set any further to the north than this and this position, and the alignment, has been determined without knowing any numerical astronomy. The site has been defined and will record the major standstill moonset position for many generations.

Although this non-mathematical written description of how to set up a lunar observatory to record the standstill may initially appear highly technical and therefore beyond the capabilities of megalithic cultures, the shocking truth is that we actually know almost nothing concerning these capabilities, yet have somehow arrogantly accorded it primitive status.

All we have done here is observe by eye where the moon sets against the horizon over an extended interval of time and marked it with stones or sticks. We can change tack and be rather more archaeologically 'scientific' and, knowing now how to erect an observatory, and the kinds of equipment and issues involved, look to see if we can find sites where someone else in the past has erected a similar observatory and left traces of platforms, stake holes or lengths in the surrounding megalithic landscape near the backsight of G, 2G or 4G. Thom identified many such sites, and the assumption that megalithic astronomers knew nothing of the complex motions of the moon is challenged when, at most alignments to the lunar standstill positions, A.T. and other researchers, such as Alan Penny, Dr John Wood and the author have found foresights highly suited to observing the current phase of the tiny $\pm\, 9'$ wobble, and hence eclipses to be predicted. These sites have often been found to contain multiples of G built into their construction.

Chapter Two - A Passion for the Past
Lunar Observatories

A Problem of Timing

We must face a remaining difficulty in observing the moon, a tricky one at that! Before we can triumphantly stake that *correct* final position for the backsight marker each month, so easily described in an earlier paragraph, an astronomical problem confronts us. Every month the moon's *potential* maximum northerly setting position against the horizon is *not synchronous* with the moment when the moon actually sets - cuts the local horizon - at the given location. Only rarely will the potential maximum set and the moment of set coincide. Within twenty-four hours of the maximum monthly set the azimuth angle may change by as much as three lunar diameters. On the ground this may translate to a stake movement of perhaps tens of feet. Our previous staking experiments would only approximate to the maximum possible position each month. Houston, we have a problem!

Before we can assess how a neolithic moon watcher would know where to place a 'super-stake' to reliably mark this elusive monthly potential maximum moon-set position, we must apply some thought as to how an observer might solve this problem today. The problem isn't nebulous - it becomes completely blindingly obvious when one begins to attempt to measure the monthly maximum setting position. A random 'error' is introduced such that we may be lucky and get very close to the elusive correct position we seek to know, but ..we may not.

The 'error' is not tiny. In the twelve hours either side of the monthly maximum declination of the moon, its declination changes by about 12'. On the ground in Britain, this translates to an azimuth change of up to nearly half a degree - the angle occupied by the moon's disc. Unless an observer lived through many standstills, until a moonset coincided with the time of maximum declination, it would be impossible to observe the 9' wobble.

The solution requires some kind of trick - a device or technique to inform the observer of the *correct* position for the extreme left stake given the layout of the *actual* stake positions marked on the ground for each observed moonset around the maximum. Neolithic astronomers engaged in staking out moonsets would ultimately have had to face the task of solving this fundamental problem of knowing where to place the extreme stake every month.

Thom applied much thought as to how this practical astronomical conundrum could be solved. We will probably never know when he came to the conclusions he did, probably around 1967, but he informs us, on page 83 of *MLO*,

> *'..recently, when studying methods of extrapolation that might have been available at the Megalithic lunar observatories, I found that I have developed a geometrical method that corresponds exactly with what is found in the Caithness rows.'*

Alexander Thom - Cracking the Stone Age Code

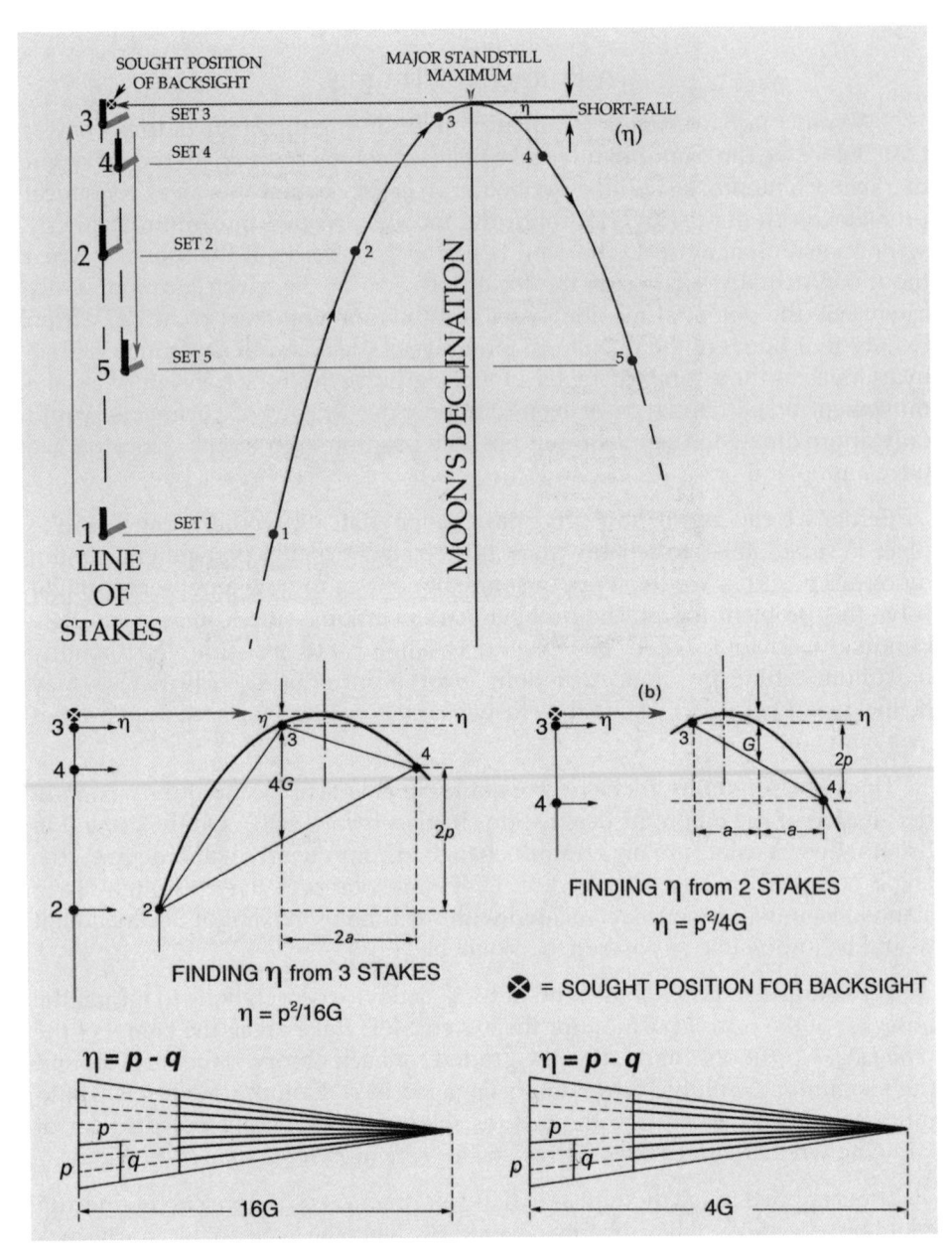

FINDING η from 3 STAKES
$$\eta = p^2/16G$$

FINDING η from 2 STAKES
$$\eta = p^2/4G$$

⊗ = SOUGHT POSITION FOR BACKSIGHT

$\eta = p - q$

$\eta = p - q$

One solution to determining where to position the backsight stake. The row of stakes on the previous diagram are here shown at the top left, with their corresponding positions as the moonsets approach and depart from the standstill position. Because the time of the maximum will not normally coincide with moonset for that day, there is a small discrepancy (η) between where the final stake (no. 3 in the sequence) is placed and where the backsight position needs to be located for future observation of the standstill moonset over the foresight. The lower diagrams show how the stone fans found at many sites possess ideal geometrical properties to enable this distance η to be determined using ropes. Other sites suggest alternative geometrical solutions. Fantasy or sophisticated astronomy?

Chapter Two - A Passion for the Past
Lunar Observatories

At Caithness, Thom identified four sites where, adjacent to the lunar observatory, lie large fan-shaped stone rows. Thom indicated that these were a suitable shape to work out or extrapolate the correct maximum extreme left stake position. With masterful understatement, the professor wrote about Hill o' Many Stanes, Mid-Clyth (*survey plan below*), that,

> '*Whether or not we accept the idea that the grid was a computer, the site is certainly a lunar computer. The chance is remotely small that these stones are situated by accident at a spot which provides foresights for e + i and - (e + i)* [both major standstill bearings, rise and set - author's comment] *with perturbations, and provides them accurately. As has been pointed out, such a site is useless without a means of extrapolation.*'

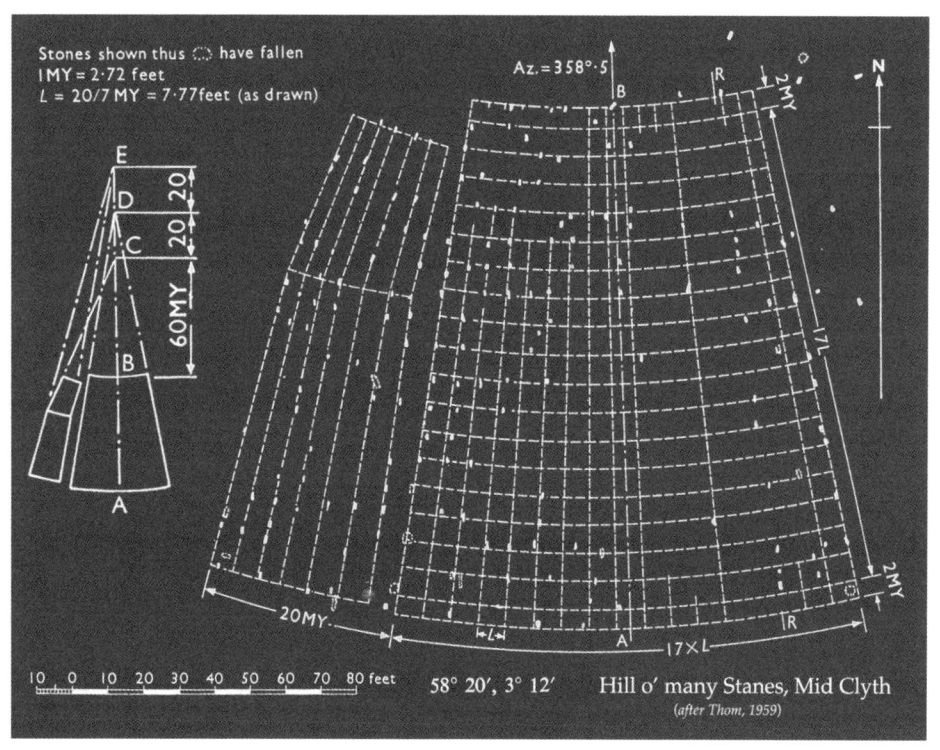

Plan of the stone fan at Hill o'Many Stanes, Mid Clyth, Caithness. Thom's original 1959 survey of this site was undertaken many years prior to his discovery of lunar observatories. It was during the later work on the moon that Thom then developed a geometrical method to determine the extreme lunar rise and set positions which could be fabricated quite readily from the layout of this site.

Later on, Thom was to find the same type of stone 'computer' at other sites. In the October 1972 issue of *JHA* (vol 3, part 3, No 8) he concludes that,

> '*A method is suggested whereby the extrapolation length can be found with sufficient accuracy for all four sites to the west of the Sea of Morbihan. ... but the peculiar square law relation shown in Table 2 cannot be the result of chance, and when we find that it gives approximately the extrapolation*

length for the mean value of G (the stake position - author) there can be little doubt that the rows were intended to be used with Er Grah (the 57 foot long, 330 ton foresight stone erected in Morbihan, Brittany - author) *in some such way as we have described.'*

Although Thom honestly informs his readers that the stone rows of Dartmoor defeated his attempts to decode any astronomical sense, Dr John Wood and Mr Alan Penny subsequently investigated a geometrical device attached to Merrivale stone rows. Their account of this solution to the problem is written up in *Sun, Moon and Standing Stones* (Oxford 1978). The present author has 'driven' this extrapolation device with student groups for some years and discovered it to offer a simple, reliable and accurate technique for establishing the maximum stake position. On one occasion we watched a National Park tractor drive right across the tiny stones that make up the row, distressing support for Thom's concluding plea in *MLO* that,

'the position of every stone near a site, however insignificant-looking, to be recorded exactly, before the information it may hold is lost for ever.'

The smaller sizes of the stone used to fabricate an extrapolation 'engine' have probably long made them extremely tempting to farmers and other interested parties looking for gateposts, lintels and wall building material. At some sites the stones are so inconspicuous that they are hard to spot on rough ground in heather or bracken.

In southern Scotland, another simpler type of device may be found adjacent to sites which align to the lunar standstill position. This variety of artefact forms suggests that the nature of the problem was universally met with whenever neolithic astronomers attempted to determine the true backsight position, but that their solutions were independently worked out. This poses a highly relevant question as to why Thom found that the Megalithic yard and the 16 month calendar were universally applied whilst the type of extrapolation device to perfect lunar observation was not.

Eclipses and Observing the Moon's Wobble

During the months either side of a major standstill, the extreme monthly moonset would be seen to oscillate by a small amount. This oscillation is readily observed because it amounts to about a half of the lunar diameter. It is normally allocated the Greek letter delta (Δ), an up and down oscillation of the Moon that varies the moon's position by ± 9 minutes of a degree with a period of 173.3 days, or just under six lunar months. The moon's disc occupies an angle of just over half a degree, or 30'.

Any observer at the established backsight would notice that, at the monthly extreme moonsets around the time of the major standstill, the moon would set at slightly different places adjacent to the ultimate extreme standstill set position. This can be expressed mathematically as a range of declinations which vary from from $(\varepsilon + i + \Delta)$ to $(\varepsilon + i - \Delta)$, the former expression being the 'super-extreme' position. This translates on the ground to an observer simply observing the maximum monthly set position vary by up to half a degree, this effect only being observable very close indeed to the actual standstill. Only when this 'super-extreme' set position was observed would an observer be assured of the possibility of an eclipse seven days either side of the extreme set - one a solar and the other a lunar eclipse.

Only at the standstills may this small perturbation be observed, and once its frequency had been established, eclipses could always have been predicted in advance. But why should neolithic people need to know how to predict such events? In the *Chronicle* film, having been asked this same question by Magnus Magnusson, Thom gives an honest if rather weak answer, "Well, that I don't know", then goes on to relate the story of the two Chinese astronomers who were executed for failing to predict an eclipse, finishing with,

> *"If you could predict an eclipse in advance then obviously you were in a powerful position."*

Perhaps such prediction gave the neolithic astronomer-priests much power over the community, an assumption taken up by Euan MacKie in *Science and Society in Prehistoric Britain* (Paul Elek, London, 1977). We simply don't know whether or not eclipse prediction formed the *Grand Prix* of Stone Age astronomy, because while it may be possible to show that such feats could have been undertaken from the sites identified and the surviving artefacts there, it is impossible to prove that the astronomers actually forecasted anything. However, it might be useful to remember that megalith moving and neolithic astronomy were activities probably supported by the local community, through the production of surplus food and other essentials needed to support the venture. Human nature normally demands a pay-off for such an arduous activity. The major megalithic sites, like Rome, weren't built in a day, and the planning and labour for such feats of civil engineering must have required food surplusses and many willing hands.

The Cultural Importance of Eclipses

There may have been another cultural reason why a lunar eclipse was considered so powerful. In addition to the tides being synchronous with the lunation cycle, so too is the human menstrual cycle. Humans are the only primate that has such a synchronous link to the lunar cycle. Dr Chris Knight's book *Blood Relations* (Yale, 1987) suggests this to be a *cultural synchronicity* linking the (male) hunting cycle with that of menstruation cycle of the tribal women. Knight suggests that hunting proceeded with the increasing lunar light in the waxing cycle, culminated at the full moon when the hunt would be brought back to the tribe to be rendered and eaten, with concomitant sexual activity coinciding with the women becoming fertile. Following the full moon, a dark gap occurs each night after sunset increasing as the waning moon rises later each night by just under an hour, making hunting at night more difficult as the new moon approaches, a time when the men prepare for the next hunt and their womenfolk menstruate.

At the time of a full moon, another spectacular event occasionally takes place - a lunar eclipse. The transformation of the full moon into a dark coppery-red orb whilst the night-sky goes from its brightest to its most dark in under an hour must have been more awesome then than now, and the subsequent light loss to a traveller or hunter at night would bring concomitant risk during such an event - in effect the night sky goes from fully lit to fully dark and back again in under four hours. We now confidently know that a lunar eclipse will normally end in about 3 hours, maybe they felt no such confidence. Factors such as these would impel the most inquiring minds of the tribe to explore the whole mechanism of lunar eclipses. (Solar eclipses are quite rare at higher latitudes, but would impel the same line of inquiry).

Summary

If it cannot ever be proved that these rows and fans were used as extrapolation devices, then all modern researchers can do is record and survey them and understand how they could have been used for such a purpose. Sadly, it appears that only a handful of people have ever done this since Thom's time. Academia has washed its hands of the whole prehistoric precision astronomy business, yet it remains the case that these geometrical devices are both fit for purpose *and* located near to identified lunar observing sites. The question is begged: for what other purpose might they have been built?

With the apparent complexities of these extrapolation devices, Thom left almost all his readers behind. What is so sad is that the practical nature of attempting to mark the monthly lunar extreme setting positions delivers the problem to be solved fairly simply and quite naturally, on a silver platter one might say. The technique may be understood within a few clear nights of observations of the moon. But treated as an assault course in advanced astronomy is quite the worst way to first meet this subject. Megalithic man was spared the necessity of needing to know all that numerical and other complex detail, and so must the casual reader of this book!

The prehistoric astronomers just watched the moon set and marked it. Then they worked out how to find the maximum setting position from the actual stake positions, this informing them when to expect the extreme standstill moonset and, eventually, to predict the timing of eclipses. Thom described the discoverer of this giant leap for mankind simply, if somewhat understated, as 'a genius' (*MLO*, p 86).

Chapter Two - A Passion for the Past
The Cup and Ring Marks

THE CUP AND RING MARKS

"I have an idea, entirely nebulous at the moment, that the cup and ring markings were a method of recording, of writing, and that they may indicate, once we can read them, what a particular stone was for. We have seen the cup and ring markings on the stone at Temple Wood, and that's on the main stone, but we can't interpret them ...yet."

Alexander Thom,
Cracking the Stone Age Code, Chronicle BBC

Throughout his career, Thom was intrigued by the occurrence at many megalithic sites of cup and ring markings. It is unfortunate that perhaps his best writing on the subject was in a little known journal called *Systematics*, a somewhat esoteric publication carrying the top-heavy subtitle, *The Journal of the Institute for the comparative study of History, Philosophy and the Sciences*. Published under the auspices of the school of philosopher and mystic J. G. Bennett, this article was commissioned by the editor.

Thom wrote sixteen pages in this journal (Vol 6, No. 3 - December 1968) which hardly anyone has ever seen, let alone absorbed. There are some fine diagrams, reproduced here (*Cardrones House, right, and overleaf*)). He accurately measured over fifty designs, from whence a length emerged which Thom termed the Megalithic inch (MI), exactly one fortieth of the Megalithic yard. Such a subdivision would deliver a foot divided into 16 divisions, exactly as would be predicted by metrologists [the twelve divisions of the English foot into inches is unusual]. Just prior to the conclusions for this article, Thom disclaimed,

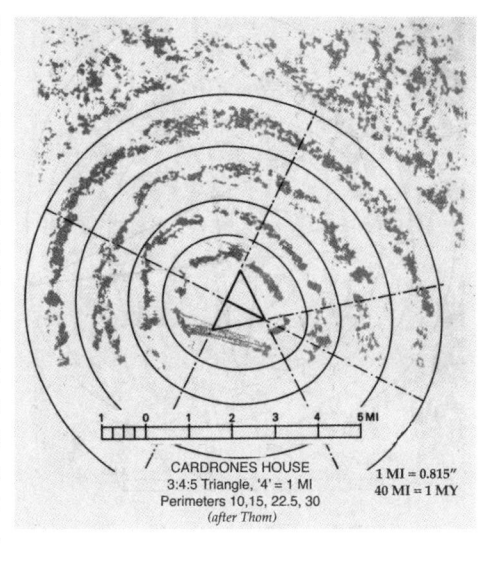

CARDRONES HOUSE
3:4:5 Triangle, '4' = 1 MI
Perimeters 10,15, 22.5, 30
(after Thom)

1 MI = 0.815"
40 MI = 1 MY

'*..all ability to invent designs to megalithic terms of reference, terms which will later be shown as remarkably sophisticated*', and '*..that the same people were responsible for the stone rings and the cup and ring marks. This is substantiated by finding in both the same kind of design worked to the same terms of reference.*'

In view of this remark, it is surprising that so little work has appeared since on either the geometry or the metrology of the cup and ring markings. However, in the 1980s, Alan Davies, then a Physics and Mathematics teacher

Alexander Thom - Cracking the Stone Age Code

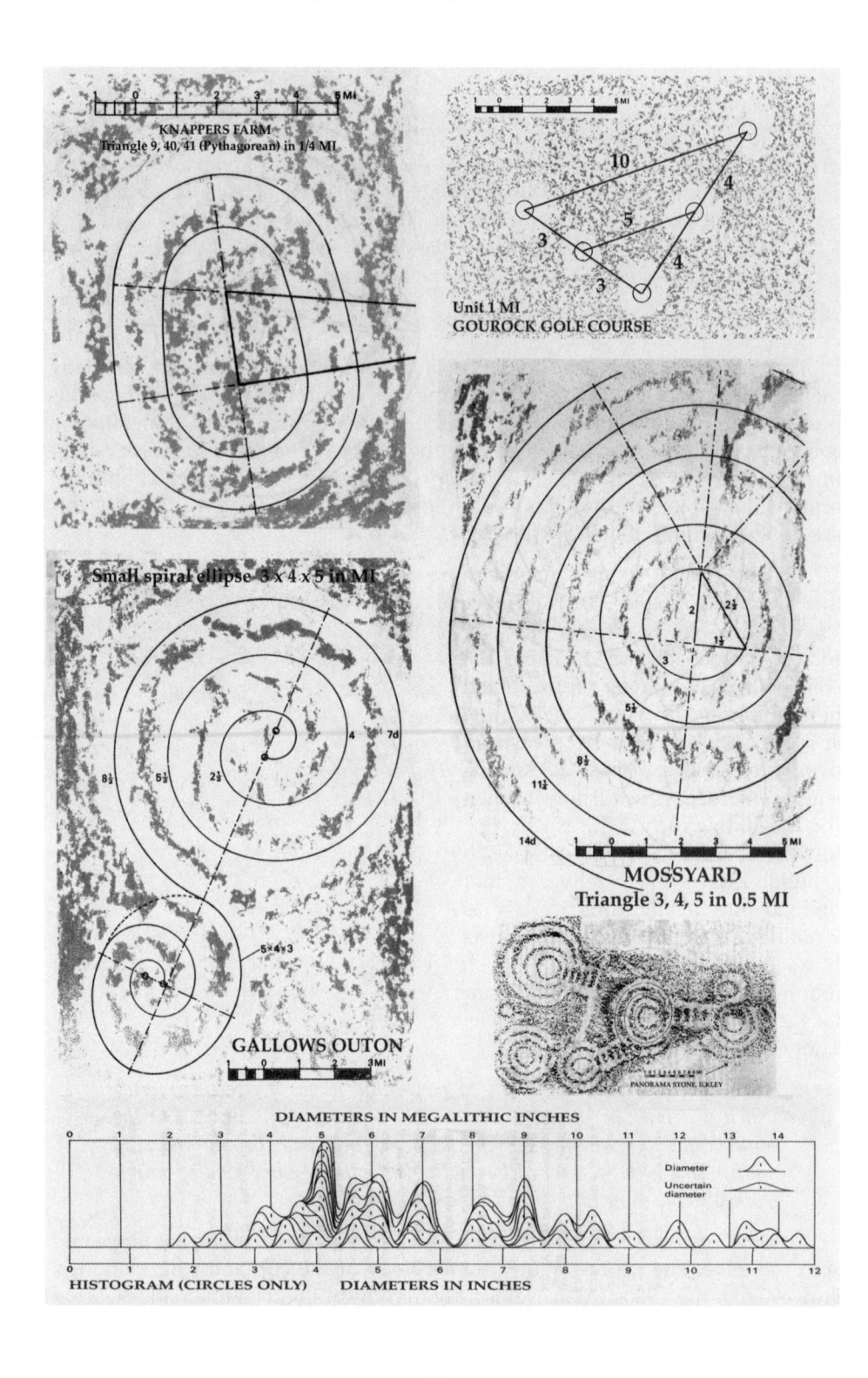

KNAPPERS FARM
Triangle 9, 40, 41 (Pythagorean) in 1/4 MI

Unit 1 MI
GOUROCK GOLF COURSE

Small spiral ellipse 3 x 4 x 5 in MI

MOSSYARD
Triangle 3, 4, 5 in 0.5 MI

GALLOWS OUTON

PANORAMA STONE, ILKLEY

DIAMETERS IN MEGALITHIC INCHES

Diameter
Uncertain diameter

HISTOGRAM (CIRCLES ONLY)   DIAMETERS IN INCHES

- 72 -

Chapter Two - A Passion for the Past
The Cup and Ring Marks

at Lancaster Royal Grammar School decided to apply his not inconsiderable skills in statistics to an assessment of their metrology, the result of which may be found in *Records in Stone* [Cambridge, 1988, pp 392-422]. This research covered only the English sites, for which Davies defined a new mathematical model and rebuilt the statistical method. He found '*strongest indications.. ..towards the use of a quantum close in value to 5MI at certain sites*' and '*evidence for a quantum close to 3MI*' at two sites. In each case he found that '*the apparent quantum seems strongly associated with ringed cups*'.

The finding of 1MI and 5MI also fits entirely supportively into the metrology of the Megalithic yard 'family' of units, for

1 Megalithic rod   = 5/2 Megalithic yards   = 100 MI

1 Megalithic yard   = 5/2 megalithic feet   = 16 x 5/2 MI (i.e. 40MI)

1 Megalithic foot   = 16 MI

Some metrological confusion needs to be clarified here. When Thom called his unit the Megalithic yard, he was cutting across a metrological convention. Thom's yard is in fact a unit more traditionally called a *step*, which is two and a half times (x 5/2) the value of its corresponding foot. All families of units in antiquity sprang from the foot. Thom's yard did not appear to have its corresponding 'foot', the division by three, as Thom himself tells us in *MSIB* (*page 55*).

The Megalithic foot can be easily identified in metrology. It is the Belgic or Drusian foot of 1.08617 'English' feet, derived from a root foot of 15/14 ths the length of the Greek foot of 1.01376 feet. The Greek foot is an ancient unit of length which lives on in nautical and navigational matters. The nautical mile is 6000 Greek feet. In geodetics, one degree of latitude is 360,000 Greek feet. (See *The Measure of Albion, p 10*). The Greek foot is often termed the 'geographic foot' for this reason.

The Megalithic foot is thus 16 MI, and times 5/2 this delivers the Megalithic yard, more correctly to be termed the Megalithic step in strict metrological classification. Another multiplication by 5/2 gives the length of Thom's Megalithic rod. The Megalithic foot subdivides into 16 Megalithic inches each of length 0.816 Imperial inches (20.7264 mm).

Davies later made visits to some of the Scottish cup and ring sites, ably assisted by Dr Euan MacKie. The strongest evidence for support of the MI was to be found at the Scottish sites. Again 5MI emerged as the strongest multiple of the unit. Thom often commented that these curious markings might represent some kind of language, a 'stone age code' which he endeavoured to crack, without much success. In *MRBB* he writes,

> '*Why should a man spend hours - or rather days - cutting cups in a random fashion on a rock? It would indeed be a breakthrough if someone could crack the code of the cups*'

Thom's legacy is that we are once again left with an exhaustive data collection and associated analysis, plus some very good photographs and rubbings of cup and ring marks, courtesy of R W B Morris and D C Bailey (printed in *Systematics*, 1968 and *MRBB*, 1978) analysed with customary Thomian thoroughness. The whole matter has been ignored almost totally since then, except for Davies, an amateur researcher who made a 'preliminary attempt' to build on Thom's start, and provided a most useful revision of the data together with a statistical analysis which confirmed the subject to be well worthy of further study.

SUMMARY

The previously described topics cover the major areas of Alexander Thom's research during his second career. They are the data, analysis and conclusions of a rational and distinguished academic who worked long and hard over nearly half a century. Was he a pioneering genius, a reincarnated neolithic astronomer come back to admonish us unappreciative moderns who have given away our civilising to Mesopotamia, or was he, plain and simply, *wrong*? Since his death we have increasingly been told that Thom was mistaken and that his findings are a fabrication, a delusion, a wish fantasy. How did this come about? Is this viewpoint itself a wishful belief, mere opinion or is there some hard evidence that Thom got it all so totally wrong? To answer these questions we must investigate matters further and deal with a paradox.

The Herring Fishers
by Alexander Thom.
c 1920, oil on canvas
(*courtesy James and Susan MacColl*)

CHAPTER THREE

The Thomist Paradox

It has traditionally been the task of anthropologists and archaeologists, not engineers and scientists, to answer questions about prehistoric human cultures. The erection of so many standing stones, stone circles, rows, henges and cursuses during the late Neolithic and early Bronze Age had been understood to represent, as Clark (1941) suggested, the *'symbols of a religious life which may ever elude us.'* But there the subject stopped in its tracks. It went no further. No one knew very much about these things until Thom. They remained an antiquarian's delight yet had not even been properly catalogued, let alone adequately surveyed. Their stones were often of impressive size, and were known to have been sometimes dragged from a considerable distance, and of course there are many legends and myths associated with megalithic sites to capture the imagination and assure them a place in folklore. But we knew almost *nothing* about why they were there, nor why they were built.

Incredibly, before Thom came along, hardly anyone had accurately surveyed them, almost certainly because archaeologists had concluded that there was nothing to be discovered by so doing. And there was apparently a good reason for not doing much to change their status. Provided the megaliths remained crude ritual artefacts, a rough derivative of Middle Eastern practices, they fitted well within the prevailing model of prehistory that archaeology was then advocating. This essentially conservative profession had predisposed researchers against considering the megalith builders of Europe to be other than an evolutionary dead-end or a cultural backwater.

When Alex Thom showed them to be something else and more, then all manner of difficulties presented themselves, as we shall now discover. The megaliths hit the archaeological fan. The Alexander Thom 'package' was the inevitable product of someone trained in the sciences, with knowledge of astronomy, surveying and metrology, someone who asked a different set of questions about prehistory and whose evidence was based on objective data.

No one could have been better placed to undertake the kind of work that Thom undertook and which needed to be carried out in order to lift the subject of megalithic astronomy and stone circles out of the waste bin of archaeology, where it had lain for years. In five centuries of confusion and uncertainty concerning their origin and purpose, the megaliths had been at sometime or another thought to have been erected during the Dark Ages, or were thought to be 'pagan', 'heathen', the work of those shadowy Celtic Druids, or even Roman in origin. In the 6th century the Church had decreed by papal decree that they were the work of the Devil, and one might assume from this that they were recognised as being pre-Christian, making the Church's assessment of dating uncharacteristically accurate! Otherwise, dating for these monuments had spanned the entire chronology of history from the Celtic Druids, Romans, the Dark Ages even right up to the Norman invasion, and it had never been contemplated that their construction might have *preceded* the great megaliths of Babylon and Egypt.

At the precise time when Thom submitted his first papers on the subject of the megalithic unit of length, archaeology was in the biggest turmoil imaginable, and was being shown to be completely in error concerning its dating of the model of European prehistory. Up to about 1960 this error had fuelled the growth of an extremely attractive and tenacious theory, one that some might say in retrospect had been rather too cosy, a theory which appeared to explain the chronology of prehistoric Europe. That theory was called *diffusionism*.

Diffusionism Rules - OK?

The first half of the twentieth century had seen rapid growth of the *Theory of Diffusionism*, whereby the path of civilisation was thought to have moved ever westward across Europe from the Middle East in a chronological sequence. Because the monuments and artefacts of the Middle East could be dated from reliable and sometimes written sources, the diffusionist theory was heavily prejudiced to reject any alternative theory suggesting that the *apparently* crude monuments of Europe were in fact older than the rather grander monuments of Egypt and Assyria.

There was superficially some quite convincing evidence for this belief. Sir Flinders Petrie had made the first step, carrying the known chronology of Egypt across to Europe. He noted Egyptian objects in the tombs of Minoan Crete, and Minoan pottery in Egypt. The northern European tombs clearly resembled those on Malta and in Crete. However, they were rather to be understood as inferior copies erected by barbarians who were gradually but inexorably being 'civilised' by trade and cultural contact with the founding civilisations of the Middle East and the Mediterranean. Oscar Montelius later devised a 'typological method' to collate European artefacts in a chronological sequence with those from Egypt and the Near East. During the first sixty years of the twentieth century, graffiti on the walls of the archaeology departments within universities universally read *'Diffusion rules - OK?'*

Some extreme books resulted from the diffusionist model, none more so than Gustav Kossinna's 1905 book *Die Deutsche Vorgeschichte eine Herr Voragend Nationale Wissenschaft*, where the supremacy of German prehistory over that of the rest of Europe anticipated and fuelled the later nationalist model of Nazi Germany. Sir Grafton Elliot Smith's *Children of the Sun*, a so-called *hyper-diffusionist* book of the Twenties, took another extreme diffusionist view - that all civilisation had originated in Egypt.

The most respected diffusionist of his day, the brilliant and shrewd academic V. Gordon Childe found a position between these two extremes and set European prehistory on a systematic footing, listing axioms that acknowledged Montelius while at the same time enabled him to chart out the way forward in investigating diffusionism. *The Dawn of European Civilisation* (1925) took each prehistoric European culture in turn and provided scientific evidence for how they fitted together. It remained the standard work on the subject until the early 70s. By calling his diffusionist assumptions 'axioms' he covered his back such that room was left to change tack. He himself stated that by taking different axioms, the prehistory of Europe would be pushed further back and look very different.

In a later book, *What Happened in History* (Pelican, 1942), Childe pronounced that there was 'no neolithic culture', and 'we cannot speak of neolithic science'. A generation of archaeology undergraduates had duly taken note of this, passed their examinations on this belief and thereafter become dumb on the matter of 'neolithic science'. It simply did not, could not, exist within the diffusionist model.

The Advent of Radiocarbon Dating

The cause of the collapse of diffusionism was the developing technique of radiocarbon dating, initially developed by Willard F Libby in New York in 1949. By the middle 1950s this new technique for dating organic matter began to seriously threaten the diffusionist model of prehistory. The technique is beautifully simple, independent of the traditional methods for archaeological dating and it works by measuring the amount of radioactive Carbon 14 within an artefact or sample of organic origin. Carbon 14 is found in the earth's atmosphere and absorbed by all living matter from the food chain, and maintains a constant percentage of the body weight. After death, this C_{14} percentage is 'frozen' within the sample and thereafter decays very slowly, with a 'half-life' of 5,500 years, into nitrogen gas. The residual amount of C_{14} left within any sample of organic matter can be accurately measured to give a statistical range of dates for that sample.

In 1960, Libby was awarded the Nobel Prize for Chemistry for his contribution to the technique. And by the late 60s radiocarbon dating techniques had been perfected, by comparison with the known age of tree rings, more specifically the annual growth rings of the Californian Bristlecone pine tree, the world's oldest living tree. Using *dendrochronology,* the counting and measurement of the relative sizes and hence dating of tree growth rings it was possible to calibrate the radiocarbon dates to a much greater accuracy, to the point where it became transparently clear that the archaeological model was completely wrong in its dating of the Neolithic and Bronze Age cultures of northwestern Europe.

In *Before Civilisation (1973)*, a best-selling book based on the effect of radiocarbon dating techniques on the understanding of European prehistory, Colin Renfrew writes at the beginning of Chapter Three, *'The First Radiocarbon Revolution'*,

> *'Radiocarbon Dating came as a godsend to archaeology. For the first time, the prehistorian could hope to date his finds, both accurately and reliably, by a method that made no archaeological assumptions whatsoever.'*

Sir Colin Renfrew

What may have come as a godsend to archaeology was at the time seen as the work of the Devil by some archaeologists, most of whom had been groomed in the diffusionist model. Many had flag-ship text books destined to become pulped, and many had built their entire careers from the diffusionist model. Professor Stuart Piggott declared, in a now famous remark, that the new date for the henge monument at Durrington Walls was *'archaeologically inacceptable'* (sic), radiocarbon dating showing it to be nearly one thousand years older than previously thought.

Beyond wiping egg off faces and revising text books, archaeologists gradually fell in line and accepted the new dating. Loss of face went hand in hand with new opportunities to better understand European prehistory. Yet in the midst of this period of adaptation, archaeologists failed to seize a *second* opportunity to enlarge their knowledge of European prehistory. Re-read Renfrew's quotation above and replace the words 'Radiocarbon dating' with the word 'Archaeoastronomy'.

Archaeoastronomical Dating

Thom demonstrated that astronomy offered another independent technique by which the date of any ancient monument accurately aligned to sun, stars or moon could be accurately ascertained. The only 'archaeological assumptions' required were that the site identified was indeed intended by the builders to form a precision alignment. If the distance from the foresight to the backsight was sufficiently large, then the precision of the alignment would provide a narrow band of dates within which the site had been constructed.

Chapter Three - The Thomist Paradox

The technique works by reference to the change in the tilt of the earth's axis over time, termed 'the change in the obliquity of the ecliptic'. Rather a mouthful for a simple truth, the earth's tilt has over the past ten millennia been reducing by a known amount within a periodic cycle of about 41,000 years. Since 3000 BC, when the tilt angle was $24°$, the tilt has reduced by about half a degree, and this drastically changes the azimuth, the clockwise angle referred from true north, of the solstitial rising and setting points of the sun at a given location. The tilt angle is now represented by the symbol ε. The standstill points of the moon are similarly changed, and for both luminaries this effect is much amplified at more northern latitudes. For example, in the Shetland Isles during the Neolithic period the moon became a circumpolar object at the major standstill - it never set - whereas today it spends a couple of hours below the horizon.

Using astronomical alignments from prehistory sites to date the site was not a new idea. There had been serious attempts to date prehistoric and ancient monuments with salient positions of celestial bodies before Thom. Even old Stukeley had noted that the avenue at Stonehenge was aligned to the midsummer sunrise. Then, in 1904, the Astronomer Royal, Sir Norman Lockyer, took a theodolite to Stonehenge and attempted to use astronomy via the change over time in the earth's tilt angle in order to date England's most famous alignment, the avenue at Stonehenge. His later 1906 article in *Nature* began the popular fascination linking Stonehenge to the calendar. The Stonehenge avenue was not the best site to demonstrate dating using astronomy. It is neither long enough (under 600 m) to deliver the precision needed nor is the Heel Stone part of that alignment, as it once formed one of a pair of stones which framed the sunrise. All those photographs of the sun rising on the Heel stone are misleading, they have been shot off-axis - the earth's tilt angle has changed since 2500 BC.

An Edwardian archaeoastronomical toy. This glass paperweight, made in 1906, has the simple instruction, 'hold to light for sunrise' (*right*) and was made to cater for the rising public interest in the astronomy of Stonehenge following Lockyer's survey of the now famous midsummer alignment. By measuring the azimuth of the midsummer sunrise at Stonehenge, Lockyer was able to make an estimate for its date of construction, about 1650 BC, a date suspiciously close to the archaeological date then in vogue. Seventy years on, in 1973, Thom used a more accurate figure for the change in obliquity of the Earth's tilt in prehistory. The date of the axis alignment fitted closely that being newly obtained from radiocarbon dating. (*paperweight from author's collection*).

For his troubles Lockyer was castigated by archaeologists for both his methodology and his result. More recent attacks on Lockyer's work are not really warranted. The rate of reduction in the earth's tilt angle was not fully evaluated, nor was there an accurate figure (for ε) available for the prehistoric era, until De Sitte's research in the late 30s, long after Lockyer's time.

The meticulous task of measuring and classifying stones was to reveal something to Thom beyond that of the unit of length used to measure them out. Thom, like Lockyer before him, saw the potential to accurately date astronomical alignments at sites set up to observe neolithic skies. Armed with impeccable academic qualifications, a good theodolite and a correct graph for the rate of change of the obliquity angle (ε), Thom was offering archaeology an independent method for establishing the date of erection of many important megalithic sites.

Because of the shift in the earth's tilt angle, these sites no longer align in our time requiring that arduous and quite complex calculations are undertaken to establish over what dates in prehistory the site 'worked' as a precision alignment. In theory this technique offered an accuracy at least as good as that offered by radiocarbon techniques. But it also required a belief that prehistoric Britons were indeed undertaking precision astronomical observations, the astonishing claim made by Thom that would later be called into question.

One might have supposed that such an independent check, in an era when dating was in ferment, would have been eagerly snapped up by archaeologists. But, already disturbed by the changes wrought by radiocarbon dating, the archaeological fraternity was both wholly unprepared and massively threatened by Thom's claims.

Thom had already pointed out, in *Megalithic Lunar Observatories*, page 16, that,

> 'It follows that if we hope to determine the mean date of the erection of the sites to within a century, we must find from the sight lines values of ε with a precision greater than an arc minute. One of the objects of this book is to show that there is a real possibility of approaching this kind of accuracy (a) from Megalithic man's solar observatories and (b) indirectly from his lunar observatories.'

Thom's measurements at Stonehenge (1973), and subsequent calculations, suggested a date of 2700 BC for the Aubrey circle, and 3380 for the Heel stone (both figures were accurate to ±300 years), and this dating fell in line with the revised archaeological dating only just being accepted at Stonehenge. Despite the apparent rigour of the measurements and the formulae applied to 'work back' the alignment, many archaeologists were still adapting to the shock of having the British Neolithic period wrenched backwards in time by up to a millennium. Serious doubts and criticisms were voiced concerning Thom's original paper on Stonehenge in the *Journal for the History of Astronomy (Vol xx)*.

Chapter Three - The Thomist Paradox

New Questions and New Data

Most of the archaeological establishment had been spoon-fed *Childean* diffusionism whilst undergraduates. When they subsequently found themselves elevated to influential positions within academia, some were driven by their beliefs to deny the entire Thom package, and suggest that Thom found what he wanted to find because he was a surveyor and engineer, that the whole edifice of his work was a mirror of himself, a psychological projection onto the surviving and crude remains left by neolithic barbarians. Thom's theories and conclusions must have appeared as a 'double-whammy' for them, threatening the foundations of prehistoric studies in much the same manner as radiocarbon dating had done just a few years earlier. The 60s was a roller-coaster decade to have been an archaeologist.

Do we accuse of psychological projection the archaeologist who remains preoccupied with sifting through graves, ancient human remains, domestic rubbish and the odd sacrifice? Of course we don't, *do we*? The study of death and its rituals have revealed important insights into the social structure of ancient man, yet it appears self-evident that one cannot hope to discover much about what goes on inside a church by excavating the graveyard. A modern churchyard reveals nothing of the present computer revolution and very little concerning modern science, so why might one assume that an archaeologist could discover "neolithic science" by excavating neolithic cemeteries, especially so if that archaeologist had been prejudiced against looking for such a thing throughout his or her training? Simply, it did not, could not, exist. And if the nearest thing to a 'church' in the Neolithic was a stone circle - might not its location, dimensions and geometry tell us something, however little, of the people who erected it?

Alexander Thom had only a scant knowledge of archaeology, a fact which he freely admitted. Initially he merely wanted to know, as engineers do want to know those sorts of things, whether the builders of all those massive stone rings, fans and rows which littered the Scottish countryside used a consistent unit of length or not. Such an innocent and obvious question! Refreshingly free from prejudice or orthodox views on such matters, and unconcerned that the historians had relegated the mute stone circles of Britain, Brittany and Ireland into the category of being almost unworthy of study, Thom began asking different questions that had not been asked previously except by Lockyer and Somerville. His accurate surveying became the British equivalent of that undertaken in Egypt at the end of the nineteenth century, when Petrie had revealed the accuracy with which the Great Pyramid had been constructed, aligned precisely to the cardinal points of the compass.

Thom accurately surveyed over 500 stone circles and perhaps 100 other sites. Initially he asked one deceptively simple question - did the builders use a standard unit of length with which to build their stone monuments? He believed that a definite answer would require an extensive mathematical, i.e. statistical, treatment. The catalyst in forming such an opinion was his experience with an early submission to *Antiquity*. The article was immediately returned and across the frontispiece was scrawled '*I do not believe your hypothesis*' by the then founding editor, O.G.S. Crawford.

Strangely, Crawford enjoyed a reputation as someone able to seize new ideas in archaeology very well, an imaginative thinker, and a highly respected archaeologist. He had immediately embraced radiocarbon dating after listening to Lord Cherwell's account of the then new radiocarbon dating technique in the Senior Common Room at Christ Church, Oxford, in 1949. Sir Mortimer Wheeler related how Crawford's 'eyes lighted up as the conversation proceeded'. Crawford's dismissive 'reply' to Thom's first sorties into the archaeological world was therefore untypical, at best it was ill-mannered and at worst unprofessional, but the effect on Thom was that he realised that he now needed to prepare, in John Michell's words, a 'statistically unassailable' case. That case is covered in depth in a later chapter.

As the preliminary results began to emerge from the increasing volume of data, in the mid-fifties, Thom consulted a *maestro* of the art of statistical analysis, Dr Simon Broadbent, in order to find the most valid method for the analysis and treatment of his surveys. In addition he consulted Dr John Hammersley, a superb mathematician charged with investigating and improving experimental and scientific techniques at Oxford. As a result of this correspondence the introductory chapter of *Megalithic Sites in Britain* is a terse five pages in length, leading to a second chapter which is nothing short of being an assault course in statistical mathematics. Thom had realised, following the curt response from the editor of *Antiquity*, that he had to get his facts and figures impeccably right to break through the barrier of peer-group exclusion he had already experienced from the archaeologists.

The real target for this difficult yet seminal book was clearly the archaeological establishment, and here Thom made a terrible mistake by alienating the intelligent yet mathematically challenged non-specialist reader who, unlike many of the archaeologists who would later refute Thom's findings, carried no cargo of prejudice or dogma. The consequences of this decision were only too clear and will be revealed as our story progresses.

It was entirely in the spirit of the scientific method so intrinsic in Thom's long career for him to search for patterns within the circles and standing stones. He asked new questions and generated a new type of data. The patterns he revealed through his careful surveys suggested to him a cohesive social structure and implied a remarkable level of communication between centres of megalithic activity. Thom showed that not only had the pieces of the prehistoric jigsaw been placed in the wrong box but that the picture on the lid was the wrong one!

This revelation cut right across the bows of the archaeologically held views of the time. Professor Gordon Childe was a contemporary of Thom and had been the first Abercrombie Professor of Prehistoric Archaeology at Edinburgh. A brilliant historian with a rare gift for popularisation, he was one of several highly qualified experts laying out the jigsaw of prehistory. Childe had said, 'There is no 'neolithic culture', but a limitless multitude of neolithic cultures'. Thom showed that this statement was not true, at least not in the British Isles, and that there was a coherent, in his words, *Megalithic science* being practised across the whole area where stone circles were to be found. The information he brought to the table cut right across the Childean diffusionist doctrine then still in vogue.

Many of the archaeologists who struggled and sometimes fought with Thom's discoveries had been weaned on Childe's many textbooks and popular books such as *The Dawn of European Civilisation* and *Man makes Himself*. These books had also been enjoyed by a large number of non-specialist readers. Now, archaeologists and non-specialists alike were faced with Thom's highly specialised textbook, a commando course in statistics, mathematics and astronomy. The non-specialists couldn't understand it, as Thom later admitted, while even those very few archaeologists who could understand it were predisposed to reject the radical implications emerging from Thom's research.

On Measuring and Classifying Stones

One such academic archaeologist who also possessed a great ability to popularise prehistory was Dr Graham Clark, a Cambridge archaeologist. In the later softback edition of the popular 1940 *Prehistoric Britain*, published in 1962, one may detect a first example of what was to become a defensive stance against the kind of research Thom was undertaking. Clark suggested,

> *'Even if we could visit Bronze Age Britain and study at first hand the rites and practices associated with them, it would be difficult enough to comprehend their underlying meaning: to probe the innermost consciousness of men who lived thousands of years ago by measuring and classifying stones, however meticulously, is manifestly vain.'*

In the second half of this statement we discover both a perfect description of Thom's methodology, and a well laid injunction against such an undertaking. In addition, during the period when this book was first written, anthropologists were making huge advances in understanding what they saw as similar cultures to the Neolithic in New Guinea, Australia, the Amazon and elsewhere, lessening the first part of Clark's hypothetical argument for ancient Britons. It is instructive to imagine ourselves as archaeologists in 5000 AD, then to re-read the above paragraph substituting the word 'Industrial' for 'Bronze Age', and 'buildings' for 'stones'. It then becomes patently obvious that Clark's logic had gone sadly awry.

Perhaps recognising that a prehistoric archaeologist still needed to have a career, Clark went on, wistfully and contradictorily, to say,

> 'Still, the stones are abundantly worthy of study, even if only as the symbols of a religious life which may forever elude us.'

Clark then shot himself in the foot with this display of logical circularity,

> 'Although in its general appearance Stonehenge may strike us as barbarous, the monument has been laid out with great precision and the sarsens themselves have been meticulously planned and shaped. The lintels have been most carefully secured to their uprights by tenon and mortice and to their neighbours by tongue and groove joints. In plan they have been perfectly curved to fit the joints.'

To have been able to write this paragraph, someone, somewhere must have been very 'manifestly vain'! Clark finally advocated keeping the lid shut on the whole megalithic can of worms with the following flourish, perhaps a recommendation!

> 'In all essentials the great circles retain their mystery.'

It is easy to detect in these extracts the shadow side of archaeology peeking through. Something very uncomfortable was being avoided, consequently an involuntary hypocrisy ran right through all of this material, and no-one, even pre-Thom, seemed able at the time to reconcile their beliefs with what was actually to be found on the ground. For example, taking Clark's own example a stage further, Stonehenge was self-evidently built by skilled precision engineers. Even Clark accepted that fact. And the father of modern archaeology, Sir William Flinders Petrie, had measured the inside diameter of the Sarsen ring in 1888 and determined it, correctly, to be 100 'cyclopean feet', a measure which, in the classification of metrology, would now be recognised immediately as being 100 'Roman' feet of 0.9732 English feet. Richard Atkinson, without knowing aught of metrology, gave an independent surveyed measurement of this same diameter in *Stonehenge* (1956), at 97.3 feet.

Were then these renowned archaeologists being 'manifestly vain'? The nub of the matter is that, on the one hand, many of these monuments carried meticulousness and precision to a perfection which could be measured, so that furthermore and astonishingly these measurements have been shown to fall within the canon of ancient measure; on the other hand, the culture which spawned such artefacts was thought 'barbarous'. Clark's revised book was a first glimmer of what Dr Euan MacKie was to later dub the '*Thomist paradox*'.

The Problem of Dating

Manifest vanity apart, during the period when Thom was initially working with the dating of these sites, radiocarbon dating was in its infancy and was unreliable for dating stone circles. Until the dating could be recalibrated by using dendrochronology, the earliest phase of Stonehenge had been dated nearly 1000 years later than it is now, with Atkinson writing, in *Stonehenge* (1956), page 82, that,

Chapter Three - The Thomist Paradox

> *'Translated into everyday terms, this means that the odds are about 2 to 1 that the date of Stonehenge I (the earliest phase) lies between 2125 and 1575 B.C., and about 20 to 1 that it lies somewhere between 2400 B.C. and 1300 B.C. The C_{14} estimation thus supports the date arrived at on archaeological grounds, but in no way increases its precision.'*

By 1970, both the accuracy and the precision of radiocarbon dating had improved immeasurably. It is the current estimation that Stonehenge I, i.e. the very earliest phase of the present monument, was constructed before 3000 BC, perhaps around 3100 BC. This is over 1000 years earlier than the date assumed in 1956. Unfortunately, the later revision no longer squared at all well with 'the date arrived at on archaeological grounds' given above, and once more we see the wedge splitting the archaeological model from the scientific evidence. As another small example of archaeology's shadow, even after quarter of a century has elapsed, it is still possible to visit the major museums in this country and find displays where the dating remains set at the earlier, incorrect values or at intermediate values. I can think of no other scientific field where such procrastination would be acceptable, and it forms another example of archaeology's inertia to change quite separate from its apparent inability to embrace Thom's package.

We need to dwell on this matter a little longer, for it is possible to catch a glimpse of what may underpin this procrastination. In the 1920s, the world marvelled when Sir Howard Carter and Lord Carnarvon pulled "wonderful things" from Tutankhamun's tomb. These remarkable artefacts, proof of advanced civilisation in Egypt, were then thought to predate the rude stone artefacts of Britain by at least 1500 years. Why would anyone think that the rough stone circles of the British Isles were other than the product of uncivilised and backward people, when apparently much older exquisite gold artefacts, fine furniture and other wonderful craft and artwork was being pulled from that Egyptian tomb by the ton-load? A century previously, Napoleon's escapades into Egypt had already demonstrated the astonishing achievements of dynastic Egypt, crowned by Champollion's brilliant deciphering of the Rosetta Stone.

Spanning this same period, in Britain, early archaeologists such as Colt-Hoare and the Cunninghams were picking and shovelling their way into barrow after tumulus and discovering almost nothing to support a high level of culture in pre-Roman Britain. Britain's megalithic culture was understandably already primed to appear as a stagnant evolutionary backwater, just as had been perceived the Australian aboriginals and the native American Indians, during the same period. The diffusionist vision of prehistory was perhaps inevitable, developed refined and advocated by Childe, Hawkes and many other archaeological sages of the inter-war and post-war period. It was a product of the culture of the time. Under its tenets, prehistoric tribes had had plenty of time to wend their way gradually but inexorably westwards, conveniently arriving on these shores just in time to fit the archaeological model. Until the revision to radiocarbon dating was made in the mid 1960s, no one had any real doubts about such a view.

It is instructive to read older archaeology books, such an exercise rapidly confirming that the subject has enjoyed no flawless track record of success where dating is concerned. This dating problem prompted historian Dr Nicholas Campion (1995), editor of *Culture and Cosmos*, to write,

> *'When Jacquetta Hawkes, since a leading opponent of archaeoastronomy, wrote confidently in 1945 that British megaliths were based on Mediterranean models, (Early Britain, Bracken Books 1945), she had no idea that the British sites would later be shown to be much older and that her self-assurance was not partially, but completely, misplaced.'*

The question as to how old were the stone circles and megalithic monuments was a wrong guess prior to the radiocarbon dating revolution, and a constantly moving platform during the twenty years when Thom undertook his main research into the level of astronomical intent built into the sites.

'One is Tempted to Disbelieve the Evidence'

The revision in dating was a real shock for archaeologists to take on board. The British Neolithic Period having now been found to be much earlier than previously thought possible, the first results coming from those pathetic scraps of carbon, wood and bone were being received with the 'utmost dismay' by many archaeologists. Now, with the diffusionist theory becoming increasingly unworkable, the circles were indeed seen to predate most of dynastic Egypt, possibly being classified as an independent cultural flowering. If Thom was correct with his accurate unit of length and his circle geometries, the circles then became cultural dynamite, and stood at the vanguard of human civilisation, the earliest known examples of metrology, geometry and precision astronomy. It was a bridge too far for many archaeologists, and apparently for anyone else, a situation that remains until this day. How historians coped with the newly arriving evidence forms an interesting cameo of how new ideas enter - or not - an established discipline.

Senior Lecturer in Prehistory and Archaeology at the University of Sheffield, Dr Colin Renfrew (now Lord Renfrew) presented this paradox to readers of *The Listener*, on January 7th 1971,

> *'...so astonishing does it seem, when we are told that our own great earthen mound, Silbury Hill, is as old as the Pyramids and Stonehenge earlier than the Mycenean civilizations, that one is tempted to disbelieve the evidence...'*

Renfrew went on to overcome his temptation and write the popular book, *Beyond Civilisation* (Cape, 1973), bravely exploring the consequences of the new dating and the chronological 'fault-lines' exposed by it. The book was quite complimentary about Thom's work. In 1974, Renfrew updated Clark's later edition of *Prehistoric Britain* (Duckworth).

Chapter Three - The Thomist Paradox

Enter Chieftains...

A new model of prehistory inevitably began to emerge during the 70s to explain the anomalies exposed by radiocarbon dating. Initially the idea was explored by Colin Renfrew but gradually the concept of a specialist group of 'Chieftains' began to appear more widely to explain the remarkable earthworks, cursusses, stone circles and large round houses, many of which had only recently been discovered. It was later proposed that an elite band of superior citizens well versed in astronomy, surveying and mathematics possessed an even more impressive skill - that of coercing the rest of the alleged barbarous population into willingly feeding and supporting them. Through such a model it was then possible to explain the high cultural artefact evidence existing in the vicinity of the round houses within an essentially nomadic, and assumed primitive, tribal population. One archaeologist attempted to test this theory further.

...and Astronomer-Priests

In 1977, Glasgow archaeologist Dr Euan MacKie published his *Science and Society in Prehistoric Britain* (Paul Elek, London), a seminal book which defined 'astronomer-priests' as a separate social grouping of wise men, keepers of the arcane wisdom of geometry and astronomy within the tribal cultures of Neolithic Britain, who gratefully housed, fed and clothed them as they planned and built huge earthworks and vast monuments of stone. Despite showing convincing evidence that these occupants of the rather grand round houses that had once littered southern Britain had been eating a rather better diet than the *commoners*, and from better made pots, it was not at all well received by many other archaeologists, who had not known that Richard Atkinson had been the proof-reader and editorial advisor to MacKie. Piggott wrote a quite waspish review of the book in *Antiquity*, apparently reversing his stance of just three years earlier, when he had spoken favourably about MacKie's theories at an event hosted by Glasgow University.

Atkinson and Piggott were colleagues, and had worked closely together many times, culminating in their massive restoration project of the fallen trilithon at Stonehenge in 1958 (*photograph overleaf*). They were two of the most famous and respected archaeologists of their period, and yet here was Piggott heavily criticising a book that Atkinson had guided through to publication. By 1977, the new evidence was causing a divide to be riven through the archaeological community. This remarkable book stands aloft as a high point in the attempt to place Thom's findings within a valid archaeological model that also makes sense of the corpus of other evidence from prehistory. MacKie later made it known that he had, in retrospect, felt that the word 'science' had been inappropriate in the title of his book.

In the popular press, another quite different model was being proposed. John Ivimy's *The Sphinx and the Megaliths*, (Abacus, 1976) captured public imagination.

Atkinson (with cigarette holder) and Piggott (centre) during the partial restoration of Stonehenge in April 1958. The re-erection of one of the fallen trilithons formed the main work. In 1958, both these archaeologists were having to deal with the new chronology being wrought by the application of radiocarbon techniques. Atkinson later bcame the editor for Dr Euan Mackie's 1977 book, *Science and Society in Prehistoric Britain*. This fact was unbeknown to Piggott, who was extremely critical of it.

In his hypothetical account of prehistory, ancient Egyptians come to Britain in order to build megaliths and study astronomy. This was diffusionism in one giant leap across Europe. The book was lampooned by the archaeology world, yet in effect all Ivimy was doing was supporting diffusionism of a sort and taking the concept of a superior class of citizen in prehistoric Britain a stage further than Renfrew and MacKie had done. Now, the archaeological record and the revised dating of the stone circles could be explained away by a few visiting Pharaonic astronomer-priests wishing to observe the moon and do other astronomical things in these islands which were tricky or impossible back in Egypt. Dr John Edwin Wood was to point out, in *Sun, Moon and Standing Stones*, (Merrivale Books, 1978), a little tongue in cheek, that Ivimy's Egyptians were unique in the history of our race in that they apparently left not one item of litter behind for future archaeologists to discover or pore over. Presumably, Stonehenge itself could not be considered as Egyptian litter, could it?

Chapter Three - The Thomist Paradox

But an even worse heresy could be found within Ivimy's book - some astonishing mathematical, metrological and geometrical connections were shown to exist between Thom's metrology and that of ancient Egypt. The Megalithic yard was shown objectively to be geometrically related to the Egyptian Royal cubit and the Egyptian remen. Ivimy related to the author in 1993 that the book had attracted some "quite dreadful flak, as I expected it would", yet he was still "entirely glad to have written it. At 65, one can do this kind of thing".

In his critical review for Ivimy's book in the *New Scientist*, Dr Euan MacKie made the obvious comment,

> *'If prehistorians are not satisfied (with Ivimy's theory), we must provide a better one.'*

MacKie was eminently suited to write this review, for he too had included within *Science and Society in Prehistoric Britain* some of the same interesting metrological and geometrical material as found in Ivimy's book. As a result of this book something odd had occurred. MacKie suddenly found himself in a club of one other archaeologist (Renfrew), one retired engineer (Thom) and two popular writers, John Michell and John Ivimy, unlikely bedfellows indeed, connected by a common desire to make sense of prehistory and provide historians with a better model. A delicious irony if ever there was one! All their models were broadly theoretically possible, they were interesting, based on much hard evidence and, except for Renfrew, drew attention to parallels existing between the mathematics, geometry and measures of Egypt and those revealed by Thom. Perhaps even more interesting is that all their books remain essential reading.

The Options

By the early 70s it was becoming clear that there were now scant few options available to archaeologists and prehistorians with regard to the anomalies and questions posed by the revised dating of megalithic monuments and the work of Thom, MacKie, Renfrew, Ivimy and Michell, to wit,

1. Keep denying the new radiocarbon dating - the 'King Canute' option.

2. Do nothing. Nod, say 'very interesting' a lot, yet leave things exactly as they were.

3. Admit the new dating yet ensure that the circles retain their primitive status.

4. Admit that the model of European prehistory is wrong and in need of revision.

5. (a) Retire immediately or (b) seek another profession.

Option one rapidly became untenable, as Piggott must have realised following his comment about the radiocarbon dates being 'archaeologically inacceptable'. Colin Renfrew, hailed as the 'leading theoretical archaeologist of our generation' moved in 1981 from Southampton to become Disney Professor of Archaeology at Cambridge, then became Lord Renfrew of Kaimsthorn in 1991, and thereby went initially to option 4, and eventually settled for option 5 (b).

Many archaeologists appear to have chosen a cocktail of option 2 and 3 above. Aubrey Burl and Clive Ruggles appear to have plumbed for option 3, whilst Atkinson, as we shall see, eventually and bravely chose option 4, as did Euan MacKie, Piggott, Case and Daniel (for a brief period). The 'loony fringe' authors all naturally chose option 4, not just because it sold books, but because from their perspective, outside of mainstream archaeology, it made sense.

Renfrew recently revealed an unexpected commonality between the orthodoxy and the so-called 'loony fringe'. In *Current Archaeology*, Nov/Dec 2005; 200,439) he relates how he defined his priorities as a prehistorian,

'My first twenty years as a professional archaeologist involved excavations in Greece as well as in Britain, in the Orkney Islands, much of it trying to make sense of the new chronology implied by radiocarbon dating and its calibration. To see developments in European prehistory, such as the Neolithic monuments of north-western Europe, in their own terms rather than as a result of diffusion meant a focus on social models. So the title 'Social Archaeology' was a natural one for my inaugural lecture in Southampton in 1973.

So too we find social models underpinning *The View over Atlantis*, *The Sphinx and the Megaliths* and to a lesser extent, suggested in Thom's publications. Later in the same article Renfrew reveals a further unexpected link with Thom,

'As it turns out, much of my work has been on what had seemed the fringes of archaeology, and trying to find a theoretical basis to incorporate them within the theoretical mainstream.'

So Renfrew had the same 'mission statement' as did Alexander Thom - they both shared precisely the same objectives! Both lived on the fringes of archaeology, but the archaeologist became a lord while the scientist became an outcast.

Archaeologists' egos were fragile and remained wounded throughout the two decades following the introduction of radiocarbon dating. Many had to accept that they had been wrong on matters concerning British prehistory. In the midst of all this, along came a chirpy retired professor of engineering with a whole new take on Neolithic and Bronze Age Britain. Thom was not made welcome.

Thom's books were published throughout this entire turbulent period in British archaeology, and they provided ample data and intellectual evidence to support the existence of 'astronomer-priests'. But even thirty years after the end of the Second World War, any theory concerning elites and superior classes of people was a dangerous place to go. MacKie even took this further, suggesting in *Science and Society in Prehistoric Britain* (page 228),

'It is easy to see how the presence of an intellectual class in Late Neolithic Britain having such abilities - which were doubtless encouraged

genetically by selective breeding and culturally by the appropriately favourable environment - could have led to most of the achievements that Thom has inferred.'

One senses the discomfort many must have felt with this comment, a single generation after the Nazis had attempted to implement selective breeding, with ghastly consequences.

Dealing with Criticism

By the mid-seventies, Thom was into his ninth decade and Archie Thom had noticed that during the *'throes of the work in Brittany* (it was 1972) *perhaps AT was tiring a little. He was seventy-nine at the time.'* [*WIATS*, page 251]. Having spent nearly four decades amassing the evidence and data to support a new view of megalithic Britain, Sandy was becoming a little weary, although he had not entirely bowed out from the mainstream debate. In 1981, he dictated the following note (*WIATS*, p 276), which perhaps best sums up his viewpoint on such matters,

> *We can divide people who tend to study archeoastronomy into three classes -*
>
> *1. Those who believe that our forefathers were able to do these things.*
>
> *2. Those who are uncertain but are prepared to read and learn, and*
>
> *3. Those who do not believe and refuse to be convinced.*
>
> *The third class is the most difficult to deal with, because its members do not want to spend the time reading; they are so convinced that they are right. Perhaps they do read a little but as they find this cuts across their preconceived ideas it makes them annoyed and they will not read any more.'*

This unsophisticated, some might say *naïve* analysis sums up in category three the entire problem Thom faced, but it also partially summarised the attitude that archaeologists found prevalent in Thom, who, in MacKie's words, was also 'so convinced that he was right'.

Archie Thom wrote a telling paragraph in *Walking in all of the Squares (p275)* about one of his father's techniques for dealing with critics,

> *'Thom received criticism aplenty. Sometimes he reacted instantly, putting his thoughts on paper - thoughts which he did not publish. If he was upset he might write a strong letter which he never posted. He seemed to benefit by expressing himself in this way.'*

Dr Arthur Hogg, a prominent and very well respected archaeologist became an outspoken critic of Thom's metrological and geometrical work following the publication of *MSIB* in 1967. Hogg was a Research Fellow in the University of Wales and the curator for the Royal Commission on the Ancient and Historic Monuments of Wales. In 1969 he wrote a very strongly worded letter to Thom's

Alexander Thom - Cracking the Stone Age Code

publisher, Clarendon Press, attacking Thom's methodology and conclusions concerning the Megalithic yard and the proposed geometrical construction of stone circles. He did not comment concerning the astronomical aspects of Thom's work. Clarendon passed the letter on to Thom, who, on the 30th September 1969, wrote a revealing letter to Robert Merritt in Ohio concerning Hogg's criticism of the Megalithic yard,

> '...About Hogg, Clarendon Press does not think it advisable to reply. It is as you say peculiar that he accepts the astronomy but discards the geometry. The latter is, to my way of thinking, much more rigidly established than the former, on which indeed it is very difficult to put a figure. Hogg ignores completely (1) the evidence of the fit of the geometry, (2) the manner in which the factor 10 appears at Avebury, (3) the evidence of the perimeters, and (4) the adjustments made in the diameter to bring the perimeters nearer to multiples of the Megalithic yard.
>
> I spent as many years gathering as long a list of diameters as possible in order to get a reliable figure of use in Broadbent's formulae (I ignored nothing). And then Hogg goes into reverse and divides the range into parts. If he goes far enough, he will end up with groups of two diameters in each - and get anything he wants. This is a misuse of the material and statistical analysis. Surely it was to avoid this sort of thing that Broadbent prepared his paper... ... I can assure you that years of work went into the thing. Why does Hogg not attack my paper on The Megalithic Unit of length in J Roy Stat Soc? Queer that this paper was accepted by a society with a very strict refereeing system on papers. I have written to you about this matter but I have not written to anyone else..'

The last sentence shows Thom's caution in discussing criticism with other people. By and large he would take the whole criticism thing on the chin, sometimes share it with his family but only very rarely would he write or say anything that might 'go public'. The *'strong letter which he never posted'* formed his main outlet for upset, anger and frustration.

In 1970, during the *Chronicle* documentary, Hogg is given free reign to announce that he believes not one calculation within Thom's research,

> "I question how many of Professor Thom's figures have been put in, inadvertently, by Professor Thom himself?"
>
> Dr Arthur Hogg
> Chronicle, BBC, 1972

Hogg was given another 'ten-seconder' slot where he was more circumspect concerning his doubts on Thom's work. Atkinson dismissed these criticisms immediately afterwards, the only occurrence within the entire programme where one archaeologist challenged another. It was a further sign of a developing split within the archaeological profession over Thom's evidence.

Chapter Three - The Thomist Paradox

Having 'starred' in the highly praised 1968 documentary about Silbury Hill, Atkinson had become the nation's representative archaeologist, and this is reflected in the commanding stance he adopted in the *Chronicle* documentary. Specifically citing Hogg's remarks he tactfully implied that, although his and other criticisms had to be listened to, the weight of evidence for the Megalithic yard meant that these criticisms need not be taken too seriously. Hogg must have been none too pleased with that, having said,

"I have no problem accepting the astronomical theory proposed by Thom, However, I do not think that he has sufficiently proved the case either for the Megalithic yard or for the proposed geometrical layouts of the stone circles".

Dr Arthur Hogg
Chronicle, BBC, 1972

Following Kendal's lecture at the 1974 Royal Society conference *Astronomy in the Ancient World*, discussed in detail later, Hogg generously conceded to Thom that he had 'won the day'. Prior to that he had been vociferous in attacking the whole basis for Thom's belief in the megalithic units of length.

Dr Arthur Hogg

It is unlikely now that any of Thom's 'strong letters' will one day turn up. They would make most interesting reading. During a visit to an outhouse at *The Hill* in 2001, the author was shown a high stack of Thom's letters and papers which were very badly affected by the damp. Stuck together, foxed and mouldy, amongst these pathetic remnants of a life's work may well have been some of this 'correspondence'. Perhaps that is how it should be, for while we might never fully understand Thom's inner reaction to those who criticised his work, one thing has been widely noted and commented on - in public he always remained composed, quietly spoken and polite.

Stoning the Heretic

Such was not always the case with his opponents. At one conference, a critic ranted at the professor so vehemently that the Chair had to intervene. This same individual, at another conference and in Thom's absence, launched into a tirade so extreme that it prompted Atkinson to reprimand the man by saying, "Words such as these are not in my book." But we might wager that similar words may once have been written on crumpled sheets of note paper thrown vigorously from white knuckled hands against the far wall and later kicked into the waste-paper basket at *The Hill*. We will probably never fully know the grief that Thom felt at his work being excluded from mainstream archaeology. His family remain both dazed and appalled concerning some of the treatment doled out to him.

Marginalised, and with his age and health running against him, one can only guess how Thom must have felt about the treatment he had received from some elements of the archaeological establishment. In effect, he had self-funded a forty-year research programme and carried it out to the highest standards of precision and rigour. In one of the last conversations I held with Archie Thom, he remained confident that his father's time - the full valuing of his contribution towards understanding prehistoric Britain - was yet to come. For that to occur, archaeologists must find ways of placing the metrological, astronomical and geometrical data to be found at the surviving monuments within the current model of prehistoric archaeology described below. Archaeologists have almost universally avoided any attempt at doing this in the past and there has been no attempt to incorporate Thom's material within the developing model of prehistory in Europe. That model, simplified from that found in undergraduate textbooks, is described below.

The Model of European Prehistory

The model of European prehistory developed by archaeology has been compared, by some critics to digging in the graveyard rather than exploring the adjacent church. While archaeologists have determined a great deal about the chronology, and diet, types of housing, clothes, illnesses, causes of death, the grave goods, position of the corpse and the clothing - the basis of social structures - they know very little of the behavioural aspects or intellectual capabilities of an evidently once vibrant community.

It will therefore be useful for the non-specialist reader to look at the very nature of archaeological evidence. It consists for the most part, as has been admitted by many archaeologists, in digging for what are essentially random items of mundane *bric a brac* stratified within dateable layers of earth. These 'fragmentary and often random pieces of the material culture' comprise artefacts, rubbish and constructions of all kinds together with whatever material traces of other hardware belonging to a vanished society has survived.

Thus one may excavate and discover a few bronze tools. Stratigraphy and dating techniques may provide the period of use. Classification experience may suggest the 'family' or type of tool, what it may have been used for and whether it was used by a right-handed or left-handed person. Metallurgy may offer help with knowing where the tin and copper were once mined, and how it was smelted into bronze and forged to make the tool. Other items discovered at the same excavation may tell of a trading arrangement, from which we may discover that the tools were transported by sea because the remains of a wrecked boat with similar tools in its hold was discovered previously on the sea bed along the proposed trading route. All of which is vital, interesting and important evidence.

But at this crucial point, when the hard won evidence emerges out from the laboratory, the archaeologist has to fall back on hypothesis and surmise in an attempt to answer any further questions from that evidence. What was the tool used for? Was it for everyday use or as a ritual token? Was it used by a tribal leader or a peasant, a man or a woman? Even this last question is likely to involve ethnocentricity in surmising that there may have been a social class system, rather like our own hierarchical and essentially patriarchal system, existing at the time the tool was made and used. Where is the evidence for this?

The answers to these kinds of questions depend on what an archaeologist thinks was the most likely explanation, qualitative answers quite separate from the quantifiable evidence. With a bronze axe-head we may feel we are on safe ground in making an assumption that it was used functionally to split or chop something. But with a monument such as a round cairn it is impossible to know the totality of function and meaning it may once have possessed within the society that originated it. The various 'hill-forts' found dotted all across Britain are often so named because they resemble similar constructions from other cultures where we know they were constructed as defended sites, but this naming is an a*ssumption of functionality*. It is a best guess or 'guestimate'. If we make the assumption that they were places of ritual and worship, can we then suggest they may have been 'churches' or 'temples'? We can then find ourselves unsure because we have to define these words. What is 'worship' and what are its limits?

In an article called *Archaeological systematics and the study of cultural process* (*American Antiquity* (Vol. 31(2), pp203-210), L R Binford identifies three kinds of behaviour on which artefacts may inform: technological, sociological and ideological. He suggests that if all artefacts relate to one or more of these forms of behaviour then it may be possible to identify the specific behaviour if it becomes possible to correctly identify the uses to which the artefacts were put. Thom's astronomical data is wonderfully suited to test this, being based on the assumption of a *technological* function for the artefacts. (They probably combine technological with sociological and ideological functions). Binford makes an important additional point,

> 'Logically we cannot do this solely with archaeological material for we would be correlating assumed evidence with assumed behavioural patterns.'

Solely depending on archaeological evidence from prehistory leads to assumptions, whence the data is discovered to be inherently without meaning, telling the archaeologist remarkably little about the people to whom that evidence once formed a vital aspect of their life and culture. Thom showed that archaeoastronomical evidence could provide an additional dimension to a site, one which could reveal objective behavioural and cultural intent. The astronomical evidence at aligned sites wrenches the archaeoastronomer free from sole dependence on archaeological evidence, for now we have *the azimuth* of the site, which is dependent in turn on *the latitude* of the site, and the *resulting date* of the relevant sun or moon rise or set which may or may not agree with the archaeological date for the site.

Charged with determining the function and meaning of solely archaeological evidence, the real danger has been for archaeologists that their assumptions have connected them analogously with a known historical or even modern human culture. This is called *ethnocentricity*. The crucial component - knowing the functional behavioural role of the artefact evidence or the dynamics of individuals and social groupings that once created that evidence, or their aspirations and thinking processes - is thereby almost always missing. The archaeologist is denied access. As an additional barrier, in the case of prehistoric Europe, written evidence to support any of the obtained evidence is wholly lacking, although oral folklore and legend sometimes offer insights that may prove tangibly useful.

Prehistoric evidence has traditionally taken archaeology to this barrier wall beyond which there can sometimes be glimpsed shadowy ancestral figures whose everyday thinking processes, in Clark's words, 'may continually elude us'. We can often know very little concerning prehistory, the nature of the evidence precludes it, yet the prehistorian must attempt to make the best, the most realistic, model from this evidence.

Nowhere may this limitation be better seen than in the problems posed by stone rings and the many 'henge' monuments. Archaeology has not yet been able to resolve the implications of the consistent level of collective thinking required in building any of the larger megalithic structures, a planning process which must have invoked a level of both numeracy and language skills, and which underpinned the building of so many stone circles, rows, henges and cursuses over such a large area of space and time. As John Michell reminds us, in *Megalithomania (T&H, 1976),*

> '...the most damning criticism of excavations at ancient sites, whether by simple treasure hunters or highly trained archaeologists, is that the sum total of all their labours has contributed scarcely at all to resolving the problem obviously presented by the substantial presence of megalithic monuments, the problem of why they were built.'

Atkinson reckoned that perhaps five stone circles were built each and every year for over 1400 years in Britain. It is definitely worth pondering why such effort should have been invested into so many ancestral artefacts whose functions remain almost totally beyond our comprehension. Clearly they were made by human hands, yet clearly their function has totally eluded modern culture, some 300 generations down the family tree. There is currently no model within archaeology to explain these curious structures.

Thom demonstrated that there is much more that we may glean from the stone monuments by asking different questions. If one takes the view that conventional archaeological theory has not delivered any workable solutions nor a model of their function, then surely it would be sensible to look outside of conventional archaeology for answers? This is precisely what Thom did, and in bringing in a new type of quantitative evidence he appeared to bridge the barrier separating that evidence from the social explanations previously assumed by analogy. Indeed he connected his objective evidence to social functions that had previously been entirely overlooked.

Difficult Implications

Thom's work suggested that some of our ancestors in prehistoric Europe were working at a higher level of astronomy, mathematics, geometry and precision measurement than previously thought possible. Thom also provided good evidence that there had been a common unit of length used in the construction of many stone circles, and also that the circles and stone rows often expressed an astronomical purpose. Finally, he showed that there was a consistent geometry to be found throughout the megalithic culture in Britain and Brittany. And while it might be thought by many that it would be a straightforward matter to accommodate these things within a new historical record, for archaeologists there are complications beyond measure, as Atkinson had realised, once we consider the *implications* of Thom's work.

For example, his claim that the builders of the non-circular stone rings had marked the site out using pythagorean triangles, some 2000 years before Pythagoras was born, would upset the whole flow of perceived cultural development. And if one one accepts Thom's findings, it is necessary to accommodate serious levels of mathematics, geometry, metrology and astronomy into the record prior to the first dynastic period in Egypt. This was the megalith-sized stumbling block which prevented Thom's conclusions finding mainstream acceptance and why they probably still occur today in the worst nightmares of some prehistorians.

This is the very essence of the Thomist paradox, well summarised at the time by the following two brief quotations, both made by that remarkably talented archaeologist and artist, the late Stuart Piggott. Juxtaposed, the dilemma is seen immediately:

Describing Skara Brae, in the Orkneys, Piggott writes, evidently shocked, that,

> *'Within the dark interiors of the huts, the air thick with acrid peat smoke, there seems to have been, at the time of their use, a state of indescribable filth and disorder. The floors are found stained with sewage and strewn with bones and shells discarded from successive meals; in the beds there fell down amongst the loose bedding not only personal possessions such as bone pins or beads, but oddments such as a calf's skull or a shoulder-blade shovel'.*

Alexander Thom - Cracking the Stone Age Code

Clearly, Piggott had never had a teenage son living at home, nor rented a property out, or had squatters move in. But following Thom's work in Brittany, note this apparent sea-change, for then Piggott and Daniel, clearly swayed by Thom's findings (Glyn Daniel was part of the entourage during the filming of Thom's survey at Carnac) jointly wrote,

> 'It begins to look as though the people of prehistoric France who were responsible for the dolmens and alignments and menhirs were not only skilled architects and builders, but had considerable mathematical and astronomical knowledge as well'.

The scholarship and diligence which went into into the production of the extant archaeological record of the period was hard won and sincerely presented, and it had revealed a squalid and unpleasant lifestyle in prehistoric Britain - Hobbes' *'nasty, brutish and short'* life. Set against this, Thom's impeccable surveys had revealed a completely different component: an intellectual and cultural high ground operating right in the midst of this same lifestyle. A strange brew indeed, a cauldron filled with archaeological hot potatoes!

Atkinson's Road to Damascus

Richard Atkinson's scathing critique in *Antiquity* of Hawkins *Stonehenge Decoded* (1965), entitled *'Moonshine over Stonehenge'*, had been written as Bob Dylan was reminding everyone that *'the times they are a'changin"*. In 1965 'tendentious' and 'arrogant' had been the two adjectives amongst many Atkinson had used to vent his spleen on Hawkins. 'Howling barbarians' is the term he had applied to describe the culture around Stonehenge in a mid-sixties TV programme about the monument, following publication of Hawkins' popular book . But Atkinson eventually and courageously made the giant leap over to Thom's model of prehistory, understanding full well that it was impossible to continue to marginalise Thom's findings just because they were so uncomfortable to archaeologists. In 1972 he wrote, with rare candour,

> 'It is important that non-archaeologists should understand how disturbing to archaeologists are the implications of Thom's work... . It is hardly surprising, therefore, that many prehistorians either ignore the implications of Thom's work, because they do not understand them, or resist them because it is more comfortable to do so. I have myself gone through the latter process; but I have come to the conclusion that to reject Thom's thesis because it does not conform to the model of prehistory on which I was brought up involves also the acceptance of improbabilities of an even higher order. I am prepared, in other words, to believe that my model of European prehistory is wrong, rather than that the results presented by Thom are due to nothing but chance.'

With this, Atkinson broke rank and the old archaeological model was seen to be fraying at the edges. Eight years after his attack on Hawkins' work at Stonehenge he recognised his words had been inaccurate and unhelpful as a model of the Neolithic. By 1972, through familiarity and study of Thom's work, he had perceived something of what Hawkins had been trying to assess - an astronomical purpose for Stonehenge. Atkinson had faced his demons!

Unfortunately, Atkinson, Glyn Daniel, Humphrey Case and Euan MacKie and a few other well known archaeologists of the period were unable to generate enough momentum to whip the rest of the profession out of its stolid conservatism. Why? Most obviously because anyone wishing to understand Thom's data was faced with a massive educational programme in astronomy (the basic motions of the Sun, Moon and principal stars as observed from the earth), mathematics (the statistical techniques applied to the metrological work), and geometry (the complex curves built into stone rings and often derived from pythagorean triangles). Without these things, hardly the normal fare of an archaeologist of the period, the ability to discern the value of Thom's work was simply not there, and like the general public, the majority of archaeologists were thereby vulnerable to being influenced by ill-informed or prejudiced opinion from within their own ranks, where undoubtedly there were vested interests in retaining the old model of prehistory.

'The Lunatic Fringe of Dotty Archaeology'

In addition to this educational vacuum, by the early 70s, the dangers of the cutting edge of archaeology being usurped by astronomers, engineers, physicists, geomantists, dowsers, ley-line enthusiasts and the 'loony fringe', with its plethora of sundry theories and curious notions, was becoming too much to cope with. The profession closed ranks and interest in Thom's work rapidly declined.

But archaeologists were not alone in the 60s and 70s with having to deal with the 'loony fringe', so too were astronomers. Both disciplines were being plagued with astonishing and often outlandish claims concerning ancient civilisations, alien intervention and historical astronomic catastrophe. It was apocalypse and UFO time - the era of Velikovsky's *Ages in Chaos*, Von Daniken's *Chariots of the Gods* and *Was God an Astronaut?*

This genre of books has since matured, developing quite a pedigree, and the 90s brought us Graham Hancock's best selling *Fingerprints of the Gods*. Just as science fiction has provided insight into the possible futures of our species, so the 'alternative archaeology' genre has provided the same for our possible pasts. On a bad day Atkinson would no doubt have referred to all of such material as low grade 'loony fringe', on a good day he might have been more generous:

> *'shots in the dark may not always be accurate: but at least they serve to wake sleepers from their beds.'*

At best, some of these books did at least further expose the incomplete nature of the model of prehistory. More importantly, they brought some people from outside the archaeological profession into the debate. Some of these went on to make a deeper study of the evidence. But at worst, almost any evidence could be wheeled in to prove whatever. In *Records of Stone*, Pierre-Roland Giot, Professor of Archaeology at the University of Rennes, fairly summed up the archaeologist's position,

> *'It is often difficult to separate more or less objective and scientific theories from the mass of esoteric coincidences and the doctrines about them which flourish in certain schools or sects. Unfortunately these lunacies have contaminated the rest. Nevertheless there are sometimes, in the usual crazy arguments of the devotees of 'alternative archaeology', interesting criticisms of the shortcomings of most orthodox archaeological publications about the significance of the stones. Ignorance, or failure to take account of comparative ethnography, can lead to failings and invite censure. In the huge mass of rubbish accumulated by the 'lunatic fringe' there do exist, if one is to be objective, some interesting observations of facts hitherto overlooked or ignored. The difficulty is to discriminate, to evaluate and exploit them, because of their dubious origin.*
>
> *On the whole topological, metrological and archaeoastronomical research has suffered from this dubious fringe, much as it has also suffered from the fact that in general it has been divorced from the study of Neolithic societies as such.'*

[RIS, pp 323-4]

Vacuums to Vacuous Theories

One major reason why so many bizarre theories found fertile ground in which to grow popular roots was in some part due to the vacuum left by archaeology in its failure to adapt its model of prehistory to include Thomian material. Nature abhors a vacuum and by the early 70s, this vacuum was being rapidly filled by the authors of many books titled like the ones listed previously. If archaeologists had only grabbed hold of it, Thom's work offered them a safe route by which the archaeology profession could have challenged some of the more ludicrous claims made by the authors of the 'alternative' and 'forbidden' archaeology books.

For example, Thom's data could have greatly assisted in debunking Velikovsky's theories. Thom had already confirmed through his work on solar alignments that the extreme solstice declinations showed continuous and predictable minute reduction back to neolithic times, proving that the earth's axial tilt had not suffered sudden change since 3000 BC. This slow change had been accounted for at the solar observatories. And in *MLO*, he was similarly able to demonstrate that megalithic sites confirmed that the moon's orbital obliquity had remained within a few seconds of the modern figure of $5°\ 8'\ 43''$ since prehistoric times. Such independent confirmation of the long term stability of astronomical constants should surely have been welcomed, for it showed that no large planetary body or asteroid could have passed close by the earth in the past 5000 years. Cosmic catastrophe had simply not happened in the timeframe quoted by Velikovsky. This fact alone would have blown out of the water the 'Velikovskian theories' currently fashionable in America concerning planetary or cometary 'near-misses' in prehistoric and early historical times. Thom had no time for such speculation, and wrote to Bob Merritt in 1974 that,

> *'I cannot understand the vogue which Velikovsky has in America. His ideas are simply rubbish. Does he think all astronomers are fools?'*

Thom, a fellow of the *Royal Astronomical Society*, continued his letter by stating that none other than the Astronomer Royal himself had once told him that,

> *'the orbit I had deduced (for a comet he observed in 1915 - author) represented things better than that from the huge observatory in Pulkova in Russia, so I am not entirely ignorant of computational astronomy.'*

Acceptance of Thom's theory of lunar observatories in megalithic times would have provided an archaeological basis by which to have refuted Velikovsky's theories.

SUMMARY

Thom's deceptively simple initial discovery that the circle builders were using an accurate measure to mark out their monuments was not simple at all - it was inseparable from the growing recognition that our model of prehistory was vastly incomplete. At the same time, the advent of radiocarbon dating techniques demonstrated that European megalith building could no longer be thought of as a later derivative of the Middle Eastern cultures. And if that, and then showing unequivocal accurate astronomical alignments at many megalithic sites wasn't enough, then their consistent and complex geometry made up a triple 'whammy' for archaeologists to take on board within the model of prehistory. And, looking more closely at the small print, we discover that the evolution of world history is radically different from that in our history books. The revised radiocarbon dating showed that Thom's revealed model places northwestern Europe ahead of Egypt and Sumeria in the development of many important cultural achievements, amongst which we may list an accurate calendar, accurate metrology, eclipse prediction, Pythagorean and Euclidian geometry and an impressive technology to solve cosmological and numerical problems. And acceptance of this collection even suggests that diffusionism might actually have run in reverse, taking culture ever eastwards!

But the door was actually closed on Thom long before the revised radiocarbon dating came along. This calibration arrived four or five years after the publication of *Megalithic Sites in Britain*. Diffusionism as a theory explaining European prehistory was then all but finished, following a process which had begun in the 1950s when C_{14} dating was first introduced. Radiocarbon techniques originated from a quite separate discipline to archaeology, and was

Alexander Thom - Cracking the Stone Age Code

ultimately ushered in as a vital tool necessary to assist archaeological research, while archaeoastronomy, via the work of Alexander Thom, was not. But even without archaeoastronomy, radiocarbon dating had created a new urgency to explain who built all those, now much older, stone circles littered across the landscape, and more importantly, why? Archaeology was unable to provide an answer to either question and also failed to grab hold of the newly revealed and crucially important components in understanding our prehistoric past, as the Thom package. The profession itself thus created the present vacuum in the model of prehistory, and this goes some way to explaining the extraordinary public fascination with 'forbidden' and 'alternative' archaeology.

This then is the *'Thomist paradox'* of Dr Euan MacKie, but unfortunately it is not the only paradox relating to Thom's researches. With Daniel's announcement on national television that "Professor Thom is not part of this (the lunatic fringe)", and with five leading twentieth century archaeologists, Atkinson, Renfrew, Daniel, MacKie and Case all disturbed by the gap between traditional archaeological evidence and Thom's evidence, the real paradox is surely that the finest, most complete and most compelling piece of astronomical and metrological research ever undertaken on megalithic sites remains marginalised to the extent that many archaeology undergraduates, let alone the lay public, have today never even heard of Alexander Thom. His work is not even discussed any more. Meanwhile those folk from the 'lunatic fringe of dotty archaeology'.. well, they often know quite a lot about Thom's work and its implications. Some even write books about it.

When, how and why did this situation come about, that the pioneering father of a wholly new discipline within archaeology has all but disappeared from that same subject so soon after his death? In chapter six an attempt to answer this question is given, together with a look at how the model of prehistory has changed since Thom's death in November 1985.

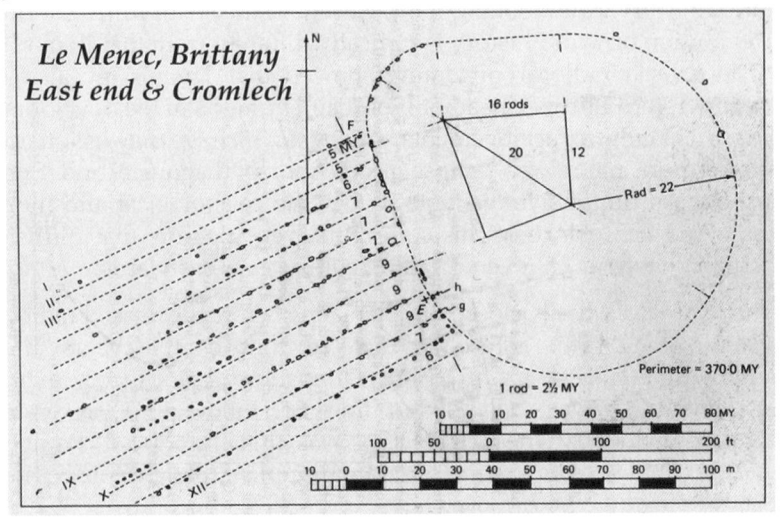

CHAPTER FOUR

The Quest for the Megalithic Yard

The fifth chapter of *Megalithic Sites in Britain*, succinctly entitled *Megalithic Unit of Length*, began with a curiously short sentence,

'Today we use the yard as a standard unit of length.'

Within thirty years, Thom's characteristically nuts and bolts statement of fact is no longer true, the yard has passed from official use in the forty years since he penned this curt sentence. Around the time of publication of *MSIB* Britain finally adopted the metre and its entourage of attendant weights and measures which make up the SI system, also called the Metric System. By a curious irony, just at the very time the British nation turned its back on its long history of use of the customary weights and measures, often referred to as Imperial measure, one of its most ancient cousins, the Megalithic yard was being (re)discovered at hundreds of megalithic sites, by Alexander Thom.

One direct result of metrication is that our children no longer know how to perform simple operations using the old system of Imperial weights and measures, and they are wholly unfamiliar with 'furlongs' or a 'hundredweight', both as words and as quantities. If you were born after 1960, it is unlikely that you are familiar with ounces, thousandths of an inch, or gallons. In a single generation the old mensuration has become quaint and another generation will probably see it relegated to the history books and the dictionary.

So how much more remote are we from 300 generations ago, a time when our ancestors were hauling huge stones over unfeasible distances for purposes that remain unanswered? What do we know of these people from whom many of us are descended? About what did they think and to what did they apply their grey matter, essentially no different to our own?

This chapter investigates the issues that Thom faced in the surveying and measuring of a large number of stone rings in order to determine any units of length used in their construction. We begin by making a self-evident assertion: measuring the primary dimensions of a large number of the same common artefact, modern or ancient, would readily reveal any unit of length which was originally intended by the designer. To identify this length, a large number of measurements would initially be taken, as accurately as possible, and these would then be analysed using mathematical techniques such as averaging and simple statistics. Such a procedure is standard practice throughout industry.

As an example, taking a few dozen old house bricks from a variety of British houses and measuring the brick's length, width and height would quickly reveal that sub-multiples of a single unit - the inch - had formed a quantized system of measurement used in their construction. English bricks once had dimensions of 9, 4 and 3 inches. Even if we had no prior knowledge concerning the inch, this unit would inevitably emerge from the measurements. And, if we measured enough old bricks, it would be possible, using the most basic statistical analysis, to work backwards in order to determine the length of the inch to high precision.

But we could learn much more than this. If many more bricks were accurately measured, the precision by which they were made would emerge. Assuming that a ruler was used to measure out the clay strip prior to cutting and firing the brick, the diagrams (*right*) show (*a*), low precision bricks; (*b*) better precision bricks; and (*c*) high precision bricks. However, for each type of brick we would be assured that the same ruler had been used and that the intended length had been L. The 'tighter' the curve the more precision been achieved. This is hardly rocket science, it is basic high school statistics.

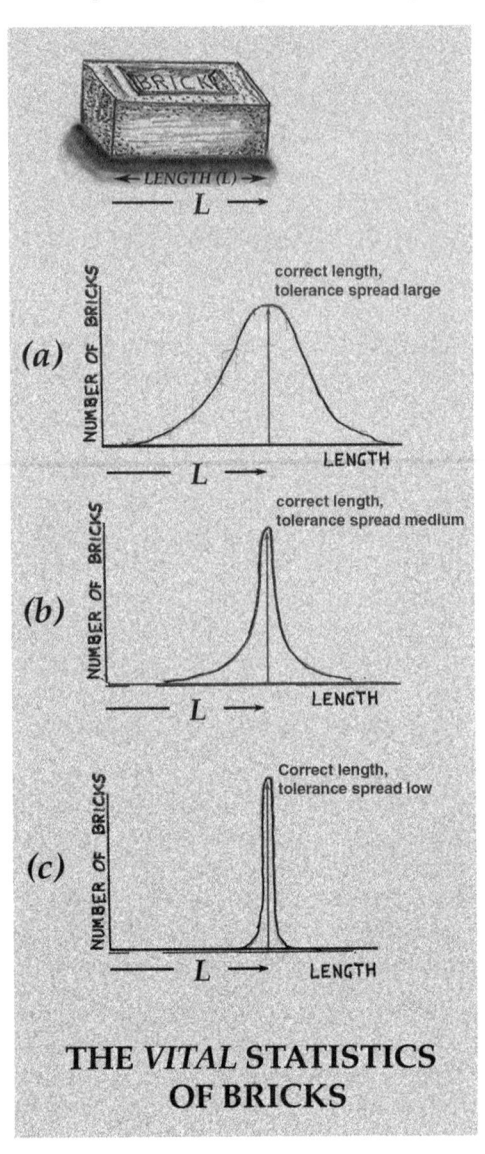

THE *VITAL* STATISTICS OF BRICKS

If one were to repeat these measurements for more modern bricks, it would become apparent that there had been a change of unit. L would have changed. Around 1970, bricks increasingly were manufactured to metric measurements, and the dimensions changed slightly. This change, although small, would be readily detectable, shifting the centre of the curves - the average or mean value to the new length. We would rightly conclude from this that the metrology of brick manufacturers had undergone a radical change - the adoption of the centimetre - and be able to date that change through an understanding of the new house designs into which these bricks were incorporated. For either old or new bricks and certainly for imperial or metric bricks of quality manufacture the precision would remain very high.

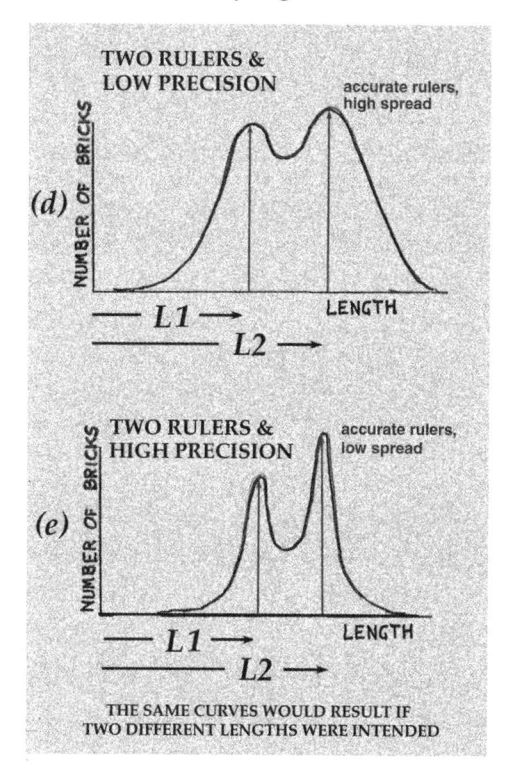

If brick manufacturers were using different values for L, however slight, perhaps through using inaccurately made rulers, we could determine the individual factory's value of L. In the simple example where two manufacturers had supplied bricks for the same house we would discover that the produced curves would now possess two 'humps'. Curve (d) shows that less low precision bricks from one factory (length L1) had been mixed with rather more poor precision bricks from the other factory (length L2). The higher 'hump' represents the higher number of bricks used with length L2. Curve (e) shows the same situation for high precision bricks. For both (d) and (e), each factory was using a different value for L, or inaccurate rulers. For either low or high precision bricks, we can determine the length intended by the factory and the quality of measurement employed, even the proportion of bricks from each factory when they have been mixed. More importantly, for measurements on bricks or stone circles, *we can spot if different rulers have been employed, or a different length intended, from factory to factory, region to region.*

Finally, buildings made from either imperial or metric bricks would be expected to incorporate dimensions which were multiples of that same unit of length. In this case an allowance would have to be made for the added dimensions of the mortar bond between each brick and each course of brickwork.

Alexander Thom was to provide similar well prepared evidence that throughout the period of stone circle building, roughly from 3000 BC to 1400 BC, the same unit of length was in use over a wide area of northwestern Europe. He named this unit the Megalithic yard, and found it to be 2.72 feet in length, or 32.64 inches (0.829 m). Thom began surveying stone circles 'around 1934'. Thereafter, whenever he had spare time from his professional duties, he surveyed sites 'on each and every possible occasion'.

Measuring Stone Circles

The problems facing Thom in surveying megalithic stone monuments were quite different to the measurements of house bricks. For a start Thom was measuring the diameters of the circles, rather than the actual sizes of the stones. A visit to just a few circles will reveal that there appears to be little or no correlation between size of stone, size of circle and the spacing of the stones around the perimeter. Secondly, although the stones are durable in themselves, far more so than brick, several factors have been responsible for moving a proportion of them away from their original position and thereby scattering their diameters away from the original length. The precision we would surely find with a modern artefact has become diffused. Thom identified the following factors in *Megalithic Remains in Britain and Brittany* as responsible for movement of stones,

Soil Creep. Over thousands of years, even a one degree angle of slope can produce flow over large areas. This is often termed *solifluction*. Long Meg is a typical example of a circle, built on a slope of 3^0, where stones have moved because of soil creep. Built on a remarkably steep slope for such a large circle, the survey plans suggest that some of the stones have moved down the slope to the north. This, coupled with the known anti-pagan assaults against this fine site in more recent times explains why the original geometry now lies in some disarray.

Trees. Stones can be entwined in the roots of trees whence, if the tree falls, the stone is uprooted with the tree. In time, the wood rots leaving almost no traces, and the stone position has been changed from its original placement. At Athgreany, Co. Wicklow, and at another site nearby, sturdy Hawthorn trees grow between the huge stones, safe from grazing sheep, and this has clearly forced stones apart.

Frost. Wet earth lifts under heavy frost, placing large forces on stones. Over many winters the positions of stones may change by a few inches. The author has seen heavy flagstones in a garden path raised like Tower Bridge during an unusually harsh frost which occurred suddenly while the soil was very wet.

In addition to this list we might also include the movement by farm animals using upright stones as rubbing posts, and stones sinking into the annual accretion of top-soil, changing what is seen and hence their profile measured above ground. Animal burrowing under stones weakens their foundation over a long period of time, and may cause stones to sink or fall in extreme cases.

Fortunately, most these movements tend to cancel out in a large enough sample. Analyse a large enough number of rings and a stone moved northwards at one site will be matched by one moved southwards at another, and so on. This type of error is termed an *accidental error* or an *'error of discrepancy'*.

Accidental errors obey the following laws:

(i). Small errors occur more often than do large ones.

(ii). In a large enough sample, there are equal numbers of positive and negative errors either side of the mean value. The mean value is the best estimate for the original position of the stone, a length very close to that surmised to have been used by the circle builders.

(iii). Very large errors do not occur.

The more the site has suffered from the elements and natural forces, the more the range of readings will spread out from the mean value of any standard length used to define the stone ring, although the mean value of that length ought to remain where it was.

Where very large errors are found, the error is taken to indicate that the stone had been deliberately moved, in some cases removed altogether, by human intent. Although this kind of vandalism can in truth appear to be accidental - stones 'restored' by some well meaning heritage group for example - we must class such activity (i.e. people tampering with stones) as a deliberate error for the purposes of any analysis.

The outcome of all this is quite depressingly clear, and Thom warns us, again in *Megalithic Remains in Britain and Brittany* that,

> *'It is only in exceptional circumstances that we can expect megalithic stones to be accurately in their original places.'*

So, how may we account for the movement of stones from their original position? In the case of deliberate errors, which are demonstrably common at stone circles, Thom first tackled this problem by avoiding very large errors, choosing instead those stone rings which appeared to him to be more or less complete and in reasonable shape. Fortunately, there were enough of these to satisfy him and others in the later statistical analyses. At the damaged or incomplete sites, Thom applied common sense, a quality he was blessed with in copious amounts. A buried stone was often located by repeated and arduous prodding with a bayonet. A missing stone could sometimes be identified by finding its original socket hole.

Fortunately, it is almost impossible to remove all traces of the hole where a stone or post once stood. Electrical resistivity mapping, sound echo imaging and even bayonetting softer ground can often reveal where a stone once stood. When even this failed, Thom was often able to assess the original position of a missing stone by averaging the spaces between adjacent stones, whilst the position of a fallen stone was similarly 'guestimated' by averaging within the implied geometry taken by the adjacent or neighbouring stones. Such 'best estimate' calculations are supported by standard formulae published in scientific tables, used throughout the industrial and scientific world.

Levels of Accuracy in Surveys

Thom rejected nearly all the site plans previously produced by prehistorians and archaeologists as 'crude'. He found the Ministry of Works survey plan for Stonehenge 'laughably inaccurate' and from this eye-opener he was eventually persuaded by Richard Atkinson to provide a new survey. In a letter to the author about the 1973 Stonehenge survey, Archie Thom explained that:-

> 'About our survey, the Ministry plan was a botch. It had two scales on itself which did not fit. It had obviously been made up from several sources. This finally persuaded A.T. to do the survey. He never trusted the work of strangers. We carefully left records of where our survey pegs had been; nobody ever asked us about it all. Our survey is the best record of things on the surface. I still keep the tracings for reproduction. We measured the stone positions to half an inch, and then repeated these measurements at original ground level, about three feet up according to what Dick (Richard Atkinson - author's addition) told us.'

Surveys at megalithic sites had never been conducted to anywhere like the accuracy required to conclusively answer Thom's questions about units of length and the geometry applied to lay out the rings. To do that, he identified that it was necessary to be working with an accuracy of 99.9%, or one part in a thousand, Thom eventually demonstrating that the circle builders were capable of working to one part in 1500. Following a communication with Professor J E Gordon, Thom was informed that 'along the grain the expansion of wood when it becomes wet is very small, being in fact comparable with the expansion due to a rise in temperature.' In *Megalithic Remains in Britain and Brittany* (1978, 42), armed with this information from an expert in the properties of materials, Thom conducted practical experiments and answered his critics directly with the following reply,

Thom 'weighing-up' a stone in the Le Menec alignment, Carnac in 1970. Surveying megalithic sites is often extremely difficult, especially when there is extensive tree cover, nettles, brambles or bracken.
(*photo possibly by Hamish Gorrie*).

'It has been stated in public that it would be impossible to use wooden rods to measure with the accuracy which we claim for the Megalithic yard. Accordingly we made an experiment on the ground under conditions identical to those under which Megalithic man must have worked. We made two wooden rods each exactly 6 ft long, and used them to set out a length of 198 ft (33 lengths of 6 ft) along the top of a ridge in a grass field, each rod supported on two pieces of wood. We then measured with a steel tape the length we had set and found it to be 197 ft 113/16 inches. Thus the error was 13/16 inch, or 1 in 2924.

We then repeated the experiment and set out 96 ft, but this time we measured across the ridges which were about 33 ft pitch and 16-18 inches deep. This was more difficult, but we did not use any special equipment. The error was 3/4 inch, or 1 in 1536. Thus there is no real difficulty in attaining an accuracy of 1 in 1500 in the field and this is equivalent to 0.0018 ft in the length of the Megalithic yard. This is of the same order as the difference which we find in the yard from various sites.' MRBB, p42

To attain either standard of accuracy demanded high standards of laying out and measuring skills from the circle builders. These same standards demand that a modern surveyor uses a good theodolite well and measures using accurate steel or *invar* surveyor's tapes if they are to do justice to the resulting plan. Thom had started his quest using cloth tapes, and later resurveyed all the early sites as a result of having recognised the importance of matching his tolerances to that of the circle builders' abilities.

The Use of Theodolites in Surveying Circles

Ever the practical engineer, Thom eschewed the leather backed armchairs of the university common room, preferring instead the wild places of the British Isles where, armed with his specially lightened theodolite, he went a-hunting for our past. Thom needed a theodolite to recover the geometry of the circles because their centres are hardly if ever marked. Because of this, it is impossible to know accurately where the centre is located prior to producing the final drawing from the theodolite survey data - the bookings - and a marked rope or tape cannot simply be used to establish an accurate radius, although a diameter can be very roughly established using tapes.

A survey plan's dimensions are only as accurate as the original base line, the measured angles to stones and the accuracy of the rulers or tapes employed. Thom used surveyor's chains to measure distances, checking these nightly against a standard, also compensating for temperature changes. At the larger sites he preferred what are known as closed traverse surveys, partly because they tend to be self-checking against human error, but also because the size of most large stone rings suited admirably this kind of work. A radial survey with tapes would be undertaken at smaller sites or at sites of less interest or where much damage had occurred. Many of Thom's original drawings show faint pencil lines and crossover arcs associated with the transference of the theodolite bookings onto the plan. There are over 200 filled notebooks in the RCAHMS collection which reveal how each survey was undertaken.

A complete survey plan of a megalithic site must ideally be done in three dimensions. Not only must a plan be drawn from the survey, the familiar bird's-eye view of the site, but for archaeoastronomical analysis the local horizon elevation must be recorded and a profile drawn. The slope of the site must be accounted for, by contouring using a surveyors stave. Thom had special staves made up, each with a circular bubble level mounted to the top to enable them to be held vertically. Add to this the need to find true north to an accuracy of a least one minute of a degree (one arc minute is a sixtieth of one degree) and it is clear that only a professional theodolite survey, using an instrument of at least what is termed *intermediate quality*, will suffice. Thom owned several such instruments, one by E.R.Watts & Sons, London, one specially lightened by Troughton & Simms, London, and latterly, for the Stonehenge and Carnac surveys, a Swiss made Wild T16, one of the best quality optical theodolites to this standard ever made. He had access to other instruments from the University of Glasgow and, sometimes, from archaeologists he had befriended.

Thom visited many sites again and again to improve on earlier work or to test some new hypothesis or where the weather had previously precluded obtaining an accurate azimuth bearing by 'shooting the sun'.In such cases, prior to a revisit, he would sight his theodolite on a reference object (RO) - a trig point, transmitting aerial, prominent stone or mountain top at as far a distance away as the weather conditions allowed, then use standard geodetic formulae to calculate the bearing (azimuth). Thom was never entirely happy with the accuracy of this technique and often revisited sites in an attempt to be on-site on a day when the sun would make a showing, whence he could determine a more or less exact azimuth for a reference object. From this the direction of true north could be established to within a minute of one degree or better. Determination of the orientation of the site forms the prime datum within any accurate survey in archaeoastronomy.

At many sites visibility can often drop down to only a few metres, especially at high altitudes. In such cases, not only may the sun not be visible during the survey, precluding the determination of accurate azimuths, but the site itself may disappear! Add to this the wind, rain and cold, being hassled by farm animals and having to deal with brambles, nettles and inconveniently placed trees, and the lot of a surveyor of megalithic sites is hardly an easy quest, although it inevitably leads to some of the most astonishingly beautiful landscapes.

It is unlikely that the quality of Thom's surveying work will or needs ever be bettered, a fact admitted by almost all who have reviewed his data and plans. On that alone, the data he obtained for diameters of the true circles tabulated in *MSIB* must be regarded as a prime data bank. Anyone could verify his results today, because the circles remain *in situ*, although several sites have much deteriorated or been damaged and even, in some cases, demolished, since the 1950s. Allan Water, an egg-shaped ring near Hawick, has in recent years suffered

Chapter Four - The Quest for the Megalithic Yard

severe cattle damage as a result of changing farming practices. Year on year, Thom undertook regular survey trips to increase his data collection and in order to support the conclusions drawn from his earlier analyses.

All Shapes and Sizes

The old stone circles of Britain have diameters which vary from as little as eleven feet to as large as 350 feet. Thom surveyed as many circles as he could and ascertained from the resulting plan the diameter of each circle. Lest the reader suspect that Thom pre-empted his results, one should note that the original centres of the circles are never marked. They may only be accurately pinpointed by first obtaining a survey plan of the ring based on the theodolite 'bookings'. No prior bias can be 'written in' to this process. Thom's notebooks, which contain the bookings from which the plans were drawn, are safely tucked away within a store-room at RCAHMS, Edinburgh, under the auspices of Lesley Ferguson, who will, given notice, kindly prepare the collection on tables for any serious researcher. All Thom's survey work may be re-checked by anyone patient enough to go through this data. Better still would be to take a theodolite to the sites and undertake a check on-site..

Thom's surveys revealed a further and most important aspect of megalithic thinking. Not only was the unit of length consistently adhered to but so too was the geometry of many stone rings, a geometry which was often decidedly non-circular. Thom was analysing both the mensuration and these geometries simultaneously during the post-war period, right up to the publication of *Megalithic Sites in Britain*. During the many surveys necessary to reveal the unit of length the builders were using, he also discovered that the circles were often not circles at all. Ellipses, flattened circles, eggs and other shapes were mixed in amongst the true circles, carefully and *consistently* laid out to very precise geometries. These geometries are the subject of the following chapter, but the reader is asked to note, firstly, that these other shapes also possessed diameters, arcs and radii which incorporated the same unit of length, often as multiples, and secondly, that many of these shapes appeared to have been formed using Pythagorean triangles whose integer dimensions *also* employed the same units of length or sub-multiples of that length. That such was the case confirmed to Thom that the Megalithic yard was 'universally used'.

Experimental Technique - Analysing the Data

By what technique could one determine any common unit of length (the 'quantum') supposedly used by the builders of stone circles. How could it best be done? Thom identified these two obvious approaches in *Megalithic Sites in Britain* (page 8),

> 'It is essential to recognize two distinct classes of problem.
>
> **Case I.** *In the first case we have come to the problem with an a priori knowledge that a quantum may exist. We have an idea of its magnitude*

and we wish to test the hypothesis that its existence is demonstrated by the measurements..

Case II. *In the second and more difficult case the quantum has come from the data themselves. We had in fact no idea beforehand that such a quantum existed nor with hindsight can we say, 'Ah, but we ought to have expected such a quantum because.....'.*

In order to discover, albeit approximately, any unit of length employed by the builders, Thom must have commenced his surveying and subsequent analysis by using a 'Case II' method - he initially had no idea what unit of length he might discover! But at some point, and it is not clear just when this occurred, Thom repeatedly found that multiples of the same regularly occurring unit of length appeared to have been used to define the diameters of many of the circles he surveyed. Thereafter, it would have been common sense to apply a 'Case I' analysis to data gleaned from subsequent surveys. This seemed to be the inevitable route for his private and self-funded research to progress in 1950-4, when Thom was no longer coming at the problem from complete guesswork nor ignorance. He had *'a priori* knowledge', a term quaintly Biblical, reminiscent of something which ought to be considered sinful.

The early surveys, prior to 1955, had already revealed the existence of what he termed the Megalithic fathom (about 5.44 feet, 1.65m) at site after site, and Thom, like all good engineers, wanted to have his cake and eat it. He wanted to take this quantum value he had assumed for the earlier surveys and apply it to the later data using a Case I methodology. But at this point he was wise enough to recognise that there may be better ways to prove the existence of a megalithic unit of length. In 1955 Thom wrote to Dr Simon R. Broadbent, a renowned Cambridge academic and expert in the subject of statistics, and also to Professor John Hammersley, who held the Readership in the Design and Analysis of Scientific Experiment at Oxford, asking each of them for help and advice in selecting the best statistical analysis to identify if stone circles had been constructed using a standard unit of length..

From then on the Class I methodology was to be challenged and then totally dumped in favour of the Class II analysis, following suggestions made by both these expert statisticians - most notably by Simon Broadbent. Eventually, through his enthusiastic and willing help, Thom was able to discern much more useful information about the way the circles had been constructed. That he took the advice given *in toto* is shown by the fact that the Case II analysis in *MSIB* derives entirely from Broadbent's work in designing a statistical treatment of the data. From Broadbent, he was also advised that, to prove the existence of the unit of length to his (Broadbent's) satisfaction, he would need to acquire more data, more surveys. So, once more, Thom went back on the road again.

Thom worked furiously to acquire the extra survey data needed to satisfy Broadbent's method, Archie Thom informing us, in *WIATS*, page 205,

Chapter Four - The Quest for the Megalithic Yard

> *'By 1956, Thom was ready, able to write that any lingering doubts he may have had were completely removed by his measurements of the diameters of circles - 'some sixty new values'.'*

As the data bank grew, the probability that Thom's quantum length was employed by the circle builders rose up from the noise level, using the Class II analysis of Broadbent's second paper. Thom had taken delivery of the best contemporary solution to his initial problem, and applied it rigorously to his data. The initial paper, published in the *Journal of the Royal Statistical Society* in 1955, and based on Broadbent's model, was then extensively revised in 1962 and again in 1964, as he perfected his understanding of the problem and added to his data collection. Broadbent published two articles in the journal *Biometrika* (Vol. 42, 1955), *'Quantum Hypotheses'*, where he quoted Hammersley and Morton's (1954) paper on *The Druid Circle Problem,* and another in 1956 (*Biometrika*, Vol. 43), entitled *Examination of a Quantum Hypothesis on a single set of data.*

Statistics without Tears

We must now stray just a little into the rarified world of statistical analysis to understand better the devastating implications of Thom's surveys and subsequent analyses for those who would have us believe that peasant farmers passed the time of day by building inaccurate stone rings in Bronze Age Britain. Thom found out that they didn't. The presumption of the existence of the Megalithic yard is one major plank in the argument, the radial accuracy of the true circles and the intricate and consistent geometries of the flattened rings, eggs and compound rings, distributed over an enormous area, are others. Combined, the evidence demonstrated to Thom that this belief was wholly untenable.

Thom's conclusions may be grasped quite simply, without wading through the commando course that is chapters one and five of *Megalithic Sites in Britain*. Thom measured the diameters of 112 surviving true circles, as well as 33 other sites having different geometries. Provided a diameter was confidently known to within one foot, he included it within his data table. From his initial surveys, Thom repeatedly found integral numbers appearing in lengths which were multiples of about 2.72 feet. This formed the 'quantum'. Assuming that he was looking for a unit around 2.72 feet, he quantised the data accordingly and this was the initial Case I approach adopted in the earlier work.

Thom originally used a standard engineering technique called 'least squares' to determine the most likely diameters for the circles, taken from drawings meticulously drawn from the survey data and whose shape he assumed had been slightly distorted by four thousand years of weathering and earth slippage. He assumed that if the diameters of circles used any quantum value, an integer multiple (1,2,3..etc) would deliver an accurate estimate of the diameter. Any error (ε), plus or minus, could be incorporated into any mathematical formula used to analyse the results. The final diameter was entered into the data set and quantised, for each ring, according to the equation,

Diameter (D) = 2.72 n + ε

The residual errors for each measurement then take the form,

ε = Diameter (D) - 2.72 n

For example, a circle of surveyed diameter 21.8 feet would be identified as most likely intended to have been set out as 8 MY, because 21.8 feet divided by 2.72 is 8.014. The quantum multiple (n) is therefore 8, the residual error (ε) from this measurement is then +0.014, the plus sign indicating that the error takes the measurement above the quantum or 'node'. These errors he termed *residuals*, the nomenclature (and technique) described in the standard work on surveying, Clark's *Geodetic and Plane Surveying* textbook, volume II (Glasgow 1923). Edited by Professor George Moncur and written by David Clark, both of whom were renowned surveyors and had instructed Thom on the art of surveying at Loch Eck way back in 1912, when he was just 18 years of age. Thom had both volumes of this classic textbook on his bookshelf.

If the sum of all values of ε in a sample is zero then the measurements fall exactly on the nodes - a *perfect* quantum (ε is the the residual error (±) from any individual measurement). Thom was able to demonstrate that the zero of the measurements did indeed fall at the quantised or node positions. Such a situation greatly added to Thom's confidence in both the use of the unit of length and in his initial assumption that, given a large enough data sample the accidental errors ought to cancel each other out.

Thom separated his circles data into two groups - Scottish sites and then combined English and Welsh sites. He treated these two collections of data as separate in order to establish that the two lengths for the Megalithic yard obtained from each set were so similar as to suggest that every circle builder had marked them out with the same length of ruler.

At a most basic level, if one takes individually the Scottish circles and adds up all the diameters, then divides by the quantum (a Class I analysis), the emerging number will lie quite near to the quantum value 2.72 feet, an *'implied quantum'* for each site that includes the error from the assumed quantum. A set of values either side of and roughly centering on 2.72 feet will naturally emerge. The Scottish data is tabulated opposite and the circle data for both Scottish and English & Welsh sites is shown in histogram form on the following page.

The 'tighter' the values huddle around the central quantum value of 2.72 feet, the more confident can we be that the circles were marked out using that unit of length. But how do we know what is 'tighter' or 'looser' here? How is 'precision defined? We now must introduce a standard of comparison, so that Thom's results may be usefully compared with data derived from circles where no quantum, i.e. no fixed ruler or length, has been employed. And where can we find such circles? Welcome to Randomland!

Chapter Four - The Quest for the Megalithic Yard

SURVEY DATA & ANALYSIS

SCOTLAND

Residuals, e = y - 2.72m, where m = No. of Quanta

Implied Quantum = y/m ft.

CIRCLES Diameters known to within one foot.

Site	Map ref.	Diameter (y feet)	m	e	Implied Quantum (y/m feet)
Boat of Garten	NH967210	10.8	4	-0.08	2.70
Temple Wood	NR827979	11.2	4	+0.32	2.80
Glenshee	NO117701	12.7	5	-0.90	2.54
Monzie	NN881241	16.4	6	+0.08	2.733
Fountain Hill	NJ880328	16.9	6	+0.58	2.816
Shin River	NC582049	20.5	8	-1.26	2.5625
Esslie, South	NO717916	20.6	8	-1.16	2.575
Loch Mannoch	NX661614	20.9	8	-0.86	2.6125
Duncracaig	NR833964	21.0	8	-0.76	2.625
Colen	NO110311	21.0	8	-0.76	2.625
Burreldales	NJ676550	21.3	8	-0.46	2.6625
Kintraw	NM830050	21.4	8	-0.36	2.675
Loch Buie	NM618251	21.8	8	+0.04	2.725
Miltown of Clava	NH751438	22.0	8	+0.24	2.75
Ninestone Rig	NY225881	23.2	9	-1.28	2.5777
Callanish I	NB213330	24.0	9	-0.48	2.6667
The Mound	ND770991	24.0	9	-0.48	2.6667
Shianbank I	NO156272	27.5	10	+0.30	2.750
Shianbank II	NO156273	27.5	10	+0.30	2.800
Blindwells	NO125314	28.0	10	+0.80	2.7364
Riverness	NH621380	30.1	11	+0.18	2.6667
Farr, P.O.	NH682332	32.0	12	-0.64	2.7080
Raedykes N	NO832907	32.5	12	-0.14	2.7833
Cullerlie	NJ785043	33.4	12	+0.76	2.7385
Little Urchany	NH866482	35.6	13	+0.24	2.6857
Ardlair	NJ553280	37.6	14	-0.48	2.8000
Dalcross Castle	NH780484	39.2	14	+1.12	2.725
Esslie North	NO722921	43.6	16	+0.08	2.7563
Loch Buie (2nd)	NM618251	44.1	16	+0.58	2.7625
Temple Wood	NR827979	44.2	16	+0.68	2.6471
Up. Auchnagorth	NJ839563	45.0	17	-1.24	2.7529
Tannagorn	NJ651077	46.8	17	+0.56	2.6944
Leys of Marlee	NO460439	48.5	18	-0.46	2.7222
Westerton	NJ706190	49.0	18	+0.04	2.7611
Aquorthies, N.	NO902963	49.7	18	+0.74	2.7450
A8/6 (Dere St?)	NT751161	54.9	20	+0.50	2.6857
Clune Wood	NO795950	56.4	21	-0.72	2.7095
Midmar Church	NJ699064	56.9	21	-0.22	2.7143
Yonder Bognie	NJ600458	57.0	21	-0.12	2.6864
Miltown of Clava	NH751438	59.1	22	-0.74	2.6909
Esslie, South	NO717916	59.2	22	-0.64	2.6954
Tyrebagger	NJ859132	59.3	22	-0.54	2.7391
Moyness	NH951536	63.0	23	+0.44	2.6667
Easter Aquorthies	NJ733207	64.0	24	-1.28	2.7125
Loch Nell	NM906291	65.1	24	-0.18	2.6760

FRH 11/99
Page 1 of 2

- 115 -

SCOTLAND

CIRCLES (continued)

Site	Map ref.	Diameter (y feet)	m	e	Implied Quantum (y/m feet)
Castle Fraser	NJ715124	66.9	25	-0.10	2.6760
Loanhead, Daviot	NJ748289	67.2	25	-0.80	2.6880
Little Urchany	NH866482	68.4	25	+0.40	2.7360
River Ness	NH621380	69.1	25	+1.10	2.7640
Tannagorn	NJ651077	73.3	27	-0.14	2.7148
Farland	NJ471052	74.1	27	+0.66	2.7444
Druid Temple	NH685420	74.3	27	+0.86	2.7519
Aquathories, N	NO902963	75.1	28	-1.06	2.6821
Aviemore	NH897134	76.0	28	-0.16	2.7143
Cauldside	NX530571	82.1	30	+0.50	2.7367
Mains of Gask	NH680359	82.9	30	+1.30	2.7633
Sunhoney	NJ716057	83.2	31	-1.12	2.6839
Drannando	NX400710	89.1	33	-0.46	2.7000
Milton	NJ550487	92.0	34	-0.48	2.7058
Clava (i)	NH757444	103.9	38	+0.34	2.7342
Clava (ii)	NH757444	104.2	38	+0.84	2.7421
Sheldon of Bo'rtie	NJ823249	108.4	40	-0.40	2.7100
Urquhart	NJ290640	110.0	40	+1.20	2.75
Farr, West	NH680335	113.2	42	-1.04	2.6952
Mains of Gask	NH680359	119.9	44	+0.22	2.725
Latheron Wheel	ND180350	188.3	69	+0.62	2.7289

TYPE A Flattened Circles

Site	Map ref.	Diameter	m	e	Implied Quantum
Loupin Stanes	NY257966	37.7	14	-0.38	2.6928
Aviemor	NH897134	43.0	16	-0.52	2.6875
Callanish I	NB213330	43.3	16	-0.22	2.7063
Cambret	NX510582	54.5	20	+0.10	2.7250
Seven Brethren	NY217827	65.5	24	+0.22	2.7292
Farr, West	NH680335	66.8	25	-1.20	2.6720
Torhouse	NX383565	69.3	25	+1.30	2.772

TYPE B Flattened Circles

Site	Map ref.	Diameter	m	e	Implied Quantum
Loch Nell	NM906291	16.0	6	-0.32	2.6667
South Ythsie	NJ884305	28.0	10	+0.80	2.8000
Garrol Wood	NO725912	58.9	22	-0.94	2.6773

TYPE I & II Egg-shaped rings

Site	Map ref.	Diameter	m	e	Implied Quantum
Druid Temple	NH685420	38.3	14	+0.22	2.7357
Allen Water	NT470063	43.9	16	+0.38	2.7438
Esslie, South	NO717916	76.1	28	-0.06	2.7179
Clava	NH757444	103.6	38	+0.24	2.7263
B'stone Rig (II)	NT560921	136.0	50	+0.00	2.7200

COMPOUND RINGS

Site	Map ref.	Diameter	m	e	Implied Quantum
Easter Delfour	NH845086	60.0	22	+0.16	2.7272

Chapter Four - The Quest for the Megalithic Yard

A Visit to Randomland

In Randomland, there are a great many stone circles laid out by people who just use an unmarked rope and a peg to define the centre. These slip-shod people just peg up the intended centre of the circle and then bale out enough rope to meet their requirement for the size of their intended circle, walk around marking the future perimeter, dig a few holes and then lug large stones and set them into the holes. Job done!

It is self evident that if the Scottish and the English and Welsh circles were laid out in the same way as were these Randomland circles, then there ought to be no major discernible difference in the shape of the histograms. Randomland circles define a histogram from which any significant increase in 'tightness' seen in an analysis of circles from other places would suggest they were erected in 'not-Randomland', i.e. depending on the 'tightness' they would show an increasing probability that they had been measured out using the quantum length. The random data thus provides a test against which suspected non-random data may be compared. The histogram for Randomland circles is shown overleaf. A computer program was written to generate random numbers in a program that generated the diameters of circles between 10 and 340 feet - the range that Thom surveyed in real circles. The number of the sample was chosen to match the sample size of the actual survey sample of Thom's data.

For Randomland circle data, the percentage of the sample falling between 2.68 and 2.76 feet (approximately ± 1 cm either side of the quantum value of 2.72 feet) would tend to 56% (in a very large sample). For the Scottish data it is 62% and for the English and Welsh data it is 67%. Even in this most basic analysis, aimed at the non-mathematical reader, it is possible to show that Thom's exhaustive but essentially limited supply of data came not from Randomland circles, whose 'tightness' is significantly less than from the British circles.

Alas, *Megalithic Sites in Britain* did not contain any such simple conclusions prior to the heavier statistical treatment, which improved on the suggested accuracy of the Megalithic yard and the probability that it and not some other length had been used, all at the expense of undue complication for the non-specialist reader. Most skipped over this material and gave it up as an academic bridge too far. The interested layperson was forced to verification of the proof from those few archaeologists who spoke out on the subject, an act of trust equivalent to leaving little Red Riding Hood with 'grandmother'. In 1967 it was true that most archaeologists couldn't understand the statistics either and those that could, and many that couldn't, were predisposed to reject Thom's conclusions, as Crawford's response to Thom's first submitted paper to *Antiquity* demonstrated - '*I do not believe your hypothesis.*'

With well over 100 well preserved rings impeccably surveyed, this data and the subsequent analyses and conclusions - first Class I and then Class II - would

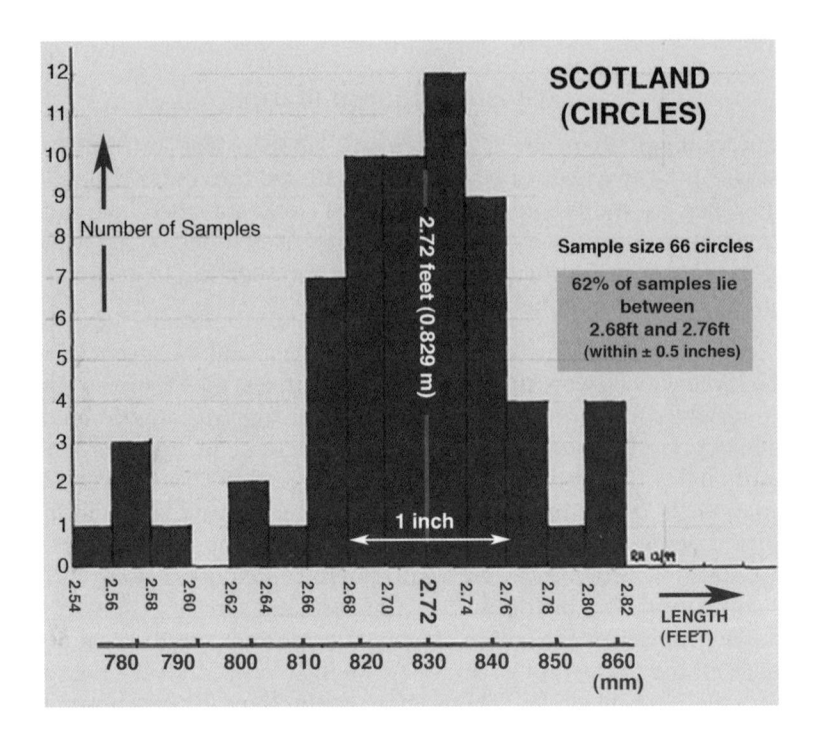

SCOTLAND (CIRCLES)

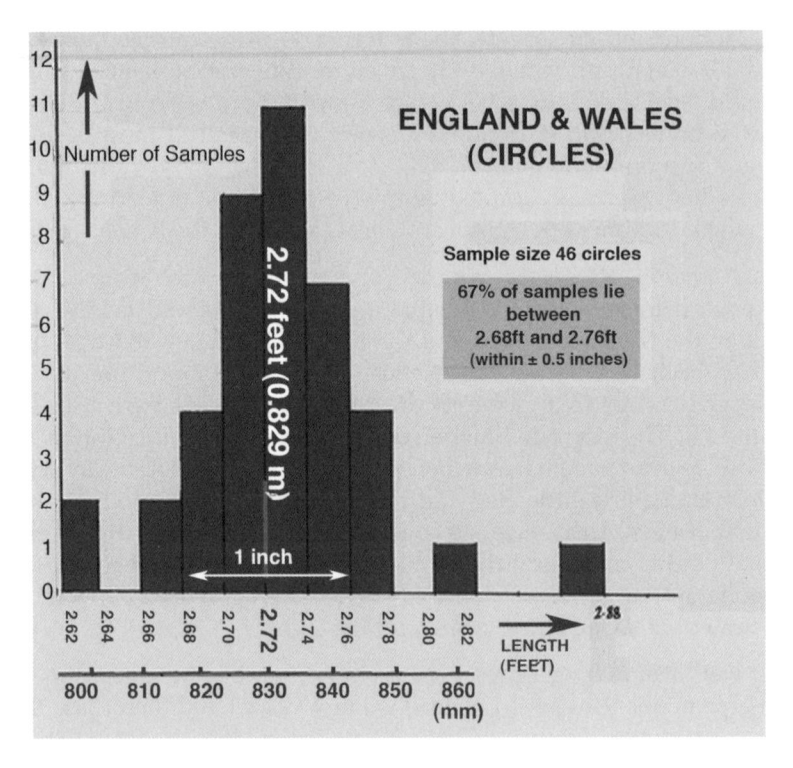

Sample size 66 circles

62% of samples lie between 2.68ft and 2.76ft (within ± 0.5 inches)

2.72 feet (0.829 m)

ENGLAND & WALES (CIRCLES)

Sample size 46 circles

67% of samples lie between 2.68ft and 2.76ft (within ± 0.5 inches)

2.72 feet (0.829 m)

Chapter Four - The Quest for the Megalithic Yard

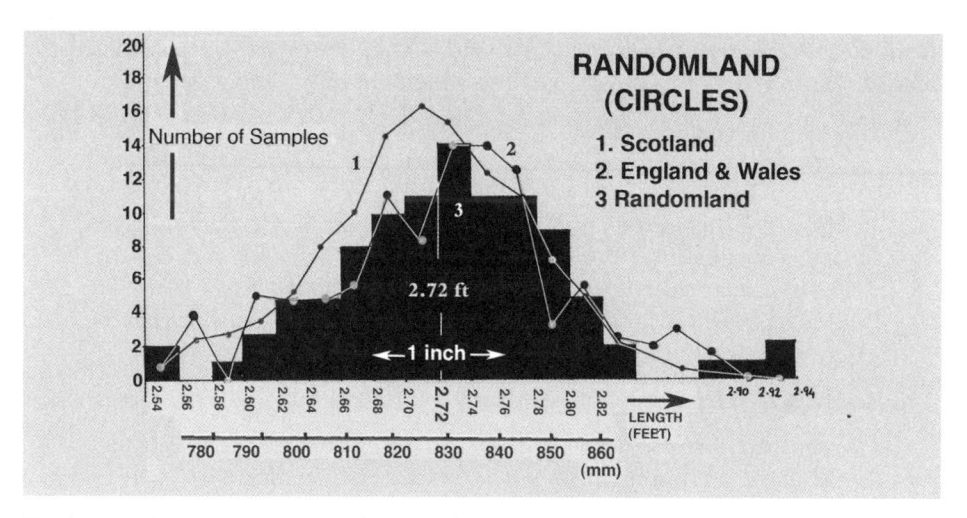

Random number data compared to that from the Scottish and English/Welsh circles shows a broader spread, even with such limited sample sizes. The spread here is 44% of circles lying between 2.68 and 2.76 feet, compared to 67% (Scottish circles) and 62% (English/Welsh circles). In an 'infinite sample' this percentage in a random sample would rise, but never exceed, 56%.

have been accepted in almost every branch of science. Indeed it had already been published in the *Journal of the Royal Society of Statistics*, not a journal noted for publishing fanciful or shallow work. Alas, it was not acceptable to many archaeologists, from which the more logical reader may conclude that their decision making was based on other factors than the pursuit of scientific truth. It is also true that many cared not to wade through the statistical treatment doled out in *MSIB*, and had they done so most simply would not have understood it.

Stage Two in the Proof

So, how does one advance on the statistical treatment from the high school first stage presented above which assumed that there *was* a quantum length of 2.72 feet? Might there have been other indications of other quanta? Let us summarize the journey so far. Having surveyed over seventy-eight stone circles prior to 1955 Thom discovered that certain lengths did indeed emerge from his surveys. He had used the 'least squares' method to minimise residual errors and thereby determined the best value for the mean in order to obtain a more accurate figure for the diameters of the circles. He had then taken things as far as he could prior to calling on the statistical expertise of Broadbent and Hammersley.

Thom described Dr Broadbent as 'a stickler' and it is not clear whether this was a compliment or a criticism! Broadbent insisted that Thom apply his second technique (Case II) to each set of data separately. The early (Scottish) data which had revealed the Megalithic fathom (2 MY) was to be kept apart from that of the later (English and Welsh) rings and with no *a priori* assumption that any quantum of length existed for the latter. In a letter to Robert Merritt, a supportive friend who had facilitated useful grants to support Thom's research from Case Western University, Cleveland, Ohio, about later criticisms of his results, Thom writes this most revealing statement of his analyses,

> 'Broadbent would not allow any division of the material, e.g., I wanted to take the Scottish circles and say that they gave 2.72 ft, one Megalithic yard, and then test this on the English circles because then I maintained I had a priori evidence for 2.72, and so could use the straight-forward analysis on English circles of his first paper. But Broadbent would have none of it and was not satisfied until I had enough diameters to use in his second method (2nd paper) (a 'class II' analysis - author) which (logically) needs no a priori evidence.'

Elsewhere in the same letter he writes,

> 'I spent many years gathering as long a list of diameters as possible in order to get a reliable figure of use in Broadbent's formulae.'

Once he had this new data, Thom diligently worked on all the data using the approach and formulae suggested by Dr Broadbent. The results were astonishing, confirming a unit of length (2.72 feet) to a much higher probability than that obtained previously and to a remarkably consistent accuracy (± 0.003 feet). In metric measure, the Megalithic yard is 0.829m ± 0.9mm

Having satisfied the two leading statisticians of the time, what do we know of Thom's reaction? Apparently he was not at all surprised. In a typically underplayed and succinct reply to the question (WIATS, p 157) he said,

> "Being an engineer myself, I realised I was dealing with other engineers."

Once Thom had the additional surveys under his belt, the data from the English and Welsh circles, analysed to Broadbent's strict criteria, i.e. with no *a priori* value for the Megalithic yard, Thom was ready. The analysis had yielded the same length for the quantum as revealed by the Scottish circles. In *MSIB*, this satisfying result was typically understated with the simple account of the probability levels revealed by each type of analysis,

> 'If there were an a priori reason for expecting that the diameters were set out in units of 5.44 ft (the Megalithic fathom and equal to 2 MY, implying that the radii were set out in units of 2.72 feet - author's note) then we... should find that the probability that the hypothesis is correct is so high that the ..probability level is of..about 0.001 per cent. If we deny that there is an a priori reason for the hypothesis, then we...can accept the existence of the fathom for the diameter and the yard for the radius with complete confidence.'

Enter the Megalithic Yard

In 1967, Thom threw down the gauntlet. On page 36 of *Megalithic Sites in Britain*, two short and well thought out sentences lit the fuse to 'a well

Chapter Four - The Quest for the Megalithic Yard

Robert L Merritt, an Ohio Lawyer associated with Case Western University, in Cleveland, helped to fund Thom's later surveys. Shown above is the survey team at the Fairlawn Hotel, Amesbury, during the 1973 Stonehenge survey. From the left, Ethan Merritt, Len Smith (Keeper at Stonehenge), Archie Thom, Alexander Thom, Prof. Hans Motz, Archie's wife, Margaret and Bob Merritt. Not shown is the photographer, Prof. Richard Atkinson, whose glasses remain on the table in the foreground.

constructed parcel-bomb delivered through the letter-box of the archaeological establishment.'

> 'We first demonstrate that there is a presumption amounting to a certainty that a definite unit was used in setting out these rings. It is proposed to call this the Megalithic yard (MY).... It will appear that the Megalithic yard is 2.72 ft.'

The Megalithic yard, the unit of length used by those enigmatic circle builders, had been discovered, measured and named - by Alexander Thom. QED. But it was not to be QED, neither in the immediate wake of Thom's pronouncements, nor during the remainder of his active life, nor thereafter. The megalithic metrology suggested by Thom was to be queried, challenged, criticised, sneered at and finally ignored in a more or less continuous process from the mid 1950s until the present time.

High Noon at the Royal Society

So, where was any rational discussion going on? Well, in one instance academia set up a conference in order to try to sort out the matter of the prehistoric astronomy and the Megalithic yard once and for all. Was Thom a heretic or a prophet? The star of the show was to be Professor David George Kendall, a ferociously competent mathematician and then head of the Statistical Laboratory at Cambridge. He had been brought in to analyse Thom's statistical methods at a two-day symposium organised jointly by the *Royal Society* and the

British Academy, and held in London on the 7th and 8th December 1972. He was probably Britain's most able statistician at the time!

Entitled *The Place of Astronomy in the Ancient World*, Kendall, then aged 54, immediately showed that he had done his homework on the situation facing him, and shrewdly began his lecture by pointing out the polarity surrounding Thom's work - in his words, people either took Thom's theories as "overwhelmingly convincing" or rejected them as "utterly preposterous." But he had also done his homework on the data set - and more. Using new and powerful statistical techniques, he demonstrated to his audience that Thom's diameter quantum of 5.44 feet rose up above the sea of random noise produced by his statistical experiment. He termed this peak 'Mount Thom' and told his audience that in the Monte Carlo experiment, where 200 independent (random) values for the quantum were run through the computer program designed to detect a quantum:-

> 'Mount Thom, like Mount Ararat, was submerged only once, and even then, only just.'

He went on to say that,

> 'even if we throw away the English and Welsh data we still find that 'Mount Thom' demands to be taken seriously'

In his concluding remarks, Kendall had this to say,

> ' If the audience were to put a pistol to my head and demand an answer to the question: 'a quantum - yes or no?', then I should plead for more observations. A significance level of 1% is normally regarded as a strong recommendation that the experiment be repeated on a larger scale, this being preceded perhaps by a cautious letter to Nature.
>
> If the audience were to put the question somewhat differently, and say, 'does the analysis of the available data justify the expenditure of public monies on a costly and sophisticated aerial re-survey of the circular sites?', then I think few would disagree with my affirmative reply'.

Here the problem of a limited sample size became only too apparent. To apply statistical techniques in this kind of experiment would normally demand thousands of items of sample data. It took Thom over 30 years to amass his sample data of 169 stone rings. To date no one has applied to re-survey or add to Thom's original data bank.

Whatever, Kendall had pointed out that the quantum was detectable and how it behaved under various experimental techniques. Thom must have returned to *The Hill* a happy man following that symposium, leaving a few red faces behind in his wake. The debate about whether or not the Megalithic fathom (5.44 feet) and hence the Megalithic Yard (2.72 feet) was the length Thom had found it to be and whether or not the builders of megalithic rings had employed it should now have been over. It was a done deal. Anyone having doubts had been invited by Kendall, politely, to go out and acquire some more data.

The Tipping Point

In a recent (2006) conversation with Euan MacKie, who had also presented a paper at the event, he told me that,

> "There was a very positive and constructive atmosphere at the venue. It felt like some kind of pivotal point had been reached. Of course it was before everything turned nasty with regard to Thom and archaeoastronomy in general. It was just about the same time that Glyn Daniel began to bias some of his editorials in Antiquity against Thom."

With Kendall's independent assessment of Thom's data, the top three statisticians in the UK at the time had all given a green light to the existence of the megalithic fathom/yard as the unit invoked in the construction of stone rings. There was no Atlantis scenario here, Thom never mentioned any Golden Age nor made any references to extra-terrestrial intervention. In fact Thom rarely speculated at all, his conclusions were always evidence based. He had simply revealed that whoever made all those stone rings was, to a significant level of probability, using the same unit of length to a very high accuracy for about a millennium and a half, all over northwestern Europe. His critics would say, "How could this be?", yet to those that still doubted Thom's quantum, Kendall had demonstrated, in front of many learned archaeologists, mathematicians, astronomers and scientists that,

> 'The hypothesis of a smooth, non-quantal distribution of circle diameters (for the Scottish, English and Welsh true circles - author), is thus rejected at the 1% level.

Surely this time it was QED?

To the author's knowledge, no subsequent rigorous statistical analysis has overturned Kendall's pronouncements. And since 1972, more evidence has been accruing for the Megalithic yard, of which the most recent material is covered in chapter seven. Euan MacKie discovered that the Megalithic yard had lingered on in the building of Iron Age Brochs. Another researcher, P.R.Freeman, wrote a paper in 1976 for the *Journal of the Royal Statistical Society* entitled *'A Bayesian analysis of the megalithic yard'*. Using this technique Freeman's main conclusion was, like Kendall's, that the Scottish sites do reveal the use of Thom's quantum. He was not so happy about the 'English' data. The use of Bayesian statistics has formed part of other threads weaving through the Thom story following his death in 1985.

From these submitted papers and later alternative statistical examinations, the circles are seen no longer as a crude by-product of a primitive tribes-people. Childe's refuted 'neolithic science' was a fact - the circles *were* accurately measured out - but how? Kendall had dismissed as 'an irrelevance' how the circles were measured out, perhaps seeing this as beyond his remit, and instead confidently asserted that, *'the primary question is not how measurements were made, but whether they were made.'* This is what he had been employed to establish and, according to all the considerable skills he could muster, there emerged a high probability that the measurements were indeed made.

Increasing Antagonism from *Antiquity*

It is very revealing to study the changing mood within archaeology throughout this decade, through that most obvious barometer of the profession, the Journal *Antiquity*. Its Editor throughout this turbulent period was Glyn Daniel, and a read through his editorials and the occasional published letter shows an increasingly hostile attitude to all things Thomian. A few examples of Glyn Daniel's increasing scepticism are given below, clearly reflecting and perhaps even driving this change of mood. This evolution starts very pro-Thom with the Halloween edition of 1970 (Vol. 44),

> *'the Editor is just getting on his broomstick to fly to the great alignments at Carnac to meet there Professor Alexander Thom who has done so much to make us think seriously about the mathematical and astronomical knowledge of the prehistoric inhabitants of north-western Europe. Serious, informed thinking on these matters is what we want, not bats, ghosts and flying saucers.'*

By 1978, a William Irvin Thompson wrote an article on megalithic astronomy in a new and very popular magazine called *Quest*. Atkinson bought a copy and wrote to Daniel via *Antiquity* (1978, Vol. 52),

> *'..you are set up as the great big fuddy-duddy of blind orthodoxy, and I as another such who suffered a lightning conversion to the new Thomian on the road to Stonehenge.. Here are some sentences from it:*
>
>> *'Glyn Daniel is very like the snobbish priest who refused to look through Galileo's telescope because he knew what the world was like... It's a marvellous irony that Daniel has become one of the stodgy old cranks he himself debunked in his The Idea of Prehistory... Daniel refused to change his mind. No doubt his colleagues reassure him over glasses of sherry that his views will prevail over any of the tommy rot argued in the popular press.''*

Daniels, who was man enough to print this bellicose rant, responds thus,

> *'He might better heed the example of Professor Atkinson, another prince of the church of orthodox archaeology, who, though known to fume against the lunatic fringe in the pages of the London Times Literary Supplement, has had the courage to publish a recantation concerning Professor Thom.'*

By 1978, the kid gloves were off and some prime examples of tribal warfare began to widen the chasm between the orthodoxy and the new kids on the

Chapter Four - The Quest for the Megalithic Yard

block. Thom had always been right in the crossfire, but now so too was Daniel. His editorials became increasingly dismissive of archaeoastronomy, as this example from 1980 (Vol. 54), illustrates,

> 'Dr Valera's Preface (to a revised edition of Antiquities of the Irish Countryside, by Sean P. O'Riordain) is short and succinct, but in his last paragraph he has something of great importance to say that is new, and deals fairly and clearly with that unsatisfactory aspect of modern archaeology which is called astro-archaeology or archaeo-astronomy.'

And by Vol. 55 (1981), the opposition to archaeoastronomy appears to have become complete. Referring to 'all this mystical taradiddle' in Martin Brennan's 8-year research programme on megalithic art, later to become written up in his notoriously controversial book, *The Stars and the Stones* (Thames & Hudson, 1983), Daniel writes,

> 'These are interesting ideas, although they smell of the Thomery that produced megalithic inches, yards and fathoms. ... We have no doubt where in this, as in so many matters of archaeological interpretation, the sensible readers of this journal will look for the truth as it appears to us in the last quarter of this century.'

In his editorial in Vol. 56 (1982), Daniel again warms to this theme,

> 'One of the mistakes, in our view, is the way in which so many people jumped on the archaeo-astronomical bandwagon. We have been described, kindly, as sceptical in these matters. We may have been politely dubious in what we wrote, but neither Alexander Thom nor his associates have ever really had the slightest doubt that we always thought their theories were mistaken.' ... When the Editor was Professor of Archaeology at Cambridge he got Thom to lecture to his students and after dinner Thom confessed that he was a worried man. "Daniel", he said, "if what I believe is true, the neolithic inhabitants of Britain knew the theory of geometry long before Pythagoras."
>
> We think they did not. ... It seems to us that what has happened in the last ten years or so is that we have passed through a curious phase in the history of archaeology - a phase in which some very reputable archaeologists and scientists and some less qualified journalists and popular writers, and many members of the general public, have shown that they wanted to believe in wise, learned men in western Europe in the third and fourth millennia BC - men who could read the skies as well as build great stone monuments.
>
> It is our view that when someone comes to write the history of archaeological thought in the second half of the twentieth century they will find the astro-archaeological episode on a par with that of the Egyptocentric hyperdiffusionist episode associated with Elliot Smith and Perry that spanned the years from 1911... ... And let us not forget, 70 years after The Ancient Egyptians, that, at first, Gordon Childe and Daryll Forde thought vary favourably of the Givers of Life and the Children of the

- 125 -

> Sun. ... Fleure in Wales, Peake on the Berkshire Downs, Childe in the library of the Royal Anthropological Institute, and Forde in California were all writing at the same time and coming to the same answers - quite wrong as we now know them to be, but a far more cogent and useful model than Elliot Smith had proposed...''

Whatever else this florid and revealing remark may say about the failings of archaeological models, Daniel's *volte face* since the heady days of the *Chronicle* documentary now becomes plainly evident - he had distanced himself entirely from Thom, undoubtedly taking mainstream archaeology with him. And a quarter of a century later, it is almost as though Thom never existed.

An Alternative Origin for the Megalithic Yard?

During the 1970s, *Antiquity* also published some interesting correspondence on the Megalithic measures. Dr Max Hammerton, of the *Medical Research Council* (Applied Psychology), at the University of Cambridge, wrote a refreshingly clear take on the possible source of the Megalithic fathom, a commentary coming at the problem from a totally different discipline. Concerning Thom's evidence and statistical analysis on the Megalithic fathom, he wrote,

> 'If we accept his evidence - as, it seems to me, we must - it becomes of interest to ask a further question, not about populations of units, but about specific instances. This is: what was the the actual value of the unit employed at each circle? Fortunately Thom himself (1967) has presented the data from which this may be answered. If we consult his table 5.1, we see that the best value of the site unit at 145 sites can be derived very easily; for, (using his nomenclature) the value we want is simply y/m_2.

> Doing the arithmetic yields a set of values whose mean is 65.6 in. with a standard deviation of 2.98 in. The <u>range</u>, however, is considerable, being from 57.8 in. to 81.6 in.; and even if we neglect the few extreme values (which we should not) there is still a range of over a foot.

> Thom has suggested (1967,43) that there was a 'standard fathom', of which copies were sent to the several construction sites.

> As an alternative I would offer the following suggestions: (i) There was no 'megalithic standard fathom'; but (ii) that the site engineer (priest?) in charge of the construction of each monument used as a unit <u>his own height</u>, or that of some local dignitary.

> On this alternative hypothesis we would predict (a) that the mean site unit would be a few inches less that the mean height of a modern population, (b) that the standard deviation would be much the same as for the height of a modern population, (c) that statistical analysis would peak sharply around the then population mean, (d) measurements within an individual site should display very little variability, (e) that there would be little if any variation over the time and space in which the monuments were built, and (f) that the range of site units would be comparable to the range of modern population heights.

Chapter Four - The Quest for the Megalithic Yard

Professor Thom has already domonstrated (c), (d) and (e). Predictions (a), (b) and (f) are confirmed by Morgan et al (Human Engineering guide to Equipment Design, New York, 1963) who give, for a population of American male college graduates, a mean of 68.8 in., a standard deviation of 2.64 in. and a 98% range (i.e. omitting the 1% extrema) of 12.4 in.

I submit, then, that this alternative satisfies the statistical properties of the circles as well as, and the range of values distinctly better than, Professor Thom's. Also, although this is necessarily a subjective judgement, it seems more sheerly credible. Indeed it appears to me so obvious that I am not a little astonished to learn (G. Daniel, pers. comm., 1971) that it has not previously been made.'

Is this the seemingly blindingly obvious solution as to how the standard length for the Megalithic yard was both maintained, transported and readily available throughout the territory in which the megaliths were erected? Was the unit enshrined in flesh and bones as the mean height of the Neolithic and Bronze Age population? Perhaps not, yet this obvious pointer to a fascinating anthropological research programme was evidently never taken up, and no answers to these two questions have ever been forthcoming. Hammerton implied it could answer a raft of unresolved issues relating to the Thom data without diminishing by one jot his assertions that these units were applied at site after site, nor lessening the value of the statistical analyses.

The Megalithic Yard in Modern Archaeology

If the issue that Thom endeavoured to settle once and for all remained decidedly unsettled in the 60s, it remains true that to mention the Megalithic yard today within archaeological papers, essays and textbooks more or less condemns the aspiring younger archaeologist to scorn and ridicule. As one archaeologist reminded me, 'it is a non-promotable offence.' While Professor John North has 'come out', he writes from a high pinnacle within the profession and, perhaps more importantly, lives and works in Denmark. Keith Critchlow has worked inspiringly with the Megalithic yard and Thom's geometry, but he is essentially an architect, with no direct influence on archaeology. Dr Aubrey Burl, a friend of the Thoms, retained an open mind and has taken the not inconsiderable time and effort required to understand the evidence. Burl informed Thom when his own survey work had suggested use of the Megalithic yard. Clive Ruggles edited out mention of the Megalithic yard from at least one important paper (about the Bush Barrow lozenge), written in part by Archie Thom. And so it has gone on..and on.

An astonishing and confidently delivered assertion - that the builders of British stone rings were all using the same accurate unit of length to define their monuments - had been placed in front of prehistorians. This exposed them, as a few years previously had the radiocarbon dating misalignment, to further challenging misalignment between the archaeological record of this period of human development and the objective facts arrayed before them - the *Thomist paradox*, in fact. As Atkinson stated, this was not at all comfortable to those charged with informing us what we are to believe about ancient history, or those archaeologists who had furthered their careers using the traditional model of human development, where all culture was Egyptian, Greek and Roman and where Europe was filled with barbarians until, depending on where one learned history, either the Celts or the Romans arrived. This comfortable picture of our 'progress' found many historians rudely awakened by Thom's assertions and needing to rethink just what exactly defined 'civilisation' - geometry and metrology had not previously been very high on the list in prehistoric Europe.

Thom had this to say on the matter (*MSIB*, p43),

> ' .. it is not possible to detect by statistical examination any difference between the values determined from the English and Scottish circles. There must have been a headquarters from which standard rods were sent out but whether this was in these islands or on the Continent the present investigation cannot determine. The length of the rods in Scotland cannot have differed from that in England by more than 0.03 inches or the difference would have shown up (in Table 5.5). If each small community had obtained the length by copying the rod of its neighbour to the south the accumulated error would have been much greater than this'.

This bold statement would not have been written without sufficient evidence, analysis and forethought. Thom was no New Age sensationalist, as his written works and lectures demonstrated. He provided evidence, from which he drew sensible conclusions, uninfluenced by the archaeological paradigm fashionable at the time. But this was not enough - he and his work increasingly began to become linked with the outer fringes of mainstream archaeology.

The truth is that Thom's findings did attract attention from within some important sections of archaeology, but that there was no model in which to secure them. In contrast, the New Age movement had an enormous capacity to propose models in which they could pour Thom's findings, which were proving widely popular within the movement. The entire 'earth mysteries' tribe was right behind any evidence that supported a Druid-styled 'Pythagorean' culture in ancient Britain - you bet! But as Dr John Wood commented in his Thom-friendly, *Sun, Moon and Standing Stones* (Oxford, 1980), 'Views based on emotional needs are not changed by rational discussion'. Although Wood's remark was specifically aimed at the 'loony fringe', this short and disparaging sentence could equally well have been applied to those academics who rejected Thom's researches *in lieu* of adequately understanding them.

For years, archaeologists have ignored or been dismissive of the 'earth mysteries' school of thought, the Pagan/Druid version of our past, and indeed anyone or any school which has put forth evidence concerning ancient cultures suggesting that great knowledge was available in the far distant past. And it is indeed true that the outer fringes of this subject are truly a very strange place to venture. The increasing popularity of television programmes and books which promise a glimpse of Atlantis, the whiff of a Golden Age or the slightest sniff of a Super-civilisation demonstrate a rising public interest in such matters, much to the chagrin of many archaeologists, who are therefore often delighted to be employed in the role of wheeled-in 'experts' to shoot down in flames anyone who has written a best selling book within this *genre* without providing adequate 'proof'. "Bring us proof, an artefact or some data!" cry these 'experts', "Repeatable data!", they add. But this is *precisely* what Alex Thom did over thirty years ago and his data and work was not picked up then and has been almost totally ignored since.

Proof as *Chimera*

Such a demand for proof wastes much time, for absolute proof is a *chimera*. Indeed, statistics deals only with *probabilities*, never proof, leaving the decision as to whether a theory or hypothesis is valid to the experience and wisdom of the person who studies the way the data has been gathered, and the nature of the statistical evidence and analysis. The great French mathematician Laplace put this rather well,

> *'We see that the theory of probability is at bottom only common sense reduced to calculation; it makes us appreciate with exactitude what reasonable minds feel by a sort of instinct, often without being able to give account for it... It is remarkable that this science, which originated in the consideration of games of chance, should have become the most important object of human knowledge... The most important questions of life are, for the most part, really only problems of probability.'*

Statistical programmes will thus always fail to furnish proof absolute of the existence of either the Megalithic yard, Atlantis or cometary catastrophe in prehistory, and therefore statistical material is only useful when the complete evidential basis for it is understood. It is far more useful to look at how the data evidence fits the model being proposed. In 1967, Thom's model did not fit the model then in vogue - he was backing a losing horse.

SUMMARY

The Megalithic yard provided the entry point from which Thom was able to enter into a new dimension regarding the capabilities of the people who built the megaliths. He was the first person to have done this, a true pioneer. His methodology was severely criticised right from the date of the very first publications announcing his results, despite two of the leading British statisticians of the day having designed the methodology of the statistical 'run'. Later a third statistician, one of the greatest mathematicians of the twentieth century, redesigned the statistics in order to then be able to affirm at the Royal Society the value of Thom's work in suggesting the length used by the circle builders. Despite this, and the repeated presence of this unit at site after measured site following Thom's initial data analysis, by Thom and others, the Megalithic yard is today ignored by prehistorians as a spurious unit of length.

Modern methodology in archaeology began in Victorian times with Flinders Petrie. He was a pioneer in the use of metrological analysis regarding it as an essential component of archaeological investigation. And it is certainly true that the input from other disciplines than archaeology has been consistently valuable in enlarging our knowledge of the megalith builders, as Aubrey Burl observed in *Records in Stone*, page 176,

> *'It is strange how rarely advances in stone circle research have been made by an archaeologist. .. Most of the discoveries about the rings have been made by non-archaeologists, surveyors, engineers, clerics, astronomers, solicitors, from the seventeenth century onwards, an illustrious pageant of true amateurs amongst whom Alexander Thom occupies an honourable place.'*

Dr Aubrey Burl admiring the huge outer ring at Avebury. Burl collaborated with the Thoms in the now rare book, *'Megalithic Rings'* (BAR, 1980). (*photograph supplied to the author by Dr Burl*).

Burl's comment suggests that a more multi-disciplined approach would benefit prehistoric research. Apart from clerics and solicitors, the professions mentioned above derive from that component of the Liberal Arts education package, known as the *Quadrivium*. This component includes astronomy, mathematics, and geometry (only harmony is missing from the list). Thom was thus ideally qualified to make 'discoveries about the rings'!

Thom saw right into a crucial aspect of the thinking processes of the circle builders. But without the discovery of the Megalithic yard the intricate geometries of the non-circular rings described in the following chapter would never have fallen into place. Whilst the circles still remained mysterious, they began to reveal their art to Thom; he had glimpsed an aspect of prehistoric life in Britain that no one in recent epochs had seen or believed possible.

CHAPTER FIVE

Megalithic Designs

The shapes which megalithic people constructed on moor and fell included an astonishing range of geometrical designs, from simple circles to complex multiple arc rings, sometimes of great size. The circles themselves formed part of this legacy and were often built as precision devices. They are not failed or 'Friday afternoon' circles. According to Aubrey Burl, referring to 'the neglected aspects of shape, design and orientation',

> *'These had been regarded, quite deliberately, by a majority of archaeologists as illusion fostered by romantics who had no understanding of the realities of prehistoric existence.'*

As Dr Burl is unarguably the foremost living expert on the archaeology of stone rings, his preface to the publication of all Thom's plans (*Megalithic Rings*, BAR 1980) provides a rare supportive comment as to their value,

> *'(Thom's) standards of planning have been far higher than those of the average archaeologist and certainly superior to most of the 19th century antiquarians whose plans of circles were often inaccurate and slipshod. It has been the misfortune of those interested in megalithic rings that often only such inexact plans have been available. ... Alexander Thom's plans .. must be regarded as the finest and largest collection of stone circle plans ever assembled by an individual.'*

> *'His work has compelled other students to consider the implications of his data. No longer is it possible to dismiss a 'circle' as devoid of any clues as to its function simply because excavation has produced nothing tangible. Even without artefacts or dating evidence a ring possesses shape and design, and it was Thom who made archaeologists think about such matters.'*

The value of having all Thom's prolific data bank and survey plans provided in this publication arrived too late to catch the initial interest in the geometry and metrology revealed by Thom's books. This sea-change can even be seen in Burl's own published output since 1980. While Burl recommended to the archaeological profession that it takes the geometry of Thom's work seriously, in his indispensable *A Guide to the Stone Circles of Britain, Ireland and Brittany* (Yale), and many other fine publications, Dr Burl curiously gives scant mention to Thom's geometries, or their metrological implications.

Precision Circles or Roughly Shaped Ovals?

What are these geometries which were recognised yet now ignored? A short answer to this question is that the non-circular shapes are comprised of arcs from radii defined by rods or ropes and measured from pegs intelligently placed. Estimating the geometry of a ring armed only with a cloth tape will never reveal the true centres for these arcs, nor will it offer any indication of the accuracy with which the ring had been planned, aligned and constructed. If, as Thom claimed, the rings were precision artefacts, then that precision can only be revealed by surveying them to an equal standard of precision.

Thom's plans revealed that about two-thirds of rings were indeed built as truly circular. The rest were not, and demonstrated a fascination for designs utilising multiple radii and struck arcs often originating from the perimeter of an originally marked out circle that was used as a guide but never built as a stone monument. Thom also discovered geometries that were often defined by right angled triangles (usually 'Pythagorean' - triangles with integer or whole number sides in Megalithic yards, sometimes as multiples or submultiples of MY). He discovered that the builders preferred to produce an integer circumference for their finished designs, and that they often used the Megalithic rod (2.5 MY) as their preferred unit by which to achieve this goal. Stones were almost always centrally placed to the intended geometry. All these things have, at various times and by various critics, been refuted, often with little or no evidence.

Thom assumed that the best of the true circles were either measured by rods to the intended perimeter starting from the centre, or staked out from a central peg by walking a rope radius around the resulting circumference. Even Thom's fiercest critics, Barnatt and Moir, in *Stone Circles and Megalithic Mathematics*, (*Proceedings of the Prehistoric Society* 50:Dec 1984) having suggested that, *'the majority of stone circles are laid out by eye to appear circular.'*, agreed that *'...in southern England and perhaps northeastern Scotland there is evidence that some stone rings were designed with more care.'*

The first part of this quotation is a *laissez-faire* comment that might have held some conviction if backed up by the authors' attempting to construct, by eye alone, circular rings which possessed, even to a small degree, the precision evidenced within most of Thom's survey plans. It is a matter of fact that all circles appear oval or elliptical when observed from the immediate location and

Chapter Five - Megalithic Designs

experience confirms quite readily that attempting to construct a circle by eye will always result in irregular oval or elliptical shapes. As a general rule, circles produced in this way will appear wholly inauthentic in comparison to their Neolithic and Bronze Age cousins and 'replicas' often look quite awful.

Taking a theodolite and steel tapes and surveying a ring will quite quickly reveal dimensions of Neolithic circle building that Barnett and Moir avoid. It is the purpose of this chapter to demonstrate that many aspects of the design and construction of stone rings support a much higher level of technological and geometrical ability. Even Barnatt and Moir go on to mention,

> '18 circles for which we believe peg and rope construction was used'

Consensus that the use of a rope and peg was known and practised by at least some of the circle builders provides an entry point into their study here.

Were the Circles Paced Out?

Although it has been postulated that the circles might have been produced by pacing out from the centre, practical attempts to approach the accuracy evident from theodolite surveys of several notable circles have demonstrated, to several archaeologists and to this writer, that this is a highly improbable hypothesis. Thom's statistical evidence confirmed this to be the case and Thom himself comments that, because the value of σ (the standard deviation - a measure of the precision achieved in marking out the circle) is almost independent of the size of the circle,

> 'If..the measuring appliance were in itself crude, then σ might be proportional to m (the diameter - author's addition) or would at least increase with m. This would happen if distances were obtained by pacing.'

Such is not what Thom measured. Had pacing been the preferred method for defining the radii, then the inaccuracies inherent in this method would accumulate as the size of the finished circle increased. Such was not found to be the case, and later, in *MSIB*, he writes,

> 'It will be seen how far wrong it would be to take σ proportional to the diameter.'

Regarding Thom's surveys and resulting plans we may also agree with Aubrey Burl, in his *Antiquity* review (November 1981, p 238) of Thom's *Megalithic Remains in Britain and Brittany*, that his surveys represent,

> 'masterpieces of detailed accuracy...will remain standard references for decades.'

Another critic of Thom's conclusions is Douglas Heggie. In *Megalithic Science* (Thames and Hudson, 1981), p 82, he concedes that,

> 'Thom's classification of the shapes of different sites is a useful one'

Having thus established a loose consensus concerning the accuracy of the surveys of the resulting plans and that the classification of the shapes is 'useful', we can now proceed to look at what Thom discovered concerning Megalithic geometry.

There are some general guide rules which form a starting basis for any study of the enigmatic rings and circles of northwestern Europe.

Six General Rules about Megalithic Geometry

(i). There is a consistency of design throughout the European megalithic catalogue and chronology. 'Type I' eggs in Brittany have identical geometries to ones found in Scotland. Early examples take the same geometry as later ones.

(ii). The marking out or staking of the site involved the Megalithic yard and/or rod (2.5 MY or 6.8 ft).

(iii). The forming triangles are regularly dimensioned with integer values of the Megalithic yard or rod, as are the circumferences of the resulting geometries. When the diameter and circumference were irreconcilable, adjustment was made to the diameter so that the circumference became closer to an integer value of Megalithic rods. The integer value for the diameter was sacrificed by lengthening or shortening it in order to maintain an integral perimeter length, normally in megalithic rods.

(iv). The stones are almost always placed with their centres on the line of the staked out geometry. Slab sided stones are normally found with their longer sides parallel to the perimeter. Whilst their spacing around the perimeter often appears random, their radial spacing - the distance of each stone from the centre of the design - was originally accurate to a predetermined marked-out geometry.

(v). There is little apparent connection between the size of a ring and size of the stones placed around it. Huge rings may be formed from small stones and vice versa.

(vi). Stones are rarely placed diametrically opposite each other.

The Merry Maidens circle (*shown opposite*) in Cornwall demonstrates many of these rules to good effect. Self evidently, its precision could not be attained by placing the 19 stones by eye, a rope (or rods) and peg were clearly employed. The perimeter is integral in Megalithic rods (36 MR). Cornwall sports several other circles containing 19 stones, a number suggestive of the nineteen year repeat cycle of the sun and moon - the metonic cycle.

Chapter Five - Megalithic Designs

THE GEOMETRIES OF STONE RINGS

To support this section it is recommended that the reader finds a relatively unpopulated section of beach or a flat field in order to emulate the geometries of our ancestors. A collection of plastic tent pegs, various lengths of non-elastic rope marked in Megalithic yard lengths and some small stakes, about half a Megalithic yard in length should be prepared, along with a lump hammer, compass, notebook, pocket calculator and a surveyor's tape (or metal tape). The geometry and two or three surviving examples of each main type of ring are illustrated in this chapter to enable the reader to grasp the design, extent and consistency of megalithic design.

ONE FOCUS - THE CIRCLE

To lay out a simple circle, stake a central point and place a rope loop around the stake, and then walk the circumference whilst placing tent pegs, pebbles, sawdust, or even megaliths around it. The finished perimeter will not appear circular from ground level, but elliptical or oval, whereby it is unsurprising that many true circles have been described in the archaeological literature as 'ovals' and 'ovoids'. Without a proper survey it is impossible to accurately perceive the shape, or its precision, nor is it an easy task to determine the centre once the peg or stake used to mark it has been removed.

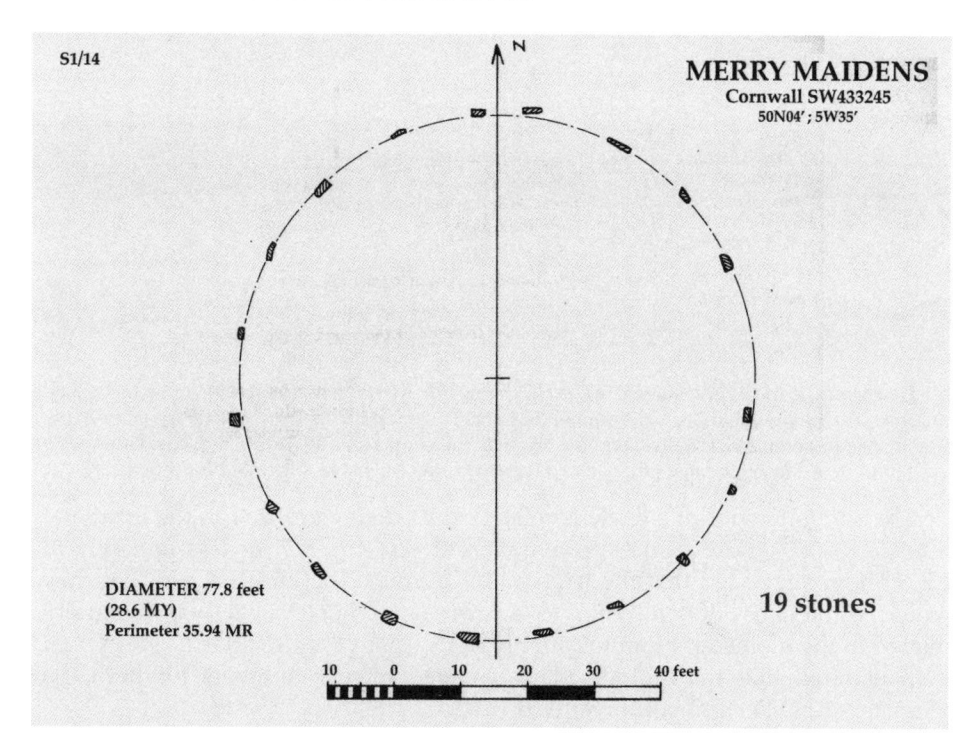

S1/14

MERRY MAIDENS
Cornwall SW433245
50N04'; 5W35'

DIAMETER 77.8 feet
(28.6 MY)
Perimeter 35.94 MR

19 stones

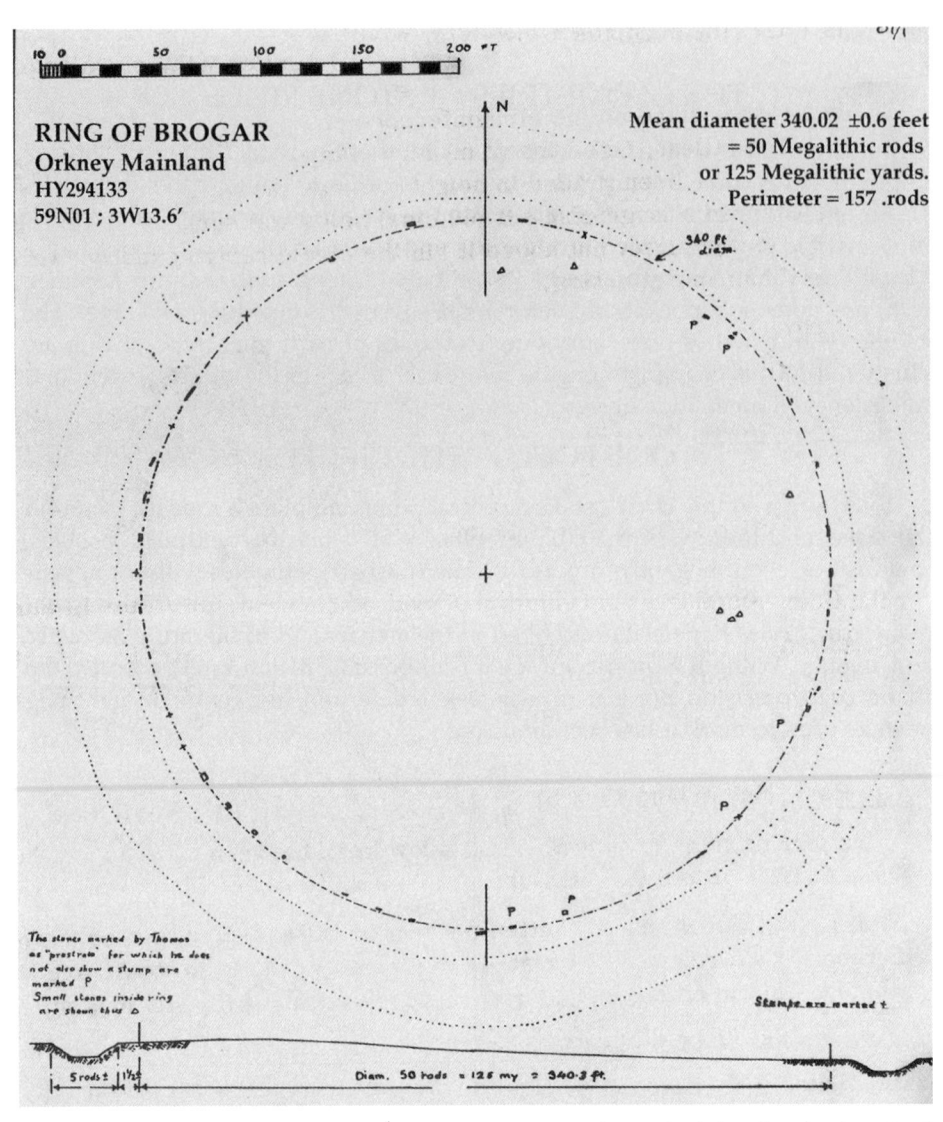

RING OF BROGAR
Orkney Mainland
HY294133
59N01 ; 3W13.6'

Mean diameter 340.02 ±0.6 feet
= 50 Megalithic rods
or 125 Megalithic yards.
Perimeter = 157 .rods

The Brogar ring is the largest stone circle in Scotland, and is only matched elsewhere by the ruined inner two circles at Avebury, which contained 29 and 27 stones. Erected within a henge monument, Brogar resembles the Aubrey circle and the original bluestone circle at Stonehenge. This latter circle was found by Atkinson to have originally contained 60 stones, just as suggested for Brogar.

The circumference of a circle is related to its diameter through the irrational number *pi* (π), whose value approximates closely to 22/7, or less precisely to 25/8 Thom suggested that the irrational π troubled the builders and that they would sometimes 'flatten' rings to achieve a perimeter that was integrally related to the diameter. From his survey at the giant Brogar circle (*above*) Thom demonstrated that the builders had achieved integer numbers for both the diameter (125 MY) and perimeter (157 MR).

TWO FOCI - THE ELLIPSE

To make an ellipse, two stakes are placed along a line which will define the major axis of the finished ellipse. With a loop of rope as used above, and placed over both stakes, the walking procedure is repeated, whence the ellipse perimeter is duly traced out. Thom showed that the right-triangle formed when the loop is perpendicular to the major axis line was often of whole numbers of Megalithic yards or rods, and that the circumference of the finished ellipse was an integer value of Megalithic rods.

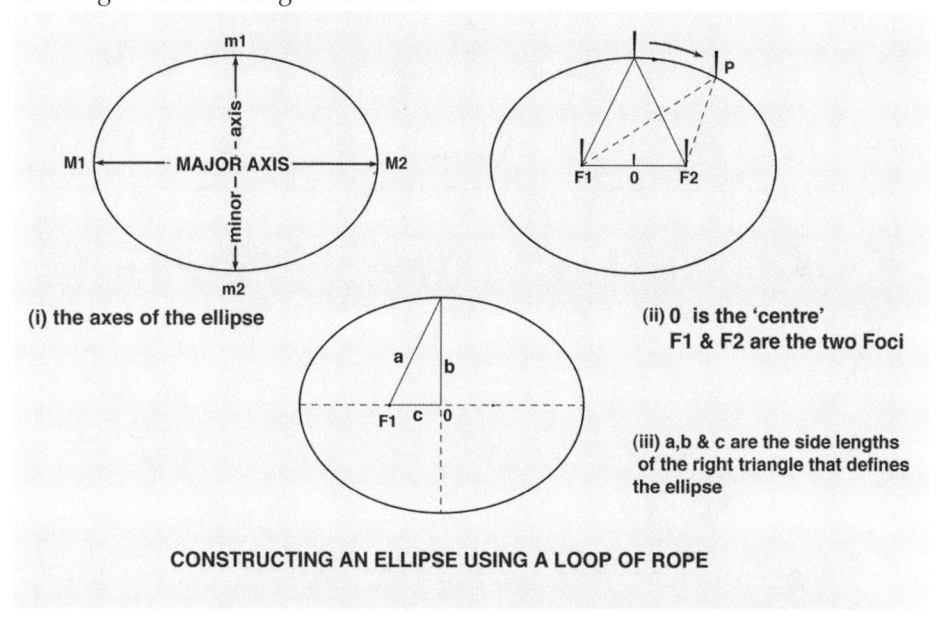

(i) the axes of the ellipse

(ii) 0 is the 'centre'
F1 & F2 are the two Foci

(iii) a,b & c are the side lengths of the right triangle that defines the ellipse

CONSTRUCTING AN ELLIPSE USING A LOOP OF ROPE

The 'flattening' of an ellipse is called its eccentricity (e), and is mathematically fixed by the ratio F2 - F1/M2 - M1, also 2c/2a. As the eccentricity gets smaller and smaller the ellipse more and more resembles a circle.

An ellipse is produced as suggested by the earlier circle construction, only now the rope is looped around the two focal pegs, F1 and F2. Megalithic ellipses rarely show a high degree of eccentricity, and without an accurate survey are usually indistinguishable from circles. Thom found that their hidden internal geometry nearly always implied a right-angled triangle with integer or very near integer lengths in Megalithic yards, or submultiples thereof. To get the perimeter integral as well, in units of Megalithic rods faced the builders with quite a challenge. They appear to have risen to the task, and in the later (1974) edition of *MSIB*, Thom lists a, b and c, together with the perimeter for 35 examples of megalithic ellipses (*see also the histogram on page 139*). The residual errors are given for each ellipse, and only five show residuals between 0.3 and 0.7 MR, the remainder adhere closely to the integer value.

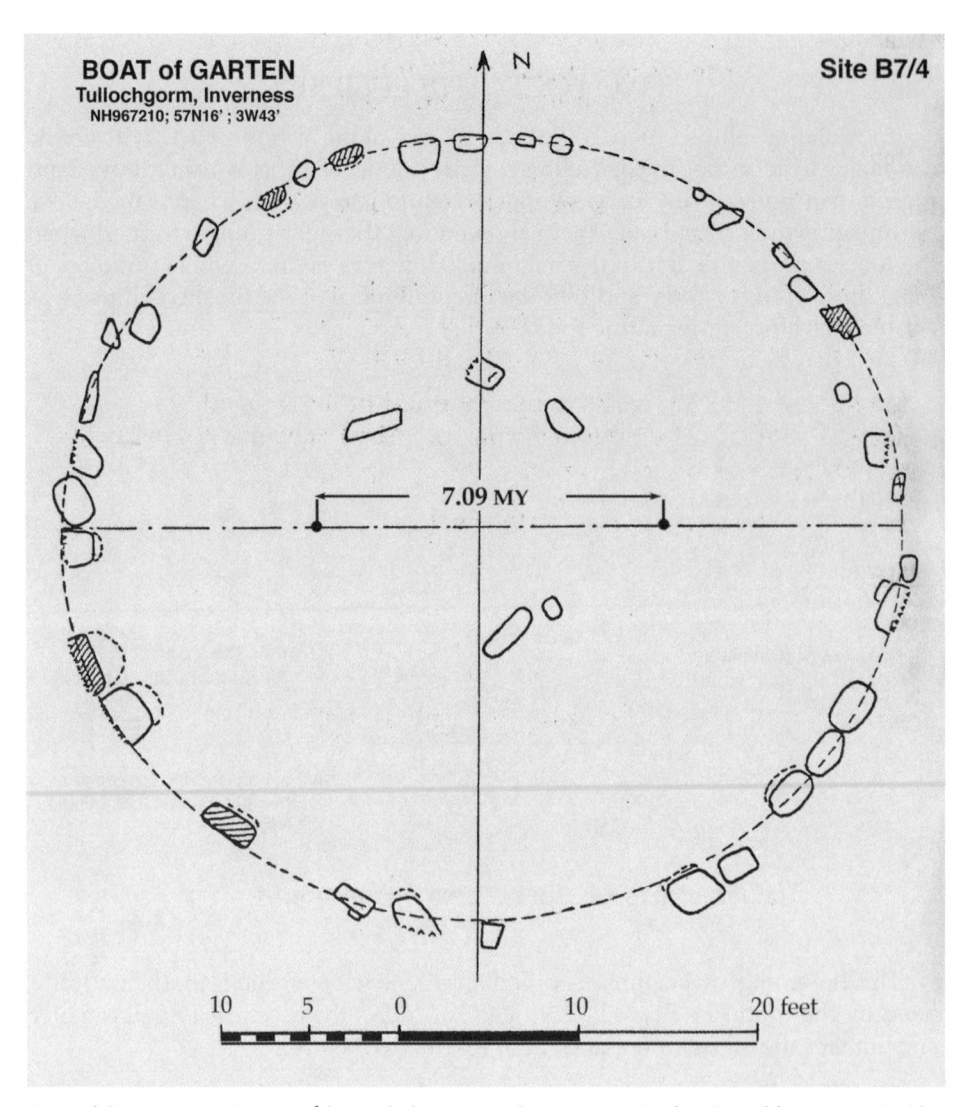

BOAT of GARTEN
Tullochgorm, Inverness
NH967210; 57N16'; 3W43'

Site B7/4

7.09 MY

10 5 0 10 20 feet

Boat of Garten comprises roughly graded stones and was categorised as 'possibly a ring-cairn' by Burl, who also mentions that the site 'has been much robbed'. A 4MY (3.3 m) diameter central area was identified by Burl suggesting that the monument was originally more complex. The outer ellipse has a perimeter of 21.1 Megalithic rods (52.64 MY).

    The ellipse at Daviot (B7/5, *opposite left*) has an 'inner' right-angled triangle that is Pythagorean, being 12, 35, 37 in units of half Megalithic yards. Similar in size to Boat of Garten, both sites have the minor axis of the ellipse aligned exactly north-south. To achieve this orientation required that the builders possessed and were incorporating astronomical knowledge into their monuments. The well preserved northerly section of the ellipse at Sands of Forvie (B1/27, *opposite right*) comprises slab-sided stones aligned along the perimeter confirming Thom's geometry. The perimeter is integral at 20 megalithic rods (50MY).

Chapter Five - Megalithic Designs

Thom noted that normally the builders had used a subdivision of the megalithic yard into halves and sometimes quarters. For Sands of Forvie he found they used eighths, subdividing a further time. Thom suggests that this subdivision *'was done here to achieve a perimeter of 50 MYs, actually 50.08'*. At Blackhill of Drachlaw (B1/24) they also used eighths, and the perimeter is 30 MY. For both ellipses the triangle is almost perfectly Pythagorean, being 48, 123, 132.03 for Forvie and 41, 71, 81.98 for Drachlaw. Major Prain's survey of Stanton Drew had suggested that two of the circles there were in fact ellipses. Thom later confirmed these to both be based on the 5, 12, 13 triangle, in units of half and third MY.

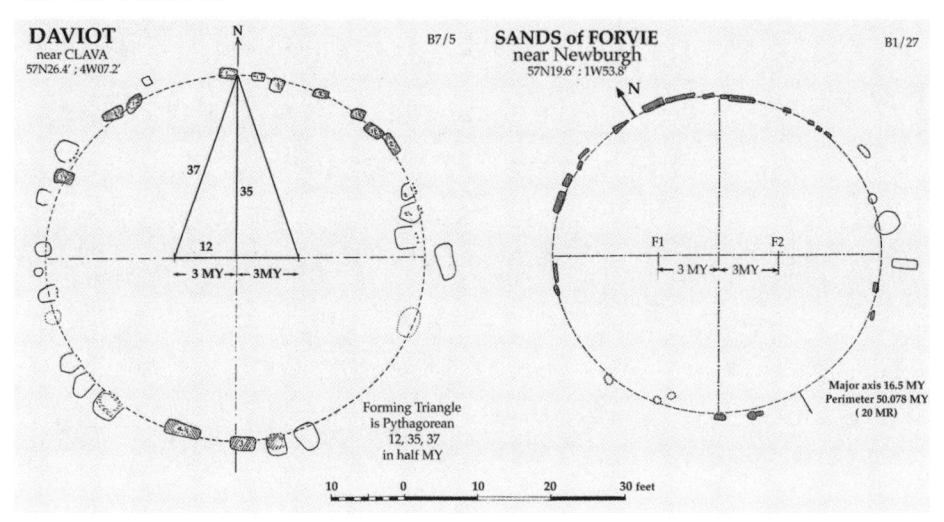

DAVIOT near CLAVA 57N26.4'; 4W07.2' — B7/5
Forming Triangle is Pythagorean 12, 35, 37 in half MY

SANDS of FORVIE near Newburgh 57N19.6'; 1W53.8' — B1/27
Major axis 16.5 MY
Perimeter 50.078 MY
(20 MR)

Daviot and Sands of Forvie are two fine examples of megalithic ellipses. Their archaeological characteristics are very different, Daviot of rough stones and Forvie of slab-sided stones laid precisely along the northern perimeter. Geometrically and metrologically these two are very similar.

Shown below is a 'folded' histogram showing how attractive it had been to the builders of ellipses to achieve an integral number of Megalithic rods in the perimeter length. Half units were clearly avoided, the sample size adequate to demonstrate this fact. And in 1974, the Thoms had published their survey on Stonehenge (*JHA*, Vol 5, part 2, No 13), suggesting that,

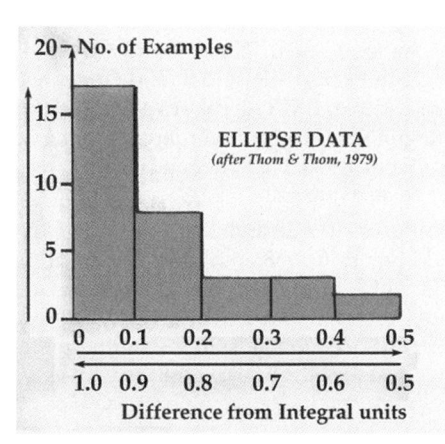

ELLIPSE DATA (after Thom & Thom, 1979)
Difference from Integral units

'a particularly good example of an almost perfect ellipse is that shown for the inner faces of the large trilithons at Stonehenge (overleaf), where major and minor axes, the distance between foci and the perimeter are, for all practical purposes, integral in Megalithic yards.'

- 139 -

Alexander Thom - Cracking the Stone Age Code

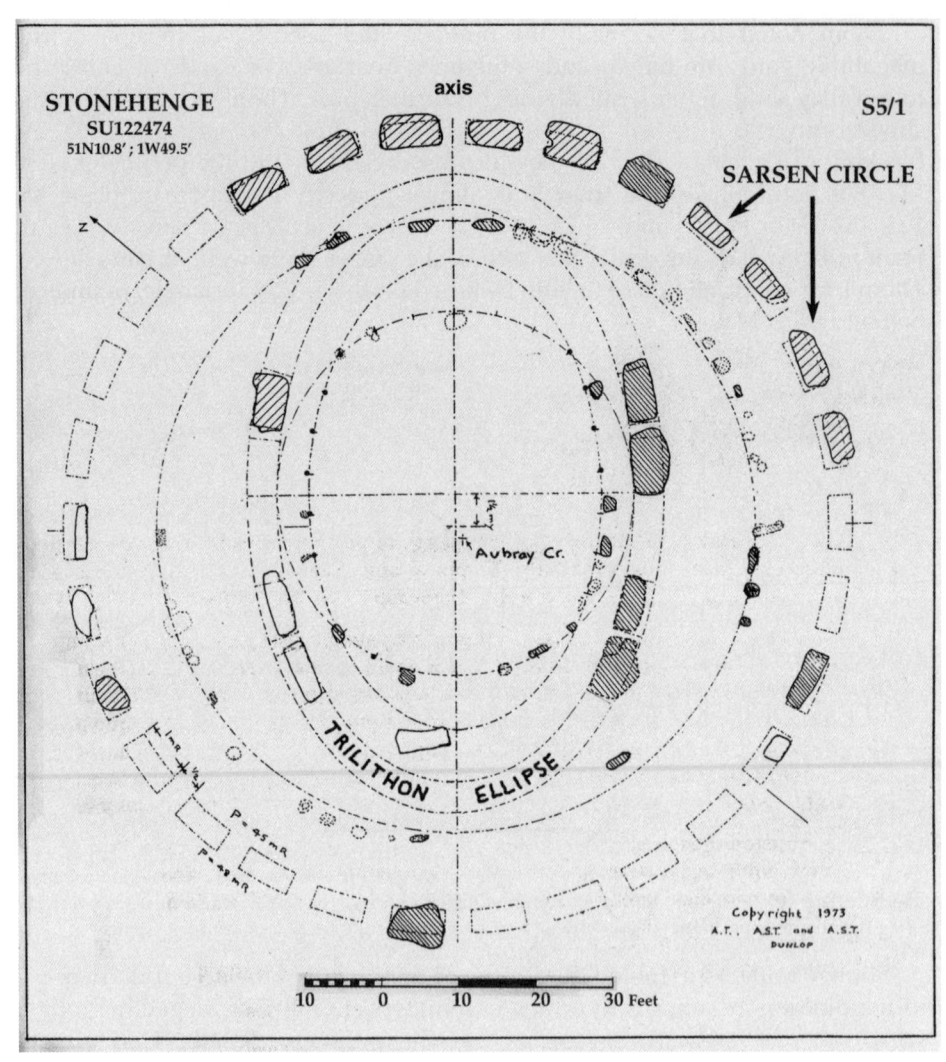

Geometry at Stonehenge. In his 1973 survey of the monument, Thom found the inside perimeter length of the sarsen circle to be 45 Megalithic rods (MR) and half a rod defined the average gaps between stones, whose average width is 1 MR, depth 0.5 MR. The trilithon ellipse perimeter at Stonehenge is also integral, the inside circumference being 28 MR. The residual error from integral was a tiny -0.01 or +0.03 MR, depending on which lengths of the forming triangle were assumed to be also integral.

Four of the trilithons lie accurately within two ellipses, 30 x 20 and 27 x 17 MY. The unshaded trilithon was re-erected by Atkinson and Piggott in 1958, into the original socket holes (*see page 88*). The massive axial trilithon, of which only stone 56 still stands, is not part of this ellipse but would touch another ellipse drawn inboard of the trilithon ellipse and upon which the geometry of the bluestone 'horseshoe' depends. In the southern section the bluestones lie on a circle of diameter identical to the minor axis of the ellipse.

FOUR FOCI - THE STONE EGGS

The egg shaped rings come in two basic forms as well - Type I and Type II. Whilst Thom's nomenclature is hardly exciting, the designs certainly are, requiring the marking out and staking of two right angled triangles placed back to back. To make a Type I egg in the field, the following procedure is required.

Making a Type I Egg

The adjacent sides of the triangle are clamped together. From their right-angles a defining radius is taken around a semi-circle. This radius is then enlarged from the outermost points of each triangle to meet the ends of the perimeter of the semicircle, and two wide arcs are drawn towards the 'sharp end' of the emerging egg. Finally, a small radius is taken from the apex of the two triangles to meet these arcs, whence the 'sharp end' of the egg is completed.

The illustration below and on the right shows the two triangles staked out. The radius of the semi-circle is defined by the length of the vertical line from the centre. This is shown as radius 1. The circle builder 'walks' a rope around the right hand part of the emerging design. This establishes the semi-circle.

The rope is then taken in turn to each of the other two stakes on the diameter line, and arcs struck to extend the semicircle to the left. These arcs are shown as radius two. Finally, the rope is fastened to the stake at the apex of the triangles and a third smaller arc is struck to complete the 'egg. This arc is shown as radius 3. The white arrows depict approximately the path walked by the circle builder.

The Type II egg has the hypotenuses of the triangle clamped together. The procedure then remains as before, only now the first radius is continued

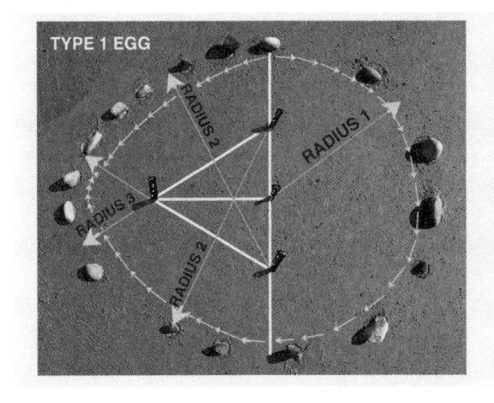

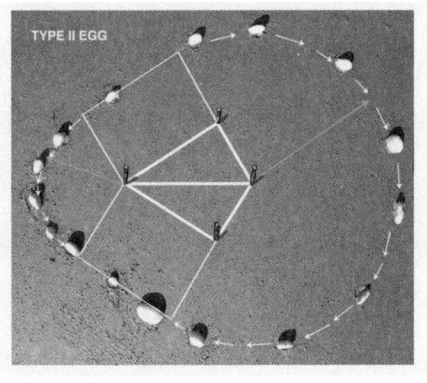

A Type I egg is made using four stakes, three make a triangle - a central stake then defines two right-angled triangles. A rope radius from each stake defines a part of the egg's perimeter. A Type II egg is made by clamping the longest sides of the two right-angled triangles together. A rope attached to either end in turn generates the radii of the egg's shape. These radii are joined by a straight line.

around beyond a semicircle until the emerging perimeter of the egg lines up with the shortest sides of the triangle, extended outwards. Make a copy of this extended line and, on the 'sharp-end' of the two triangles lay it perpendicular to the adjacent side. The third radius, as for the Type I, is taken from the point of the triangles to meet this rope. Of all the megalithic designs, this 'pulleys and fanbelt' design is perhaps the least aesthetic.

Allan Water (*below*) is a good example a Type I Egg. Slab-sided stones are aligned to the geometry and the triangle is 'good', being 11, 13 and 17 in units of half a Megalithic yard. The ring is situated on the top of a very steep hill, part of a ridge along which the axis of the ring is aligned. Although Thom does not note it, the egg also points in the direction of the major standstill moonrise (38

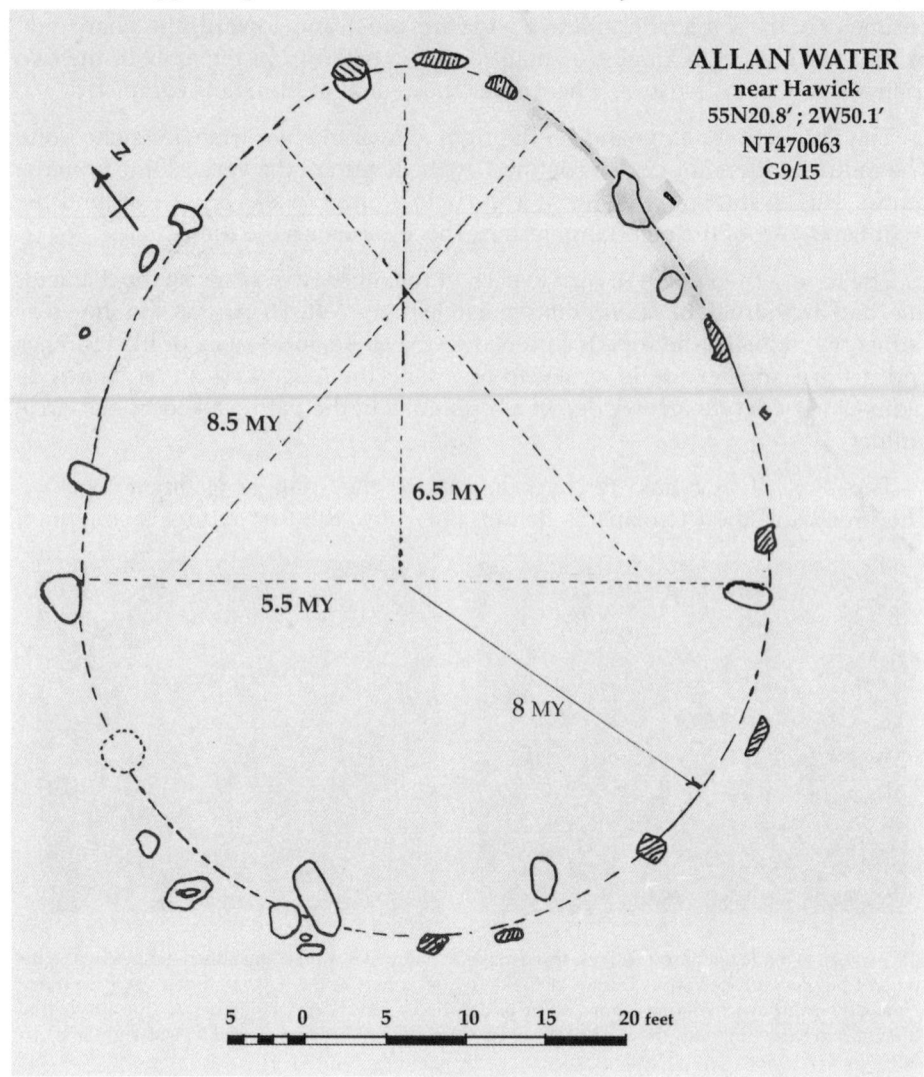

ALLAN WATER
near Hawick
55N20.8' ; 2W50.1'
NT470063
G9/15

Chapter Five - Megalithic Designs

degrees), making this a most interesting site where the landscape itself defines a significant aspect of the astronomy of the latitude.

Thom's survey of the Twelve Apostles is given below. It is a very early survey, from 1939, and yet Thom is clearly confident in the units of lengths employed and is already marking out the internal dimensions of surveying rings in megalithic yards. The triangle is a 3, 4, 5, in units of 6 Megalithic yards.

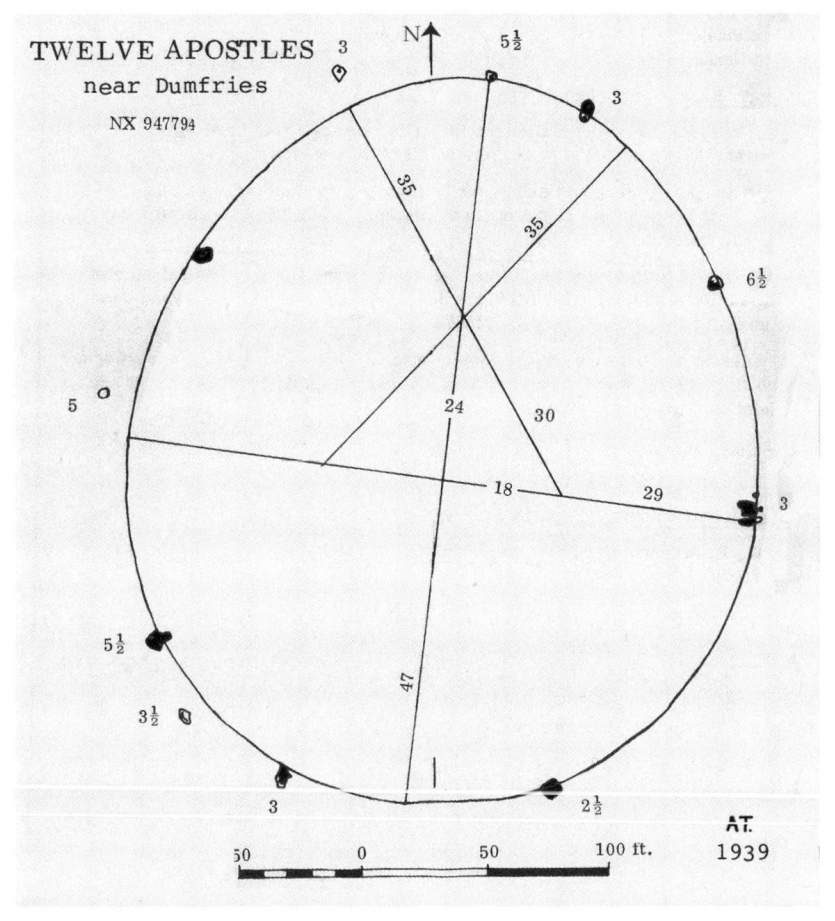

Thom's original 1939 survey of the Twelve Apostles, near Dumfries. It is a huge ring, and seven stones remain on Thom's proposed geometry. The heights of the stones (in feet) are printed outside the perimeter, the internal dimensions marked in Megalithic yards. This suggests that Thom had *a priori* knowledge of the unit by 1939 and was already assuming the rings were built using this length in their construction.

Only a dozen Type I eggs were in adequate enough condition to make an accurate survey worthwhile, although the design was quite commonly chosen throughout northwestern Europe. Usually it is found built into the smaller rings, an example being Druid Temple, near Inverness, based once again on a 3, 4, 5.

- 143 -

The Type II egg is rarer, although in 1970 Thom found a well preserved example in Brittany, marking the eastern end of the *Le Menec* alignment (see page 102). Borrowston Rig, previously quoted by Thom as 'the best example of a Type II ring', is singularly visually unimpressive, although its geometry is impressive enough and follows the general format identified by Thom.

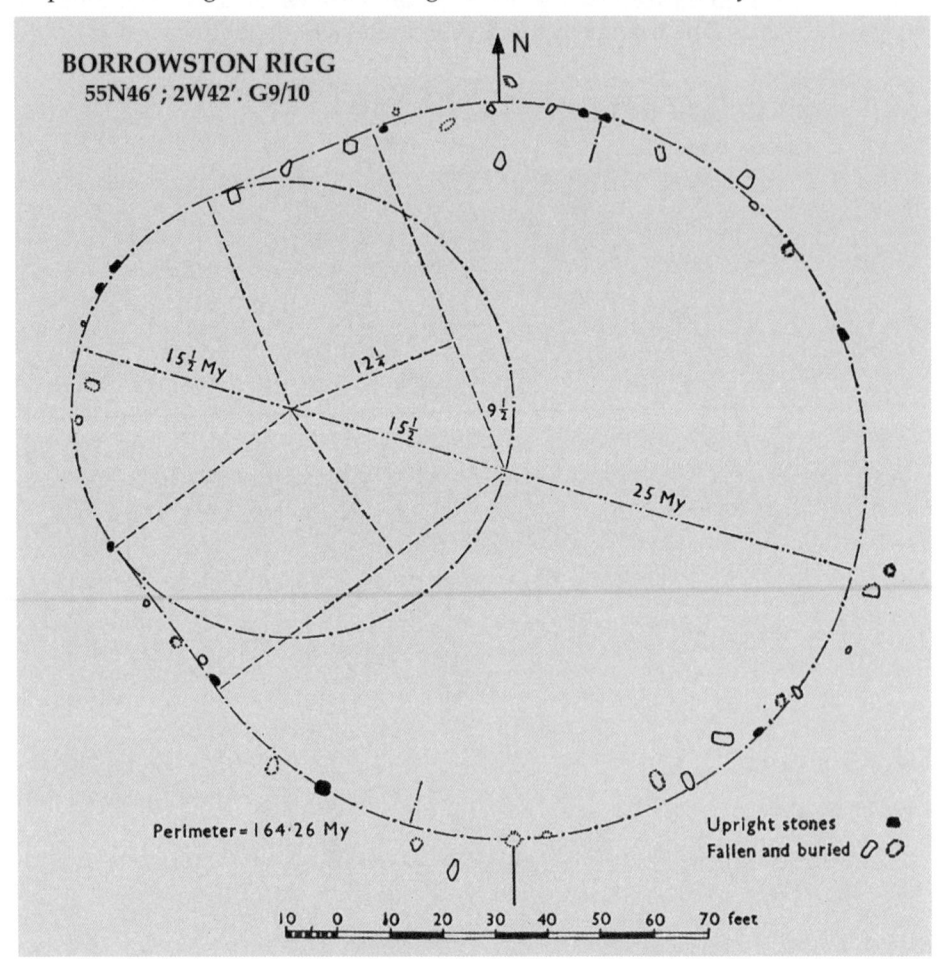

BORROWSTON RIGG
55N46' ; 2W42'. G9/10

Perimeter = 164·26 My

Upright stones ●
Fallen and buried ◌ ◯

Borrowston Rigg, near Dalkeith, is a disappointing site to visit. The stones are hardly visible on the rough ground, and there has clearly been much damage done to the site. Fortunately some of the stones that have not fallen have their long edges aligned around the proposed geometry, and Thom was able to reconstruct what he felt sure was the original shape of the ring. Borrowston Rigg is unique in that the smallest arc is part of a circle that intersects the centre of the large circle.

Some eggs have elliptical and not circular ends. These are more related to the 'Woodhenge type' of geometry than to the Type II egg. An example is illustrated later in this section. For both types of egg, Thom noted that they offered their builders some leeway in matching integral lengths throughout the design.

Chapter Five - Megalithic Designs

FLATTENED CIRCLES

The flattened circles form a quite different family to the previous rings. Unlike the ellipses and eggs, both types conform to a definite design and are geometrically similar. There is no evidence of any attempt to make the perimeter integral in megalithic yards or rods. At least forty examples are known.

The Type A Flattened Circle

The Type A geometry is shown compared to that of the Type B in the diagrams below. See also the design of Castle Rigg (*page 58*). The Type A design requires that the circumference of the circle is divided into six equal sections. This defines the limits for the angle of the flattened arcs, which can be seen to be less flattened than for the Type B. The technique for making a Type A flattened circle on the ground is given below, and visually depicted overleaf,

(i) Place a central stake and use a rope loop to define the desired radius of a circle, as described for the circle previously. Mark the circumference. Then divide the circumference into six equal parts. Most children perform this task using compasses while at school, it is an elementary geometric construction. In the field it is necessary to use the loop of rope that defined the radius. Remove the central stake and swing it and the freed end of the loop to the next 'cut' along the circumference. Stake this point and continue around the perimeter in the same manner until it is divided into six equal parts.

(ii). Bisect any two radii separated by 240 degrees. The technique for doing this is shown in illustration (ii) overleaf. Peg the bisection points A and B.

(iii) Take a pegged rope from the 'bottom' of the design and bring it up to one of the bisection pegs and then out to the perimeter marker peg.

(iv) Now 'walk' the rope to the opposite circumference, as shown. The flattened top section of the ring will now be traced out automatically.

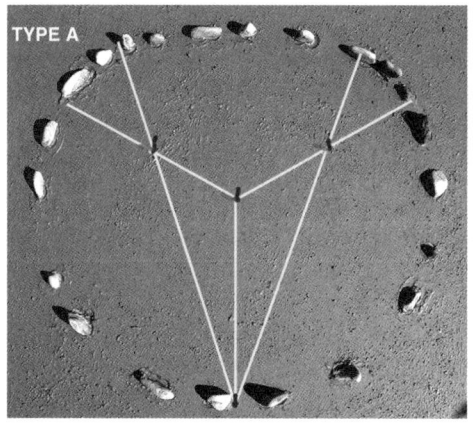

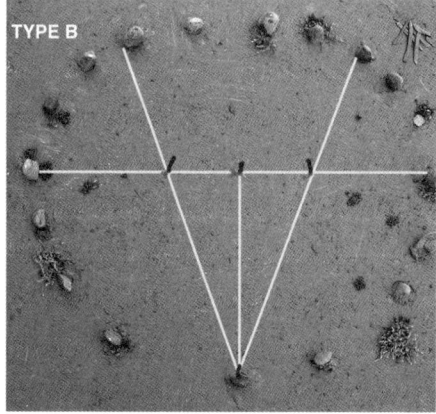

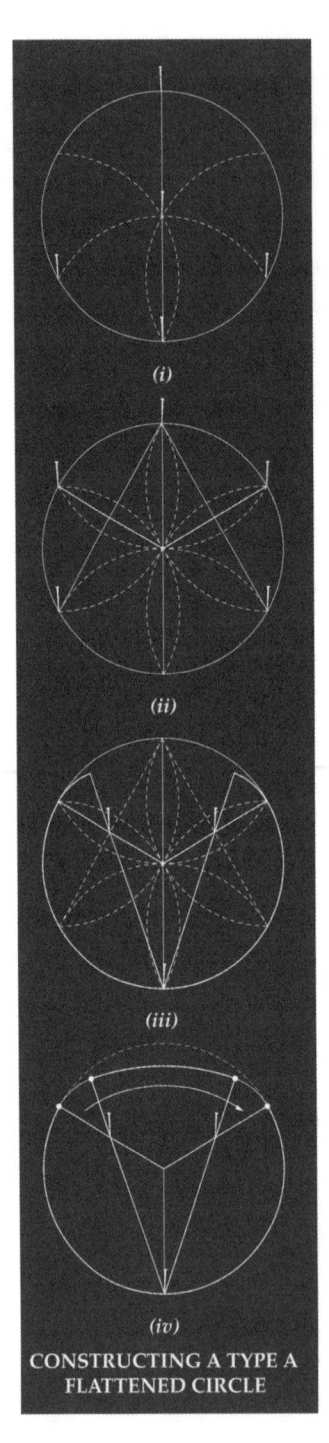

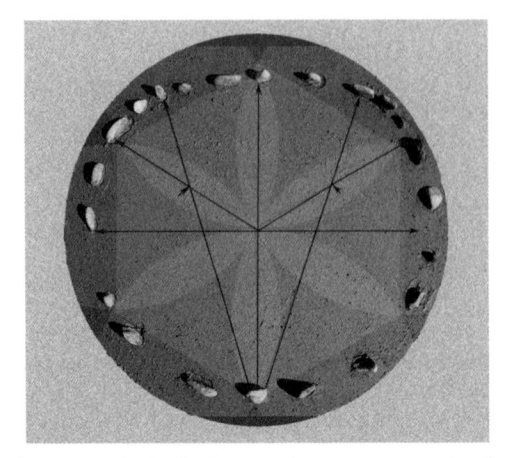

The essentially hexagonal construction is shown in the illustration above, where the scribing arcs form a 'flower of life' pattern within the ring. The Type A ring is essentially a circle over two-thirds of its perimeter. At either end of this regular curve the curvature increases through two arcs centred on the pegs (shown marked with arrows)which then lead into the flattened arc at the top of the diagram. The conformity of this design is demonstrated by Thom's superimposition of four Type A rings (*below*). Although of differing sizes, the geometry is clearly similar. At least fourteen good examples survive on the British mainland and the design may also be found in Ireland and in Brittany.

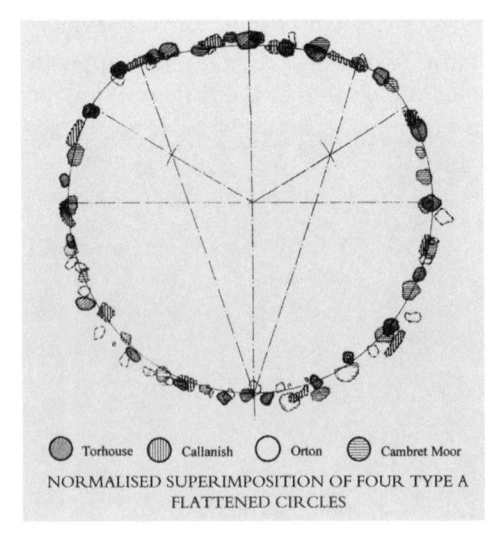

(i)
(ii)
(iii)
(iv)
CONSTRUCTING A TYPE A
FLATTENED CIRCLE

● Torhouse ▥ Callanish ○ Orton ▤ Cambret Moor
NORMALISED SUPERIMPOSITION OF FOUR TYPE A
FLATTENED CIRCLES

Chapter Five - Megalithic Designs

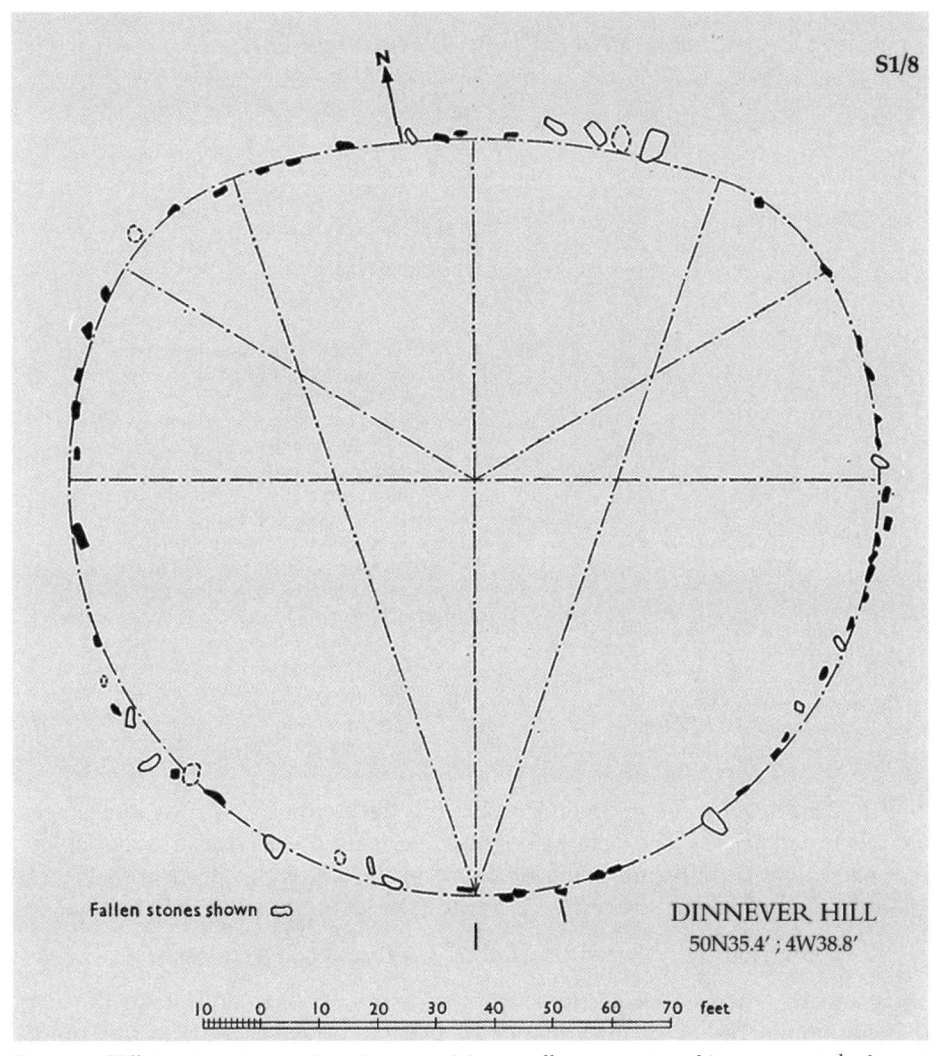

Dinnever Hill is not an impressive site, comprising small stones yet ranking amongst the largest stone rings in Britain. The remaining stones have their longer sides aligned along the perimeter.

The Type B Flattened Circle

Superficially, the Type B rings resemble the Type A. The two small radius 'corners' look less pronounced but this belies the fact that the design of a Type B ring draws on quite different design rules. The circular part of the perimeter of a Type B is a semicircle, whereas for a Type A it is two-thirds of the circle.

A Type B flattened circle begins life by placing three equidistant stakes on a straight line. The final size of the ring is given by its radius, which will be three times the space between each stake.

Constructing a Type-B Flattened Circle

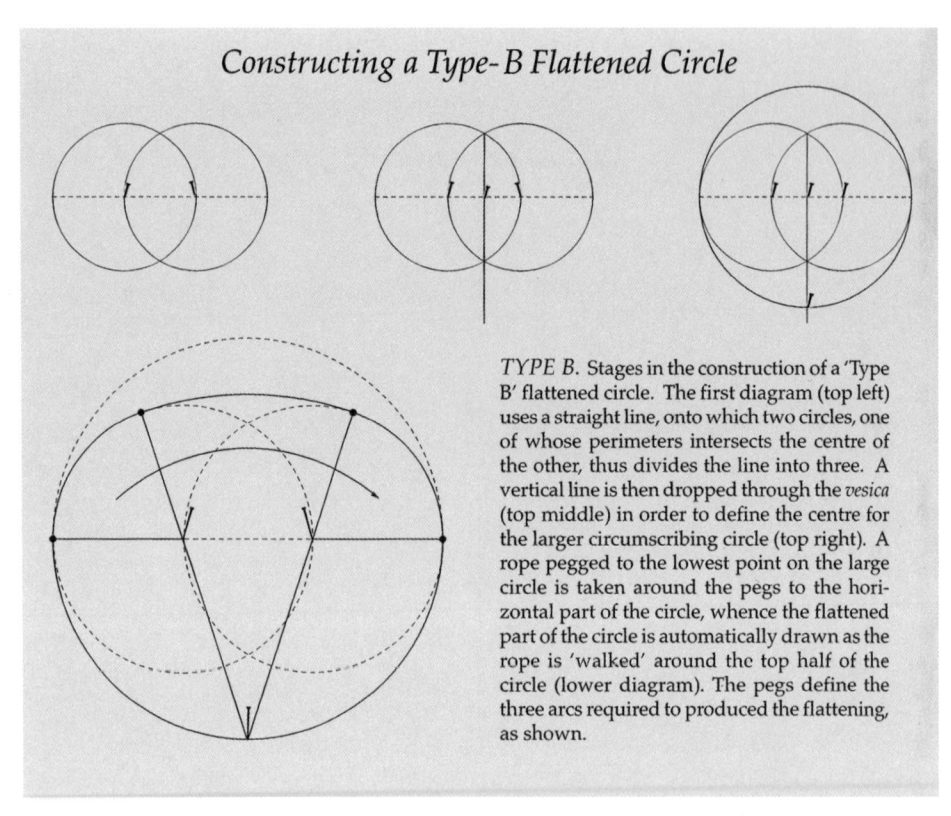

TYPE B. Stages in the construction of a 'Type B' flattened circle. The first diagram (top left) uses a straight line, onto which two circles, one of whose perimeters intersects the centre of the other, thus divides the line into three. A vertical line is then dropped through the *vesica* (top middle) in order to define the centre for the larger circumscribing circle (top right). A rope pegged to the lowest point on the large circle is taken around the pegs to the horizontal part of the circle, whence the flattened part of the circle is automatically drawn as the rope is 'walked' around the top half of the circle (lower diagram). The pegs define the three arcs required to produced the flattening, as shown.

There are several variations for producing the geometry. The various stages are illustrated (*above*). The '*vesica piscis*' method is used to divide an original line that becomes the diameter of the finished ring. It is easy to produce a Type B geometry to high accuracy in the field using the technique illustrated above.

A second, slightly different method of construction is as follows,

(i) Define three equal sections along a length of line and stake the two division points. Bisect the middle section, placing a stake at the bisection point.

(ii) Using a rope radius attached to this central stake, mark out or otherwise define the large circle whose diameter is the original length of the line.

(iii) A perpendicular is now dropped from the central stake down onto the perimeter of the circle produced, using standard geometrical procedures, where a stake is fixed.

(iv) a rope is fastened to this stake and its end taken up and around one of the two stakes that divide the line into three. Once the rope is engaged with this stake, take the end to the perimeter. Mark the rope at this distance and then walk this rope length around the 'top' half of the circle, making sure that the rope disengages from the first stake and, after drawing out the long arc, engages with the second stake prior to ending up on the opposite side of the design.

Chapter Five - Megalithic Designs

A Type B circle being constructed on a beach. Despite all rings appearing oval in shape when viewed from the ground, the construction above shows clearly the two 'vesica' circles, the perimeter of the ring, and the pegs used to mark out the geometry. The flattened section is in the background.

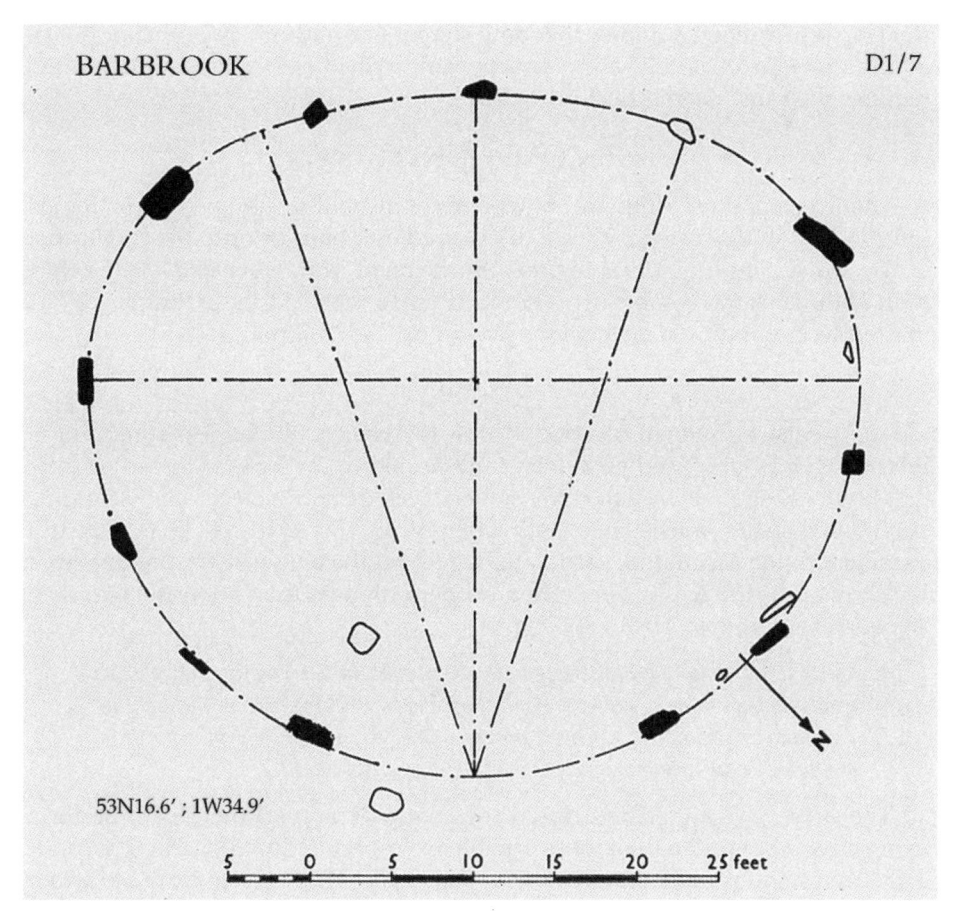

BARBROOK   D1/7

53N16.6' ; 1W34.9'

Bar Brook in Derbyshire is a good example of a Type B flattened circle. The stones are slab-sided, and support the proposed geometry. This geometry, and that of the other rings, was clearly important.

This is the shape of Thom's 'Class B' flattened circle - a walkover, one might say. Interestingly, it is only when practically constructing this shape with ropes and pegs that the 'secret' of how to make the shape becomes so obviously apparent. Construction on paper using compasses cannot reveal this ease of construction. A couple of practice runs and Thom's geometry becomes easy to recreate.

Is this how the builders created the shape? One interesting confirming piece of evidence is that some of the flattened circles, like the egg excavated by Jack Scott (*see page 60*), revealed their internal markers. In addition, and already discussed on page 58, some circles, like Castle Rigg, have stones accurately placed to support Thom's geometrical construction for the Type A geometry.

An apparently simpler procedure for constructing both Type A and Type B flattened circles is described by T. Cowan in 1970 in *Megalithic rings, their design construction, (Science,* 168, pp 321-5). Again, all that is needed is a rope and some stakes, the technique supplies the same shape. The author's two 'anchor points' and the two 'pivot points' are precisely as described above, and to place these requires the same geometrical procedures.

THE COMPOUND RINGS

Thom's compound rings are showpieces of megalithic design. Originally, just four designs in this category were discovered by Thom prior to the publication of *Megalithic Sites in Britain* in 1967. Subsequent work revealed some others built with the same complexity. Thom's surveys revealed these designs to be a masterpiece of multiple arc geometry and precision metrology.

Avebury

The most well known compound ring is Avebury, the largest stone ring in Britain. Thom's proposed geometry, built around a 3:4:5 pythagorean triangle, has been questioned by later researchers, yet certain aspects of his original survey suggested consistency with other rings. Because the later statistical treatment of the Megalithic yard data had found the evidence for the English & Welsh data insufficiently clear, Thom undertook a further extensive survey of Avebury. He wrote in MRBB (1978),

> '*But there are many other strong indications that the yard really existed apart from a list of diameters...We consider that because of its size and the fact that we know its geometry, Avebury provides the best site for determining, from a single site in England, the value of the megalithic yard.*'

The survey, a seven-sided closed traverse took several months to perform, using steel tapes and a theodolite capable of resolving down to ±5 arc seconds. The seven stations remain marked with steel nails. The traverse closed to within 'an inch or two' and the position of every surviving stone, stone hole and even the burning pits used to break the stones in the eighteenth century were thus

Chapter Five - Megalithic Designs

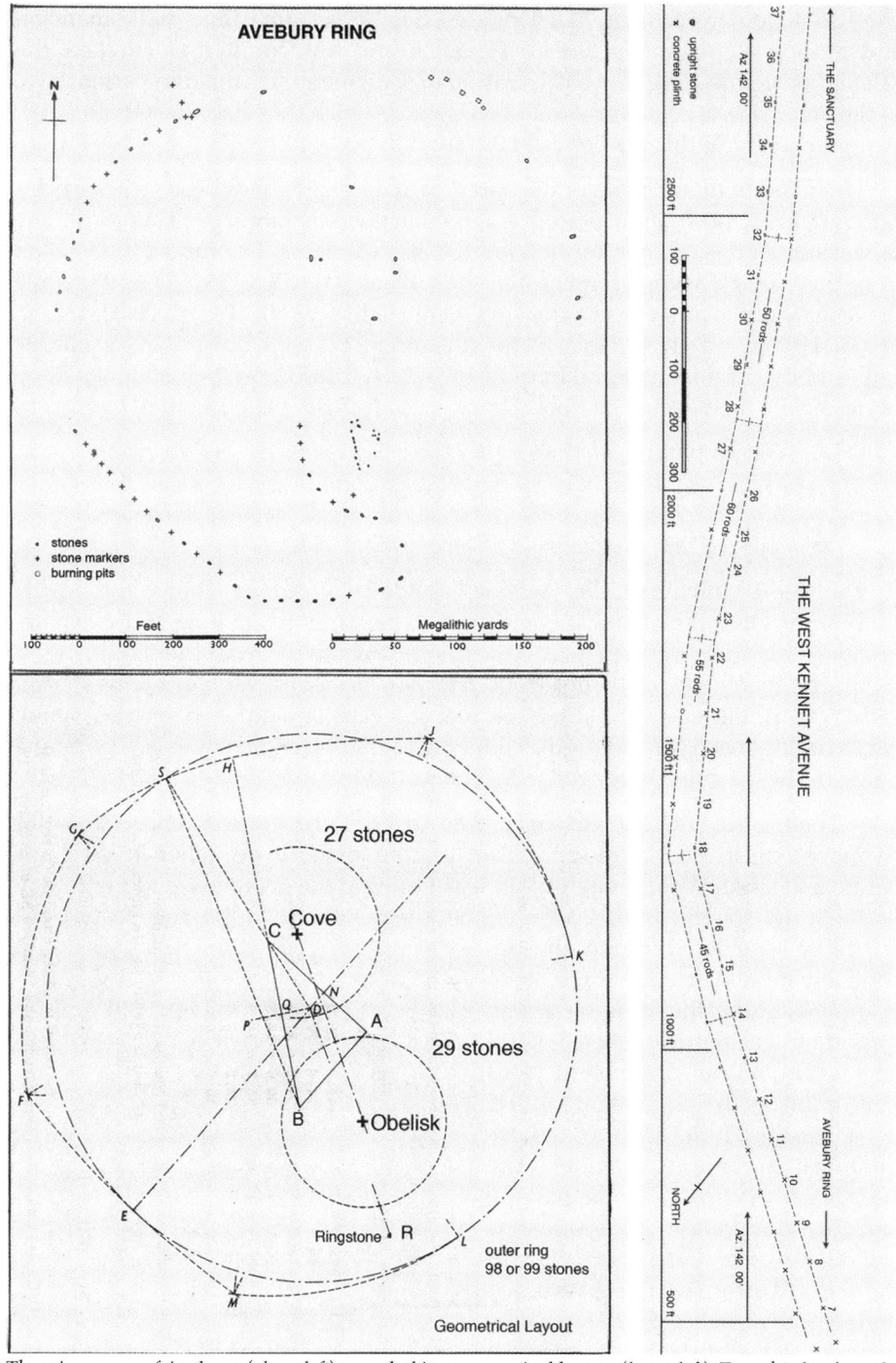

Thom's survey of Avebury (*above left*) revealed its geometrical layout (*lower left*). Two-thirds of a mile in perimeter, Avebury ring connects to the Sanctuary via the West Kennet Avenue (*right*).

- 151 -

fixed to a similar accuracy. Dr Douglas Heggie, a Cambridge mathematician and author of *Megalithic Science* (Thames and Hudson, 1981) checked the calculations, providing also a calculation of the probability that the various arcs of the outer ring at Avebury would be integral, which they had turned out to be. The probability of this lay between 0.1 and 1%.

Thom found that the arcs of the outer ring could only have been struck from a right-angled 3, 4, 5 triangle placed as shown in the illustration (*previous page*). The dimensions of this triangle are *30, 40 and 50 megalithic rods*. The various radii taken from this triangle were all integral in rods, BS as 104, CS as 56, CD as 24, while the lengths of the arcs of the outer ring were , in MY, 97.50, 117.50, 200.00, 130.00, 150.00, 195.00, and 412.00. Thus all the measurements were integral in Megalithic rods and five of them integral in units of 10 MR. In addition the two inner stone circles held a diameter of 50 rods. Thom wrote (*MRBB*, page 38), that,

> 'The accuracy with which this ring has been set out is clearly remarkable; the stones fit every theoretical arc and the overall dimensions are satisfied within close limits.. The erectors did it without theodolites, without steel tapes and without trigonometrical tables.'

The survey included the Avenue, assisted by Archie Thom and Mr K McWhirter. Once the plan was committed to paper, all 8 foot long of it, the pairs of stones that dog-leg their way towards the Sanctuary from the main ring at Avebury began to reveal their secrets. The pairs of stones were seen to be spaced 18 MY apart, measuring to stone centres, and each straight 'run' of the Avenue was a multiple of 5 MR in length. Thom could find no explanation as to why the parallel rows of stones changed direction as it does.

Thom also failed to discover how or why the erectors chose to build Avebury ring in such a design, but in that he joined every other investigator before and since. What Thom did do was to reveal the geometry and metrology of the ring, together with an eloquent demonstration that the shape was not to be considered 'rough' or slipshod any more. The current refusal to acknowledge that the site possesses an important geometrical, metrological and astronomical component does not optimise the immediate future of a World Heritage Site, whose qualification criteria include '(The site)..*must represent a masterpiece of human creative genius*'. Unless someone can demonstrate that Thom's work at the site is in error, this refusal is based merely on disbelief in the creative genius of our ancestors, a form of ethnocentricity or racism in time.

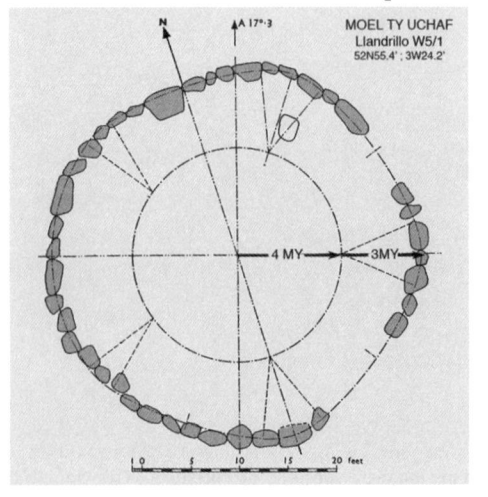

Chapter Five - Megalithic Designs

Moel ty Uchaf (*above and plan, opposite*) sits on a tiny plateau at the summit of a steep hill near Llandrillo, Bala, Wales. It enjoys panoramic views. Nearby is a cairn constructed of white quartz, and numerous outliers surround the vicinity. It is undoubtedly one of the best preserved and most important stone rings in Britain, and provided Thom with great insight into the capabilities of the neolithic geometers.

Moel ty Uchaf

The geometry of Moel ty Uchaf has already been discussed on page 59. To complete matters Thom's original survey plan is included opposite. The geometry is based on two concentric circles, of 4 and 7 Megalithic yards in radius, upon which a complex pentagonal geometry was constructed. The dimensions remain within a couple of inches of the geometry originally described by Thom, and it is possible to recreate the stages of construction on site to confirm this. Thom offered this explanation for the geometry of the ring in *MSIB* (*page 84*)

> '*They started with a circle 14 yards in diameter and therefore 44 yards in circumference. But this was not enough: they wanted also to have a multiple of 2.5 yards in the perimeter. So they proceeded to invent a method of drawing flattened portions on the ring which, with a minimum of distortion, would reduce it to 42.5 MY. To introduce these flattened portions they had to use at least two radii and each had to be integral. Finally, the finished ring had to have, like nearly all others, an axis of symmetry.*'

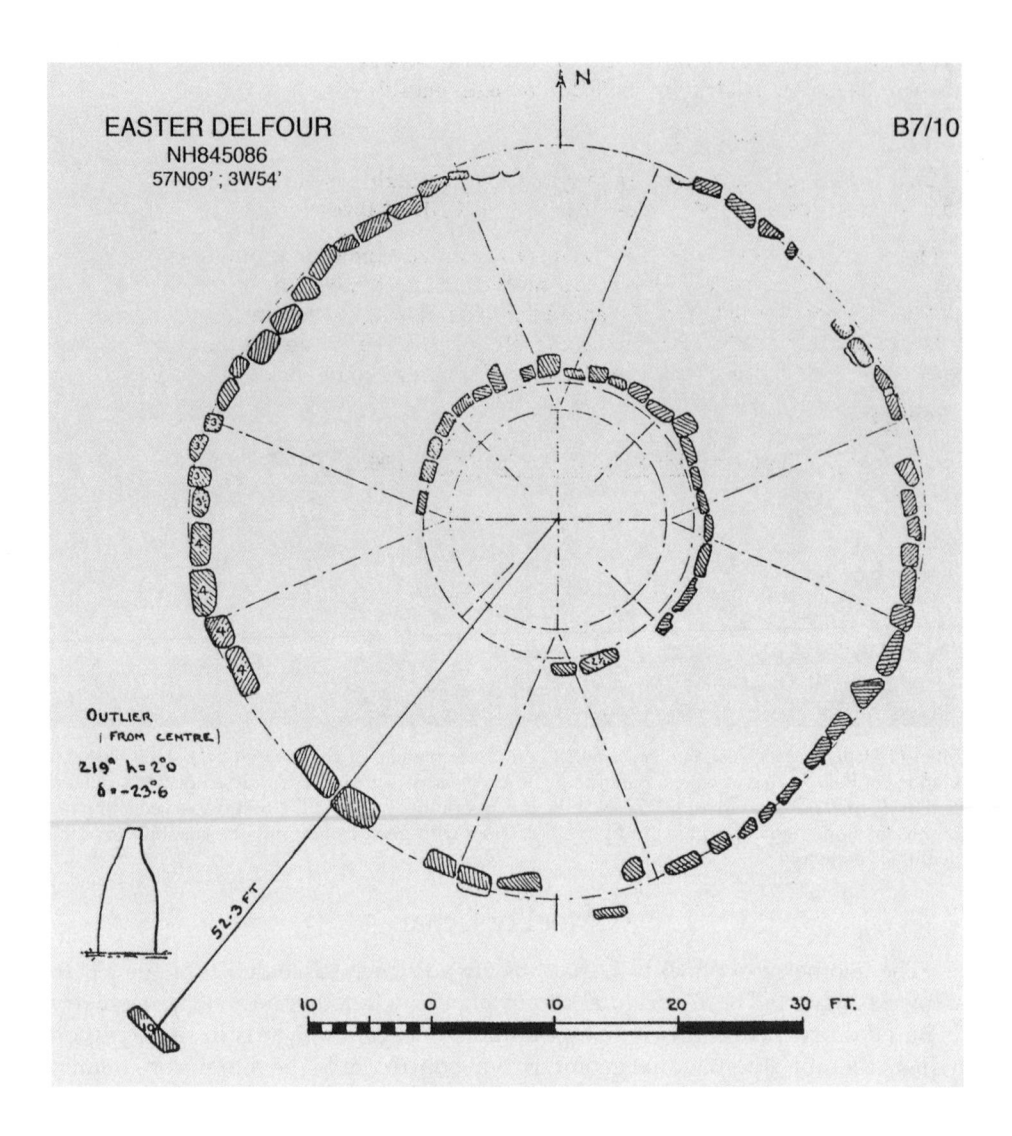

Easter Delfour

Constructed on the Spey valley floor two miles north of Kincraig, this ring draws on the same techniques as that shown in Moel ty Uchaf, but this time the geometry is four-fold, a 6.5 MY inner circle being used to define the outer ring. The minimum diameter of the outer ring is 21.01 MY and its maximum diameter 22 MY. The perimeter is calculated as 67.52 MY or 27.00 Megalithic rods.

Unlike Moel ty Uchaf, Easter Delfour is a built concentric structure, a category of monument that is largely confined to Scotland. However, the geometrical techniques used in its construction, and the metrology, are to be found throughout the British Isles, Brittany and Ireland.

Chapter Five - Megalithic Designs

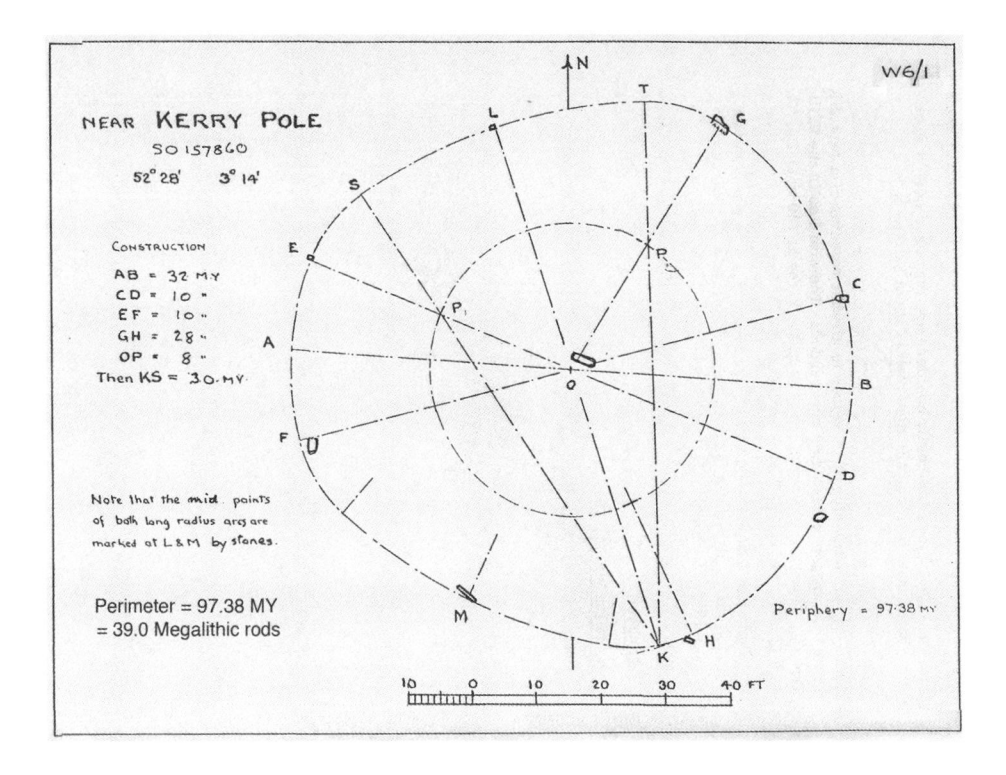

```
NEAR KERRY POLE
SO 157860
52° 28'   3° 14'

CONSTRUCTION
AB = 32 MY
CD =  10 "
EF =  10 "
GH =  28 "
OP =   8 "
Then KS = 30. MY

Note that the mid points
of both long radius arcs are
marked at L & M by stones.

Perimeter = 97.38 MY
= 39.0 Megalithic rods

Periphery = 97.38 MY
```

Kerry Pole

Kerry Pole (*above*) provides a further example of a visually disappointing ring whose survey reveals a great deal that confirms Thom's general design criteria. Fortunately, the ring has been little disturbed, and the nine purple stones that comprise the perimeter are all apparently in their original positions.

The multiple arcs that make up the perimeter geometry resemble a hybrid construction between Moel ty Uchaf and Avebury. These arcs have lengths of 8, 10 (twice), 28, 30 and 32 MY, and the perimeter is integral in Megalithic rods, at 39.0. Thom also noted that the midpoints of both large radius arcs were marked by stones, marked L and M on the plan.

Archie Thom once said that his father was not sure "enough stones remained to determine the geometry" prior to drawing up the plan. Then, "with no little satisfaction he discovered that the site closely emulated the techniques of nearby Moel ty Uchaf." In print, Thom described the site as 'most interesting'.

The compound rings provided Thom with more insight into the techniques the builders were using, and this showed their ability using more complex geometry within their structures. The author has resurveyed the Welsh sites, and has found no discrepancies in either the published plans nor in their proposed geometries and dimensions.

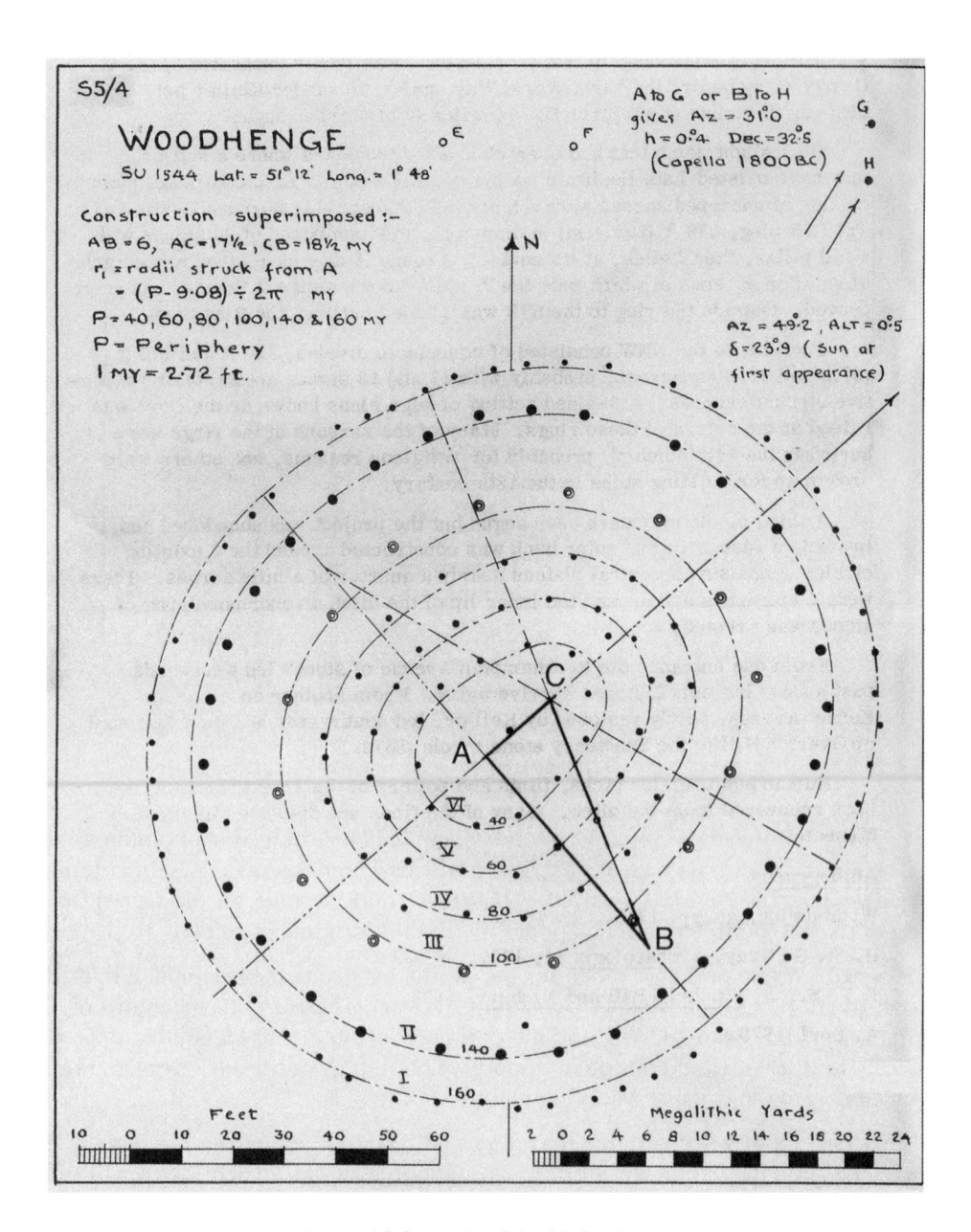

THE 'WOODHENGE' GEOMETRY

Several other complex arc shapes have been surveyed, particularly in Brittany. In Britain perhaps Woodhenge is the representative wooden example of this geometry, based on a Pythagorean 12:35:37 triangle. Thom's survey, which he describes as 'very careful', revealed the following geometric qualities for this wooden post structure, listed on page 73 of *MSIB*, and given overleaf.

- 156 -

Chapter Five - Megalithic Designs

The Woodhenge Geometry

Six egg-shaped concentric layers, each derived from the perfect Pythagorean triangle, 12, 35, 37, built using half Megalithic yards (6, 17.5, 18.5). The shortest side of this triangle lies along the axis of the monument and both coincide with the rising point of the midsummer sunrise in 2000 BC.

The perimeters of each ring are 40, 60, 80, 100 140 and 160 MY. In rods these are 16, 24, 32, 40, 56 and 64.

(1) the arcs at the large end have a common centre at A,

(2) the arcs at the small end have a common centre at B

(3) the distance AB between these centres is 6 MY,

(4) the arcs are equally spaced with one gap,

(5) the radius at the small end is in each ring 1 MY smaller than the radius of the large end.

Thom's survey was undertaken by measuring to the centres of the concrete cylinders that the Ministry of Works placed into the socket hole positions identified by archaeologists, most notably the Cunningtons (*Woodhenge*, 1929). Further commentary seems unnecessary.

ELLIPTICALLY ENDED EGGS

Thom surveyed two good examples of what turned out to be eggs that had elliptical 'blunt ends' rather than the usual semicircular ends. Named Type III, the best example of the type was surveyed by John R Hoyle, Hirnant cairn circle in North Wales. The ellipse and the triangle are both integral in quarter yards.

The geometry of Hirnant cairn circle (*shown right*) clearly draws from the same technique that produced Woodhenge. A right-angled triangle is first laid down with its shortest side coincident to the axis. Flattening arcs are then struck from the perimeter. It would follow that interchange of geometrical knowledge took place between the 'Wessex culture' that built Stonehenge, Woodhenge and Avebury and people who lived in what is now North Wales, or they shared a cultural heritage that included a high level of understanding in metrology and geometry. Either warrants study.

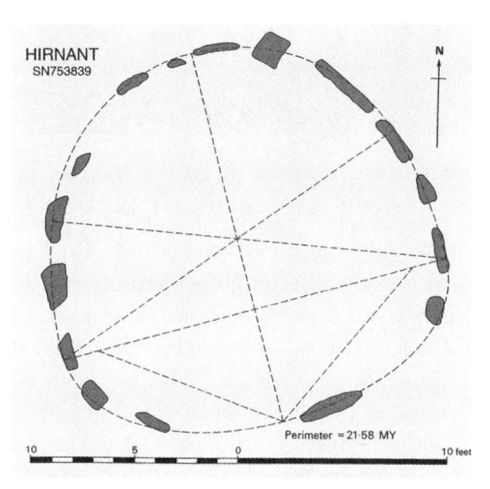

Alexander Thom - Cracking the Stone Age Code

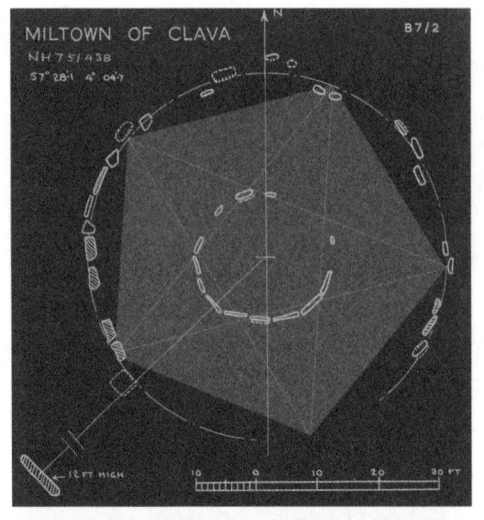

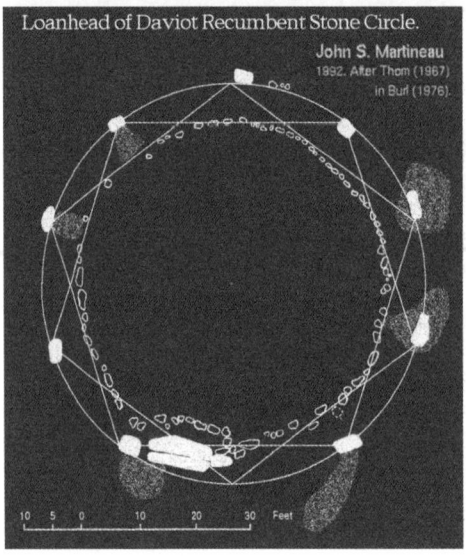

RECTANGULAR RINGS

During his surveying trips to Brittany, Thom came across a unique site where a rectangular enclosure of stones revealed a significant confirmation of the general rules he had found applied to the British sites. Apart from the oddness of the shape, Crucuno possessed side dimensions of 30 and 40 Megalithic yards, making the diameters 50 of the same units. One diameter was aligned accurately to the midsummer sunrise at the latitude of Crucuno in megalithic times. The site is currently enjoying a revival, following interest from several metrologists.

CONCENTRIC GEOMETRIES

Scotland holds many concentric sites, although Stonehenge and Woodhenge both display concentricity. Loanhead of Daviot and Miltown of Clava (*left, upper*) are two fine examples. The graphic of Milltown of Clava shows Thom's original survey plan overlain with a pentagon. The diameter of the inner kerbed cairn, fits well into the 'star-arms' of the inscribed pentagram. The original discoverer of this geometric property of many Scottish rings was the late Anne Macaulay, and acknowledgement for the supply of the original graphic is given here.

At the Loanhead site Aubrey Burl made a rare reference to the Megalithic yard, where he is supportive of the unit when describing a previously undiscovered central area to the main circle, found to be 5 Megalithic yards in diameter. The outer circle is 25.0 MY in diameter, the inner is 20 MY. If five-ness is suggested by the dimensions, so too may it be found in the geometry, and researcher John Martineau has demonstrated (*left, lower*)) that two circumscribed pentagons drawn within the large ring accurately define the kerb. I am indebted to John for permission to use and adapt his original graphic.

- 158 -

Chapter Five - Megalithic Designs

STONEHENGE

Professor Richard Atkinson eventually persuaded Thom to undertake a survey of the ground plan of Stonehenge in 1973. The results were published in the *Journal for the History of Astronomy* (Vol. 5, part 2, No 13) in June 1974.

It is not necessary to repeat too much detail concerning the dimensions and geometry of Stonehenge. These things can be found in other books, and the sarsen circle and trilithon ellipse have been covered here on page 140. However, as Stonehenge is considered to be the *non pareil* of stone circles, it is important to discover if the same rules applied here as they did in 'the lesser circles on Scottish hills and Welsh moors'.

Amongst the earliest constructions at Stonehenge was the Aubrey circle, whose 56 holes were possibly dug to provide a wooden proto-Stonehenge. Atkinson identified the centres of these holes during the survey and Thom was able to make the following statement concerning the accuracy by which this circle had been laid out,

> '*The standard deviation of the radii to the holes is 0.56 feet and the mean radius is 141.8 ±0.08 feet... The above value of the radius gives a figure for the circumference of 891 feet, i.e. almost exactly 131 rods.*'

This means that two thirds of all the holes had been dug within half a foot (30 cms) of a perfect circle 283.6 feet in diameter (86.46 m). This is 99.8% accuracy, and such a circle would be impossible to construct by eye, and quite difficult even with modern surveying equipment. It is a precision circle.

In the 108 page consultation draft of the *Stonehenge World Heritage Site Management Plan* (September 1999, Chris Blandford Associates), there is no mention of any geometry in relationship to Stonehenge. All there is concerning its construction may be found included in a single sentence under the heading 'spiritual values' (page 19). Section 2.4 12 tells the reader that,

> '.*Stonehenge is enigmatic. While theories about the reason for its construction, the manner of its use and its role as a sacred place abound, these can be but speculation.*'

From Thom's survey of Stonehenge, there emerged a recognisable geometrical structure within Thom's general rules (*see page 140*). For example, the station rectangle is a 5, 12 rectangle in units of 8 MY, its diameters form a 5,12,13 Pythagorean triangle. An octagonal 'star' is defined by the station rectangle and the heel stone. The stones and stone holes that once defined the rectangle sit less than a foot inside the Aubrey circle and their diagonals are 104 MY in length (13 x 8 MY: Thom's value of 283.6 ft for the Aubrey circle is 104.26 MY). This is anything but speculative, and the educational poverty caused by leaving this kind of geometrical component out of our national monument short-changes us, separating us from our ancestral legacy. It is an incredible sin of omission.

Alexander Thom - Cracking the Stone Age Code

Thom at Stonehenge, during his survey of 1973. Then seventy-nine years of age, Professor Atkinson, who assisted on the survey and was thirty years his junior, complained that he "could hardly keep up with him". Working on theodolite 'bookings', fur hat and Curta calculator by his side, pocket stuffed with pipe and tobacco, this photo is about as representative of Alexander Thom and his work as one could hope for.

SUMMARY

For four decades Thom undertook surveys of stone rings which he then transcribed into accurate plans from which he discovered the geometries that the erectors of the non-circular rings had been following. "No one, I am sure, is going to question the accuracy nor the comprehensiveness of the evidence that Professor Thom has put before us", said Richard Atkinson on the *Chronicle* documentary. Arthur Hogg, a fellow archaeologist said something quite different. Having "no great difficulty" in accepting Thom's astronomical theories, he then went on "Where I do have difficulty is in accepting Thom's case for the Megalithic yard or for the use of pythagorean triangles in laying out stone circles". His critics were not kind to him, failing to recognise that without these plans they would have precious little material to criticise. Some made patronising commentary on his achievements, Thaddeus Cowan, an American psychologist writing in *Megalithic compound ring geometry* (RIS, page 379),

> '..we are indebted to Alexander Thom who took the first steps towards understanding the geometric structure of these monuments. First steps are always the boldest and most difficult, and Thom deserves considerable praise for taking them. But they are necessarily faltering.'

No one ever gave a detailed critique describing in what way Thom's proposed geometrical constructions for the rings were 'faltering steps'. Thom said they were simply the best fit he could determine for the recorded shapes he had surveyed. In many cases Thom would describe a 'difficult' site as 'possibly an ellipse' (Carsphairn, G4/1) or 'possibly circle and standing stone' (Nine Ladies, D1/3)'. For this latter ring, Cowan indeed managed a much better fit of all the stones using an equal-width geometry, a most convincing alternative to Thom's 'possibly circle'. However, the diameter remained the same at 13.0 MY, making Cowan's criticism of Thom curiously irrelevant,

> 'It sometimes seems that he (Thom) selected his geometric patterns to fit his purposes rather than the data, e.g. Nine Ladies.'

To Cowan, the 'hypothetized prehistoric unit or measure' lay at the root of Thom's 'purposes', and this apparently had made him blind to the diameter being, in both solutions to the 'fit' of Nine Ladies ring, 13.0 Megalithic yards long. Thom's initial quest was, after all, to accurately establish the diameters!

Other people have attempted to find alternative techniques to fit the surveyed shapes, most notably I.O. Angell, yet unless we can determine exactly how the builders actually constructed the rings, these solutions remain, like Thom's geometries, hypothetical. They remain 'best fit' solutions. But Thom had an additional advantage up his sleeve. His discovery of the Megalithic yard and rod, in integral values, throughout many examples of every design of ring, supported the geometry. It did not 'fit his purposes', it augmented the likely reality that the constructors were using both the yard and the geometries.The yard was discovered implanted within the rings *after* Thom had drawn up the plans following the survey, and in most cases these were not directly measurable on site. *Thom's metrology and geometry mutually supported each other*.

The geometries of the non-circular rings represent a planned and developed expertise - *a technology*. While such may seem very different from our technological aims today, in its manifestation the practical or engineering component is identical and immediately recognisable, and it can immediately reconnect a modern constructor with aspects of the mindset of the original designer(s). Any modern act of marking out these geometric patterns is partaking in an original ritual that took place around 4000 years ago. In addition, and grossly understated, the rings represent *the earliest coherent example of landscape art in northwestern Europe*. Astonishingly, both these dimensions of our cultural heritage remain almost completely ignored.

Alexander Thom was the first person in modern times to enter into the enchanting world of the geometry of stone rings. His survey plans offer an easy access to understanding the rules of megalithic designs. They surely are a triumph of human creative genius, from four millennia ago.

Thom pondering the massive surveying task that confronted him on his arrival at Carnac, 1970.
[photograph by Hamish Gorrie]

CHAPTER SIX

Disposing of the Evidence
(Archaeoastronomy Post-Thom)

The approach adopted by archaeoastronomy towards Thom's research began long before Sandy Thom passed away, Dr Aubrey Burl writing in 1981 that,

> *'A catholic approach is needed by anyone contemplating the problems of archaeoastronomy. A single-minded belief in shamans, magicians and witch-doctors may be unhelpful. Equally, an obsession with astronomer-priests and the miniscule perturbations of the moon may lead an investigator a long way from the truth'*
>
> By the Light of the Cinerary Moon, ed. Ruggles & Whittle, 1981, BAR p 270

No radical developments in this package, better to concentrate on the middle ground, and a less than subtle suggestion that MacKie and Thom might be considered obsessive and were barking up the wrong tree. But even this wasn't a new stance that Burl was taking in 1981, for two decades earlier he had been urging archaeologists and archaeoastronomers alike to *avoid* looking for precision astronomical alignments,

> *' For nearly twenty years the writer has been urging archaeologists and archaeoastronomers to turn from the study of single sites, searching for high precision alignments, and, instead, to look for 'a group of similar monuments with the same orientation in a restricted locality'. Where this has been done... generalised and approximate but recognisable alignments have been demonstrated. .. . The lines discovered are never so fine that they could have been used for celestial prediction but they are consistent enough to show that in the Neolithic and Bronze Ages of the British Isles people had an obvious interest in the sun and the moon.'*
>
> (RIS, 1988, p 200)

Burl's recommendation to concentrate on 'approximate' alignments suggests to both students and non-specialists alike that maybe Thom had been mistaken in his assertion that such precision alignments existed. With the implicit suggestion that the alignments 'could never have been used for celestial prediction' but were just 'an obvious interest in the sun and moon', Burl jumps Thom's ship. The replacement word *orientation* creeps in, and eventually it became the preferred alternative to the word *alignment*.

Dr Burl then issued an astonishingly perceptive mantra for archaeologists, a mantra that somewhat contradicted his earlier assertions,

> *'More research, coupled with scepticism but unimpeded by prejudice, will bring us closer to an understanding of what such alignments...meant to the communities that laid them out. It is, after all, the pursuit of the whole past, not just the comfortably preferred elements of it, that should be the preoccupation of all who possess an interest in antiquity. No less than architecture and artefacts, astronomy and its alignments are a legitimate part of that pursuit.'* (RIS, p 200)

In this apparently well considered statement it appears that Burl had filtered out his own 'comfortably preferred elements' identified in the earlier quote 'urging archaeologists and archaeoastronomers to turn away from...searching for high precision alignments'. However, the entire future of archaeoastronomy at this time hinged on identifying the locations of sites suspected of having been used as precision astronomical alignments and evaluating the evidence for them ever having been used for these purposes. Analyses of those sites would have clarified and enlarged on Thom's hypotheses concerning alignments.

Unless archaeoastronomers were (and are) able and encouraged to estimate the level of precision at such sites, the subject stalls. A dozen stone circles having a recumbent stone roughly marking the southwestern horizon says one thing, but a twenty mile alignment aligned to a sunset whose angle gives an accurate archaeological date for the foresight monument says something quite different. A long distance lunar alignment that may have enabled a megalithic observer to know when to expect eclipses says something else again - each represents a different level of cultural achievement.

Like all other disciplines, archaeoastronomers need a regular supply of new data in order to move the subject forward. How else could they begin to satisfy what one considers to be 'proof' of such alignments - be that the statistical approach advocated by Ruggles *et al*, or the measurement of stones indicating and aligned within a minute of arc to a notch in a distant hillside where, in the Bronze Age, the major standstill moon rose or set?

The Entry of Clive Ruggles into Archaeoastronomy

During the final decade of Thom's life a newcomer began to establish himself within the archaeoastronomy scene. This newcomer was Dr Clive Ruggles, a Cambridge mathematics graduate with an interest in archaeoastronomy, based in the Department of Archaeology at the University of Wales, Cardiff. His first major impact on the subject was to revisit and check out many of the Western Scottish sites for which Thom had claimed to have found precision alignments.

Chapter Six - Disposing of the Evidence

Financed by a hefty SERC grant, and with a letter of recommendation from Thom himself, Ruggles armed himself with an equally hefty collection of theodolites and helpers, and strode off into Scotland.

The results of this research first appeared in a 1981 *British Archaeological Review* publication called *Astronomy and Society in Britain*. Ruggles co-edited this collection of essays with fellow Cardiff archaeologist Alasdair Whittle. In 1984, *BAR* published the report on the Scottish sites under the title *Megalithic Astronomy, A new archaeological and statistical study of 300 western Scottish sites*. As we shall shortly discover, the tenor of this report was not at all favourable to precision alignments, nor to other archaeoastronomers, including Thom.

This written charter for the future of archaeoastronomy post-Thom was therefore being laid down just before Thom's death, Ruggles making this telling identification of the situation,

> 'The main problem is that the archaeoastronomers have effectively been doing no more for some years than arguing amongst themselves about what constitutes reliable archaeological evidence. They are not yet ready to supply archaeologists with dependable evidence which can be considered in its social context alongside more conventional data.'
>
> *Megalithic Astronomy*, BAR 1984, p 15

All previous archaeoastronomical evidence was apparently not dependable, suggesting that archaeoastronomers cut off entirely from their past, a dismal start for building on previous work. Ruggles amplifies this theme and, having criticised the archaeoastronomers *en masse*, he now focusses on Thom,

> 'On the one hand some leading archaeoastronomers, notably Alexander Thom (whose intensive and high-quality fieldwork has formed the backbone of British archaeoastronomy for many years) refuse to accept that their evidence is in question at all, and go on to interpret it in manifestly ethnocentric terms quite unrelated to current thought about the social context (hence talk about "Megalithic Man").. . ..On the other hand, archaeologists have been keen to interpret and discuss what astronomical evidence there is, and some have tended in an equally high-handed way to select certain astronomical evidence as reliable and dismiss the rest.'
>
> *Megalithic Astronomy*, BAR 1984, p 16

In archaeology the 1980s were a love affair with 'social context', and being 'ethnocentric' was just about the worst sin an archaeologist could commit. By writing this quote in the *British Archaeological Review*, Ruggles was here surfing the archaeological wave of the time whilst at the same time rebuking some of those 'high-handed' archaeologists who, forever to their shame, had 'been keen to interpret and discuss what astronomical evidence there is', but had failed to jump over the 'selection bias' barrier, as defined by Ruggles and wheeled out by him in various publications (some to be cited later), in order to cast doubt on

Thom's precision alignments. Indeed the final phrase in the above quote very succinctly sums up Ruggles' own approach to archaeoastronomical evidence.

This quote represents a terrible school report, despite Thom's 'intensive and high-quality fieldwork' being given an A*. 'Alex has had a good term but needs to try and stop being so *ethnocentric* and to be more open to the fact that his evidence may be wrong'. The ethnocentricity could in fact be Ruggles' own, forgetting that Thom was brought up in Edwardian times, *sans* political correctness. 'Megalithic man' and 'The Boys' may not suit today's audiences, but as generic terms for the prehistoric astronomers it was an obviously suitable choice for a man brought up before women even had a vote.

Whilst both archaeology and astronomy claim to be sciences, the methodology of each is so radically different as to make any marriage of these two disciplines extremely difficult and often confusing. Ruggles labours the point,

> *'In this atmosphere of confusion, it is clear that a reasoned approach is urgently needed to investigating possible astronomical influences on the design of megalithic sites. Apt methods of analysis of putative astronomical orientations and alignments need to be formulated by the archaeoastronomers and presented clearly to the archaeological community at large for constructive criticism. Only when a reliable basic approach has been accepted can meaningful astronomical evidence be incorporated into the theories of prehistoric society'.*
>
> Megalithic Astronomy, BAR 1984, p16

It would be impossible not to agree with the admirable goals being expressed here, yet how did the work of Alexander Thom not fit into this suggested formula? Did Thom not find 'apt methods of analysis' and did he not present clearly his findings? Was his not a 'reasoned approach'? This statement is another veiled attempt to turn people away from Thom's astronomical findings. Thom openly admitted he was not qualified in archaeological matters, but then neither is Ruggles. Thom certainly 'presented clearly', academically and rigorously his findings to the archaeologists. By and large, they were ill-equipped to understand it, although some built up their careers criticising it.

Perhaps even in the words *archaeoastronomy* and *astroarchaeology* we may detect a clumsy awkwardness. The marriage twixt the two subjects has never really been recognised by academia. For it to be one day consummated, multidisciplinary skills will be needed to reunite the artefacts with their astronomy and their numbers.

Megalithic Astronomy - The End of Alignments?

With the publication of *Megalithic Astronomy - a new archaeological and statistical study of 300 western Scottish sites*, in 1984, Clive Ruggles emerged from all the uncertainty and confusion concerning the place of archaeoastronomy within archaeology as the heir apparent to Thom, who, aged 90, frail, blind and housebound, was in the final year of his life. The only other clear candidates would have been archaeologist prehistorians Euan MacKie and Aubrey Burl.

MacKie had been the first archaeologist to use the word *archaeoastronomy* in print (in 1971) and had learned the required skills in the subject, attempting thereafter to provide archaeological evidence to support astronomical intent at sites. The erudite Burl, whose first degree had been in languages, has provided through both popular and academic texts, an outstandingly useful catalogue of all matters relating to the archaeology of stone circles, including some aspects of their astronomy and metrology. Both knew Thom personally and held a high respect for him. While it could have been argued that Burl and MacKie lacked the necessary mathematical and statistical skills, Ruggles lacked the many years of archaeological experience gathered by MacKie and Burl..

Megalithic Astronomy was a tipping point in the history of the subject. From the original SRC grant, and initially welcomed by Thom, there emerged a work which appeared to discover that Thom's claims were at best over-enthusiastic and, at worst, flawed. Surveys were undertaken from 1973 to 1981 from 'an initial list of 322 sites of free standing megaliths in certain areas of western Scotland. After an archaeological reappraisal, 189 were considered for analysis.'

> *'At the most precise level, there is marginal evidence of a preference for six particular declination values to within a precision of one or two degrees.. three of the declinations may indicate a specific interest in the edges of the lunar limiting bands (the lunar 'standstills'), and would imply that organised observations were undertaken over periods of at least twenty years. However, there is no evidence of any interest in the other lunar standstill declination. The fourth preferred declination is - 25°, and may indicate an interest in the winter solstice. The fifth value (- 22.5^o)* has no particular solar or lunar significance and the last (+ 33°) is well outside those declinations attainable by the sun or moon.*
>
> *Although there is clear evidence of lunar orientation, and marginal evidence of orientation upon the winter solstice, there is no evidence whatsoever for an interest in the summer solstice or equinoxes (indeed, declinations in the vicinity of the equinoxes are strongly avoided). We find no evidence of astronomical orientations of a precision greater than one degree.'*

(* A declination of - 22.5^o is however identical to that defined by two of the 'months' in Thom's 16-month calendar structure.) + 33° remains anomalous.)

The authoritative style and the apparently thorough nature of this re-check of Scottish sites made it the only such work that could stand in comparison to Thom's exhaustive work in the same area of Scotland. That said, like Thom's book, it is difficult to access, for different reasons - and the methodology is strangely different.

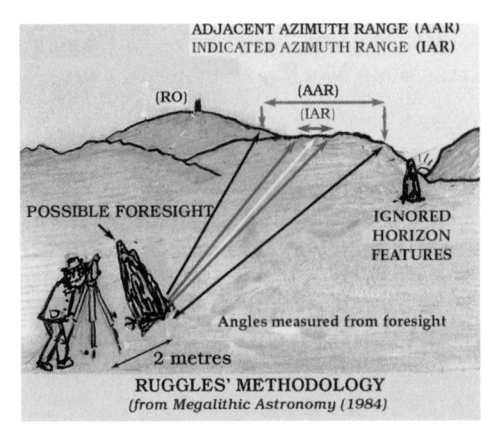

Ruggles' Methodology

The surveying methodology is defined on page 60 of *Megalithic Astronomy*,

'We define the <u>indicated azimuth range</u> (IAR) as that range of horizon which can reasonably be supposed to have been indicated by a given configuration on the ground, taking into account,

(i) different possible ways of providing the indication, e.g. in the case of an alignment of menhirs, lining up the uppermost points of the menhirs or lining up their sides; and,

(ii) possible changes in the direction indicated due to movement of individual menhirs.

We shall only quote the edges of an IAR to an accuracy of $0°.2$. Greater accuracy is seldom justified because of uncertainties in the deterioration of an indicating structure since its erection. Thus no IAR can have a width of azimuth of less than $0°.2$. (12', a fifth of one degree)

Suppose that the width of the IAR is I. We define the <u>adjacent azimuth range</u> (AAR) as a range of horizon extending for an azimuth A on either side of it, where,

$A = 1°$ *when I is up to* $1°$

$A = I$ *when I is between* $1°$ *to* $2°$; *and*

$A = 2°$ *when I is above* $2°$.

The horizon range could, when $I = 2°$, be as high as 6 degrees, $\pm 3°$ either side of the central azimuth position, shown in white on the diagram above.

The Two Methodologies Compared

Thom's methodology (*left*) was based on a survey of all the identified monuments in and around the vicinity of the site, which were first accurately surveyed. From each monument the horizon would be profiled, with particular attention paid around the four critical angles where extreme sun and moon rises and sets occur, plus the equinoctial positions. True north would be established if and when the sun made an appearance, or geodetic formulae applied to a distant reference object.

Chapter Six - Disposing of the Evidence

Thom would then draw up a large scale plan of the site and calculate all the horizon angles for the date of the site as determined (where possible) by archaeologists. In the process he attempted to identify how the site 'worked'. To do this, he specified that a minimum accuracy of better than one minute of one degree was necessary. On the other hand Ruggles paid little attention to the horizon (*left,upper*), and instead concentrated on the angle of orientation of slab-sided single orthostats (upright megaliths), pairs of stones or rows. The limits of the angular range as determined from 2m behind the supposed backsight stone would be used to determine which angular range on the horizon was relevant. Crude computer graphics (it was the 1980s) produced a profile of this range upon which declinations were marked, this removing any need to specifically date the site. The best accuracy was limited to twelve minutes of one degree (0.2 degrees) and was usually much worse than this.

Both methodologies have their limitations, as in any scientific experiment. It is true that Thom was actively looking for precision alignments, while Ruggles was commendably attempting to remove 'selection bias' from his experiment, by looking for evidence of aligned foresight stones without noting if they pointed at the horizon where significant celestial events happened. Thom thought that if a site pointed very accurately to a horizon rise or set, then any aligned stones near the identified foresight acted as low precision indicators of the direction an observer should be looking to observe it. Ruggles drew his conclusions with much less regard to natural landscape features that might define an alignment. He paid almost no heed to the horizon and his report drew almost exclusively from the backsight, and any foresight on the horizon had to be further away than 1km from the backsight.

To his credit, Dr Ruggles designed an experiment to test Thom's findings and then undertook the considerable work needed to test his hypothesis. If his methodology was different, if one disagreed with his conclusions, then so what? It was long overdue for Thom's work to be set alongside other work. With the publication of Ruggles' report there was at least the potential for further debate and discussion within the subject of precision alignments. Alas, Ruggles report, like Thom's books, was only aimed at specialists in the subject, and by 1984 there were very few people in this category. Ruggles thus had very few specialists to communicate with on his level, while a great many archaeologists stood on the sideline waiting to be told what to believe, by Ruggles. It was not a particularly healthy environment for an open debate on the results.

MacKie's critical review of *Megalithic Astronomy*

MacKie was quick to point out in his review of the book for *Archaeoastronomy* Vol VII (1-4), 1984, that this methodology inherently *prevented* the discovery of accurate alignments,

> 'It is actually important to understand - since it is not actually clearly explained - that the basic unit of study is the backsight only, in its various direction indicating

combinations. The parts of the horizon pointed at are defined objectively by looking along the oriented artificial features from a position 2m behind them and marking the approximate outer limits of the zone which could be indicated, usually between 0.25^o and 1.0^o wide.

In other words all the configurations of the horizon, except its altitude, have been altogether ignored and the assumption evidently is that only oriented stones are being dealt with... It is true that many of the the drawn horizons are rather flat and featureless but it still doesn't matter if there is a conspicuous peak or notch slightly away from the literal alignment of the stones (of the backsight). It is ignored.

This procedure was of course decided on to avoid falling into the trap of looking, even unconsciously, for 'suitable' horizon foresights and then accepting them, and from a praiseworthy desire not to take the alignment theory for granted. However, this method of analysis has by its very nature to preclude absolutely the identification of accurate alignments, and it is hardly possible to agree with the author's claim to have disproved their existence. He has simply prevented them being considered, in the same way that he has ruled out all sight lines with horizons nearer than 1 Km.'

It was surely a curious decision not to take into account any need to identify any significant foresight feature - a notch, prominent hill-slope or outcrop on the horizon, within the angular range suggested from the backsight. By taking such a decision the data collection presented here was rendered incomplete and usefully might have contained at least some indication of just what is to be found on the horizon within the astonishingly wide 'bandwidth' chosen by the treatment of the backsight. The enviable list of high quality theodolites listed on page 69 would hardly have been necessary to measure angles to $0^o.2$, twelve minutes of a degree and this list must be seen as window dressing to add weight to the seriousness and validity of the work. By only looking along orientations (low precision indicators of solar or lunar key positions) of slabs, pairs of stones and sometimes rows of stones at an identified possible backsight, high precision alignments were thus excluded.

Mackie had exposed this flaw and had also found this methodology 'not clearly explained', concluding,

'There is therefore no reason to accept the author's conclusion that only approximate orientations were intended, because it is forced on him by the way his data on the potential accuracy of the stones was collected - at the backsights only. One cannot prove that only rough sight lines existed by permitting only such lines to be considered.'

MacKie had identified the key issue: Ruggles' methodology at the 'Thom' sites was fundamentally different to Thom's and had led to different conclusions. Thom himself picked up on the same issue, aged 90 (full citation on page 23). In an ideal world Ruggles and MacKie should have joined forces as an endangered species within archaeology. However, scratch the thin veneer of professional

Chapter Six - Disposing of the Evidence

politeness and one can quickly find evidence that this was never going to be the case. Following Thom's death in 1985, Ruggles oversaw the preparation of a collection of 'papers in memory of Alexander Thom', under the title *Records in Stone* (Cambridge). The only open criticism in the book is directed at MacKie, within Ruggles' own contribution, an essay entitled, *Stone Alignments of Argyll and Mull: a perspective on the statistical approach in archaeoastronomy*. The footnote at the bottom of page 233 suggests that Ruggles was still smarting from MacKie's review,

> 'This survey concentrated on the possibility of astronomical orientations of lower precision than those envisaged by Thom in his later work, and its results must be considered in conjunction with the earlier papers of this author where the high-precision alignments were comprehensively assessed. It is, for example, quite misleading of MacKie (1986), in a review of this work, simply to ignore the earlier work and then criticise the survey of 300 sites on the grounds that it did not take into account possible high-precision alignments.'

There are interesting details in this comment. The 'high-precision alignments' that were 'comprehensively assessed' in 'the earlier papers of the author' were a) not the only high-precision alignments in Thom's catalogue and therefore b) were selected by Ruggles. This too is not made very clear. And had Mackie mentioned the earlier material in his review he would surely have had to ask a difficult question: If from the 'earlier papers' there appeared to be no evidence for precision alignments, was it another form of selection bias, that of the author, that precluded him looking more closely at the horizons in the later work - had he already made up his mind on the matter?

One of the earlier works being referred to here is Ruggles' *A Critical Examination of the Megalithic Lunar Observatories*, BAR 88, published in 1981, where the use of long distance foresights had already been dismissed in the conclusions thus,

> 'No overall evidence remained for the preferential observation of the lunar limbs.' .. and 'It was argued that the presence of apparently significant trends ... is tantamount to proof of bias in the selection of data.' .. and 'It was found that no evidence whatsoever remained for observations of the 9' wobble.'.. and ' Taken together these factors lead us overwhelmingly to the conclusion that lunar motions were *not* in fact observed and recorded to high precision by the megalith builders' BAR 88, pp 196 - 197.

I am aware that the reader may find all of this a pain in the backsight, yet the whole future of archaeoastronomy hung in the balance on this and other contemporary major research reports. Further, the history of the subject will remain incomplete without more people understanding what lay between the lines of such material, or the underlying political motives. Compared to Thom's approach to alignments, this new methodology seemed to obfuscate the subject.

For example, a significant paragraph on page 380 of *Megalithic Astronomy* needs to be far more widely quoted, whenever the subject of precision alignments is mentioned, or their reality called into doubt in popular books and press releases, some examples of which are given later in this chapter,

> 'We have not examined our data for very high precision indications using distant horizon features such as notches, on the grounds that there is no motivation from our data at lower precisions to do so.'

The possibility of there being high precision alignments has not been eliminated, nor could it have been under the conditions of the methodology applied. The point is now sufficiently made. Ruggles' data offered too low an angular precision to show precision alignments in the results. MacKie blew the whistle on this in his review, and Thom also queried the methodology,

> 'This does not make sense and we must look further. ...Ruggles' conclusions must be wide of the mark. ... It seems to me that he has introduced a new set of problems for statisticians to solve when they try to explain his peculiar results.'

By now, Thom's days of 'looking further' were virtually over. He was 90 and almost blind when he dictated this for Hilda Gustin to type up and air-mail to his friend and supporter Robert Merritt in Ohio. According to Thom's daughter, Beryl, Thom and his son Archie,

> "..asked Dr Ruggles to explain certain aspects of his work. His reply was peremptory,"Oh, I'm just doing it to make sure everything's alright", which infuriated my father. During the last ten years of his life, my father became very sad concerning the avalanche of criticism and denigration he struggled against. He would frequently shake his head and say, 'If only they would help me, we could... ...'"

According to John Michell, Thom *'deplored the quibbling approach of modern statisticians who, he said, are no longer prepared to listen to a reasoned argument'*.

The King is dead, Long live the King

With the publication of these two volumes, with contributions from various archaeologists, the *British Archaeological Review* effectively oversaw the demolition of Thom's astronomical hypotheses, during Thom's last years. In the epilogue to the above quoted paper, having seemingly discounted all Thom's work on lunar observatories, Ruggles adopts what is almost a standard formula eulogy to Alexander Thom, to be repeated in most of the other contributors' concluding paragraphs,

> 'Whatever subsequent work may prove or disprove, Professor Thom's contribution, in megalithic astronomy as in megalithic mensuration and geometry, is of incomparable importance in a pioneering sense.'

Chapter Six - Disposing of the Evidence

The Old King was dead, intellectually speaking, and the throne of archaeoastronomy was now vacant. With these reviews, essays and analyses, Ruggles took the crown from Thom, eventually becoming Professor of Archaeoastronomy within the Social Sciences Department of the University of Leicester, in January 2000. He has recently (2006) become President of the Prehistoric Society.

However much archaeologists must have been glad to be spared the complexity of Thom's research, however happy they were that the burden of understanding the astrophysics, geometry and metrology required to understand Thom's findings had been lifted off their shoulders, they were now in effect handing over the keys to the car of archaeoastronomy to one man. The subject had moved from one specialist (Thom) who had said one thing based on apparently rigorous scientific evidence, to another (Ruggles), who was saying another thing and had refuted much of the Thom package. Monopolies are never very healthy things, doubly so within the supposedly intellectual atmosphere of universities. In 1988, with specific regard to archaeoastronomy, Ruggles defined the following 'fundamental problem',

> *'The fundamental problem is that evidence acceptable to a numerate scientist is of a very different nature from that acceptable to his counterpart trained in the humanities. It is the view of this author that much of the controversy stirred up by archaeoastronomical investigations stems not from sheer prejudice, as is often claimed on both sides, or even from the lack of detailed background knowledge or ability in mathematics, astronomy or archaeology; but merely from this simple fact. In an interdisciplinary area such as archaeoastronomy two very different approaches to the interpretation of evidence meet head-on, and in order for progress to be made they* **must** *be reconciled so that the available evidence can be considered in its entirety in a satisfactory way'*

(RIS, p 249.)

Nearly 20 years after this mission statement was penned, and there is no sign whatsoever that the two different approaches to interpretation have been reconciled. And the sad truth is that, largely due to these fine essays written in the late 1970s and early 1980s, there is almost no one in the profession out there looking for any kind of alignment, precision or otherwise, any more, and even a suggestion of an orientation may bring scorn. Such issues are now left to amateurs - the vacuum mentioned in an earlier chapter. Although the problem has clearly been identified and a solution proposed, the boat of academic archaeoastronomy in Britain remains at anchor, its sails luffing idly.

It is important to remember that while Ruggles challenged the astronomical aspects of Thom's work, he has to date made few convincing inroads into the other aspects - those items covered in chapter two. The geometry and metrology of megalithic architecture are also conveniently forgotten by academia.

Archaeoastronomy - the Re-write

Despite all the high rhetoric and defining of goals to unite astronomy with archaeology, it is hardly possible to take any academic course of study in archaeoastronomy anywhere in Britain, in contrast to 27 colleges doing just that in America. Even worse was to come. The platform created by this apparently unassailable debunking of Thom's megalithic astronomy now enabled the popular press to confidently print glib overview statements that influenced non-specialists away from considering the original evidence. Authority on such matters had now moved away from Thom. In *Astronomy before the Telescope* (BCA 1996), Ruggles made the following vague statement in a chapter entitled *Archaeoastronomy in Europe*, concerning Thom's 16-month calendar being the forerunner of the Celtic 'half-quarter-days' (*sic*),

> *'The sites themselves are not calendrical instruments, it is much more likely that that by incorporating alignments upon a certain calendrical date, they express the symbolism with the ceremonies taking place on that date, and thereby reinforce those ceremonies.'*

So what exactly does *this* unclear statement mean, that they are 'not calendrical instruments' but they indicate, via alignments, certain calendar dates, i.e. dates on which a salient sun rise or set occurs along the alignment, upon which ceremonies are held? How do such sites then differ from a calendrical instrument? How is the 'certain calendrical date' determined without reference to the heavens? Even a Neolithic burial arranged with the cadaver lying east-west in its grave cannot be undertaken without reference to the heavens.

Ruggles continues, in his more definite final paragraph,

> *'There is no evidence of the use of astronomical observations for practical purposes such as determination of the time of year.'*

The suggestion is again implicit that we pack up our theodolites and go home. And is it true, as Ruggles claims it to be, again in the above essay, that 'such activities would not tend to leave a trace in the archaeological record'? In a curious emulation of Graham Clark (*see page 83*), he appears to make the career of archaeoastronomer untenable - after all, there is nothing much to do!

If Ruggles appears to have saved us all from a lot of wasted time and misguided effort there remains plenty of evidence, not just from Thom, but also from other archaeoastronomers throughout the world that solar alignments were widely used to determine the time of year. One may argue endlessly concerning their precision, and the other matters previously discussed, but this kind of blanket statement lays a false trail to the non-specialist reader. It says that there exists no evidence when it really means, in *Crawfordesque* style, "I don't believe the evidence." The word believe is the crucial one, Ruggles does not believe the evidence, based on his methodology, because he believes, as Thom did, that

Chapter Six - Disposing of the Evidence

his methodology is the correct, even the only way to approach the subject. He wheeled it out to discount precision alignments earlier in the same article,

> 'Other claims for high-precision astronomy... have now been discounted on the grounds that they can be explained away through data selection effects.'

Again the implication that Thom, and other archaeoastronomers, were wasting their time, calendrically determined or otherwise. The other, and much worse implication is that Thom was twisting his data to suit his hypothesis. To further dismiss precision alignments, a 'wild-card' is introduced,

> 'The argument for high-precision alignments at prehistoric sites also conflicts with recent evidence from modern astronomy, which indicates that day to day variations in atmospheric refraction are much greater than previously thought'

'This unidentified 'recent evidence' conveys the message to an aspiring archaeoastronomer that there is little worth investigating in the subject's past, in Thom's data. The subject is done with. Thom's 500 measurements of horizon refraction variation, and the following analysis and conclusions, published in the *Journal of the Institute of Navigation* apparently count for naught.

Naturally, this negative attitude towards Thom and archaeoastronomy in general has been picked up by astronomers and archaeoastronomers from outside Britain. Professor Bryan Penprase, Director of Brackett Observatory and Associate Professor of Astronomy at Pomona College, Claremont, California told me during a recent visit to West Wales that,

> "The subject (archaeoastronomy) appears to be wallowing in self-doubt in Britain, as if everyone is afraid of the consequences of putting a foot wrong."

Don't Mention the Megalithic Yard

Such fear of upsetting the apple-cart of orthodoxy has cowed even the more adventurous of our leading modern academic archaeologists. Professor John North, despite having moved from Oxford to the relative safety of the University of Groningen, Denmark, writes in the preface to his huge book *Stonehenge* (HarperCollins, 1996),

> 'Many will be horrified at my defence of the Megalithic yard, and even more so by its occasional use in plans. By this I do not mean to prejudge the question of whether it was in use, but merely to simplify the task of judging whether it might have been so.'

The caveat in that stunning second sentence says it all, North must have been up all night getting the wording right to gain this papal dispensation! And glancing through modern books about prehistory aimed at today's undergraduates, it is rare to find Thom listed in the index. In the main body of the text the reader may occasionally find a line or two about his 16 month calendar and its connections with the ritual 'cross-quarter days' of the later Celts. One recent book that does include a mention of the Thom 16-month calendar, as well it might, is *The Archaeology of Time* (Routledge, 2005) by Gavin Lucas, Assistant Director of the Institute of Archaeology in Rekyjavik,

> *'Thom's interpretations were never fully accepted, but he did make the idea of astronomical knowledge in prehistory hard to ignore.'*

Inconvenient of Thom to have done that, but most modern archaeologists have nevertheless managed to ignore most of it completely. For an academic book carrying such a title to have reduced Thom's input to this trivial comment demonstrates how far back Thom has receded in importance in prehistoric studies of time and cycles.

Thom-bashing has also crept into some academic textbooks. In Dr Ronald Hutton's book, *The Pagan Religions of the British Isles* (Blackwell, 1991) he wrote,

> *'Alexander Thom's assertions were received in silence by most mainstream prehistorians. This was because they did not feel competent to reply to them. To do so required a training in archaeology, astronomy and statistics, and the specialists in the monuments concerned usually had only the first of these. On the other hand, Professor Thom actually had none of them, and as a result made some obvious gaffes...'* (Hutton, 1991, p 112)

As Thom had taught classical statistics for at least thirty years, had papers published by the Royal Statistical Society, ground his own 12 inch telescope lenses, advised a Russian Observatory on the (correct) orbit of a comet and had been a Fellow of the Royal Astronomical Society, it appears that Hutton is the one who has made all the gaffes. Hutton begins his next paragraph,

> *'By the end of the 1970s, the collusion between archaeologists, astronomers and statisticians necessary to consider Alexander Thom's work had begun. By now he was dead and unable to answer his critics, but perhaps it was just as well that he was spared what ensued.'* (Hutton, 1991, p112)

This premature report of Thom's early death some 15 years before it happened perhaps suggests wishful thinking, and through this further gaffe the final attempt at sympathy for Thom over the hammering he received is rendered meaningless. One notes the appearance of the word *collusion*, 'a secret agreement for fraudulent or illegal purpose; conspiring.' (Collin's Dictionary).

Hutton takes three further pages to more or less debunk Thom's entire life work with the megaliths. On the flimsiest of cited evidence, he suggests that the astronomy was misguided, the alleged geometries of stone circles were simply because the builders were sloppy, and that they had laid them out by eye - no ropes and pegs here! The criticisms of a scant few archaeologists are cited where no mention is made of Kendall's *Royal Society* lecture nor of the measuring rods, unearthed from unpronounceable places in Denmark, which were marked up in fifths of Thom's unit of length. The Megalithic yard is not indexed.

It is not Hutton we are reading, it is what Hutton has read. It is the product of the Thom-bashing that originated in the 70s. In a final patronising paragraph - the formulaic eulogy - that Thom was also well spared, Hutton writes,

> *'Nevertheless, any prehistorian has reason to be grateful that Alexander Thom lived and worked. It is not merely that he was a magnificent personality, nor that he greatly stimulated interest in this aspect of prehistory. It is also because he was, pre-eminently, a first-rate engineer, and most of the plans which he made of so many monuments are not merely excellent, but in many cases the only surveys that we have.'*
>
> (Hutton, 1991, p 114)

Hutton's book is an admirable attempt to revise our knowledge of ancient British religious beliefs and supply academics and 'earth mystics' alike with a workable textbook about pagan Britain. And Hutton does at least give an account of Thom's output and the impact it had. But he toes the party line, debunking Thom in the process, along with MacKie and other notable archaeologists, New Age writers and the 'loony fringe'. Despite this, the cover notes inform us that,

> *'Dr Hutton shows how a host of recieved* (sic) *ideas have been demolished, and how the pagans of ancient Britain were far more creative, complex, enigmatic and dynamic than has previously been supposed.'*

But despite all these wonderful attributes the forefathers of these same pagans never once undertook precision astronomical observations nor developed units of measure or indulged in any geometrical wizardry.

I once enjoyed lunch with Hutton in The Bear Hotel, Devizes. He has an enviable grasp of his subject. But in writing against Thom in the manner presented, the gaps in his scholarship surely demonstrate the effectiveness of the bias induced by the standard Thom-busting formulae which had begun in the 70s. In a sense, Hutton was correct - by the late 1970s Thom was already dead, within academia.

Back to the Land - the Rise of Phenomenology

In a more recently adopted archaeological model, collectively referred to as *phenomenology*, the circles and their alignments have become 'symbolic' and 'ritual', (stance three in the list of options on page 89) and symbolic alignments and a subjective assessment of sites replaces the hard scientific analyses of Alexander Thom. The pioneer of this new approach was Christopher Tilley, whose book *A Phenomenology of landscape: places, paths and monuments* (1994) attempted to provide an ethnographically based system of field observation that embraced 'sacred geography' within Neolithic culture.

Phenomenology was very persuasive, largely because it encompassed material that had been left out of academic study, and which had previously been enjoyed and employed by the 'earth mysteries' people, ley hunters, dowsers and sacred geographers. Indeed, some academic phenomenologists have written articles that would not at all have been out of place in *The Leyhunter Journal* or the later *Society of Leyhunters* newsletter.

If golf is 'a good walk spoiled' then phenomenology is, at least, 'a good walk enhanced', but better than that, phenomenology took people out of their heads and books and placed them back out into the landscape, looking at the context within which the monuments were located as a method of gaining insight into the social meaning of the overall structure. The way aligned sites were assessed by Thom was initially not at all dissimilar to this, yet the manner by which he then gleaned his evidence could not have been more different than Tilley's approach.

Phenomenology could be almost totally subjective, and textbooks appear liberally sprinkled with phrases such as, '*a highly significant hill*' (Cummings and Whittle, *Places of special virtue: megaliths in the Neolithic landscape of Wales* Oxford, 2004, p 82) and '*the rock outcrops simultaneously make the monuments visible and invisible*' (Tilley, *A phenomenology of landscape: places paths and monuments*, Oxford 1994, pp 96, 99). In *The Materiality of Stone* (Oxford, 2004) Tilley launches an attack on positivism, claiming that '(the)..*thin technicist archaeological description* (makes the past) *thin and sterile*', to which Thom might have replied, "No, not if it enables me to demonstrate a high cultural level of astronomy, metrology and geometry within prehistoric societies. What is thin and sterile about that?"

Phenomenology has enjoyed quite a ride of academic acceptance within the Universities. One phenomenologist actually commended to his audience at the recent *Megalithomania* conference (May, 2006), "throw away your theodolites". This remark takes subjectivity to a new level, by in effect recommending that all accurate measurement of field evidence, in archaeology as well as for ancient astronomy, is ceased. One is left wondering if phenomenologists ever use maps, rulers or compasses.

One half of the landscape is, of course, the sky, yet phenomenology fails to incorporate orientations and alignments of the sun and moon within its output. Here is an Aladdin's cave filled with landscape geometry, earth-related units of length and solar and lunar rise and set positions that need investigation as the holistic interpretation of a landscape. If ever there was a subject crying out to embrace *Thomian* material, it is phenomenology. Why it has not done so is surely in part due to the pre-conditioning of the archaeology profession against such material. And that hardly anyone can do the sums.

Experienced and well respected archaeologists have launched serious academic criticism against phenomenology. Professor Andrew Fleming, a highly influential prehistorian, wrote a scathing attack on this interpretive model in *Antiquity* (Vol 79, 2005, pp 921-932),

> '*Archaeological fieldwork has been well served over the years by a combination of empiricism, logical positivism and critical scepticism, supported by careful observation and recording. It comes as something of a shock to encounter a version of 'landscape archaeology' (Cummings*

and Whittle, 2004, p 17 & 22) which is much more dependent on rhetoric, speculation, argument by assertion, and observations not always replicable when checked.'

'Of course prehistorians are free to believe in Neolithic ritual specialists noted for the idiosyncracies and heterogeneity of their locational and architectural decision making within small neighbourhoods - people who were incapable of reaching much agreement about cosmically significant targets and changed their minds over short (and sometimes very short) periods of time, and who were capable of both architectural perversity and 'careful orchestration'. Such a vision might 'make sense' of the claims and suggestions made by Tilley and Cummings. After all, human life and thought are usually untidy. But has this Neolithic incoherence been revealed, or is it a by-product of the investigators' wishful thinking?'

Fleming finds himself between a 'highly significant' rock and a meaningful hard place. As a leading and influential prehistorian he has, according to the strapline of his article *'taken phenomenology by the horns'*, yet in the same critique he also rejects Thom, lumping him in with Alfred Watkins, failing to recognise that Watkins and Thom were poles apart in how they defined and researched alignments.

'Watkins and Thom, working in positivist frameworks, documented their views in considerable detail. But the rules of argument which they set up were simply not rigorous enough to satisfy archaeologists' normal requirement for the validation of claims for patterns and relationships in archaeological data. Eventually, Watkins and Thom were vulnerable to archaeological common sense; credulity was strained by the notion that prehistoric people travelled in straight lines, or employed, over a considerable area, a unit of measurement standardised with tolerances best expressed by citing the thickness of a wasp's leg.'

Fleming's statement that Thom's arguments were 'simply not rigorous enough for archaeologists', is untrue, and the reverse would be more accurate. The 'wasp's leg' analogy had been borrowed from Burl, and this brief and incomplete look at modern attitudes to archaeoastronomy brings us full circle from Burl's opening quotation earlier in the chapter. These quotations maintain the mantra - Thom's material is not worthy of study.

It may be thought that the divide between archaeoastronomy and that of the phenomenologists cleaves a mighty chasm within archaeology, yet both claim to be evidence driven, Tilley writing surprisingly, in 2004, in *The Materiality of Stone* (Oxford) that,

'Our work here is open...to new interpretations... since anyone can visit these stones and experience these places themselves, make new observations and check old ones.'

Old Thom could have said these very words. Interpretations may differ, and they do, but the evidence remains on the ground for anyone bothered enough to visit the sites and explore the territory. Only a single and limited facet of the subject to aspiring students - the astronomy - has been critiqued. The geometry and metrology remain fully operational aspects of prehistoric culture available for other archaeologists to explore. There is space for other views and interpretations of data, particularly when practically gleaned from quality fieldwork.

The Fall of Archaeoastronomy as an Academic Discipline

Two well written and unbiased popular books to emerge on the subject of archaeoastronomy supported Thom's work into the 1980s. *Sun, Moon and Standing Stones* (Oxford, 1978) by John E Wood presented the evidence for and against leaving his readers to make up their own mind on the matter. A member of the Royal Archaeological Institute and also the Deputy Director of the Admiralty Surface Weapons Establishment, Dr Wood melded a popular treatment with important and unbiased academic detail. The universities, one feels, in the language of the assessment, 'could do better' in failing to match this work. The other book was by a Cambridge mathematician. Douglas Heggie's *Megalithic Science* (T&H, 1981), gave an excellent account of the evidence, yet the author pulled back somewhat from his earlier convictions (*Antiquity* 181, 1972) where he concluded,

> 'Thom's evidence that megalithic man observed the moon is so strong that it may be accepted without hesitation.'

In the prologue to this article the editor, Glyn Daniel, concluded,

> 'no reasonable archaeologist can do other than give Thom's work the most serious consideration.'

Books like these, readable, clearly illustrated and written from outside of the archaeological profession, were able to deal with the complex issues raised by Thom's work. Such have have not appeared since. The tacit message from this fact is now, I trust, crystal clear. The collective tide of interest in such matters has ebbed away, partly for the reasons spelled out in the previous pages. Thom has disappeared from the scene.

It cannot be overemphasised that students of archaeology are offered little if any opportunity to compare the party line on archaeoastronomy with the evidence available from Thom and other contributors. Here is Piggott's refuted 'closed shop', alive and well, the complete antithesis of academic freedom, debate and argument. An archaeology undergraduate in 1986, prehistorian Dr Trevor Kirk recently wrote to the author,

> 'As for archaeoastronomy when I was an undergraduate, I don't recall any real discussion of the subject at all. It was 20 years ago, so perhaps I'm forgetting some isolated and obscure seminar. But that's probably where archaeoastronomy was discussed, if it appeared on the radar at all.'

Chapter Six - Disposing of the Evidence

In 1999, a curious paragraph written by Ruggles in *Astronomy in Prehistoric Britain and Ireland* (Yale, 1999) reveals something else of what has gone wrong with archaeoastronomy,

> *'More recently, the particular emphasis on supposed alignments has been questioned and they are now generally seen in proper perspective as merely one aspect of the evidence relating to astronomical practice that might be retrievable from the material record. Despite this, many archaeoastronomers still seem to view any attempt at quantitative assessment with suspicion, regarding this as inevitably 'positivistic'.*

The subject of astronomical alignments has been made to appear largely an irrelevance, as reinforced above by the loaded phrases *'supposed alignments'*, and *'merely one aspect of the evidence relating to astronomical practice'*, and *'might be retrievable'* (should anyone need to bother!). However, the real revelation is to be found in the final sentence. Can it be the case that archaeoastronomers are actually trying to avoid 'quantitative assessment', a euphemism for mathematical analysis, within a subject where a high degree of numeracy is an essential pre-requisite in order to enable determination of almost all the astronomical and geodetic parameters in any research? If this be true then truly Thom's era is over.

The Problem with Numbers

In his inaugural lecture as Professor of Archaeoastronomy at Leicester University, Clive Ruggles underplayed the mathematical component,

> *'Laughable as most archaeologists found 'megalithic man', very few indeed felt themselves competent to judge Thom's mathematical arguments and one who did - Richard Atkinson, the excavator of Stonehenge - actually came down in his support. Arguments sparked off by Thom's work raged throughout the 1970s with leading archaeologists, astronomers, historians and statisticians all wading in, while the silent majority preferred to watch intently, but safely, from the sidelines. In fact, the technical concepts underlying a great deal of archaeoastronomy are really very simple..'*

Archaeoastronomy, no.25 (JHA xxxi (2000)

The decline in facility in mathematical skills is a factor that cannot be ignored in explaining some of the reasons for the decline in archaeoastronomy - which in spite of the final sentence quoted above remains a highly mathematically based subject.* This is even confirmed by Ruggles's own lecture notes, given out by the School of Archaeology and Ancient History at the University of Leicester, where one may read, incredulously,

> *'Thom's "megalithic astronomy". In the course we do not consider the work of Alexander Thom and its reassessment in any detail, partly because the subject is a very technical one and partly because many of the issues are no longer of archaeological interest'*

---

* GPS devices and computer programs have greatly simplified matters since 1990.

Which is it, 'the technical concepts underlying a great deal of archaeoastronomy are really very simple', or, 'the subject is a very technical one'? Whichever it is, and there is clearly some confusion here, there will obviously be no reassessment of Thom's work at Leicester. But even if one dismisses the astronomical components of Thom's output, can anyone honestly believe that 400 accurate survey plans, ten major geometrical designs of stone rings, the consistent and linked metrology of the rings and the cup and ring marks are 'no longer of archaeological interest'? Of course not. The evidence has been disposed of because something is being avoided here.

One noted archaeologist has ably summed up the profession's inabilities to assess numerically based evidence. The late Livio Stecchini, Professor of the History of Science, an archaeologist himself and the greatest metrologist of the post-war era, wrote about his own entry into historical research that,

> 'I was gradually forced to accept the fact that scholars of ancient history do not read numbers, neither in ancient texts nor in research papers. .. I was told that "numbers do not constitute evidence in ancient studies." Finally I learned that I had no choice but to pursue my interests in splendid isolation.'

This strongly worded and revealing account of the archaeological profession ignoring numerically based evidence is reinforced by one of the most respected archaeologists of his day. During a visit to the Thom family in the early 70s, in connection with the planning of Thom's forthcoming survey of Stonehenge, Professor Richard Atkinson told Thom's daughter, Beryl Austin, that,

> "I could hardly add five plus five before I met the work of your father and then made time to understand the mathematics in his work. Through this I was able to see some missing components of the incomplete picture I had held of the prehistoric culture."

This problem is not confined to archaeologists, it pervades the whole of the educational system. It is worth citing the magnificently outrageous title of John Hammersley's famous article in the *Bulletin of the Institution of Mathematics and its Applications* (Vol 4, 4), October 1968, pp 66-85, entitled,

> 'On the enfeeblement of mathematical skills by 'Modern Mathematics' and by similar soft intellectual trash in schools and universities'.

This article was another well constructed parcel bomb from one of our top academic mathematicians directed at Britain's inability to train mathematicians or to accord due value to the numerate sciences. Sandy Thom would surely have read it, and would equally surely have nodded resignedly.

The Need for Postgraduate Training Programmes

Later in his inaugural lecture, Professor Ruggles makes the following concluding remarks, a 'mission statement' for the future of archaeoastronomy,

Chapter Six - Disposing of the Evidence

'Academics are very prone to constructing 'brick walls' around their own disciplines. Yet the majority of academics working in archaeoastronomy have found themselves breaching disciplinary boundaries in earnest. Like myself, most have probably been several times through the process of realizing the depths of their own ignorance in another field, and having to work fast to achieve an acceptable level of discourse with previously undiscovered sets of academic peers. Being interdisciplinary involves being aware of the non-superiority of one's own disciplinary view, being brave enough to admit one's own deficiencies when stepping into a new field, and being prepared to listen to what those already there have to tell us.

Difficult as this may be for the established academic, it is a formidable problem for young workers in the field. There is a serious issue here that can be addressed only through good interdisciplinary postgraduate training programmes.'

Archaeoastronomy, no.25 (JHA xxxi (2000)

The fine aspirations of the final paragraph are *exactly* what has been needed to encourage archaeoastronomical work. Despite this, a recent MA postgraduate course entitled *Archaeoastronomy and Landscape Archaeology*, prepared by the author and archaeologists at the University of Wales, Lampeter, was dropped by the University largely as a result of Professors Ruggles' and Parker Pearson's negative validation reports. It is hard to believe in the fine words above within the context of their author actually discouraging from happening what he purports to support. It remains true that it is not possible to take an undergraduate or postgraduate course in archaeoastronomy anywhere in Britain, a situation which, in view of the obvious importance of the subject, is a dismal and wholly unsatisfactory state of affairs.

SUMMARY

In preparing this chapter I sometimes became quite depressed at the demolition job undertaken on Thom's evidence during the late 70s and throughout the 80s. It seemed at the time, and it remains true to this day, that no other person had opened up such an insight into previously unknown and culturally important components of prehistoric life - even the reasons for the circles, rows and standing stones being put there in the first place.

It continues to amaze me how much anger one can find expressed in archaeological circles when Thom's name is mentioned, often accompanied by a commensurate amount of ignorance if one pursues the matter. The extent of this hostility is a sure sign that Thom's package has deeply affected, if not all archaeologists, then the subject of archaeology itself, which presently remains in more or less total denial of the evidence Thom revealed, primarily because of the implications of that evidence. As for the archaeoastronomers who have criticised Thom, some of these resemble the kind of people who happily accept an invitation to a party but then complain to the host that it's a lousy one, or that one or two of the cut crystal glasses are chipped. For forty years, Thom threw and was the host of a fantastic party, yet his guests mostly arrived late, many gatecrashed, and one feels most might have been much more gracious.

Dr Ruggles did a very thorough job producing the required re-assessment of Thom's work, challenging it to the point where it appeared to offer very little evidence for any kind of alignment, solar or lunar. As a result Thom has been almost completely airbrushed from archaeoastronomy in Britain, despite being the originator of that discipline as we understand the term today and despite Anthony Aveni writing, in *Records in Stone*, that,

> 'Nowhere has the impact of the Thom methodology been more deeply felt than in the Americas, where alignment studies have been conducted with varying degrees of success in cultures ranging from the prehistoric period to the Spanish Conquest and from New England and south-west Canada to Peru. ... Thom raised the engaging question; do the remains of ancient civilisations reflect a knowledge of astronomy by virtue of the way they are laid out in the landscape? Thom offered us a methodology for seeking the answer to this question.'

To reject a new model of reality that threatens to radically change an established 'safe' model can be compared with an organism rejecting an infection. The boundary 'skin' of the subject becomes strengthened against the intruding virus, through peer group exclusion in journals, and by ensuring that nobody is able to inject the new ideas directly into the cell structure of the culture that holds fast to the established (i.e. 'right') model. Antibodies appear as authoritative publications which are often 'fast-tracked' to 'prove' how the new idea or model is seriously flawed, and hence risible and or dangerous.

In academia, this process takes place through removing the offending material from the curriculum in undergraduate studies, and by adopting a format for PhD and other post-graduate programmes where the thesis is normally encouraged to be about 90% established material and no more than 10% new material produced by original research by the student. This procedure ensures that the status quo is understood, nothing changes quickly, and that the keepers of the traditional belief can probably retire safely prior to any shake-up of the particular discipline involved.

The most alarming event that can happen when adopting this stance is if new evidence arrives on the doorstep from outside the establishment, coupled with public or media demands to make sense of that new evidence. Such was once the case with the Thom material, which unlike the radiocarbon dating revolution, arrived via a retired professor working in virtual isolation. It was very much easier to deal with. The new model of prehistory that Thom set in place was evidently deeply threatening to archaeology, and it has taken most of forty years to remove the offending material from within its ranks. The task has been undertaken with vigour.

CHAPTER SEVEN

A Fitting Tribute

Like many other people who have read Alexander Thom's work, I owe an inestimable amount to the man. Ever since the early 80s, when I first began to study the megalithic monuments which richly endow the British landscape with a deep sense of unfathomable history, it has been Thom's two major publications - *Megalithic Sites in Britain*, and *Megalithic Lunar Observatories* - that have been my most useful guides to the astronomy, geometry and metrology of these prehistoric sites. These books encouraged me to follow and eventually understand the cycles of the skies in a manner which must have been quite similar to that undertaken by skywatchers in the Neolithic and Bronze Age.

At some point I incorporated a theodolite into my site visits, in order to accurately measure angles and distances and to begin to look in more detail at what Thom had claimed of the original skywatchers. I learned how to do the sums in order to translate the sky back in time to how it appeared in prehistoric times, an essential technique. Thom explained it thus, '*"I can't go back and look at it in 1800 BC. They could but I can't, that's why I need a theodolite."* He also needed a *Curta* calculator and a *Nautical Almanac*, while I just have a computer.

A Celebration of Sites

This final chapter celebrates some of the joys and benefits that Alexander Thom has brought to the study of megalithic monuments. There follows some aspects of my own and others' personal journeys into this territory. Various strands of Thom's research are brought together, so that the geometry, metrology and the astronomy are seen to augment each other, revealing a holistic 'Megalithic science', thereby completing the story begun by Thom and described throughout this book.

The Integration of Thom's Researches

Thom's researches were presented as three main packages of work. His early published works, following the surveying of well over a hundred stone circles, resulted in the mid 1950s with the discovery and metrology of the Megalithic yard. Then, in 1965, Thom published his first major account of his astronomical work at sites in *Vistas in Astronomy (Pergamon Press, Vol 7)*. In 1967, *Megalithic Sites in Britain* presented the statistical analysis of the metrological work together with the work he had subsequently undertaken into the geometry of the non-circular stone rings, where he showed that integral numbers of the Megalithic yard and rod had been used to generate the radial arcs of the perimeters. Through this Thom was able to show some integration between the metrology and the geometry. In both these major publications, Thom made no link between the geometry and the astronomy. His comment in his letter to Robert Merritt concerning Dr Hogg's criticism of the geometry of the stone rings (*quoted here on pages 92 & 93*) affirms that this was indeed the case.

At the end of his life, Thom's waning energy coincided with the main attacks on his work. Although this clearly exasperated him, he already knew that what he had discovered held lasting importance for the history of science. But truly sad is that Thom did not live long enough to see his pioneering work developed.

A Geometrical Origin for the Megalithic Yard

In 1974, John Ivimy first showed in *The Sphinx and the Megaliths* (Abacus, 1974) that the Royal cubit and the Megalithic yard could be derived *geometrically*, from the diagonals of a square and a 2 by 1 rectangle whose side lengths are the Egyptian remen. Petrie had previously discovered the $\sqrt{2}$ relationship between the remen and the Royal cubit, in 1926, but Ivimy's $\sqrt{5}$ discovery was new and very accurate, giving a value for the Megalithic yard of 2.720 feet.

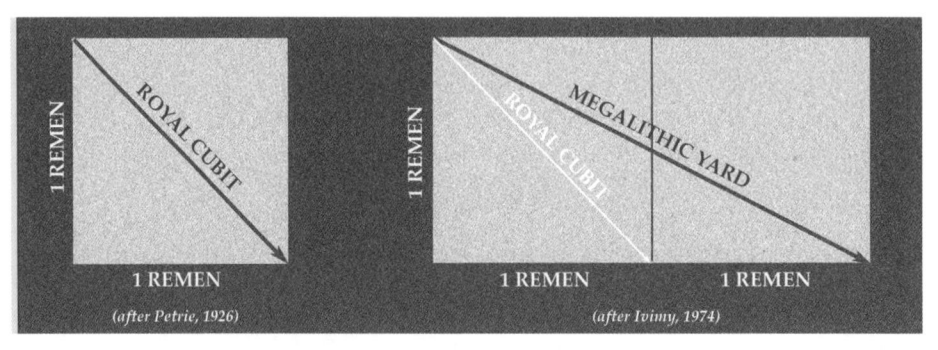

A geometrical connection between the remen, the Royal cubit and the Megalithic yard. The difference between the Megalithic yard and the Royal cubit, 2.72 - 1.72 reveals the English foot (1.00), the root length of all ancient metrology. The astronomical relationship of the lunation period to the year may also be found here, for if the Megalithic yard is taken to represent the lunation period, then the 'English' foot represents the 'silver fraction', the difference between 12 lunar months and the length of the solar year.

Chapter Seven - A Fitting Tribute

Researching into Geometry

One person who devoted a large proportion of her life to the investigation of stone circle sites was Anne Macaulay, a Scot from Balerno, near Edinburgh. Before her early death in 1998, Anne had amassed a large amount of information on the geometry and metrology of stone circles. Unfortunately she never published this material, and only in 2006 has the collection been edited, amplified and brought up to date by Richard Batchelor, a geologist from St Andrews University, and Vivien Lineacre, a Perth surveyor and expert on customary weights and measures. Published by Floris Books, Edinburgh, *Megalithic Measures and Rhythms* presents an extension of Thom's work that he would surely have enjoyed discussing with its author.

In generous tribute to Alexander Thom, Macaulay wrote in the original typescript for her proposed book,

> *'Without the accurate and pioneering work of Professor Thom and his ability to approach the megalithic remains without the limitations of the standard theories, this research (of mine) would have been impossible.'*

The diagram of concentric rings shown earlier (*page 158*) came from correspondence with Anne during 1993, and indicates that the circle builders were using regular polygons to place concentric inner circles and cairns within stone circles. Based on this idea, prior to the posthumous publication of her own work, I had prepared graphics to illustrate the importance of Anne's discoveries, and developed her original discovery.

Farr West (*right*) relies on decagonal geometry to define and locate the inner ring. The placement of the stones in the outer ring confirm this. At the top of the plan the axis of symmetry for the whole site plus four of the original standing stones and one fallen stone are spaced approximately at intervals that would divide the perimeter into ten. The three remaining stones in the lower half of the plan are similarly, if more approximately arranged so, but these fail to mesh in with the decagonal pattern established by the top half. The inner circle is a Type A flattened circle. The axis of the entire monument is aligned north-south.

Research into geometry. Farr West (*right*) and Castle Rigg (*overleaf*) both demonstrate regular spacings of stones around their perimeters. Both sites also possess astronomical properties.

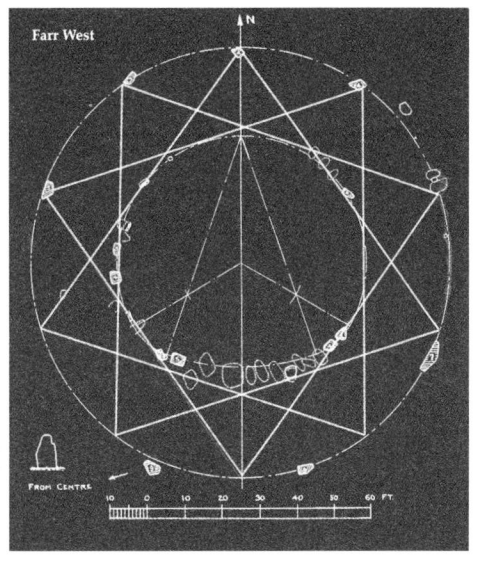

How were the builders achieving this regular spacing? Had they begun by spacing by eye, then measured the chord between pegs by laying a rope between them, with a view to obtaining a more even spacing, the geometry would have appeared directly in front of them, but would not have been seen to best effect unless viewed from high above the construction. Castle Rigg may have been laid out using twelve equally spaced markers, rather than by using the construction suggested on page 58.

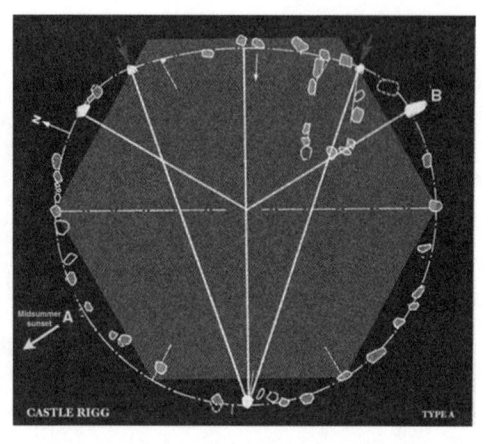

A closer inspection of some circles where stones appear more randomly located around the perimeter is highly revealing. One good example is Sunhoney (B2/2, *below, left*), where division by ten and by twelve occur mixed together to complete a clockwise pattern from north: four times thirty degrees (÷12), one times thirty-six degrees (÷10), twice thirty degrees (÷12) and four times thirty-six degrees (÷10). In this design a total of one half of the perimeter is defined by the division by ten (five gaps), and the other half by the division into twelve (six gaps).

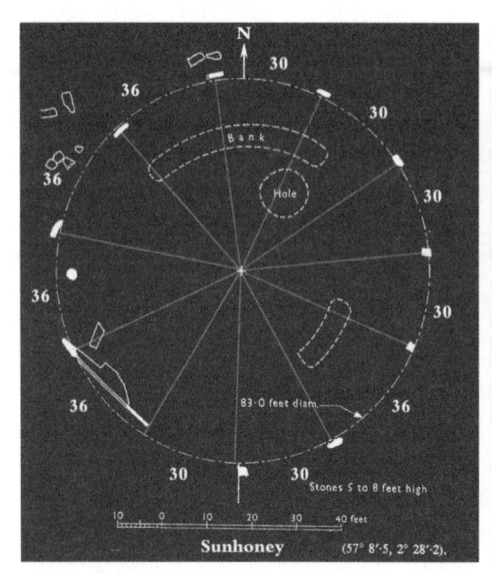

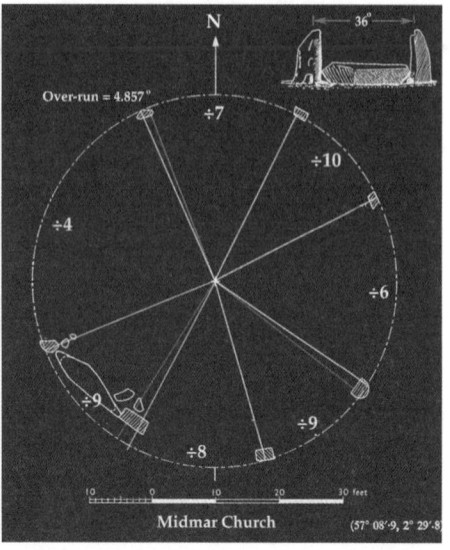

At nearby Midmar Kirk (B2/17, *above right*), the perimeter spacings appear much more haphazard, yet this turns out not to be the case at all. The geometrical game moves into a new phase, where division by four, six, seven, eight, nine (twice) and ten complete the round. Adding these up as fractions gives 1.00674, leaving a small over-run of 2.43 degrees above 360°.

Chapter Seven - A Fitting Tribute

The division of the southwestern recumbent area may be better understood as division by ten (*see inset*), whence the adjacent division by eight becomes a division by seven, and the fractions accrete to over-run by 4.857 degrees. However one decides to define the spacings, they are *not* random, being low integer divisions of the whole circle, including the prime numbers seven, eleven and thirteen.

The final example shown here (*below*), is Easter Aquorthies (B1/6), another one of many Aberdeenshire recumbent stone circles (RSCs), which Aubrey Burl showed were often oriented to the extreme southerly moon sets. Division by nine, ten, eleven and twelve completes the full circle to within a degree.

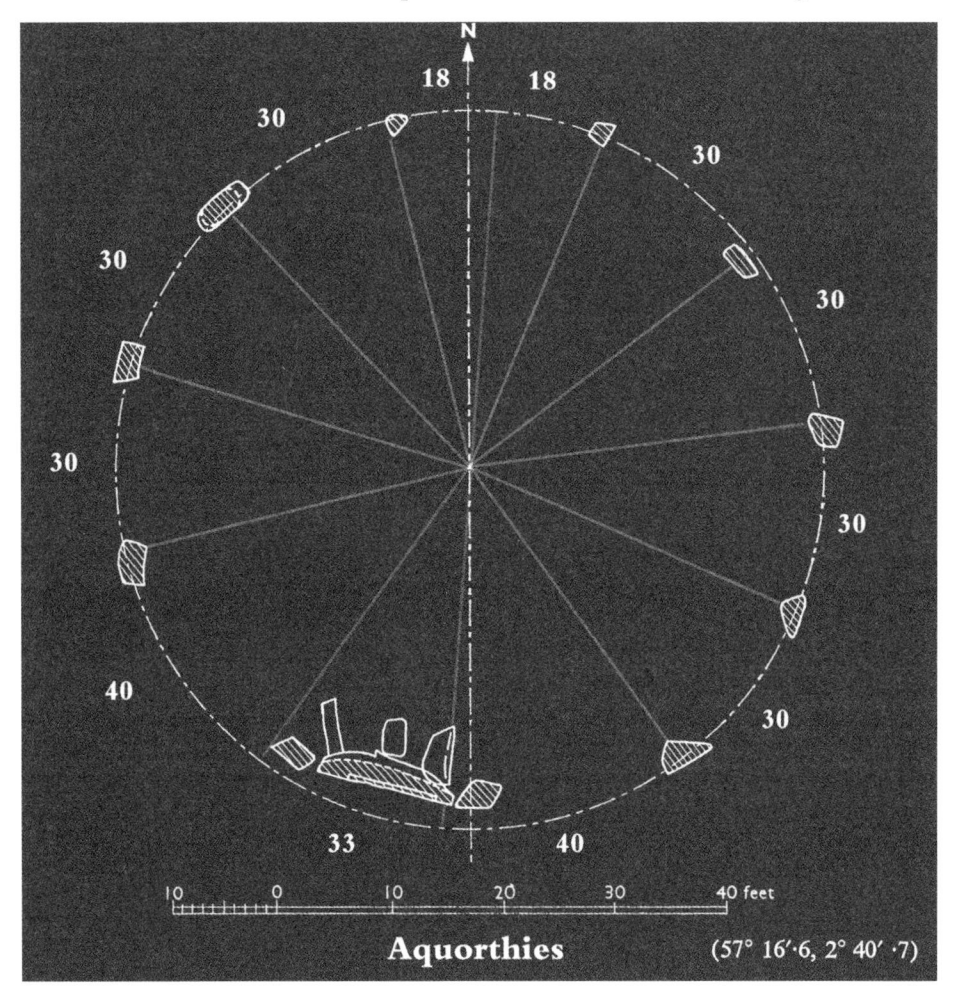

Easter Aquorthies - one of many Aberdeenshire recumbent stone circles. Research by Aubrey Burl revealed that the large recumbents were often oriented to the extreme southerly moonsets, as in this example. The stone spacings divide the circle into low digit divisions, here marked up in degrees, the total is 359 degrees. Seven divisions at (÷12), one at (÷11) one at (÷10), and two at (÷9). The interplay of numbers, angles, divisions and geometry is clear. And some astronomy too!

Alexander Thom - Cracking the Stone Age Code

Solid geometry. These curiously shaped stone artefacts are prehistoric, and over 300 examples have been discovered, mainly in northeastern Scotland, most notably Aberdeenshire and Perthshire. Although often labelled as 'ritual objects', examples of all five Platonic solids have been found. (*photograph above courtesy of Challifour photographs, from the book* Time Stands Still *by architect and geometer Professor Keith Critchlow, shortly to be republished. Photograph below courtesy of John Martineau*).

Prehistoric Geometry in Two and Three Dimensions

Other research into geometry was taking place in this same region of Britain contemporary with the plane geometry shown in the previous pages. Over the years a large collection of neolithic carved stone balls has been recovered from freshly ploughed fields and other locations in Aberdeenshire and Perthshire. In his lectures and book, *Time Stands Still*, architect and geometer Professor Keith Critchlow has demonstrated that each of the five platonic solids has been unearthed, and the photograph above shows an example of each one. The explanatory diagram (*below, courtesy John Martineau*) shows the geometry of each one. From left to right, they are cube, tetrahedron, dodecahedron, icosahedron and octahedron. These figures confirm Thom's assertion that the circle builders were, "well, they were researching into geometry", and make it clear that something quite astonishing in the cultural development of our race was taking place in Britain two thousand years before Plato was even born.

The importance of this combined evidence is inestimable for the understanding of history, and if archaeologists cannot fathom out what it all means, then perhaps mathematicians, geometers, architects, anthropologists, astronomers and psychologists would make rather better guardians of the ancient wisdom clearly displayed in Thom's surveys, and in the geometrical analyses briefly illustrated here. The Aberdeenshire RSCs demonstrate that geometry was being implemented *together* with an astronomical function for the rings in

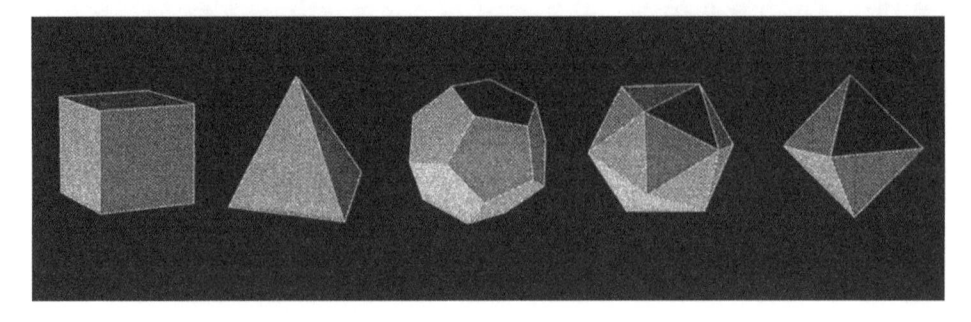

Chapter Seven - A Fitting Tribute

northeastern Scotland. But evidence of the same kind of experimentation can be found wherever there are megalithic remains. One remarkable location for the study of such things may be found some 250 miles south of Aberdeen.

In the Lake District they went in for huge and often flattened circles after a grand fashion, and subsequently we have allocated them quintessentially English names - Burnmoor, Castle Rigg, Orton, Swinside, and Seascale (Grey Croft).

Long Meg and her Naughty Daughters

Long Meg and Her Daughters is colossal, the largest Type B flattened circle known, with a diameter of 359 feet (110 m). It is larger than the Ring of Brogar or the two inner circles at Avebury, which all have the same diameter of 340 feet (104 m). Only the large ring at Avebury occupies a larger area. Comprising 70 large blocks of local porphyritic stone, even in its present vandalised state it is self evident that Long Meg once held immense importance to its builders. It is also clear to anyone who visits the site that the ring is not especially well sited, on irregular sloping ground astride a farm path near Little Salkeld. The siting could not be more different to Castle Rigg.

This ring has not fared as well as Castle Rigg since prehistoric times. In the eighteenth century explosives were used in an attempt to destroy the ring. According to one story from 1698, Long Meg's 'daughters', were in fact Meg's 'sisters' who had solicited her 'unto an unlawfull love by an enchantment' and were thus all turned into stone. Such an occurrence would probably have been the most exciting thing that ever happened in Little Salkeld since the ring was built had it not been for the anti-pagans responsible for the blasting falling prey to their own superstitious fears when a wholly unexpected and violent thunderstorm erupted during the proceedings. So fearful were they that they panicked - and some of the stones were even replaced.

Thom's plan of the ring is given overleaf. He accorded it a 'Class III' status, finding that it was too despoiled to be confident of the original dimensions. But despite the state of the geometry now being

Long Meg (*top, left*) inspecting her daughters (*top, right*) on the crest of a long shallow ridge near Little Salkeld, in the north-east of the English Lake District. Thom's site plan (*overleaf*) omits to mention an astronomical alignment between the site and one of the tallest mountains in the Lake District, Helvellyn. Long Meg (*right*) is an 'aligned indicated foresight' in this midwinter alignment.

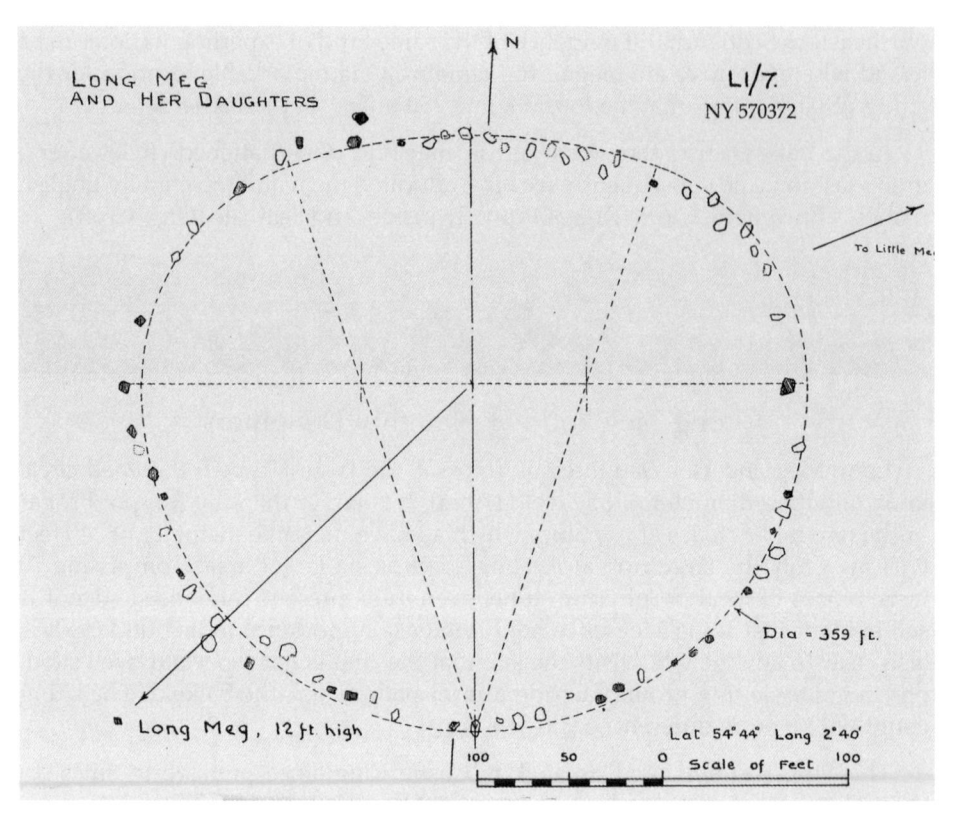

disappointing, a combination of both the vandalism and soil creep, the ring was still clearly identified by him as being a Type B. Its axis of symmetry is orientated to the four cardinal points of the compass, with two massive stones standing at east and west. This could not have been achieved without reference to and measurements from the sky.

Long Meg herself is a 12 foot (4 m) high pillar of red sandstone (*see previous page*) situated to the south-west of the ring at a distance of 82 feet (25 m) away. Burl suggests that the stone was 'possibly brought 1½ miles from the Eden Valley'. There is an anti-clockwise spiral carved in the side of the stone facing away from the ring, leading Burl to suggest that 'the outlier and ring are not contemporary.' He also tells us that, 'the stone stands in line with the midwinter sunset', while Thom points out that this orientation is only when viewed from the original centre of the ring. Here is a second linkage between the geometry and astronomy.

My first visit to the site, in 1992, made clear to me that the astronomical significance of this site was far greater than simply a large outlier some 25m from the ring's centre. Calculations showed that from the centre of the ring, past Long Meg, one can see the second tallest mountain in the Lake District, Helvellyn, some 3118 feet high (950m) and nearly 20 miles away. This raises the astronomical status of the site enormously, turning Long Meg from an outlier foresight into an

Chapter Seven - A Fitting Tribute

'indicated foresight' to a foresight which was nearly 20 miles away, Helvellyn summit. The problem was, and often is, that in the climatic conditions of this part of Northern Britain, the peak was not visible during my visit. In such a situation, not uncommonly met with, the suspected alignment must be checked out using OS Maps or GPS devices. Or one waits for a better day.

The geodetically calculated azimuth from the centre of Long Meg ring to Helvellyn turned out to be 223.2443 degrees. I returned home to find that Thom had 223.4 degrees as the azimuth from the ring centre to Long Meg. That is a match to within one sixth of a degree, surely suggestive as to why the ring was located where it was, and demonstrating one of its functions - *as an observatory to watch the midwinter sun setting into Helvellyn.* Euan MacKie also noted this potential alignment (*SSPB*, page 98 where he points out that the 'strength of the evidence for the astronomical theory is often understated in Thom's works).' And so it proved to be here, colossally understated, with no significance whatsoever given to the orientation marked on the plan.

There is no need to elaborate on how good an observatory Long Meg would have been, whether it might have been possible to record the exact day of the solstice, the date when the site may have been used or whether refraction would have made viewing less reliable. This has all been done to death at other sites and has produced statements like, ' *The sites themselves are not calendrical instruments...',* and *'Other claims for high-precision astronomy... have now been discounted..'.* Long Meg had just shown me that these statements were simply not true, they certainly weren't helpful, and from then on I decided to get on with the task of enjoying my dialogue with sites free from outside interference.

Why Flattened Circles?

The astronomical 'secret' of Long Meg ring was that in prehistoric times one needed to stand at the centre of the ring at midwinter solstice to observe the sun setting on distant Helvellyn with Long Meg silhouetted in the foreground, some 262 feet away. To know this astronomical 'secret', one must have been initiated into a second one, the 'secret' of knowing where to stand, and this implies *a priori* knowledge of the geometrical 'secret' of knowing how to determine the centre of a circle when it is not marked. Then, on the right day, right time, right epoch, having performed the right action, the site would have revealed its secret calendrical function.

This alignment no longer works, due to the change in the earth's tilt angle, and the nearest you can get to observing the ritual today will require that you possess the formulae and calculating skill to work out how far to the left of Long Meg to position your body in order to simulate what a prehistoric astronomer would have seen at the ring centre around 2500 BC. Long Meg will no longer be involved. Alternatively, you may have to run rather quickly on the day of the winter solstice at around 3:18 pm, from the centre of the ring towards the large trees.

So why was a Type B flattened circle chosen to lie directly behind the alignment between Long Meg and Helvellyn? It could have been any old circle, but a Type

B was selected. To discover why a Type B was chosen, it is necessary to return to the cycles of the sun and moon, which have remained constant since the circles were erected in the late Neolithic and the Bronze Age. It is the astronomy that will be found to support the geometry used in the flattened circles.

Lengths of Time

If observations of the cycles of the sun and moon were being recorded by the prehistoric astronomers, how could the process leave a permanent record of these cycles to be passed down through the generations over a substantial period of time? Notches, knots spaced on ropes, weaving and pottery decoration patterns may have been techniques for recording such things. Whichever medium was used, *lengths of time become converted into plain lengths*, either as numbers of notches or knots, zig-zags on pottery or geometrical patterns on cloth. The fundamental unit of time represented by such markings would naturally be the day, multiples of days making up the lunar month (29½ days) and the year (365¼ days). The sidereal month (27.32 days) might also be found, and if eclipses were being studied, then the eclipse year (346.6 days) might also be expected to occur. These are the fundamental lengths of time that control the cycles of the heavens and hence those of human life on earth.

Art & Design - Secrets of the Type B

The first astro-geometrical property of flattened circles is revealed when their perimeter is compared with the 'unflattened version', i.e. if the circular part had been extended to complete the circle. If it is assumed that this perfect circle is a 'year-circle' whose perimeter represents the annual cycle of the sun - 365¼ days, then the flattened circle perimeter has a shorter perimeter equivalent to the eclipse year, accurate to 99.19%. While this may be thought coincidental and not very accurate, the same procedure applied to the Type A design reveals a shorter perimeter equivalent to the lunar year, accurate to 99.64%. As already explained,

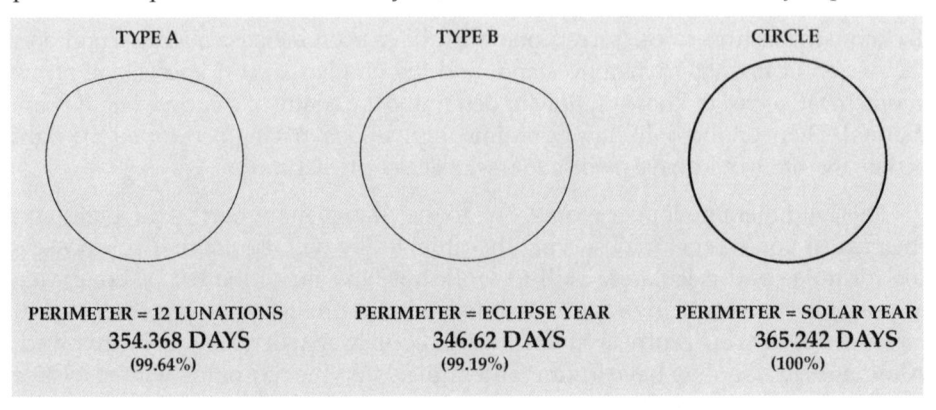

TYPE A	TYPE B	CIRCLE
PERIMETER = 12 LUNATIONS	PERIMETER = ECLIPSE YEAR	PERIMETER = SOLAR YEAR
354.368 DAYS	**346.62 DAYS**	**365.242 DAYS**
(99.64%)	(99.19%)	(100%)

The perimeter lengths of Type A and Type B flattened circles when compared to a true circle of same radius, present the lunar year and eclipse year as ratios, accurately calibrated to the solar year. Here we discover geometry responding to and replicating the major cycles of the sun and moon.

both are crucially important astronomical periods required in understanding celestial cycles and calendars (*see diagram below*).

Counting Lunations

If a counting process is initiated to mark the number of days between new moons, by observing the first visible sliver - the tiny crescent following the new moon - then after twelve lunar months, twelve new moons would have been observed. Following this twelfth observation of the new moon, and before the next lunation, the original calendar date that marked the start of the observations is returned to. Sometime after that, the thirteenth lunation is observed.

In the diagram below, one might imagine the process of recording to have begun on the same date as the winter solstice sunset, at any one of the observatories identified by Thom and others as suitable for recording the solstice sunset. As the sun sets, the tiny crescent of the new moon would have been visible not far to the left of the sun, and following it into the twilight.

Following the elapsing of a year, at the next winter solstice, twelve such crescent moons have been observed, and about eleven days later, at the solstice, the moon is seen at an angle of about 120 degrees to the left of the sun, in the eastern sky, and is gibbous or nearly full in appearance. About eighteen days following the year's return, another crescent new moon will be observed.

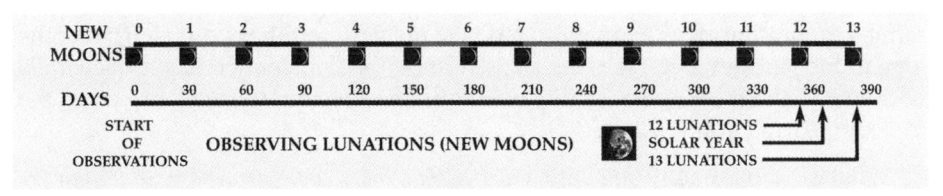

Recording new moons (lunations) as lengths of days recorded as notches on stone or wood, or as evenly spaced knots on rope, will eventually link time cycles to physical lengths. The diagram above shows the kind of pattern that emerges after a single year. The number of lunations in the year will be seen as lying between twelve and thirteen, the year ends with a nearly full moon.

The Silver Fraction

However such observations had been recorded, the understanding of how the lunations are placed within the solar year leads to the thirteenth lunation being split by the interception of the solar year. The fractional relationship that determines when this split occurs is the single most important item of knowledge in understanding the calendar, and we might expect to find this fraction imprinted or recorded at sites where the astronomers were studying the calendar.

The *silver fraction* may be understood as being the division of one lunation into two parts, the smaller being 0.368 of a lunation (very nearly 7/19ths) and the larger part being 0.636 lunations (very nearly 12/19ths), as shown overleaf. Indeed, observations over 19 years would reveal that 235 lunations had occurred,

Alexander Thom - Cracking the Stone Age Code

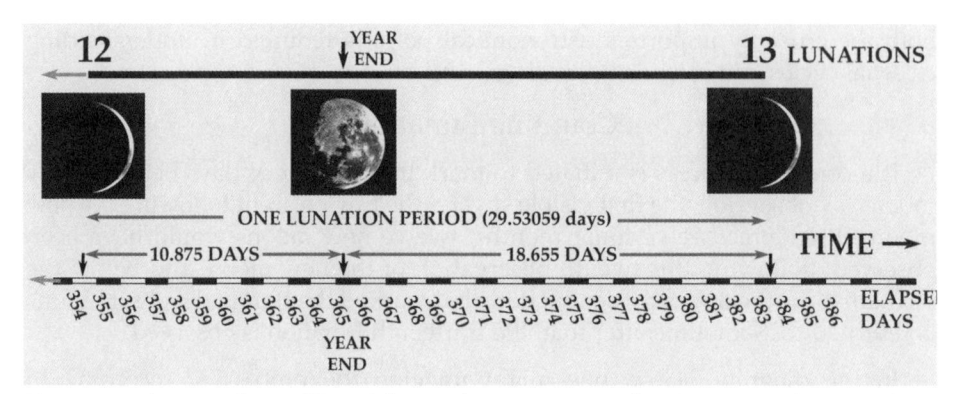

Observations between the twelfth and thirteenth lunation reveal the elapsed days (*lower scale*) and the phase of the moon (as nearly full) as one year passes. There are just under eleven days between the twelfth lunation and the year end, and just under 19 days between the year end and the thirteenth lunation. These numbers emerge from the most basic regimen of systematic naked eye observation.

the final one to within two hours of the original observation, on the same date in the calendar nineteen years previously.

The *silver fraction* may be normalised as a ratio, such that if the smaller part is made one unit, the longer part becomes 1.72 units, and the whole length - the lunation - then becomes 2.72 units in length. Due to Alexander Thom, and the fact that the English foot forms the root of all metrological units in antiquity, this number, representing the lunation, has become very familiar as the length of the Megalithic yard, in feet. Here the same number is seen connected *astronomically* with two of the most ancient units of length known from the ancient world, the foot and Royal cubit (1.72 feet).

What is immediately relevant here *is that these same ratios are built into the geometry of the flattened circles*, as the ratio of the radius of the circle to that of the flattened arc (*overleaf, left*), which is 1 : 1.72. The flattened circles were never found to fit the format of preferred integer diameters and perimeters found in the other designs. They stood apart, with diameters varying between 140 down to 16 feet. The Type B has an unique geometrical design. Implicit in this design - and available from the Type A - are two major constructional features - the radius of the circle and the radius of the flattened arc. In addition, the *vesica*

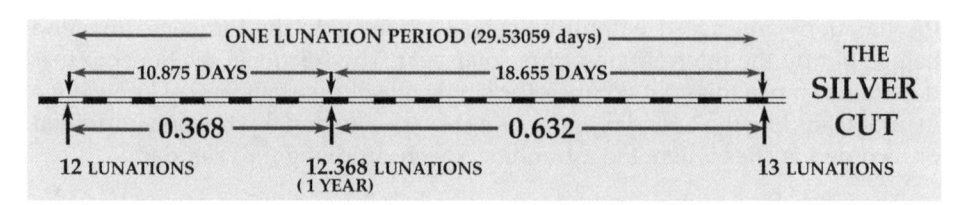

Understanding the calendar. There are 12.368 lunations in one year, the thirteenth lunation is split unequally into two, in the ratio 1 : 1.72, by the first repeat of the date of the start of observations. Understanding the numerical relationship between lunations and years is vital; without it an understanding of the patterns and cycles of eclipses, tides and the phases of the moon cannot proceed.

Chapter Seven - A Fitting Tribute

circles used to divide the diameter into three also define the two right-angled triangles (*shown below right*).

There is more astronomy stored within the flattened circle design. Referring to the adjacent illustration (*below, right*), the radius line OP compared to the line AP is in the ratio 3 : √10 (the triangle has side lengths in the ratio 1 : 3 : √10). If AP is used to represent linearly the solar year, then line OP represents the eclipse year, this time accurate to 99.97%. And there are more cosmic challenges here. If AP is made to represent a lunation cycle, then the *vesica piscis* circle cuts at a point 0.368 of its length, the essential shortfall period, already calibrated in lunations, between the end of the lunar year and that of the solar year, accurate to 99.80%. In other words, there are two ways by which the silver fraction may be extracted as a ratio from within the geometry of the Type B. The design is not only beautiful, but entirely functional as an astronomical aid.

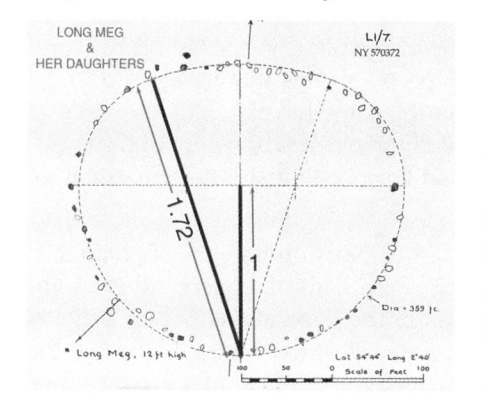

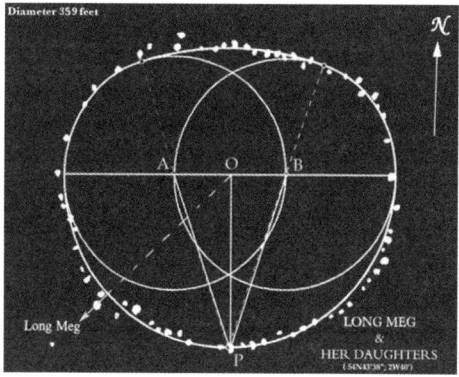

Inherent in the design of the geometry of the Type B flattened circle are two examples of the 'silver fraction' ratio 1 : 1.72, one to 100% accuracy, the other to 99.80% accuracy. In addition the design also contains the ratio of solar year to eclipse year, accurate to 99.97%. That this is so suggests that Thom's critics have been entirely in error to dismiss his claims and his evidence for precision astronomy being practised at megalithic sites throughout northwestern Europe.

Cosmic Transducers

The simple geometry of Britain's few dozen surviving flattened circles is seen to contain within itself a complete package of astronomical constants accurate enough to integrate the lunar phases within a solar calendar, and to predict eclipses to the day, years in advance. How might this have been undertaken? If the longest side of the internal triangle is taken to represent the solar year, the radius represents the eclipse year. The ratio between the lengths is 0.9490.

Once one is in possession of these two lengths, replication of the solar year rope laid end on end with the original will represent years. Laid alongside this line of year lengths, the 'eclipse year' lengths indicate the times when a full or new moon would be likely to be eclipsed. To evaluate the dates when full and new moons are going to occur in advance during the year, the longest side of the triangle (AP) is taken to represent a lunation period (29½ days). Twelve of these lengths laid end on end plus the extra 0.368 part derived from where the vesica cuts the line AP, delivers a total length of 12.368 x length AP. This new length represents the solar year *already calibrated into lunations*. Many of these lengths laid end on end will give the dates of lunations far into the future. For eclipse prediction, it remains that one places the eclipse seasons alongside this calibrated 'lunations' length. As shown earlier, OP represents the eclipse year, and if this length is also multiplied by 12.368, its ends define the eclipse year period of 346.62 days. Halving this length then marks eclipse 'seasons', times when a new or full moon will cause an eclipse, although not always visible from the location of the observatory.

This knowledge changes the perspective by which we assess prehistoric astronomy. The flattened circles store astronomical information as a form of geometrical 'writing' that can be recreated by means of a rope and pegs anywhere on the planet - providing one knows the constructional 'secret'. The fact that Type B flattened circles contain these astronomical constants stored as ratios - and the same information is contained in the Type A - means that those critics who have dismissed Thom's claims for precision astronomy have now to reassess that decision. The builders evidently had evaluated the numerical nature of the cycles of sun and moon to high precision - how had they done that if not via extensive and accurate observations over many years?

Archaeoastronomers have pondered for forty years on how the astronomical information needed to sustain long term astronomical observations might have been stored or transmitted down through the generations. When Magnus Magnusson asked Thom, referring to the geometry of the rings, "I suppose the definition of pure research is that it hasn't really any practical purpose. They didn't require to make the stone circles in this shape?", Thom himself actually provided a stunningly perceptive answer,

> *"They could have drawn any old circle and said, 'there's a circle, boys, but they didn't. They wanted the thing to have this hidden significance. The man in the street - the ordinary man who helped them set it out - wouldn't have any idea what was hidden or involved in this thing. The experts, the astronomer-priests or whatever you call them, they knew what was in it. This hidden information was stored away in this construction."*

Thom was here referring to the inner pythagorean triangles and the integer use of the Megalithic yard in the rings. With the discovery of the astronomy of the lunation and the eclipse year embedded within the geometry of the flattened circles, they can now be seen to store a profoundly *practical* function as descriptions of the way the cycles of the sky are experienced by an observer on earth.

Could it have been that Neolithic skywatchers were so attuned to their skies that their "research into geometry for its own sake" was leading them on to discover geometric patterns that emulated the cosmic patterns we know, through the work of Thom, they *were* monitoring, and that during the process they discovered a revelation

Chapter Seven - A Fitting Tribute

- that the imperturbable cycles of the sun and moon were arranged such that they could be incorporated into beautiful yet simple geometrical designs? It must have seemed like a glimpse into the mind of the Creator. If the Neolithic geometer-astronomers understood full well what these constructions represented, the subject moves beyond archaeology and enters the subject of cosmology, and we come much closer to understanding why Thom uttered his highly intuitive comment on the *Chronicle* programme,

> "I think they were, as far as brain power is concerned, my superiors."

The flattened rings are about as simple a geometrical construction as can be imagined, yet they store a range of astronomical constants sufficient to recover the principal motions of the sun-moon-earth system as experienced by an observer on the earth. In terms of connecting the sky to the earth, they do this more directly than any Gothic cathedral, whose architects' purported aim was to connect spirit with matter, sky with earth, the 'above' to the 'below'. How difficult it has been for academics to connect these things in the subject of astro-archaeology, now archaeoastronomy, yet the circle builders evidently managed the task so well!

These properties of the flattened rings have emerged only because of Thom's discovery of their geometry. While they remained 'ovoids', their secret was safely "stored away". Now, using ropes and pegs, anyone knowing the secret contained within the perimeters of either Type A or Type B flattened rings may track events in local space and time. And unlike the solar alignment at Long Meg, which is now out of alignment, the flattened circles still work, as transducers converting the cycles in the sky into stone rings on the earth. A more perfectly executed design to do this is impossible to imagine, although there is one, but that must wait until we have further investigated the metrological properties of Thom's Megalithic yard.

An Astronomical Origin for the Megalithic Yard

The silver fraction is accurately 0.368266 lunations, the difference between 12 lunations (354.368 days) and the solar year (365.242199 days). If this is represented by the English foot, then the Megalithic yard represents one lunation and should have a theoretical length equal to 2.7154291 feet.

This length is 99.8% of Thom's central value. However, it is a recognisable unit of length within the canon of ancient metrology, being a 'step' based on the 'Drusian' foot, 1.08617 feet in length.

The metrology is simply expressed thus:

Greek foot (1.01376 feet) x 15/14 = Drusian foot

Drusian foot x 5/2 = 'Step' of 2.71542857 feet.

This length is indistinguishable from the astronomically derived value for the Megalithic yard given above. Indeed, it is only one part in 500 lower than Thom's revealed value for the length.

Confirmation for this origin for the Megalithic yard may be found at Stonehenge, where the station rectangle is laid out as a 5, 12 rectangle, whose diagonals complete two 5, 12, 13 pythagorean triangles. This structure exactly measures 50, 120 and 130 in units of two Drusian feet, and 40, 96 and 104 in units of Megalithic yards, as derived above.

Stonehenge provides additional confirmation that the circle builders were well aware of the numerical ratios present in understanding the calendar. The two principal circles at Stonehenge define the ratio 1 : 1.72, the outer Sarsen circle diameter is given by various archaeologists as being 104.27 feet, and the Aubrey circle was surveyed by Thom at 283.6 feet. The ratio is 0.36766. This means that a rope laid from the centre of Stonehenge along the axis to the Aubrey circle may be calibrated at 0.368 of its length directly under the wider axis portal of the Sarsen circle. The monument both confirms and calibrates the ratio (*below*).

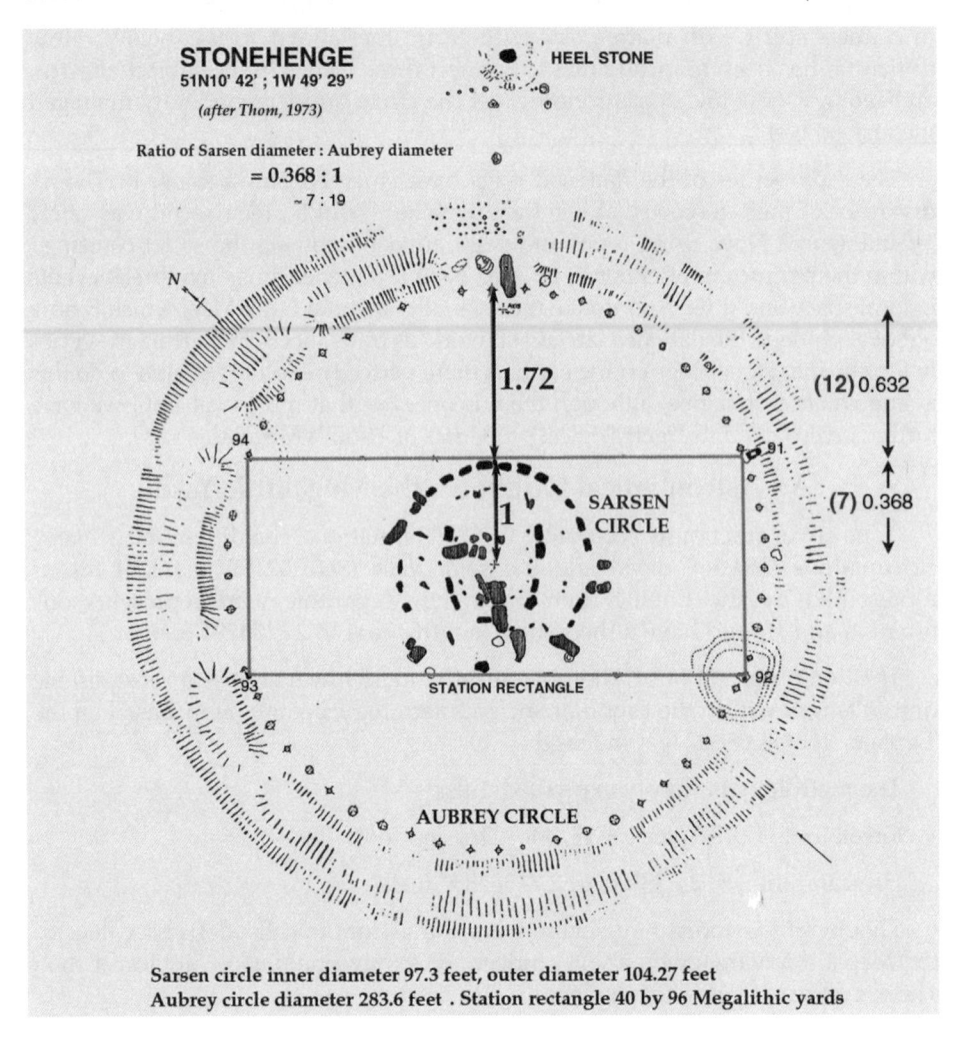

Sarsen circle inner diameter 97.3 feet, outer diameter 104.27 feet
Aubrey circle diameter 283.6 feet . Station rectangle 40 by 96 Megalithic yards

Chapter Seven - A Fitting Tribute

Nowhere is this integration better displayed than within the 5, 12, 13 Pythagorean triangle. Constructed in units of Megalithic yards, the principal astronomical structure of the sun, moon, earth system is stored in a form that enables the production of accurate soli-lunar calendars and eclipse prediction (*illustration on following page*). The Lunation triangle contains the silver fraction, 7/19ths (or in decimal format 0.368), as the English foot, and the remaining 12/19ths (0.632) of a Megalithic yard as one Royal cubit, as per Ivimy's diagram on page 186. Buried within this construction are profound questions concerning the implicit cosmology of local space, where an underpinning order can so readily be discovered just below the surface of the seemingly random orbital arrangements of the earth, sun and moon. The circle builders regularly used the 5, 12, 13 triangle, and Stonehenge implicitly contains one (*previous page, left*), enshrined in Thom's Megalithic yards, where the 7/19th ratio defines the two main radii of the monument.

The Prediction of Eclipses

If a Megalithic yard is split into the silver fraction, the two lengths, foot and Royal cubit lie end to end. Astronomically, we have seen how this represents one lunation period. 12 such lengths *plus a foot* define the solar year calibrated into lunations, 12.368 lunations, leaving one Royal cubit outside of the year which connects it on to the thirteenth lunation. The way the time periods of the sun and moon are arranged now offers a wholly unexpected bonus in predicting eclipses, for if the Royal cubit is folded back along the previous year's lunations, already marked out, then its end defines the correct length for the eclipse year accurate to 99.99%. This gift from the gods provides the final link in being able to understand in advance when eclipses are likely to occur, which type they are likely to be, solar or lunar, and whether or not they will be total or partial.

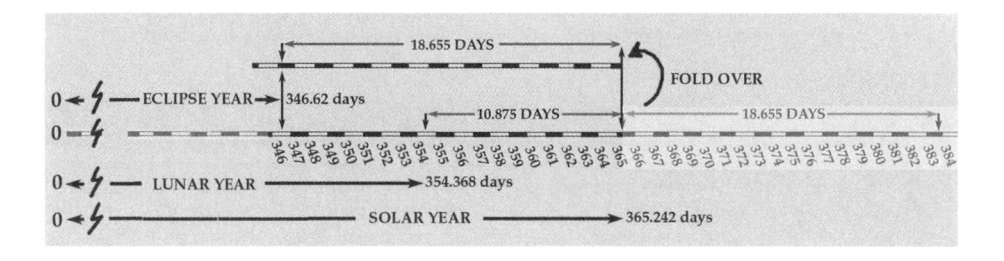

Serendipity in the sky. The difference in time between the end of the solar year and thirteen lunations just happens to be the same as that between the eclipse year and the end of the solar year. Folding back a rope (marked out as described earlier (*page 194*) and marked up to thirteen lunations) at the end of the solar year will accurately locate the eclipse year. If a separate rope marking this length is made up, then folding it in half will mark the two eclipse seasons, those two periods within the year when eclipses will occur at full and new moons. This is accurate astronomy using only marked ropes, and the ratios between the key astronomical constants are implicit in the geometry of the flattened circle.

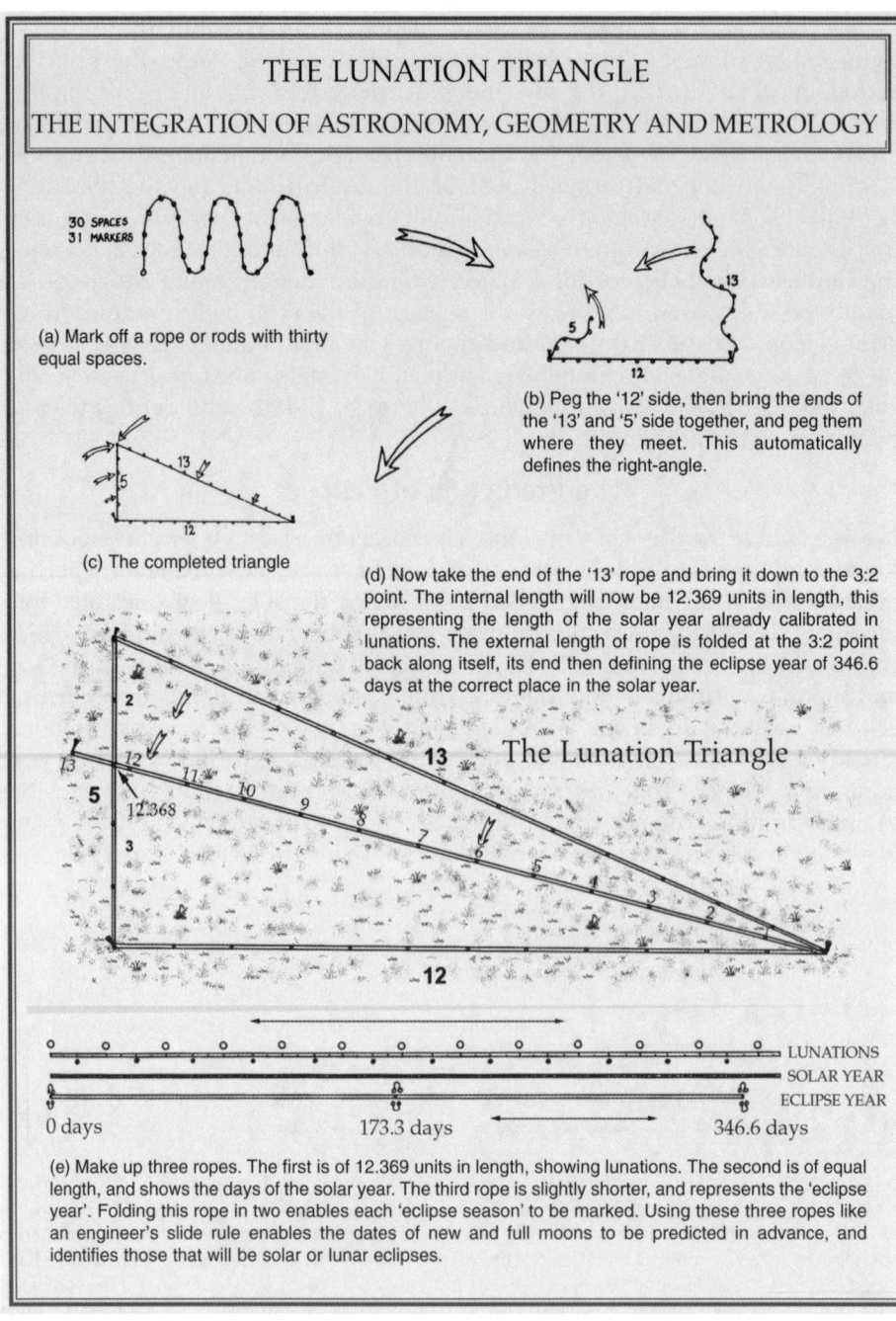

THE LUNATION TRIANGLE
THE INTEGRATION OF ASTRONOMY, GEOMETRY AND METROLOGY

(a) Mark off a rope or rods with thirty equal spaces.

(b) Peg the '12' side, then bring the ends of the '13' and '5' side together, and peg them where they meet. This automatically defines the right-angle.

(c) The completed triangle

(d) Now take the end of the '13' rope and bring it down to the 3:2 point. The internal length will now be 12.369 units in length, this representing the length of the solar year already calibrated in lunations. The external length of rope is folded at the 3:2 point back along itself, its end then defining the eclipse year of 346.6 days at the correct place in the solar year.

The Lunation Triangle

0 days — 173.3 days — 346.6 days

LUNATIONS
SOLAR YEAR
ECLIPSE YEAR

(e) Make up three ropes. The first is of 12.369 units in length, showing lunations. The second is of equal length, and shows the days of the solar year. The third rope is slightly shorter, and represents the 'eclipse year'. Folding this rope in two enables each 'eclipse season' to be marked. Using these three ropes like an engineer's slide rule enables the dates of new and full moons to be predicted in advance, and identifies those that will be solar or lunar eclipses.

The pythagorean 5, 12, 13 triangle demonstrates a perfect integration of astronomy, geometry and metrology. If Thom's megalithic yard is made the unit, then the device produces the 0.368 'silver fraction' as an English foot and the 'over-run' to the thirteenth lunation as the Royal cubit. The triangle thereby poses cosmological and philosophical questions far beyond the remit of archaeology.

Chapter Seven - A Fitting Tribute

A Question of Latitude

Latitude Matters at Stonehenge

During his correspondence with Newham in the early 1960s, Thom would have become aware of Newham's discovery that the station rectangle at Stonehenge was (a) based on a Pythagorean 5, 12, 13 triangle, and (b) the alleged calendrical alignments that Newham surveyed using the rectangle implied that the construction would not 'work' if located more than a few miles north or south of Stonehenge. Hawkins' later work in *Stonehenge Decoded* would have made it clear to Thom that this property of the station rectangle, if deliberate, implied knowledge of the way the extreme sunrises and sets changed with latitude.

The station rectangle is located such that its shorter sides are aligned parallel with the 'midsummer' axis of the monument. This was first noted by Duke in 1846. Newham discovered that the longer sides aligned to the major standstill moonset, which at this latitude occurred at 90 degrees to the summer sunrise around 2500 BC. But Newham also reported that the diagonals aligned to the four 'quarter days' in the calendar, suggesting another latitude based feature of Stonehenge. This can be confirmed by calculation. In 2500 BC, the half-rise of the rising sun on the February and November quarter-day, Imbolc and Samhain, on a level horizon occurred at an azimuth of 117.5 degrees, while the station rectangle diagonal (stone 93 to stone 91) is aligned to an azimuth of 117.34 degrees. For the two other quarter-days, May and August, Beltane and Lammas, the setting sun's half-set occurred at azimuth 297.5 degrees, while from stone 91 to stone 93 the azimuth is 297.39 degrees.

This calculation does not account for the horizon elevations at Stonehenge, but these are low and the length of the orientation short. However, from day to day at the November and February quarter-days, consecutive sunrises occur further along the horizon than the sun's apparent diameter - over half a degree An observer using the station stones would readily be able to 'clock' the correct date for the quarter days.

Geometry and Astronomy in Brittany

In the course of his surveying work in Brittany, Thom surveyed a curious rectangular construction that revealed a link between its geometry and the astronomy of its location. The Crucuno rectangle revealed itself to be a 3 : 4 rectangle, in units of 10 Megalithic yards, and therefore contained diagonals of length 50 yards. In effect it was comprised of two 3, 4, 5 triangles constructed in units of 10 Megalithic yards.

Thom was quick to note that the location of this anomalous construction was unique. Only at this latitude would the summer solstice sunrise align across the diagonal of the rectangle. In *Megalithic Remains in Britain and Brittany*, he makes the obvious point,

CRUCUNO, nr. Plouharnel, Brittany 47°37' 30" ; 3°07' 18"

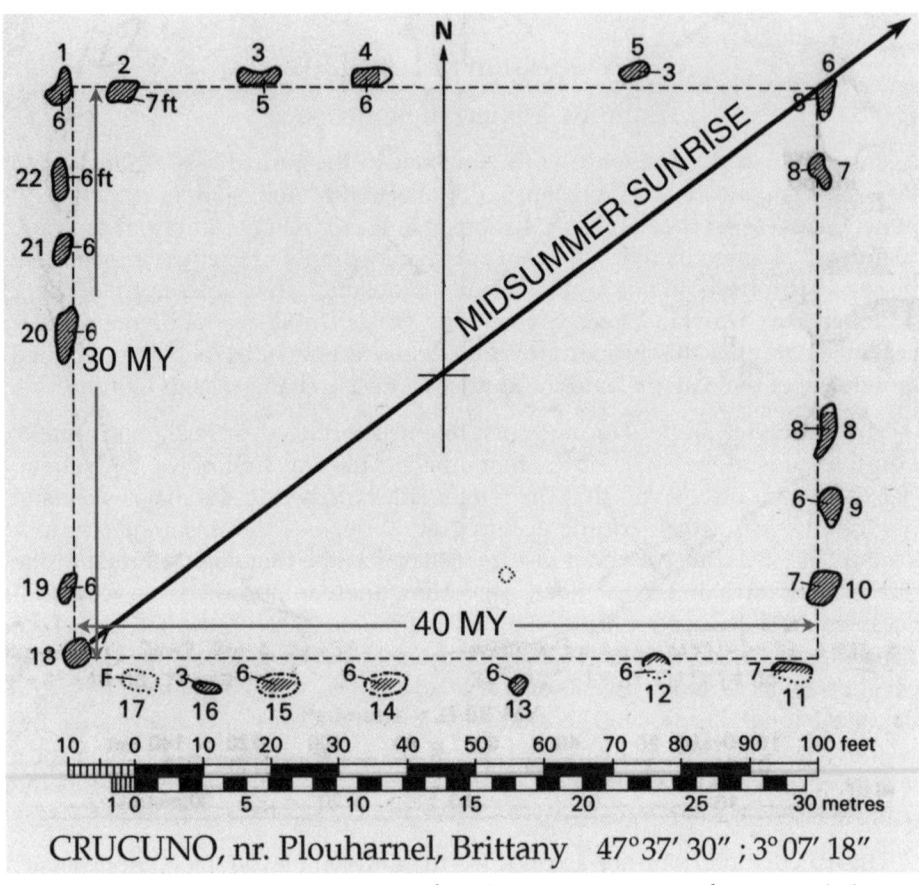

A rectangular stone 'circle'. Crucuno, near Plouharnel, Brittany, is unique in that it can only function as an observatory of the solstices at the latitude of its location. Based on the familiar 3, 4, 5 triangle so commonly found at other sites, here the construction uses units of 10 megalithic yards to define the geometry. The link between the geometry, metrology and astronomy is self-evident.

'(Crucuno) *consists of 21 menhirs ranging from 3 to 8 feet in height, but it is known that most of these have been re-erected. The stones are built around a rectangle of 30 MY by 40 MY so accurately placed east and west that the re-erectors, without instrumental aid, could not have been responsible for the orientation. This and the dimensions show that the site is Megalithic and dispose of the claim that the whole thing is not prehistoric. In Thom et al. 1973 we show that only in the latitude of Crucuno could the diagonals of a 3, 4, 5 rectangle indicate at both solstices the azimuth of of the sun rising and setting when it appears to rest on the horizon. We assumed the altitude of the horizon to be +14' and while we could not check this by measurement, it seems from the map contours to be reasonable. The long sides of the rectangle indicate to the west the setting equinoctial sun with lower limb on the horizon.*

Without distant marks, however, no accuracy would be possible and we conclude that Crucuno was a symbolic observatory.'

Symbolic or not, Crucuno is unique as a rectangular stone 'circle', based on a 3, 4, 5 design in units of ten megalithic yards, which uniquely responds to the solar astronomy of its exact latitude. Thom, as an experienced astronomer and surveyor would have understood only too well the implication that the builders had understood that the 3, 4, 5 only 'worked' in this way at that location, and it is regrettable that we have no accounts of Thom's further thoughts as to whether or not the builders understood the concept of latitude.

The Latitude of Avebury

Thom never noted that the giant ring at Avebury is located at latitude $4/7$ ths of the distance from the equator to the poles. That exact latitude ($51\,3/7$ degrees) passes just north of the Cove, and passes through the duck pond at the Stones cafe, the Keiller museum and Avebury Manor. It has additional significance because the Egyptian culture sited Thebes (now Luxor) at precisely $2/7$ th of that same distance quoted above, at 25.7143 degrees. An elaborately carved omphalos dedicated to the ram-god Amun marked the exact latitude.

That Avebury is located thus may be thought of as mere coincidence, yet Stonehenge is located at a latitude exactly one quarter of one degree of latitude south of Avebury, a distance of 17.28 miles, a observation first made by John Michell in *The Measure of Albion* and one which led him to some remarkable conclusions concerning prehistoric knowledge of the size of the earth.

Latitude, Geometry and Astronomy on Anglesey

One archaeologist who has revived the concept of aligned sites is Dr Steven Burrow, presently the Curator of the Cardiff Museum. Burrow recently managed to revive interest in the midsummer axis alignment at Bryn Celli Ddu, a passage tomb on Anglesey first surveyed by Sir Norman Lockyer while on holiday there in 1904. The film of the (now misaligned) solstice sunrise made by Burrow appeared on the local news in Wales and the resulting exhibition and book offered the public a rare chance to reckon with the possibility that prehistoric astronomy was being undertaken in Wales before 2900 BC, the latest date for the monument based on radiocarbon dating of samples. At a recent lecture in the Department of Archaeology and Anthropology at Lampeter University, Burrow bravely announced that, "*Alignments did seem to be important.*"

Alexander Thom never surveyed megalithic sites on Anglesey, a challenge the author has not been able to resist. In late March 2004, I undertook a theodolite survey of the geometry of the henge and, using the sun, accurately measured the azimuth of the passage axis, which turned out to be 53° 5'. In early April 2006, a second survey was undertaken to check and to confirm Dr Burrow's estimation that the axis alignment coincides with the right hand stone of a row of five small stones placed some 12 feet from the passage entrance.

The location of Bryn Celli Ddu is most interesting, because both the (built) axis angle and the solstice sunrise angle in 3000 BC fall extremely close to the larger internal angle of the 3, 4, 5 triangle - which is 53° 7' 48". It is the high horizon

Alexander Thom - Cracking the Stone Age Code

BRYN CELLI DDU,
YNYS MON

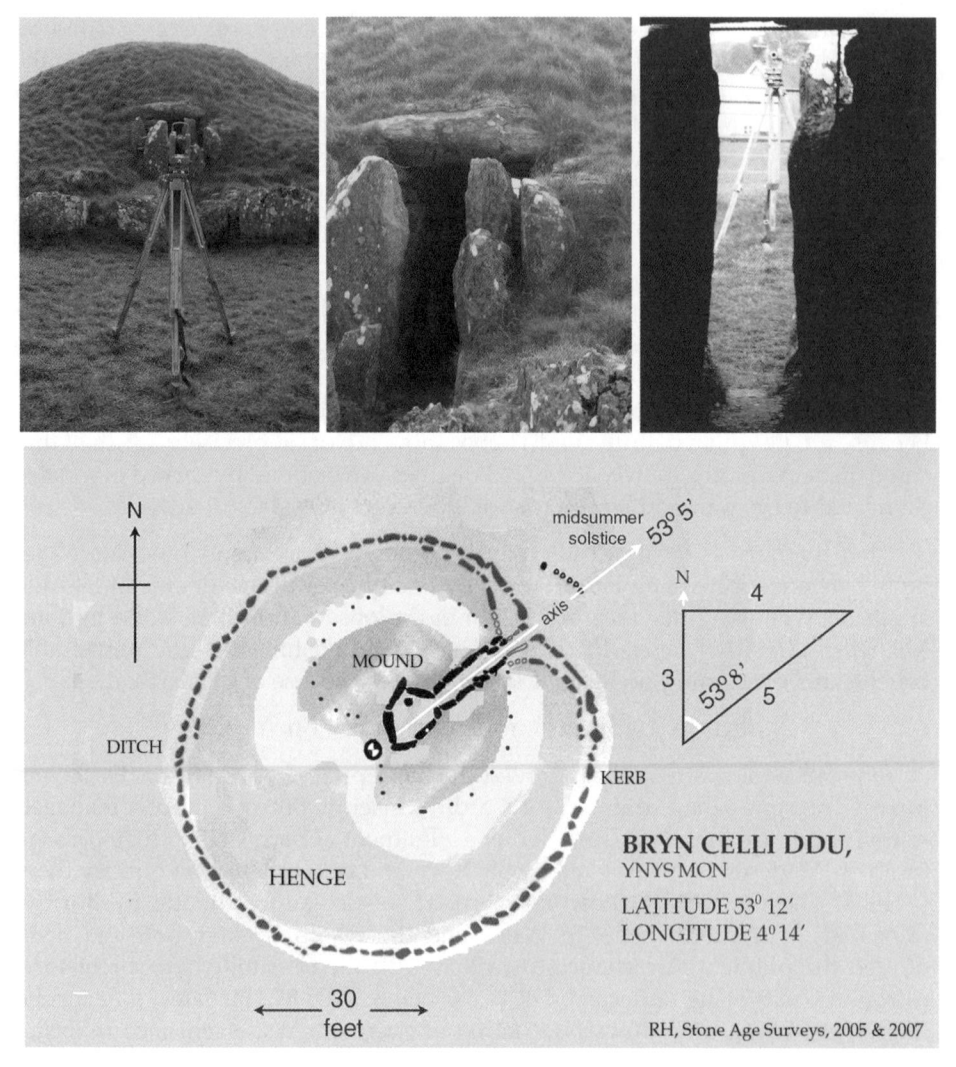

LATITUDE 53° 12'
LONGITUDE 4° 14'

RH, Stone Age Surveys, 2005 & 2007

The Passage Tomb of Bryn Celli Ddu. Despite a modern farmhouse blocking the alignment, it is possible to determine that the midsummer solstice sunrise in 3000 BC was aligned to the angle of the passage, and both are so close to the latitude of the site, and to the larger angle of a 3,4,5 triangle as to suggest that there may be a connection between all three. The other major passage grave on Anglesey, Barclodiad y Gawres is located *at the same latitude* as Bryn Celli Ddu, some 13 miles to the west.

elevation (+3° 36') at Bryn Celli Ddu that produces this increased azimuth of sunrise. Around 3000 BC, at 3:59 am, on the morning of the solstice, rays from the rising sun would have illuminated the veins of quartz on the lower half of the large blocking stone that defines the rear wall of the chamber.

The latitude of Bryn Celli Ddu is itself the same as its axis azimuth, its sunrise azimuth and one angle of the 3, 4, 5 triangle. There are astronomical odds against all these things being a coincidence, and perhaps the site demonstrates that the

- 206 -

builders were showing off their skills in integrating geometry, astronomy and surveying. The other major passage tomb on Anglesey, Barclodiad y Gawres, is located just under 13 miles and directly to the west of Bryn Celli Ddu, within 80 feet of the same latitude. If this too is other than a coincidence, then the builders established an accurate east-west correspondence between the two sites accurate to 4.5 minutes of a degree.

The Integration of Astronomy, Geometry and Metrology

When Thom said of the Temple Wood site on the *Chronicle* documentary, referring to the prediction of eclipses, "*If you put me here in megalithic times I could have worked this thing, knowing what I know now*", this displayed the practical nature of his engineering background, and was no idle boast. Any one of the thirty or so surviving flattened circles in the British Isles could still be 'worked' to perform accurately the calendrical operations described in this chapter. So too could Stonehenge. The development of the practical astronomy stored away at other sites and illustrated in this chapter has an immediate relevance. Firstly, it alters our picture of prehistoric British society, displaying what its aspirations were and what it was capable of. Secondly, because the archaeological profession has rejected Thom's astronomical research and its conclusions, they have doomed themselves to miss this clear integration of metrology, geometry and astronomy. Finally, this integration refreshes the whole subject and makes it worthy of study in a way that makes it directly relevant to disciplines other than archaeology.

The Cosmology of the Circle Builders

One outcome of this exploration of megalithic designs is to recognise that the circle designers were exploring a cosmology that our culture has either rejected since or ever failed to connect with. Their discovery that the cycles of the sun and moon in the skies above the earth were related and that this could be translated through metrology and geometry in order to bring the sky down to the earth must have been a revelatory period of enormous growth in the history of human development.

Another outcome of this revelation would have held an immediate practical value, the ability to structure time cycles to form working calendars and thereby to understand the nature of tidal rhythms, eclipses and the long-term stability of the principal cosmic cycles. It was the birth of astronomy, centred on the earth through monuments that reflected the patterns observed in the sky.

But there would have been still further outcomes, none more profound than the dawning recognition that whatever created the patterns in the sky had done so in a manner that was decidedly logical and geometrical. The raw numbers recorded from the sky, with their inconvenient fractional components, appear to offer no connection between the length of the year, the length of the lunar month or the timings of eclipses. Our modern science thinks this to be the case. The circle builders would have known otherwise, that the simple geometrical shapes incorporated into their monuments using integer lengths and simple triangles revealed an underlying order existing between these cycles, one which enabled the celestial patterns to be framed quite simply onto the earth. Alexander Thom glimpsed this truth, and in so doing, challenged the major beliefs of our age. He gathered evidence of aspects of prehistoric thinking that show a cosmology and a culture quite different from our own, yet connected across the epochs by its recognisable and measurable numerical and geometrical content.

His good friend, Professor Richard Atkinson said this of Sandy Thom at the beginning of his obituary in the *Journal for the History of Astronomy*, in 1986,

> *'It is not often that a man can be said to have created, single-handed, a whole new academic discipline. Such a one was Professor Alexander Thom, who died on 7th November 1985, aged 91. Had it not been for his relentless pursuit, over more than forty years, of megalithic sites in Britain and Brittany it is doubtful whether the subject of archaeoastronomy would have existed at all. There would have been no archaeoastronomy supplement for JHA, and probably no Archaeoastronomy Bulletin from the University of Maryland, because his influence in the Americas has been at least as great as in Britain and Europe. From small and disregarded beginnings his work grew in stature and acceptance to being published by the Oxford University Press in three successive volumes, to forming one of the focal points of a joint symposium of the Royal Society and the British Academy, and ultimately to becoming part of the canon of the early history of science. Few men could have achieved such recognition in their own lifetime; and fewer still as a by-product of a distinguished professional career in a different field.'*

Aubrey Burl wrote the following concluding paragraph of his paper in memory of Alexander Thom, published in *Records in Stone* (*page 202 - 203*). His eloquent tribute recognises Thom's contribution towards understanding both the circles and their builders. Despite Burl's reticence to wholly embrace Thom's conclusions, his attribution of 'a symbol of the cosmos' to the circles surely recognises both the theme of this final chapter and the genius of the man, thereby providing a perfect conclusion to this work.

> *'This may have been what a stone circle was to its people, a place where axes and gifts were exchanged, a place where annual gatherings were held, a place to which the bodies of the dead were brought before burial, but, above all, a place that was the symbol of the cosmos, the living world made everlasting in stone, its circle the circle of the skyline, its North point the token of the unchangingness of life, a microcosm of the world in stone, the most sacred of its places to its men and women.*

Chapter Seven - A Fitting Tribute

Should this interpretation be correct, then it will not have come out of the work of excavators but from the plans and analyses of Alexander Thom and others before him without whose information and stimulus such research would not have begun. Years ago John Aubrey wrote that he had brought the stone circles 'from an utter darkness to a thin mist' (1665-1693, I:25). The mist remains, a little thinner today, but through it, with the work of Alexander Thom, the sun is rising.'

Alexander Thom, 1894 - 1985

APPENDICES

A Brief History of British Archaeoastronomy
by Irene Earis MA(Oxon), MA in Cultural Astronomy

The history of archaeoastronomy began with a gradual recognition of the existence and importance of prehistoric sites in the country. Once recognised as man-made engineering projects, gradually the records and plans were made of the sites which now enable people to calculate their relationship with the sky.

This recognition came late in British history. In literature and records before the seventeenth century there are very few references to prehistoric monuments. One exception is a picture of a rectangular Stonehenge (obviously not drawn from life!) in a fourteenth century manuscript now in a Cambridge college library and another, in a French manuscript, shows a giant Merlin in the act of building Stonehenge. Even Shakespeare seemed to have overlooked stone circles or megaliths in the British countryside although so many features of country life are included in his plays and poems. Local folklore and tradition about the ancient sites continued, often connecting the stones to particular solar festivals in the year, but somehow they escaped the attention of the educated and literate.

However King James I visited Stonehenge in the early seventeenth century and ordered his court architect Inigo Jones to prepare a plan of it and give some indication of its date and purpose. Inigo Jones assumed that Stonehenge was a Roman temple and proposed that it was dedicated to the god *Coelus* (the sky). He felt that Druids were not likely to have built it as they had no reputation for architecture and were thought to have worshipped in simple outdoor ceremonies among groves of trees! Although an architect, Jones felt no need to pay detailed attention to the remaining stones at Stonehenge when he produced his plan. He drew an idealised version, more as he as a classical architect would have built it than as the archaeology suggested it had actually looked.

Another theory of the time, put forward by Dr. Walter Charleton, who published a book called *Chorea Gigantum* in 1663, was that Stonehenge must have been built by Danes for their kings. He felt that a Roman dating of the structure would be too early.

The first person to look more closely and accurately at some of the great British prehistoric monuments was John Aubrey (1626 – 1697). He had read Inigo Jones' manuscript *Stonehenge Restored* and it annoyed him that Jones had imposed his own ideas on how Stonehenge might have been rather than studying the remains as they were. Aubrey knew the area well, having been born and bred near Malmesbury, thirty miles away, within riding distance for the son of a country gentleman who liked to go hunting across the Wiltshire countryside.

Aubrey is best known as the author of a collection of anecdotes and gossip about many of the famous men of his day (*'Brief Lives'*). He was also one of the original fellows of the Royal Society. He lived in an age that did not separate out the arts and sciences, so his rational observations of historical monuments did not have to fit into a single academic discipline. The fact that it combines astronomy, archaeology and history has since been one of the problems that archaeoastronomy has had to face and, as a result, it has been marginalised by all sides.

Around Christmas time in 1648 Aubrey was out hunting and rode into the stone circles and avenues at Avebury. He was struck with amazement and talked about it to all his friends ("*it did much excel Stoneheng, as a Cathedral does a Parish church*") so that word got

Appendix One - A Brief History of British Archaeoastronomy

back to Charles II. Eventually, in 1663 the king then made a visit to Avebury and climbed Silbury Hill with Aubrey and others. He ordered Aubrey to prepare a report for him about both Avebury and Stonehenge. He also told Aubrey to dig out the depressions marked on his plan of Stonehenge, since known as the Aubrey holes, to try to find human bones, but Aubrey wrote *"I did not doe it"*.

Aubrey presumed that these and other ancient monuments were Temples of the Druids and that they were prehistoric. *"These Antiquities are so exceedingly old that no Bookes doe reach them…"* His notes and plans were gathered together after his death and published under the title of *Monumenta Britannica*. His contribution to their study was to draw them to the attention of the authorities as important national sites and also, by his plans and notes, to help record them before further destruction took place. For example there would originally have been about 200 megaliths at Avebury, Aubrey's plan shows 80, Stukeley in the next century recorded 70 and now there are about 50. Such detailed knowledge of the sites and accurate plans are necessary to give archaeoastronomy a firm foundation.

William Stukeley (1687 – 1765) was the most important contributor to the subject in the century after Aubrey. He was a prototype of the eccentric antiquarian with a wide-ranging knowledge of many subjects and an interest in anything old and unusual. He loved to travel round the country visiting churches and ancient sites and gradually concentrated his attentions on prehistoric monuments. Amongst many other books and manuscripts, he read Aubrey's *Monumenta Britannica*. His great contribution, however, was not so much his writing as the drawings and plans he made as he travelled about. His engravings of prehistoric sites, with their combination of excellent technical draughtsmanship with a Romantic imagination, have left an important record. His inclusion of Druid figures among the ruins helped to link the sites with imaginary Druid rituals in the popular imagination, leading to the revival of the tradition in the nineteenth century. An example of the importance of his artistic records is one engraving of a stone circle on Overton Hill dated 8 July 1723. This is now known as the Sanctuary, part of the Avebury complex. Within a year of Stukeley's engraving it had been destroyed by local farmers.

Stukeley actually used a theodolite for his surveying, but his azimuths were not very accurate as he relied on a magnetic compass. However he did raise the standard for accurate surveying and usually included the axes of orientation of the sites he visited. On the basis of his observation that Stonehenge was aligned on sunrise at the summer solstice, he came to the conclusion that it was probably a temple for worship of the sun. John Wood, the famous Bath architect, also made a survey of Stonehenge at this time and published his plan together with measurements of all the stones. The megalithic sites were becoming worthy of scientific attention and record at last.

Wandering around the hills of the Lake District in the late eighteenth and early nineteenth centuries, the poet William Wordsworth described the "circles, lines, or mounds" he came across as

"Shaped by the Druids, so to represent
Their knowledge of the heavens."

(The Prelude. Book XIII lines 338 – 341)

He had no doubt, in other words, about their astronomical alignments. This may have been from his own observations alone, but it might also be directly attributable to Stukeley whose popular engravings could be found on the walls of houses all over Britain. Indeed,

Appendix One - A Brief History of British Archaeoastronomy

few of his books have survived intact because they were cut up so frequently to extract the drawings.

In the nineteenth century a professional astronomer turned his attention to the ancient sites for the first time. This was Sir Norman Lockyer (1836 – 1920). His achievements as a scientist and astronomer were unquestionable. He founded the journal *Nature* and edited it for nearly fifty years. He was a Fellow of the Royal Society, Astronomer Royal and Professor of Astronomical Physics at the Royal College of Science. His particular academic interest was in the sun. He became fascinated by archaeoastronomy in his fifties when on holiday in Greece, where he noticed that the axes of temples, such as the Parthenon and the temple at Eleusis, had been changed over the centuries. His friend, F.C.Penrose, continued the work on Greek temples and Lockyer himself turned his attention first to Egypt and then later to British ancient monuments, especially Stonehenge.

In Egypt he measured the orientations of many temples and showed how they were aligned carefully to capture the light of the rising or setting sun at key moments in the solar year and even to observe the star Sirius that appears on the horizon just before sunrise at the summer solstice, which coincides with the Nile inundation and the Egyptian New Year. He attempted to date some of the temples from the astronomical alignments, which was theoretically possible but relied on understanding the changes in the buildings over many centuries. This led to disagreements with some archaeologists over ancient Egyptian chronology and was a precursor of the problems astronomers were to continue having with archaeologists at sites around the world. Before measuring the alignment of a building or megalithic site it is essential to know from archaeology the exact building sequences. The two subjects of astronomy and archaeology are deeply intertwined and need to be studied together.

In 1894 Lockyer published *The Dawn of Astronomy*, using his own discoveries and those of others which he gathered and edited. Then in 1906 he published *Stonehenge and Other British Stone Monuments Astronomically Considered*. At Stonehenge he calculated backwards from the midsummer sunrise in 1901 and concluded that it was designed and founded in 1680 BCE, much closer to the present estimate which, it is worth noting, has been moved further and further back by archaeologists themselves during the last fifty years. All this work was pursued for the sheer intellectual interest of it in the time he could spare from a busy and successful career, in a manner similar to that of Professor Thom. Lockyer hoped that others would take up his preliminary work on many monuments in this country and abroad, but sadly it still awaits serious archaeological interest.

Continued popular acceptance of astronomical alignments at ancient sites can be seen however in the famous conclusion to Thomas Hardy's novel *Tess of the D'Urbevilles*, published in 1890. Tess, the heroine, is arrested for murder at Stonehenge where she has taken refuge by night. In the story Hardy's characters assume that Stonehenge was a Temple of the Sun and that the sunrise would take place beyond the Heel Stone.

In 1908 an Irish naval expert in underwater surveying, Captain (later Admiral) H. Boyle Somerville, read Lockyer's book on the British monuments, was intrigued and decided to test out the ideas on the ancient monuments of his local area, Donegal. He quickly found many sites with alignments to solstices, equinoxes and cardinal points that supported Lockyer's claims. Later he surveyed other Irish sites such as Lough Gur and many monuments in

Appendix One - A Brief History of British Archaeoastronomy

Scotland, including those at Callanish and on Uist. He published his findings in various journals and Professor Thom recalled these when he started his own research later.

It is also worth mentioning in this brief history the books of Alfred Watkins, such as *The Old Straight Track*, published in 1925. Watkins was the man who started the interest in ley-lines, which subsequently have often been confused with astronomical alignments at prehistoric sites. The result of the movement he started was to rouse popular interest in looking at the landscape with fresh eyes and many people have begun with an interest in ley-lines and then moved on to the more rigorous and verifiable study of astronomical alignments. Many archaeologists, however, have failed to see the distinction between the two approaches and have dismissed them both together as if they were the same.

Before Professor Thom published his *Megalithic Sites in Britain* in 1967, another book had moved the subject of archaeoastronomy forward and at the same time seized the popular imagination. This was *Stonehenge Decoded* published in 1965 by Gerald Hawkins. He was an Englishman, with degrees from Nottingham and Manchester Universities in physics and astronomy, who was appointed Professor of Astronomy at Boston in 1957. He combined his astronomy with the new computer technology being developed at that time and applied his knowledge and techniques to Stonehenge, the great national monument of his home country. His book was a bestseller and was given much press coverage, so it was difficult for archaeologists to ignore. Richard Atkinson did try to satirise and debunk Hawkins' ideas by writing an article in *Antiquity* called *Moonshine on Stonehenge*, but thedistinguished astronomer Professor Sir Fred Hoyle, checking Hawkins' theories, not only confirmed them but felt that Hawkins had not gone far enough in his claims. Hawkins, like Thom, was not of course an archaeologist and was therefore probably resented by the profession for coming up with new ideas in their academic field. Hawkins also took for granted the high levels of intelligence of people in prehistory, which archaeologists disputed from the evidence of remains of settlements and other facets of cultural life. In the preface to *Stonehenge Decoded* Hawkins wrote that his hypothesis had been:

"If I can see any alignment, general relationship or use for the various parts of Stonehenge then these facts were also known to the builders......In retrospect it is a conservative hypothesis for it allows the Stonehenger to be equal to, but not better than, me. Many facts, for example the 56-year eclipse cycle, were not known to me and other astronomers, but were discovered (or rather rediscovered) from the decoding of Stonehenge."

This is of course reminiscent of Professor Thom's remark at the end of *Megalithic Sites in Britain*:
"Whatever we do we must avoid approaching the study with the idea that Megalithic man was our inferior in ability to think."

At about the same time as Hawkins was working with his computer on the possible alignments at Stonehenge another keen amateur astronomer from Yorkshire, C.A.Newham, had already independently come to similar conclusions. Hawkins acknowledges his work and supported Newham's conclusions in *Stonehenge Decoded*. Newham illustrates again the lack of any academic home for archaeoastronomy which continues to be developed by dedicated amateurs working in their own time and at their own expense, but with much opposition from the archaeological profession which has not moved radically in its theories about prehistoric sites over the last century. Only the external scientific discovery of carbon-dating has forced prehistorians to alter some of their thinking in recent years.

Appendix One - A Brief History of British Archaeoastronomy

When *Megalithic Sites in Britain* was published in 1967 no one else besides Professor Thom had contributed so much to the subject. The standard of academic excellence that he applied to all his research moved archaeoastronomy up to a new level. The details are contained in this book and need not be repeated here. The extraordinary outcome of the application of such a distinguished academic to the subject of archaeoastronomy, however, has been that his work has been met with almost total rejection and resistance by the professionals who stand most to gain from the new impetus he gave to the study of prehistoric archaeology. Even now the subject is generally excluded from university archaeology departments in this country, despite its obvious intellectual interest.

Professor Ruggles, who as a young man led the team of researchers into Thom's conclusions, created an optional undergraduate module in archaeoastronomy as part of the archaeology degree at Leicester and has been the only British Professor of Archaeoastronomy. By altering the methodology that Thom employed, however, naturally he came to different results, and his subsequent forays into statistical approaches have made archaeoastronomy seem more dense and difficult than has ever been necessary.

Under the influence of Professor Ruggles archaeoastronomy has become focussed almost entirely on the problem of how to authenticate astronomical alignments at prehistoric sites as intentional rather than coincidental. Since it is obviously easier to come down on the side of coincidence, astronomical alignments at site after site have been dismissed or thrown into doubt and Thom's place within the whole subject of archaeoastronomy has been held back in its development. The desire to test out theories with thorough diligence is laudable. In practice, however, by making extreme efforts not to assume any particular motivation on the part of the megalith builders, the truth behind the megaliths can equally be missed.

The story of archaeoastronomy began with folklore, place-names and traditions that linked ancient sites to the movements of the sun, moon and stars. Strangely, it has now come full circle, with most lay people being willing to accept the link between sky and landscape revealed in the carefully chosen location of stones, cairns, circles and other monuments. Images of Stonehenge, for example, on television or in magazines almost inevitably include the presence of the sun or moon. When told that at most prehistoric sites this connection is not supported by the majority of archaeologists, people are amazed.

Almost every week there is a new report in the newspapers and on television of an ancient site with astronomical alignments being discovered in, for instance, South America, North Africa or China. In the United States there has been a *Center for Archaeoastronomy* at the University of Maryland since 1978. Yet little work is being done on our own sites in Britain in support of the astronomical alignments, except by enthusiasts outside professional archaeology, such as Margaret Curtis at Callanish or indeed Robin Heath himself, the author of this book, while all the time stones that mark alignments are being moved for agricultural and building purposes.

Professor Thom has provided the groundwork of the subject by his thorough and painstaking surveys and his understated theories about the implications of his work. The next stage in the history of archaeoastronomy will hopefully be the willingness at last for some university or other higher education institution to build on the sure foundations already laid and for the subject area to become an integral part of at least some degrees in archaeology, if not an academic subject in its own right.

Appendix Two - Alexander Thom: Archaeoastronomical Publications

APPENDIX TWO - THOM: ARCHAEOASTRONOMICAL PUBLICATIONS
(based on original document supplied to the author by Dr Archie Thom, November 1994)

ALEXANDER THOM - BIBLIOGRAPHY AND PUBLICATIONS
(in chronological order)

1955
'A statistical examination of the megalithic sites of Britain'   *Journal of the Royal Statistical Society* A 118 275–95

1961
'The egg-shaped standing stone rings of Britain'   *Archivs Internationales d'Histoire des Sciences* 14 291–303
'The geometry of megalithic man'   *Mathematical Gazette* 45 83–93

1962
'The megalithic unit of length'   *Journal of the Royal Statistical Society* A 125 243–51

1964
'The larger units of length of megalithic man'   *Journal of the Royal Statistical Society* A 127 527–33

1966
'Megaliths and mathematics'   *Antiquity* 40 121–8

1967
Megalithic Sites in Britain   Clarendon Press, Oxford

1968
'The metrology and geometry of cup and ring marks'   *Systematics* 6 173–89

1970
Megalithic Lunar Observatories   Clarendon Press

1971
Thom, A & Thom, AS
The astronomical significance of the large Carnac menhirs'   *Journal for the History of Astronomy* 2 147–60

1972
'The Carnac alignments'   *Journal for the History of Astronomy* 3 11–26
'The uses and alignments at Le Menec, Carnac'   *Journal for the History of Astronomy* 3 151–64

1973
'The Kerlescan cromlechs'   *Journal for the History of Astronomy* 4 169–73
'A megalithic lunar observatory in Orkney'   *Journal for the History of Astronomy* 4 111–23

1974
'The Kermario alignments'   *Journal for the History of Astronomy* 5 30–47
'Stonehenge'   *Journal for the History of Astronomy* 5 pt 2 71-90

1975
'Further work on the Brogar Lunar Observatory'   *Journal for the History of Astronomy* 6 100–114
'Stonehenge as a possible lunar observatory'   *Journal for the History of Astronomy* 6 19-30

1976
Avebury(1): A new assessment of the geometry and metrology of the ring'   *Journal for the History of Astronomy* 7 183–92
Avebury (2): the West Kennet Avenue'   7 193–7
   Thom, A; Thom, AS & Foord TR
'The two megalithic lunar observatories at Carnac'   7 11–26
   Thom, A; Thom, AS & Gorrie, JM

1977
Megalithic Astronomy'   *Journal of Navigation* 30 1–14 (1977)
A Fourth Lunar Foresight for the Brogar Ring'   *Journal for the History of Astronomy* 8 54–55

1978
A reconsideration of the Lunar Sites in Britain'   *Journal for the History of Astronomy* 9 170–179
Megalithic remains in Britain and Brittany   Clarendon Press, Oxford

Appendix Two - Alexander Thom: Archaeoastronomical Publications

1979
The standing stones in Argyllshire'   *Glasgow Archaeological Journal* vi 5–10

1980
'A new study of all lunar lines'   *Journal for the History of Astronomy*
                                              ; Archaeoastronomy 2 S78—S94

Astronomical foresights used by Megalithic man'   *JHA* 11 S90– S94

Megalithic Rings Thom, Thom and Burl,   BAR Megalithic Rings
Plans and Data for 229 monuments in Britain

1982
Statistical and philosophical arguements for the   in DC Heggie
astronomical significance of standing stones   (ed) Archaeoastronomy in the Old World
Statistical and philosophical arguments for the   CUP (Cambridge University Press)
astronomical significance of standing stones,   53–82
with a section on the solar calendar'

1983
Observations of the Moon in megalithic times'   Archaeoastronomy no 5 S57–66 p S57

1984
The two major Megalithic observatories in Scotland'   *Journal for the History of Astronomy*

1990 (posthumous publication)   15 S129–S148

Stone Rows and Standing Stones Britain Ireland & Brittany   BAR International Series 560 (i)

APPENDIX THREE - GLOSSARY OF TERMS USED IN ARCHAEOASTRONOMY

AZIMUTH - The angle from true north, measured clockwise. Thus 'east' is azimuth 90°, south is 180° while west is 270°.

CELESTIAL EQUATOR - The plane of the earth's orbit around the sun

DECLINATION (symbol δ) - The angle of a celestial body measured from the celestial equator. Measured as positive when a celestial object is above the celestial equator and negative when below it. Independent of the latitude of a location, almanacs and ephemerides usually list declinations for the sun, moon and planets for any given date and time.

ELEVATION - The angle of a celestial body or reference object above the local horizon. 0° is taken to mean a level horizon (zero elevation or altitude).

OBLIQUITY (symbol ϵ) - The angle of tilt of the earth's axis with respect to the celestial equator. Presently 23.47°, this has fallen from just over 24° since 3000 BC, causing the ancient observatories to fall out of alignment, the reason all the sums are needed. In 2000 BC, the obliquity was 23.93°, for 2500 BC it was 23.98° and for 3000 BC it was 24.03° for 3500 BC it was 24.07°, and for 4000 BC it was 24.11° (*De Sitte's formula on page 224*).

PARALLAX - A correction that must be applied to the position of the Moon quoted in almanacs and ephemerides (astronomical tables), which, in order to be applicable for any location gives a single value of the position as seen from the centre of the earth. Lunar parallax averages at 0.95°. Solar parallax is usually negligible, at 0.002°.

REFRACTION - the visual distortion caused by the earth and its atmosphere on celestial bodies or reference objects. Increases rapidly as the elevation falls below 20°, and is particularly high when objects lie on or near the horizon (typically 0.55°) - *see graph of average refraction against altitude for two temperatures shown on page 218*).

Appendix Three & Four - Glossary and Formulae in Archaeoastronomy

APPENDIX FOUR - FORMULAE USED IN ARCHAEOASTRONOMICAL WORK

(a) ASTRONOMICAL FORMULAE
ON A LEVEL HORIZON, ANY CELESTIAL BODY CUTS THE HORIZON AT THE FOLLOWING AZIMUTH ANGLE

$$\text{Azimuth angle } (°) = \cos^{-1}[\sin(\text{Declination})/\cos(\text{latitude})]$$

Example 1. At latitude 52°, what is the horizon rise and set points for the sun when it's the summer solstice and its declination equals earth's tilt angle of 23.47°?
Answer - 49.69°. The rise angle is from north as given, the set angle is 360° minus this number, i.e. it is 310.3°.
Example 2. Try the same sum for 3000 BC, with declination = 24°. Or for the winter solstice positions, when the declination is -23.47° in 2000 AD and was -24° in 3000 BC.

ACCOUNTING FOR HORIZON ELEVATION (Altitude)
Only rarely will the horizon elevation be zero (level). In the above formulae a correction factor h must be applied, and this complicates considerably the calculations.
CURVATURE OF THE EARTH
Then, to ensure the best accuracy, you may have to account for the curvature of the earth, which is 0.007244 degrees per mile distance between you and the horizon feature.
PARALLAX
Finally for the moon one must account for lunar parallax, which varies between 0.9 and 1.0 degrees when the moon is near the horizon. For the sun it's a negligible 0.002 degrees.
REFRACTION
Then there is the problem of atmospheric refraction. Refraction is never constant and can vary quite a bit over quite a short space of time. A band of cooler or warmer air between you and a setting or rising sun can change the angle by up to a quarter of a degree in extreme cases. Refraction also varies with h such that an h of 5° gives an average one tenth of a degree of refraction, an idealised level horizon gives about 0.6° refraction, while a downward elevation may rise to well over a degree. The graph (*overleaf*) gives a guide to average values. If the sun and moon are visible, it may be measured accurately on-site.

Taking all these factors into account, the formula now changes to

$$\text{Azimuth angle}° = \cos^{-1}\left[\frac{\sin(\text{Dec}) - \sin(\text{Lat}) \times \sin(h)}{\cos(\text{Lat}) \times \cos(h)}\right]$$

where   h° = horizon elevation - curvature correction + parallax - refraction

Computer programs exist (e.g. *Solar Fire*) to solve this sum for those who go weak at the knees over mathematical formulae. Here one enters in the date, time and location (latitude and longitude - from GPS or OS maps) and immediately obtains a print out of the declination, azimuth, elevation and other useful information on the sun and moon, accurate to a minute of one degree. *Solar Fire* offers user options to account for typical refraction and/or

Appendix Four - Formulae used in Archaeoastronomy

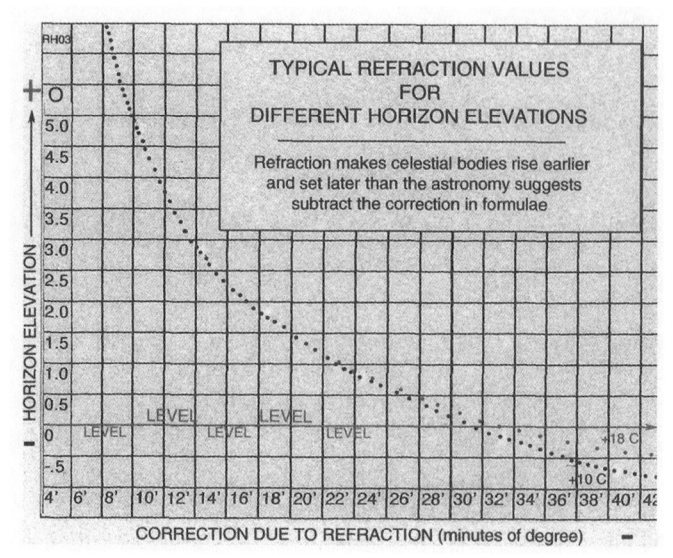

TYPICAL REFRACTION VALUES FOR DIFFERENT HORIZON ELEVATIONS

Refraction makes celestial bodies rise earlier and set later than the astronomy suggests subtract the correction in formulae

CORRECTION DUE TO REFRACTION (minutes of degree)

place the sun or moon on the horizon to determine rising or setting times. For research into the astronomy of ancient sites, such a program is invaluable. A superb example is the moon's major standstill rise in the north as seen from the 'spine' of Glastonbury Tor. Only twice or three times at each standstill would the moon be seen to rise to the left of the Tor, *Solar Fire* giving the time of this rising moon, its azimuth and its elevation over time, enabling a photographer or surveyor to be on-site at the right time and looking in the correct direction to catch that once-in-a-lunar-standstill photograph.

(*Overleaf:* author's composite photo of the 2005/6 standstill moonrise at Glastonbury Tor).

(b) GEODETIC FORMULAE

CALCULATING THE DISTANCE BETWEEN SITES AND THEIR RELATIVE AZIMUTHS AND ELEVATION

These formulae are given in full in *The Measure of Albion*, with worked examples. A GPS device can be most useful in giving accurate figures (to about 20 feet) for the latitude and longitude of a site, although these coordinates may also be taken directly from an OS map. From this data, the distance apart of two sites and also their azimuth and elevation angles between them may be determined. Years ago, the author wrote programs in BASIC that greatly simplify the calculations, and these still provide quick and accurate information from the data. They would be adaptable by suitably experienced researchers to suit other programming languages. Print-outs from GEODESY.BAS and QUICKAZ. BAS are shown opposite, each directly relevant to sites covered elsewhere in this book.

Opposite lower: Sample print-outs of two BASIC programs used by the author. On the left, the data is used to provide accurate azimuths of the moon as it sets at Bryn Celli Ddu; on the right, the distance from Long Meg to Helvellyn is calculated, together with the azimuth angle between the sites and the elevation angle.

Appendix Four - Computer Programs used in Archaeoastronomy

GLASTONBURY TOR – MAJOR STANDSTILL MOONRISE
moonrise at 5:33 pm, november 18th 2005, azimuth 41°35', composite photograph

Solar Fire v5

*** ANALYSIS REPORT ***   ENTRY - DATE, TIME AND LOCATION

Transits 18 Nov 2005 – **GLASTONBURY TOR - MAJOR STANDSTILL MOONRISE - 17:30 PM**

ELEVATION (h)

CHART POINTS							
Point	Longitude	Travel	Latitude	Rt.Asc.	Decl.	Azi(0°N)	Alti.
☽	28° Ⅱ 49'15"	+12°39'	+04°59'	088°40'	+28°25'	041°11'	+00°15'
☉	26° ♏ 28'35"	+01°01'	+00°00'	234°10'	−19°22'	252°20'	−10°42'

STONE AGE SURVEYS 31/3/2007; T16; sunshoot
BRYN CELLI DDU - OUTLIER STONE (SW).
Azimuths from sun-shoot (average) - RH edge 237° 7'; centre top 237° 39; RH edge 237° 53'

This calculation is running with the following data (all in degrees)
Minor Moonset -(e - i)
The proposed alignment lies in the SW quadrant.
Declination = -18.855
Latitude = 53.2069
Horizon Altitude = -.85
Correction for Earth's Curvature = .01
Parallax Correction = .95
Refraction Correction = .4
Cosine of the Azimuth = -.5381887

        ****
        Disc on Horizon (southerly set) =   237.4396 degrees
        Disc half set =   237.8348 degrees
        Last flash =   238.6182 degrees
        ****

****** ***** GEODESY PROGRAM - DATA FROM PROPOSED ALIGNMENT **

LONG MEG to HELVELLYN
**** The distance from LM to HV is 19.47678 miles,
**** at an azimuth angle of 223.2443 degrees,
**** the horizon elevation angle (corrected for Earth's curvature)
**** is .8194114 degrees

****   The foresight bearing is south- west of LM

*** The E-W distance is 13.34374 miles, the N-S distance is 14.18766 miles,

**** SITE DATA:- LM 54.72748 2.6668 HV 54.52222 3 degrees
           - SITE ELEVATIONS (in feet):- LM 552 HV 3118

************************* Robin Heath, Stone-Age Surveys *******************

Appendix Five - Recent Discovery of a Megalithic Ring on Lundy Island

APPENDIX FOUR - THE LUNDY EGG

As this book was about to go to press, the author was involved in taking a surveying party around Lundy Island, in the Bristol Channel. Some members of the group suggested that a group of stones to the southwest of Halfway wall was, or had been, a stone circle. A quick radial survey to the centre of every stone was undertaken in under an hour with theodolite and carbon fibre tape. Upon my return home the results were plotted and a provisional survey plan drawn up. This is given below - a more thorough survey awaits. The Lundy Egg was built as a Type I egg, with its forming triangle being a 3,4,5 of units in Megalithic rods. Despite the evident damage done to the right-hand boundary of the ring, enough stones remained, precisely on the geometry of a Type I egg to confirm the intentions of the builders. The axis is aligned to the tump at the centre of the island (see *The Measure of Albion*) and to the minor moonrise in the north, around 3000 BC.

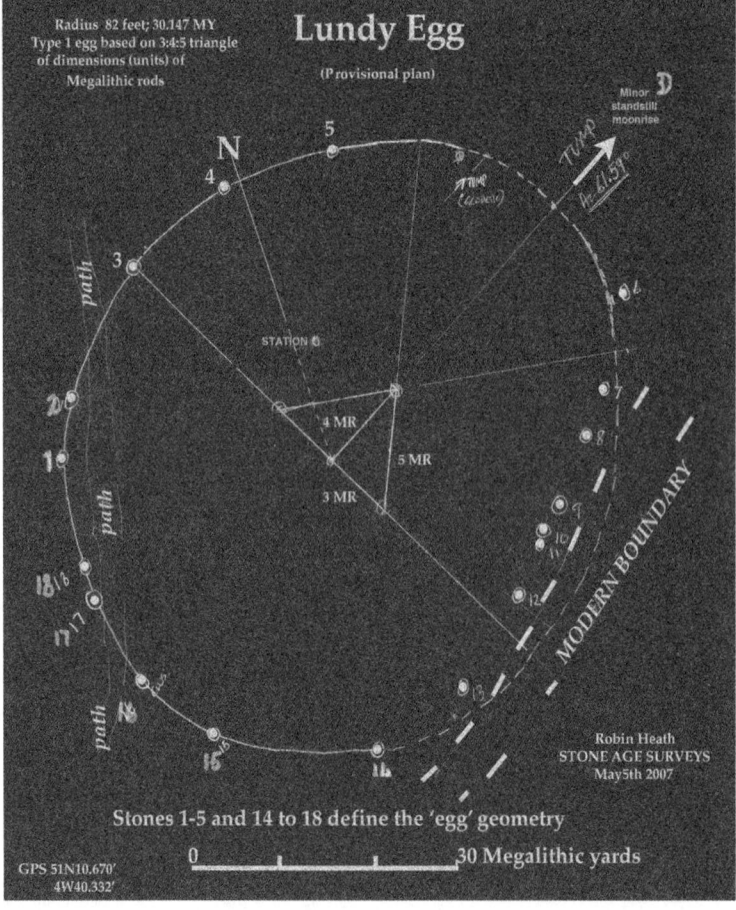

Classic Thom. A large Type I egg discovered on Lundy Island, May 2007. by members of the *Society of Ley-hunters* and surveyed by the author, assisted by Hugh Newman, Adrian Hyde and Pat Toms. Enough of the original monument remains to confirm the original geometry, metrology and astronomical properties.

BIBLIOGRAPHY

Ashmore, Patrick (2000). *'Archaeoastronomy of the British Isles'*. Archaeoastronomy, no.25 (JHA, xxxi), 78-85.
Atkinson, Richard J.C. (1968). Review of *'Megalithic Sites in Britain'*. Antiquity 42:77.
Atkinson, Richard J.C. (1956) *Stonehenge*. Unwin, & (1960) Penguin, Harmondsworth.
Bender, Barbara (ed.)(1993). Landscape Politics and Perspectives. Providence/Oxford: Berg.
Brennan, Martin (1983). *The Stars and the Stones*. Ancient Art and Astronomy in Ireland. London: Thames and Hudson.
Buck, Caitlin E., William G.Cavanagh, and Clifford D.Litton (1996). *Bayesian Approach to Interpreting Archaeological Data*. Chichester:Wiley.
Buck, C.E., Kenworthy, J.B., Litton, C.D. and Smith, A.F.M. (1991).*'Combining archaeological and radiocarbon information: A Bayesian approach to calibration'*. Antiquity, lxv, 808-21
Burl, Aubrey (1981). *'Holes in the Argument'*. Archaeoastronomy, Vol.IV, no.4: 19-25.
Burl, Aubrey (1981). *'Moving in the Wrong Circles'*. Archaeoastronomy, Vol.IV, no.2: 35-37.
Burl, Aubrey (1981).*'The Enigma of Stonehenge'*. Archaeoastronomy, Vol.IV, no.2: 38-39.
Burl, Aubrey (1993). *From Carnac to Callanish*. The Prehistoric Stone Rows and Avenues of Britain, Ireland and Brittany. New Haven and London: Yale University Press.
Burl, Aubrey (1983). *Prehistoric Astronomy and Ritual*. Aylesbury, Bucks.: Shire Archaeology.
Burl, Aubrey (1995). *A Guide to the Stone Circles of Britain, Ireland and Brittany*. New Haven and London: Yale University Press.
Childe, V. Gordon (1936) *Man Makes Himself*. London: Watts.
Cotter, C. H. *The Astronomical and Mathematical Foundations of Geography*.(1966) Hollis & Carter.
Critchlow, Keith. (1973) *Time Stands Still*. London: Gordon Frazer (*republished 2007*).
Curtis, Margaret and Curtis, Ronald (1990). *'Callanish: maximising the symbolic and dramatic potential of the landscape at the southern extreme moon.'* Archaeoastronomy in the 1990s: 309-316. Loughborough: Group D Publications.
Evans, James (1998). *The History and Practice of Ancient Astronomy*. New York and Oxford: Oxford University Press.
Freeman, P.R. and Elmore, W. (1979). *'A Test for the Significance of Astronomical Alignments'*. Archaeoastronomy, no.1 (JHA, x): 86-93.
Harding, Jan (2003). *Henge Monuments of the British Isles*. Stroud, Gloucestershire: Tempus.
Hawkins, Gerald S. (1966). *Stonehenge Decoded*. Glasgow: Fontana/Collins.
Hayman, Richard (1997). *Riddles in Stone*. Myths, Archaeology and the Ancient Britons. London: The Hambledon Press.
Heath, Robin. (1993). *A Key to Stonehenge*. Cardigan, Wales: Bluestone Press.
Heath, Robin. (1998). *Sun, Moon and Stonehenge*. Cardigan, Wales: Bluestone Press.
Heath, Robin. (1999 & 2006). *Sun, Moon and Earth.*. Glastonbury: Wooden Books.

Bibliography

Heath, Robin. (2000). *Stonehenge.* Powys, Wales: Wooden Books.
Heath, Robin and Michell, John (2004). *The Measure of Albion.* Cardigan, Wales: Bluestone Press.
Heggie, Douglas C. (1972). '*Megalithic Lunar Observatories: an Astronomer's View*'. Antiquity 181: 43-48.
Heggie, Douglas C. (1981). *Megalithic Science.* London: Thames and Hudson.
Heggie, Douglas C. (ed.)(1982). *Archaeoastronomy in the Old World.* Cambridge: Cambridge University Press.
Hicks, Ronald (1981). Review of '*Megalithic Remains in Britain and Brittany*'. Archaeoastronomy, Vol.IV, no.2: 40-43.
Higginbottom, Gail and Clay, Roger (1999). '*Reassessment of Sites in Northwest Scotland: A New Statistical Approach*'. Archaeoastronomy, no.24 (JHA, xxx): 41-46.
Hutton, Ronald (1991). *The Pagan Religions of the Ancient British Isles.* Their Nature and Legacy. Oxford: Blackwell Publishing.
Ivimy, John. (1974). *The Sphinx and the Megaliths.* London: Turnstone Books.
Johnson, Matthew. (1999). *Archaeological Theory.* An Introduction. Oxford: Blackwell.
Johnson, Aylmer. *Plane and geodetic Surveying.* (2004) Spon Press, London.
Knight, Chris (1987) *Blood Relations.* Yale: Yale University Press.
Lucas, Gavin. (2005). *The Archaeology of Time.* London: Routledge.
Lynch, Frances, Stephen Aldhouse-Green and Jeffrey L.Davies (2000). *Prehistoric Wales.* Stroud: Sutton Publishing.
MacKie, Euan W. (1977). *Science and Society in Prehistoric Britain.* London: Elek.
MacKie, Euan W. (1984).'*Megalithic Astronomy*'. Journal of Archaeoastronomy. Vol VII (1-4): 144-150.
Macaulay, A. *Megalithic Measures and Rhythms.* (2006) Floris Books, Edinburgh.
Martineau, John (1995). *A Book of Coincidence.* Wooden Books.
McCluskey, Stephen C. (2000). '*The Inconstant Moon: Lunar Astronomies in Different Cultures*'. Archaeoastronomy, Vol.XV: 14-31.
Michell, John (1969). *The View Over Atlantis.* London: Sago Press.
Michell, John (1969). *Astro-archaeology* (1976). Thames & Hudson.
Michell, John (1969). *Megalithomania. (1985).* Thames & Hudson
Michell, John. *Ancient Metrology. (1980).* Pentacle Press.
Neal, J. F. *All Done with Mirrors - Op 2.* (Ancient Metrology) (2000). Secret Academy.
Newham, C. A. *The Astronomical Significance of Stonehenge.* (1967) Moon Publications.
Norris, R.P., Appleton, P.N.and Few R.W. (1982). '*A Survey of the Barbrook Stone Circles and Their Claimed Astronomical Alignments*' in Heggie: Archaeoastronomy in the Old World. Cambridge: Cambridge University Press.
Norris, Ray (1988). '*Megalithic Observatories in Britain: real or imagined?*' Records in Stone. Cambridge: Cambridge University Press. 262-276.
North, John. (1996). *Stonehenge.* A New Interpretation of Prehistoric Man and the Cosmos. New York: The Free Press.
Patrick, Jon. (1979). '*A Reassessment of the Lunar Observatory Hypothesis for the Kilmartin Stones*'. Archaeoastronomy, no.1 (JHA, x): 78-85.

Bibliography

Ponting,M.R. and Ponting, G.H. (1982). *'Decoding the Callanish Complex – A Progress Report'*. Archaeoastronomy in the Old World (ed. Heggie). Cambridge: Cambridge University Press. 191-203.

Ponting, Gerald and Ponting, Margaret (2000). *New Light on the Stones of Callanish*. Stornaway: G & M Ponting.

Read, D.W. (1974). *'Some comments on the use of mathematical models in anthropology'* in American Antiquity 39(1): 3-15.

Renfrew, Colin). *Before Civilisation*. (1973 (Cape) & 1999 (Pimlico, Random House).

Ritchie, J.N.Graham (1982). *'Archaeology and Astronomy: An Archaeological View'* in D.Heggie (ed.) Archaeoastronomy in the Old World. 31. Cambridge: Cambridge University Press.

Rosenfeldt, G. (1984). *'A Statistical Method of Evaluating Megalithic Observatories'*. Archaeoastronomy, no.7 (JHA, xv): 111-118.

Ruggles, Clive L.N. (1983).*'A Reassessment of the High Precision Megalithic Sightlines,2.'* Archaeoastronomy, no.5 (JHA, xiv):1-34.

Ruggles, Clive L.N. (1984).*'Megalithic Astronomy: A New Archaeological and Statistical Study of 300 Western Scottish Sites.'* Oxford: BAR (British Series 123).

Ruggles, Clive L.N. (ed) (1988). *Records in Stone*. Papers in Memory of Alexander Thom. Cambridge: Cambridge University Press.

Ruggles, Clive L.N. (ed.)(1993). *Archaeoastronomy in the 1990's*. Loughborough: Group D Publications Ltd.

Ruggles, Clive L.N. (1996). *'Archaeoastronomy in Europe'* in Christopher Walker (ed.) Astronomy Before the Telescope. London: British Museum Press. 15-27.

Ruggles, Clive L.N. (1997). *'Whose Equinox?'* Archaeoastronomy, no.22 (JHA, xxviii): 45-50.

Ruggles, Clive L.N. (1999). *Astronomy in Prehistoric Britain and Ireland*. London and New Haven: Yale University Press.

Ruggles, Clive L.N. (2000 a). *'Ancient Astronomies – Ancient Worlds. Inaugural Lecture'*. Archaeoastronomy, no.25 (JHA, xxxi)

Ruggles, Clive L.N. (2003). *Orion! A Clarification*. http://www.le.ac.uk/archaeology/rug/orion.html (Accessed 15 July 2004).

Ruggles, Clive L.N. (2004). Review of *"Bayesian Approach to Interpreting Archaeological Data* by Buck, Cavanagh and Litton. http://www.palass.org/pages/archive/bookreviews35.html. (Accessed 17 October 2004).

Ruggles, Clive L.N. with Frank Prendergast and Tom Ray (eds). (2001). *Astronomy, Cosmology and Landscape*. Bognor Regis: Ocarina Books.

Ruggles, Clive L.N. and Nicholas J. Saunders (1993). *The Study of Cultural Astronomy*. in Clive L.N. Ruggles and Nicholas J. Saunders (eds.) Astronomies and Cultures. Niwot: University Press of Colorado. 1-31.

Russell, Miles (2002). *Monuments of the British Neolithic*. Stroud, Gloucestershire: Tempus.

Shanks, Michael and Tilley, Christopher (1992). *Re-Constructing Archaeology*. Theory and Practice. London and New York: Routledge.

Somerville, H. Boyle (1912). *Prehistoric Monuments in the Outer Hebrides and their Astronomical Significance*. Jnl.Royal Anthr. Inst. Gt.Brit. and Ireland, 42, 23-52.

Bibliography

Somerville, H. Boyle (1922-3). *Instances of Orientation in Prehistoric Monuments of the British Isles.* Archaeologia 73: 193-224.
Somerville, H. Boyle (1927). *'Orientation'.* Antiquity 1, 31-41.
Temple, Robert (1999). *The Crystal Sun.* London: Arrow Books.
Thom, Alexander (1967). *Megalithic Sites in Britain.* Oxford: Oxford University Press.
Thom, Alexander (1971). *Megalithic Lunar Observatories.* Oxford: Oxford University Press.**Thom, A. and Thom, A.S.** (1978). *Megalithic Remains in Britain and Brittany.* Oxford: Clarendon Press.
Thom, A and Burl, A. *Megalithic Rings* (229 plans plus interpretation) BAR 1980.
Thom,A. and Thom, A.S. (1980). *'Astronomical Foresights used by Megalithic Man'.* Archaeoastronomy, no. 2 (JHA, xi)
Thom,A. and Thom,A.S. (1982). *Statistical and Philosophical Arguments for the Astronomical Significance of Standing Stones with a Section on the Solar Calendar.* In D.Heggie (ed.) Archaeoastronomy in the Old World. 53-82. Cambridge: Cambridge University Press.
Thom,A. and Thom, A.S. (1988). *'The Metrology and Geometry of Megalithic Man'* in Records in Stone. Papers in Memory of Alexander Thom. (ed. Ruggles). Cambridge: Cambridge University Press.
Thom, A S. *Walking in all of the Squares* (1995) Argyll Publishing.
Thomas, Julian (1993). *'The Politics of Vision and the Archaeologies of Landscape'* in Landscape: Politics and Perspectives (ed.Bender). Providence/Oxford: Berg.
Tilley, Christopher (1994). *A Phenomenology of Landscape.* Oxford: Berg.
Tilley, Christopher (2004). *The materiality of Stone.* Oxford: Berg.
Walker, C (ed.) *Astronomy before the Telescope* (1996). British Museum Press.
Wood, John Edwin (1978). *Sun, Moon and Standing Stones.* Oxford: OUP.

THE CHANGE IN THE EARTH'S OBLIQUITY OVER TIME

De Sitter's formula gives the variation of the earth's obliquity (ε) over time as

$$\varepsilon = 23° 27'8.29'' - 47''.080t - 0''.0059t^2 + 0''00186t^3,$$

where t is measured in centuries forward or backwards (as -t) from 1900 AD.

THE VALUES FOR PREHISTORIC EPOCHS ARE LISTED IN APPENDIX TWO

Batteries not needed. A box housing one of Thom's 'Cat's whiskers' - crystal rectifiers used in self-powered crystal sets during the first decade of amateur radio construction in the 1920s.
Thom's love of practical outcomes made radio construction a must, and he built sets for many family members and friends.

Index

Index

Please note: italic entries denote publications, bold print entries denote photograph

Symbols

56, Stonehenge - stone 34 140
16 month calendar 68
16 month solar calendar 54

A

A Bayesian analysis of the megalithic yard 123
Abercrombie Professor of Prehistoric Archaeology at Edinburgh 83
Aberdeenshire recumbent stone circles (RSCs) 189, 190
A Critical Examination of the Megalithic Lunar Observatories, (BAR 88) 171
Admiralty Surface Weapons Establishment 180
Ages in Chaos 99
A Guide to the Stone Circles of Britain, Ireland and Brittany (Yale) 132
A Key to Stonehenge xiii
All-Saint's Day 55
Allan Water 110
Allan Water, survey plan 142
American Antiquity 95
Angell, I O 161
anti-pagans 191
Antiquities of the Irish Countryside 125
Antiquity 13, 82, 98, 124, 126, 133, 178, 180
Apeld Dr C J, iv, 9
A Phenomenology of landscape: places, paths and monuments (1994) 177, 178
Archaeoastronomy, journal 46
Archaeoastronomy, no.25 181, 183
Archaeoastronomy Vol VII (1-4), 169
Archibald Thom, Thom's father, *frontispiece*
Archimedes 32
Argyll Publishing, *acknowledgements,* xiii
Aristotle 32
astronomer-priests 88, 90
Astronomy and Society in Britain, Ruggles & Whittle, 1981, 165

Thom on his first sailing trip on open waters following the end of the second World War, in 1946. By now he had taken up his appointment at Brasenose College, Oxford. During the summer vacation he always returned to his beloved Scotland, where he took various family members sailing around the waters of the Western Isles.

- 225 -

Index

Astronomy before the Telescope (BCA 1996) 176
Astronomy in Prehistoric Britain 38
Athgreany stone circle, Co Wicklow 106
Atkinson (**photo**) 18
Atkinson, Prof Richard *coverpage*, v, ix, xi, 15, 17, 38, 84, 87, 88, 92, 93, 96, 98, 99, 102, 108, 121, 124, 128, 136, 140, 159, 160, 182, 208
Atlantis 129
Atlantis scenario 123
Aubrey, John 209
Aubrey circle 80, 136, 159
Austin, Beryl (*née* Thom) 22, 23, 24, 172, 182, see also Thom, Beryl
Avebury 152, 155, 191
Avebury, as World Heritage Site 152
Avebury, Keiller museum 205
Avebury, latitude 205
Avebury, survey 29
Avebury, survey plans 151
Avebury, the Cove 205
Avebury Manor 205
Aveni, Prof Anthony 206

B

Bailey, D C 74
Baird, John Logie 1
Balerno 187
Balinaby 22
Ballochroy 49
Ballochroy Alignment 37
Banavie, Fort William 24
Bar Brook III, survey plan 149
Barclodiad y Gawres 206
Barnatt 132
Bass Rock, lunar alignment 43
Batchelor, Richard 187
BBC *Chronicle* documentary 5, 15, 17, 19, 20, 21, 25, 32, 34, 44, 51, 52, 57, 61, 69, 71, 92, 93, 126, 160, 199
BBC Radiophonic Workshop 20
Before Civilisation viii, 24, 78, 86
Belgic or Drusian foot 73
Beltane 54, 203
Bennett 71
Bibby, S J, soil scientist 38
Binford, Dr L R 95
Biometrika, journal 113
Blackhill of Drachlaw, ellipse 139

Blakeley Moss, lunar alignment 43
Blood Relations 69
Boat of Garten, survey plan 138
Bob Dylan 98
Bonfire Night 55
Borrowston Rig, survey plan 144
Bossom, Mike, *acknowledgments*
Brackett Observatory, California 175
Brainport Bay 49
Brasenose College 1
Brasenose College, Oxford v, 9
Brennan, Martin 125
Bristlecone pine 77
British Academy 122
British Neolithic Calendar Buildings 27
Broadbent, Dr Simon 82, 112, 113, 119, 120
Brunsvega, calculator 29
Bryn Celli Ddu 205
Bryn Celli Ddu, survey plan 206
Bulletin of the Institution of Mathematics and its Applications (Vol 4, 4), October 1968, pp 66-85 182
Burl, Dr Aubrey, *acknowledgements*, 15, 24, 80, 130 - 133, 138, 158, 163, 164, 167, 179, 189, 192, 208
Burl, Dr Aubrey (**photo**) 130
Burnmoor 191
Burrow, Dr Steve 205
Bush Barrow lozenge 127

C

Caithness 61, 65
Caithness, fan 67
Caledonian Canal 24
calendar quarter-days 203
Callanish 5, 27, 32
Callanish V, lunar alignment 43
Cambridge University 121
Campbelltown, lunar alignment 43
Campion, Dr Nicholas 86
Camster 61
Canadian Pacific Railway network 2
Cardrones House, cup & ring marks 71
Carnac, in Brittany 20, 21, 47, 98, 108, 124
Carnac, survey 28
Carnac, Thom at (**photo**) 162
Carnarvon, Lord 85
Carradale iii, 1
Carsphairn 161

Index

Carter, Sir Howard 85
Case, Dr Humphrey 17, 90, 99, 102
Case I and II, statistical analysis 111, 112
Case Western University, Cleveland, Ohio 120
Castle Rigg 10, 11, 58, 146, 150, 188, 191
Castle Rigg, survey geometry 187
Castor and Pollux 62
Chair of Engineering Science 9
Champollion 85
characteristic distance 64
Chariots of the Gods 99
Cherwell, Lord 82
chieftains 87
Childe, Prof V Gordon 15, 77, 82, 85, 123, 125
Children of the Sun 77
Christ Church, Oxford 82
Circles, pacing out 133
Clarendon Press, Oxford viii, 92
Clark, Dr David 2, 114
Clark, Dr Graham 15, 75, 83, 84, 86, 96, 174
Colt-Hoare, William 85
Comet 1, jetliner 7
COMPOUND RINGS, geometry of 150
CONCENTRIC GEOMETRIES, geometry of 158
Cornwall, 19 stone rings 134, 135
Corra Beinn 37
Cowan, Thaddeus 150, 161
Crawford, Dr O G S 82, 117
Crinian Canal v
Critchlow, Prof Keith 16, 127, 190
Crucuno rectangle, Brittany 158, 203, 204
cultural synchronicity 69
Culture and Cosmos, journal 86
Cummings, Vicky 178
Cunninghams, archaeologists 85
Curator of the Cardiff Museum 205
Current Archaeology xiv, 90
Curta calculator 29, 160

D

Dalkeith 144
Dambuster raids 7
Daniel (**photo**) 18
Daniel, Dr Glyn E 13, 17, 20, 90, 98, 99, 102, 123, 124
Dartmoor xvi, 60, 68

Davies, Alan 71
Daviot ellipse, survey plan 138
dendrochronology 77, 84
Deneb 50
Department of Aeronautics 4
Derbyshire, Delia 20
De Sitte (formula for e) 80
Die Deutsche Vorgeschichte eine Herr Voragend Nationale Wissenschaft 77
Diffusionism 76, 101
Dinnever Hill, survey plan 147
Dirlot 61
Disney Professor of Archaeology at Cambridge 90
Doctor Who 20
dowsers 177
Dr Balfour, 'nature-curist' iv
Druid-styled 'Pythagorean' culture 128
Druid Temple, Inverness 143
Drusian foot 199
Dunlop, Ayrshire iii, 3, 21
Durrington Walls 78

E

Earis, Prof Roger and Irene, *acknowledgements, Appendix 1*
Early Britain (1945) 86
earth's angle of obliquity 33
Earth Magic 16
earth mysteries 177
Easter Aquorthies, geometry of 189
Easter Delfour, survey plan 154
Eclipse year 42, 46
Eden Valley 192
Egypt 76-77, 81, 85-86, 88-87
Egypt, measures 89
Egyptian remen 89, 186
Egyptology 32
Elliot Smith, Sir Grafton 77, 126
Encaustic arts, *acknowledgements*
English foot 71, 196, 201-202
English Lake District 59, 191
Equation of Time 9
Eratosthenes 32
Er Grah, Grand Menhir Brisé 68
Euclid 59
Eudoxus 32
extinction angle 50

Index

F

'flower of life' pattern 146
Farr West, survey geometry 187
Fay, Dr Peter 38
Ferguson, Lesley, *acknowledgements*, xiv, 111
Field Computation in Engineering and Physics 9, *see also* Apfeld, Dr C J
Fingerprints of the Gods 99
FLATTENED CIRCLES, geometry of 145
Flattened rings: astro-geometrical properties 194
Fleet, Hampshire v, 7
Fleming, Prof Andrew 178, 179
Fort William, Banavie vi
Fort William Hospital 24
Fowlis Wester, lunar alignment 43
Frazer, Ian, *acknowledgements*
Freeman, P R 123

G

Gallows Outon cup & ring marks 72
Gemini 62
Geodetic and Plane Surveying 114
geographic foot 73
geometry, of stone rings 111
Giot, Prof Pierre-Roland 100
Gladwin, Col. 38
Glasgow University iv, xiii, 3, 4, 9, 38, 87
Glastonbury festival 20
Golden Age 123, 129
Gordon, Prof J E 108
Gorrie, Hamish *acknowledgements*, 162
Gosport. iv
Gosport Aircraft Company iv, 2
Gouroch Cup & Ring marks 73
Grainger, Ron 20
Great Pyramid 32
Great Pyramid, cardinal alignement 81
Greek foot 73, 199
Greek Mathematics 32
Groningen, Denmark 175
Gustin, Hilda 23, 27, 172

H

Hadassah, yacht 6, 27
Half-moon Wood 49
Halloween 54
Hammersley, Dr John 82, 112, 119, 182
Hammerton, Dr Max 126

Hancock, Graham 99
Handford, David, *acknowledgements*, xvi
Hawick 110
Hawkes, Dr Jacquetta 17, 51, 85-86
Hawkins, Dr Gerald S 13-15, 46, 98,99, 203
Heggie, Dr Douglas C 46, 133, 152, 180
heliacal rising 52
Helvellyn peak 281, 282
Hewlett Packard '25' programmable calculator 29
High Speed Wind Tunnel (HST) v, 7
Hill o'many Stanes, Mid-Clyth 61
Hill o' Many Stanes, Mid-Clyth 67
Hirnant, geometry of 157
Hirnant, survey plan 157
Hitching, Francis 16
Hobbes 98
Hogg, Dr Arthur 17, 57, 91-93, 160, 186
Hopkins, Anthony 16
Horizon (BBC) 20
Hotel Celtique, Carnac 31
Hoyle, John R 157
Hoyle, Prof Fred 23
Human Engineering guide to Equipment Design 127
Hunter, Samuel, journalist 28
Hutton, Dr Ronald 176

I

Imbolc 54, 203
Imperial weights and measures 203
'indicated foresight' 35
Institute of Archaeology in Rekyjavik 176
Institute of Navigation 12
Iron Age Brochs 123
Isle of Lewis 27
Ivimy, John 87, 89, 186, 201

J

Jeanie 'sis' Thom, *see* Thom, Jeanie
Johnson, Paul 17
Journal for the History of Astronomy xi, 12, 80, 159, 208
Journal of the Institute of Navigation 175
Journal of the Royal Statistical Society 9, 92, 97, 113, 123

K

Kame of Corrigal 47

Index

Kendall, Prof David George 93, 121-123, 176
Kerry Pole, survey plan 155
Kilmartin House Museum 49
Kintraw xi, 36, 38, 49
Kintraw (winter solstice) 37
Kintyre, lunar alignment 43
Kirk, Dr Trevor 180
Kirkwood, Jeanie, 2
Knapper's farm cup & ring marks 72
Knight, Dr Chris 69
Knowth, Boyne Valley 54, 56
Kossinna, Gustav 77

L

Lammas 54, 203
Lancaster Royal Grammar School 73
Lang, Fritz 9
Laplace 129
Latitude of sites (section) 203
le Grand Menhir Brisé 47, 68
Leicester University x
Le Menec egg, Brittany 102
Lewis, archaeologist 33
Lewis, C S 16
ley hunters 177
Libby, Willard F 77
Liberal Arts education 130
Liechtenstein 29
Lilian Thom (née Strang), *see foreword*
Lineacre, Vivien 187
Little Salkeld 191
Llandrillo, Bala, Wales 153
Lloyd Davies, Janet, artist 35, 36, 37
Loanhead of Daviot, survey plan 158
Loch Eck 2, 114
Loch of Yarrows 61
Loch Roag, Lewis 5, 27
Lockyer, Sir Norman 32, 33, 79, 80, 205
Long Meg 106
Long Meg (survey plan) 192
Long Meg, orthostat 191
Long Meg and Her Daughters (section) 191
Lucas, Gavin 176
Lugnasadh 55
lunar 'wobble' 44, 49, 64
lunar double peak histogram 45
lunation cycle/synodic cycle (lunar month) 39
Lunation triangle 201, 202

M

Anne Macaulay *acknowledgements*, 158, 187
MacColl, James 22
MacColl, Susan xiv, 45
MacColl, Eóghann, Duncan and Shona, *acknowledgements*
MacKie (**photo**) 19
MacKie, Dr Euan W, *acknowledgements*, x, xiv, 15-17, 21, 26, 37-38, 69, 73, 84, 87 - 90, 99, 102, 123, 163, 167-172, 193
Magnusson 15, 17, 19-20, 69
Man makes Himself 83
Martineau, John, *acknowledgements*, 158, 190
May day 54
McCardle, David, Brother in law 4
McLay, Jack, cousin ix
McWhirter, K 152
Medical Research Council 126
Meet the Ancestors xiv
Megalithic Astronomy 172
Megalithic Astronomy, A new archaeological and statistical study of 300 western Scottish sites, BAR, 1984 165
Megalithic Astronomy, BAR 1984 165
Megalithic compound ring geometry (RIS, page 379) 161
megalithic equinox 53
Megalithic fathom 30, 112, 119, 122, 126
Megalithic foot 73
Megalithic Geometry, rules 134
Megalithic inch 73
Megalithic inch (MI) 71
Megalithic Lunar Observatories 5, 14, 36, 45, 80, 185
Megalithic Measures and Rhythms 187
Megalithic Remains in Britain and Brittany 14, 22, 47, 106-108, 133, 203
Megalithic Rings, (BAR, 1980) 130, 131
Megalithic rings, their design construction, (Science, 168, pp 321-5) 150
Megalithic rod 31, 73, 134, 137
Megalithic rod, in geometries 132
Megalithic Science (Thames and Hudson, 1981 133, 152
Megalithic Sites in Britain viii, 14, 31, 51, 52, 54, 82, 101, 103, 111, 113, 117, 120, 150, 185, 186
Megalithic yard 30, 57, 68, 71, 73, 103, 109, 114, 122, 127, 129, 130, 134, 135, 137, 142,

Index

158, 161,176, 186, 196, 201, 203
Megalithic yard, 2.72 feet, 106
Megalithic yard, astronomical origin 199
Megalithic yard, in geometries 132
Megalithomania 96
Megalithomania, conference 178
Merritt, Robert L v, 20, 22, 23, 70, 101, 119, 172, 186
Merritt, Robert L (**photo**) 121
Merry Maidens, circle 134
Metrology of Megalithic yard, 71, 186, 199
Michell, John 16, 89, 96, 172, 205
Midmar Kirk, geometry of 188
Miltown of Clava, survey plan 158
Minoan Crete 76
Minoan pottery 76
Moel ty Uchaf 155
Moel ty Uchaf, Bala, Wales 59
Moel ty Uchaf, **photo and survey plan** 153
Moir, Gordon 132
Moncur, Prof George 2, 114
Monte Carlo analysis 122
Montelius, Oscar 76
Moon, 'wobble' 42, 44
Moon, 18.6 year cycle 39, 62
Moon, circumpolar 79
Moon, eclipses 42
Moon, eclipse season 42
Moon, Eclipse year 42
Moon, lunar nodes 40
Moon, major standstill 40, 47
Moon, north & south node 40
Moon, orbital obliquity 100
Moon, the lunation 195
Moon and tides 6
Moonshine over Stonehenge 98
Morbihan, Brittany 68
Morgan et al 127
Morris, R W B 74
Mossyard cup & ring marks 72
motorcycles, FN combination 5
motorcycles, love of 4
Motz, Prof Hans 47
Motz, Prof Hans (**photo**) 121
Muir, Richard 46
Müller 46

N

Napoleon 85
Nature, Journal 79

Nautical Almanac 34
nautical mile 73
neo-pagans 55
Neolithic platonic solids 190
Neptune's Gates 24
Newham C A 'Peter' (**photo**) 14
Newham, C A 'Peter' 13, 14, 24, 56, 203
New Scientist 46, 89
Nine Ladies site 161
Norman Thompson Flight Company 2
North, Prof John 175

O

O'Riordain, Sean P 125
Observing the Moon's wobble 68
Osborne, Tricia, *acknowledgements*
orientation, replaces alignment 164
Orion 62
Orkney, Dr Ian 60
Orton 191
Outer Hebrides 28
Oxford University x

P

Panorama Stone, Ilkley vi, 72
Paps of Jura 38
Parc y Meirw 48
Parc y Meirw, lunar alignment 43
Parker Pearson, Prof Michael 183
Pattern of the Past 16
Penny, Alan 64, 68
Penprase, Prof Bryan 175
pentagonal geometry 59
Petrie 76
Petrie, William Flinders 32, 81, 84, 130
Phenomenology 177
Piggott, Prof Stuart *coverpage*, 17, 78, 86-90, 97, 140, 180
Plato 32
Platonic solids 60
Plouharnel, Brittany 204
Polaris 27
Pole Star 27
Pomona College, Claremont, California 175
Ponting, Margaret 27
Postgraduate Training Programmes in archaeoastronomy 182
Prain, Major 139
Prehistoric Britain 83, 86

- 230 -

Index

Prehistoric Society, President 173
Principal Scientific Officer 7
Pythagorean 12:35:37 triangle 156
Pythagorean triangles 19,20, 30, 32, 57, 132, 157, 159, 201, 203
pythagorean triangles 97, 150, 202

Q

Quadrivium 130
Quest 124

R

radiocarbon dating 77
'RCAHMS, Edinburgh 111
Records in Stone 27, 73, 100, 130, 171, 184, 208
RECTANGULAR 'RINGS' geometry of 158
Renfrew, Dr Colin viii, 24, 78, 86-89, 102
Renfrew, Lord, of Kaimsthorn 90
resistivity mapping 107
Rhythm of the Stars 45
Riddles in the British Landscape 46
Ring of Brogar 47, 136, 191
Rollright stones 12
Roman foot 84
Rosetta Stone 85
Roy, Prof Archibald xiii
Royal Aircraft Establishment (RAE) iv, x, 1, 7
Royal Archaeological Institute 180
Royal Astronomical Society 101, 176
Royal Commission for Ancient and Historic Monuments, Scotland, (RCAHMS) xiv, 26, 28
Royal Commission on the Ancient and Historic Monuments of Wales 91
Royal cubit 89, 186, 196, 201, 202
Royal Society 121, 129
Royal Society conference 93
Royal Statistical Society 12, 176
Royal Technical College, Glasgow 1, 2
Ruggles & Whittle, 1981, BAR p 270 163
Ruggles' Methodology (section) 168
Ruggles, Dr Clive xiv, 22, 23, 46, 90, 127, 164, 166, 167, 170, 172, 174, 181, 184

S

'Social Archaeology' 90

sacred geographers 177
Samhain 54, 203
Sands of Forvie, survey plan 138
Schultz, Joachim 45
Science and Society in Prehistoric Britain 69, 87-90
Science Research Council xiv
Scott, Jack G, archaeologist xi, 60
Scottish circle data 115-116
Sea of Morbihan (lunar sites) 67
Seascale (Grey Croft) 191
SETTING UP A MODERN LUNAR OBSERVATORY (section) 62
Shadowlands 16
Sign of Cancer 62
silver fraction 196
Sirius 50, 52
Sir William Arrol and Company 2
SI system of measures 103
Skara Brae 97
slide rule, calculator 29
Smith, Len (keeper of Stonehenge) 121
Smoley's Tables 32
Society of Leyhunters newsletter 178
soil creep 106
solifluction 106
solstitial angles 33
Somerville, Admiral Boyle 28, 54. 55, 81
sound echo imaging 107
Sound of Harris 27
Southampton University 90
Stanton Drew 12, 139
statistical analysis 82
statistics, simplified 103
Stecchini, Prof Livio 182
Stellar Alignments (section) 28
Steward, Julian 24
Stillaig, lunar alignment 21
Stone Alignments of Argyll and Mull: a perspective on the statistical approach in archaeoastronomy 171
Stone Circles and Megalithic Mathematics, (Proceedings of the Prehistoric Society 50:Dec 1984) 132
Stonehenge (1956) xi, 84
Stonehenge (1996), by John North 175
STONEHENGE (section) 159
Stonehenge, 1973 survey 28-29, 108, 139-140, 159
Stonehenge, as Egyptian litter 88

Index

Stonehenge, astronomical purpose 99
Stonehenge, Aubrey circle 200
Stonehenge, avenue 79
Stonehenge, bluestone 'horseshoe' 140
Stonehenge, bluestone circle 136
Stonehenge, concentric circles 158
Stonehenge, dating 80
Stonehenge, fallen trilithon 87
Stonehenge, heel stone 32, 79
Stonehenge, midsummer alignment 79
Stonehenge, MOW survey Plan 108
Stonehenge, Sarsen circle 200
Stonehenge, sightlines 46
Stonehenge, station stone rectangle 200
Stonehenge, station stones 203
Stonehenge, survey plan 140, 200
Stonehenge, Thom at (photo) 160
Stonehenge, trilithon ellipse 159
Stonehenge, wooden prototype 159
Stonehenge Decoded 13, 15, 98, 203
Stonehenge I, revised dating 85
Stonehenge World Heritage Site Management Plan (September 1999, Chris Blandford Associates) 159
St Pierre, Quiberon 47, 61
Strang, Sam, *frontispiece, foreword* 1
Strang, Uncle Willie *frontispiece*, 2
Stukeley, William 79
Sun, Moon & Earth, Wooden Books 40, 45
Sun, Moon and Standing Stones 62, 68, 88, 128, 180, *see also* Wood, Dr J E
Sunhoney, geometry of 188
Super-civilisation 129
Swinside 191
Systematics 71, 74

T

Tarbert, lunar alignment 43
Temple Wood 49
Thalassa iv, 3, 8, 10, 23, 29, 45
The 'Thom Collection' xiv
THE ALIGNMENTS (section) 32
The Archaeology of Time (2005) 176
The Astronomical Significance of Stonehenge 13
The Bear Hotel, Devizes 177
The Bungalow 9, 45
The Cabin 21
THE CALENDAR (section) 52

The Celtic calendar 55
THE CIRCLE, geometry of 135
THE CUP AND RING MARKS (section) 71
The Dawn of European Civilisation 77, 83
The direction of true north (azimuth) 110
THE ELLIPSE, geometry of 137
THE EXTRAPOLATION DEVICES (section) 61
THE GEOMETRIES (section) 57
THE GEOMETRIES OF STONE RINGS (section) 135
The Glasgow Herald 28
The Herring Fishers (painting) 74
The Hill iii, xiv, 2, 3, 4, 9, 20, 23, 29, 57, 93, 94, 122
The Institute of Navigation 36
The Listener 86
The Lunar Alignments (section) 39
The Materiality of Stone (Oxford) 178, 179
The Measure of Albion 73, 205
THE MEGALITHIC YARD (section) 28
The Model of European Prehistory 94
The moon's orbital plane (5.145°) 39
Theodolite 4, 33, 34, 57, 80, 109, 111, 185
Theodolite, 'shooting the sun' 110
Theodolite, reference object (RO) 110
Theodolite, types and quality 109
The Old Straight Track 12
The Pagan Religions of the British Isles (1991) 176
The Prediction of Eclipses (section) 201
The Sanctuary, Avebury 152
The Secret Life of John Logie Baird 1
The sidereal or tropical month 17
The Silver Fraction (section) 195
The Solar Alignments (section) 33
The Sphinx and the Megaliths (1974) 87, 90, 186
The Stars and the Stones (1983) 125
THE STONE EGGS, geometry of 141
The Theory of Culture Change 24
The Thom Building, Oxford v, 9
The Type A Flattened Circle (section) 145
The Type B Flattened Circle (section) 147
The View over Atlantis (1968) 16, 90
Thom, 16-month calendar 174
Thom, Alan v, 3, 7
Thom, Archibald Strang *acknowledgements*, v, xiii, 3, 7, 10, 16, 28, 31-33, 45, 52, 91, 94, 108, 112, 121, 127, 152, 155, 172
Thom, Beryl *foreword*, xiv, 3, 7, 9, 10

Index

Thom, Jeanie 5, 6, 10, 22
Thom, Margaret 7, 121
Thomas, Dr Neil 27, 56
Thomist Paradox xiv, 84, 97, 102, 127
Thompson, William Irvin 124
Tilley, Dr Christopher 177-178,
Time Stands Still (1980) 16, 190
Time Team xiv
Time Watch xiv
Tutankhamun 85
Twelve Apostles, survey plan 143
Type A and Type B flattened circles 194
Type A flattened circle 58
Type I egg 19
Type I & Type II Egg, geometry of 141
Type II egg 144

U

Uncle Sam. See also Strang, Sam
Underwood, Guy 16
University of Cambridge 126
University of Glasgow 110
University of Leicester 181
University of Leicester, chair in archaeoastronomy (1996) 173
University of Rennes 100
University of Sheffield 86
University of Wales 91
University of Wales, Lampeter xiii, 183

V

Velikovsky, Immanuel 99-101
Vistas in Astronomy 14
Vistas in Astronomy (Pergamon Press, Vol 7) 186
Von Daniken, Dr Eric 99

W

'Woodhenge type' of geometry 144
Walking in all of the Squares xiii, 91
Wallace, Sir Barnes 7, 9
Was God an Astronaut? 99
Watkins, Alfred 12, 179
Wellington bomber 7
West Kennet Avenue, survey plans 151
West Kennett Avenue 152
What Happened in History 77
Wheeler, Sir Mortimer 82

Whittle, Dr Alisdair 165
Wood, Dr John Edwin 62, 64, 68, 88, 128, 180
Woodhenge, concentric rings 158
WOODHENGE, geometry of 156
WOODHENGE, survey plan 156

Y

Yorkshire Post 46

Alexander Thom - Cracking the Stone Age Code

For further information concerning *Sky & Landscape* courses, or to order further copies of this or any other book published by Bluestone Press, go to

www.skyandlandscape.com.

Published in 2007 by Bluestone Press, Cardigan